GENERALS SOUTH
GENERALS NORTH

GENERALS SOUTH
GENERALS NORTH

THE COMMANDERS OF THE CIVIL WAR RECONSIDERED

★ ★ ★ ★

ALAN AXELROD, PhD

LYONS PRESS
Guilford, Connecticut
An imprint of Globe Pequot Press

For Anita and Ian

To buy books in quantity for corporate use
or incentives, call **(800) 962–0973**
or e-mail **premiums@GlobePequot.com**.

Lyons Press is an imprint of Globe Pequot Press.

Text design: Sheryl P. Kober
Layout artist: Mary Ballachino
Project editor: Kristen Mellitt
Maps by Trailhead Graphics Inc. © Morris Book Publishing, LLC

Library of Congress Cataloging-in-Publication Data is available on file.

ISBN 978-0-7627-6149-4

Printed in the United States of America
10 9 8 7 6 5 4 3 2 1

Contents

Introduction vi

PART ONE: GENERALS SOUTH

Chapter 1
P. G. T. Beauregard 2

Chapter 2
Joseph E. Johnston 14

Chapter 3
Robert E. Lee 27

Chapter 4
Thomas J. "Stonewall" Jackson 41

Chapter 5
Albert Sidney Johnston 53

Chapter 6
Braxton Bragg 63

Chapter 7
John Hunt Morgan 73

Chapter 8
Nathan Bedford Forrest 82

Chapter 9
J. E. B. Stuart 92

Chapter 10
James Longstreet 103

Chapter 11
John Bell Hood 115

Chapter 12
Jubal Early 125

PART TWO: GENERALS NORTH

Chapter 13
Winfield Scott 138

Chapter 14
George B. McClellan 147

Chapter 15
John Pope 161

Chapter 16
Ambrose E. Burnside 173

Chapter 17
Henry Wager Halleck 183

Chapter 18
Ulysses S. Grant 196

Chapter 19
William Tecumseh Sherman 211

Chapter 20
Joseph Hooker 226

Chapter 21
George H. Thomas 240

Chapter 22
Winfield Scott Hancock 252

Chapter 23
George Gordon Meade 266

Chapter 24
Philip H. Sheridan 278

Bibliography 293

Index 297

About the Author 312

INTRODUCTION

Of the roughly 1,556,000 soldiers who served in the Union army during the Civil War, 359,528 were killed, and 275,175 were wounded. Of the estimated 850,000 men in the forces of the Confederate states, at least 258,000 died, and some 225,000 were wounded. Thus 41 percent of the Union soldiers and 57 percent of the Confederate soldiers were either killed or wounded in action.

They were sons, brothers, husbands, fathers: soldiers.

The population of the Northern states in 1860, the year before war began, was twenty-two million, including four million men of combat age. The population of the Confederate states was nine million (of whom almost four million were slaves), including 1,140,000 men of combat age. The 1,117,703 killed or wounded on both sides represented 3.6 percent of the total U.S. population. Consider only that portion of the population that was of combat age, and the figure is 22 percent, more than a fifth, killed or wounded from 1861 to 1865.

While watching the bloody repulse of a Union charge at the Battle of Fredericksburg (18,030 killed, wounded, captured, or missing on both sides), Robert E. Lee, the most universally revered general of the Civil War, perhaps in all of America's wars, remarked, "It is well war is so terrible, or we should grow too fond of it."

Given the lives and treasure that were lavished upon it—the United States spent $15 billion (in mid-nineteenth-century dollars) on the Civil War in an era when a common laborer earned perhaps a dollar a day—no impartial judge could be faulted for concluding that Americans had already grown too fond of war. "Americans love to fight," Lieutenant General George S. Patton Jr. explained to troops preparing for D-Day some eighty years after Fredericksburg. "All *real* Americans love the sting of battle."

And yet so few of us have harbored any affection for the military.

Among the very reasons Americans welcomed the "sting of battle" in the fight for independence that began in 1775 was the British insistence on maintaining a standing army in the colonies, even for the purpose of defending them. The Constitution makes the president the commander in chief of the nation's armed forces; however, it puts the emphasis not on a standing national force but a "well-regulated militia." Before the Civil War, Americans had fought the "French and Indians," had fought a revolution, had fought the Indians some more, had fought the War of 1812, had fought Indians again, and had fought a war with Mexico. That the standing army was perpetually minuscule, poorly trained, for the most part indifferently led, and almost always inadequately equipped did not discourage entry into any of these conflicts. In hindsight, there were lessons aplenty. Without the aid of the French, the American Revolution would almost surely have been lost. If the British hadn't been preoccupied with Napoleon, the War of 1812, mostly a series of American defeats, would have been an out-and-out disaster. If Mexican soldiers had been any better trained, led, cared for, and equipped than the Americans, the U.S.-Mexican War might well have ended very differently. Yet, in 1861, the nation set about fighting with itself no better prepared for war than it had been since the eighteenth century. Americans might have proven that they were warriors, but they consistently refused to be soldiers.

At the start of 1861, with secession under way, the United States Army consisted of 15,259 enlisted soldiers presided over by 1,108 officers. Of the officers, 239 would resign their commissions to fight for the Confederacy—which, of course, had no regular army when it came into existence on February 8, 1861—and a goodly portion of the officer corps was, in any event, too old to fight; they were carried on the muster rolls because the U.S. Army had no system of retirement before the Civil War. As for the highest levels of command, on the brink of the conflict, there were just four general officers and nineteen colonels.

The popular American assumption—it was more in the nature of an article of faith or perhaps nothing more than magical thinking—was that, in a national emergency, the citizens would rally, and a militia of volunteers would somehow instantly coalesce into an effective army. Never mind that it had never turned out this way in the past.

Surprisingly, many men did volunteer all through the Civil War. Although both the North and the South introduced conscription, the majority of the armies on both sides consisted of voluntary enlistees. Professional military officers were at a premium, of course, as were those who had formerly served, especially during the war with Mexico. Most of these rallied to the cause of the Union or the Confederacy out of patriotic motives, but many, including those with no military experience, saw service in the war as a ticket to commercial or political prominence. Both sides were so desperate for commanders that the appointment of so-called political generals—officers with good connections but no military background—was commonplace. A few of these turned out to be remarkably able. Most, however, got in over their heads. As General Henry Wager Halleck, the army chief of staff, wrote to William Tecumseh Sherman on April 29, 1864, "It seems little better than murder to give important commands to men like Banks, Butler, McClernand, Sigel, and Lew Wallace"—all political appointees—"and yet it seems impossible to prevent it."

By the time the war was over, 583 generals had served in the Union army and 572 in the Confederate army. Doubtless, many should

never have held command. But many others learned on the job and did their utmost—or even gave their utmost: 139 were killed in combat, and even more were wounded.

Qualified or not, competent or not, brilliant or not, all were faced with a mission daunting beyond our ability to imagine. They commanded regiments, brigades, divisions, corps, and armies bigger than any ever before fielded on the North American continent. These were armed with more powerful musket-rifles, artillery, and ammunition, all produced in greater quantities than ever before. And, for all practical purposes, both sides started from scratch, building very large armies from forces minuscule or nonexistent and planning the strategy and tactics of warfare on a scale and of a nature no one had even contemplated.

Given the awesome magnitude of the generals' mission, it may seem presumptuous to write a book like this, which chooses from 1,155 generals South and North the two dozen who had the greatest impact on the course and outcome of the war, presents a biography of each, narrates the major engagements in which each fought, and explores the reputation of each based on historical sources as well as the opinions of current Civil War researchers. If this is presumptuous, then the numerical rating accorded each general may be judged downright blasphemous:

★   A losing commander
★ ★   A competent commander
★ ★ ★   A winning commander
★ ★ ★ ★   A standout commander

But the narratives, the comparisons, the evaluations, and even the ratings are not meant to be invidious. On the contrary, they are presented as the components of an inquiry into how the most important generals of the Civil War solved the monumental, often unprecedented problems of the conflict. On this 150th anniversary of the start of the Civil War, *Generals South, Generals*

North is intended to appeal to all readers interested in the conflict—from the casual browser and neophyte enthusiast who wants the equivalent of a "scorecard" to identify each commander, to the committed buff, a class of reader who perpetually craves rankings and comparisons for the purpose of settling (or starting) arguments.

All of the subjects deserve respect and admiration, regardless of their rating, and the order of their presentation reflects nothing more or less than the broadly chronological sequence of each general's appearance in the Civil War as a key commander.

PART ONE
GENERALS SOUTH

Chapter 1

P. G. T. BEAUREGARD

RATING: ★ ★

P. G. T. Beauregard. NATIONAL ARCHIVES AND RECORDS ADMINISTRATION

EVALUATION

The first general officer of the Confederacy, P. G. T. Beauregard was certainly well below the level of Robert E. Lee, Joseph E. Johnston, Stonewall Jackson, and Nathan Bedford Forrest, yet he may be seen as the archetypal Confederate commander—in heritage, appearance, manner, popular appeal, grandiose vision, and theatrical manner. While some have dismissed him as something of a blowhard, others have

seen his spasms of overheated battlefield rhetoric as inspiring (they sometimes were) and his flair for the dramatic as quite effective (as it was at the "Siege" of Corinth). He was impulsive, too often animated by an anachronistic sense of honor, poorly disciplined, weak in organization and logistics, sometimes wanting in tactics, and unrealistic in his formulation of broad strategy (though unshakable in his conviction that he was right), yet he was often an effective leader of men, a general capable of winning the confidence and cooperation of civilians (especially in Charleston), and a brilliant engineer, whose work on Confederate fortifications was more valuable than a field army corps. In short, his was a contradictory nature, and he combined an idiosyncratic unreliability with unprecedented longevity in command.

Principal Battles

PRE–CIVIL WAR

U.S.-Mexican War, 1846–1848

- Contreras, August 19–20, 1847
- Churubusco, August 20, 1847: Performance in these closely related battles earned Beauregard a brevet to captain
- Chapultepec, September 12–13, 1847: Played a key role in planning the assault on this fortress, was wounded, and received the personal thanks of General Winfield Scott

CIVIL WAR

- Fort Sumter, April 12–13, 1861: In South Carolina; planned and commanded the bombardment of the fort; ordered the first shot of the Civil War; forced the surrender of Fort Sumter
- First Battle of Bull Run, July 21, 1861: In Virginia; planned the battle, and though he yielded its overall execution to Joseph E. Johnston, was credited with the victory

- Shiloh, April 6-7, 1862: In Tennessee; second in command to Albert Sidney Johnston; assuming command after Johnston was mortally wounded, he lost the battle
- "Siege" of Corinth, April 29-May 30, 1862: By a skillful ruse, duped H. W. Halleck into allowing his army to withdraw intact
- First and Second Battles of Fort Wagner, July 10-11 and 18, 1863
- Second Battle of Fort Sumter, September 9, 1863: Environs of Charleston, South Carolina; in charge of Charleston's defenses, in these three battles, Beauregard repulsed Union attempts to capture the city
- Ware Bottom Church, May 15, 1864: In Virginia, the Bermuda Hundred Campaign; Beauregard defeated Benjamin Butler's Army of the James, bottling it up and effectively neutralizing it on Bermuda Hundred
- Second Battle of Petersburg, June 15-18, 1864: In Virginia, the Petersburg Campaign; made a daring stand against superior Union numbers, buying the crucial time Lee required to build up defenses here; denied the Union a momentous victory
- Bentonville, March 19-21, 1865: Served as J. E. Johnston's second in command in this final battle between Sherman and Johnston

For many, P. G. T. Beauregard—as a West Point cadet, he thought the first three of his names sounded too French and decided to use his initials instead—was and remains the very image of a Southern general. His florid mustache and neat, almost vestigial goatee, trimmed in the "imperial" fashion of Napoleon III, his chiseled jaw, a fine nose verging on aquiline, the high, broad forehead, his impeccably tailored uniforms, his obsession with "honor" (to the point of dueling), and the pride he took in counting himself a child of the Creole aristocracy, all were and are still part and parcel of the magnolia and moonlight picture. If all this seems too superficial to make Beauregard a truly meaningful icon of the Southern cause, the fact is that most icons are, by their nature, superficial, but Beauregard did have considerable substance as well.

He never wavered in his loyalty to his native state, Louisiana, although he was often at odds with the Richmond government, especially President Jefferson Davis. He served in the entire war. It was he who ordered the conflict's first shots, against Fort Sumter on April 12–13, 1861; he played a major role in the first major battle of the war, First Bull Run on July 21, 1861; and he fought in both principal theaters of the war, serving from the very beginning to the bitter end, joining Joseph Johnston and the Army of Tennessee to fight William T. Sherman in Georgia and the Carolinas. Photographs of Beauregard before, during, and after the war reveal nary a hint of a smile, but neither do they suggest much pain. Unlike a number of his even more illustrious contemporaries in gray, his service was never interrupted by a serious wound, and, of course, he lived through it all, the war that his command had begun. He seemed never to regret any of it.

THE YOUNG ARISTOCRAT

Pierre Gustave Toutant Beauregard was born on May 28, 1818, but he might just as well have emerged from the pages of some romance novel set in the deep South. His home was a sugarcane plantation called "Contreras" in St. Bernard Parish, Louisiana, twenty miles outside of New Orleans. He was the third of seven children—three brothers, three sisters—in the French-Spanish Creole family of Jacques Toutant-Beauregard and Hélène Judith de Reggio Toutant-Beauregard.

The Beauregards raised their children to be French men and women. Pierre Gustave attended a French-speaking private school in New Orleans until his eleventh year, when he was put on a train to New York City to continue his education at a preparatory school run by former officers of no less a figure than Napoleon. The boy was twelve before he spoke a word of English. And that was just fine with his parents, who, however, were appalled when he came back from his Napoleonic education with a powerful desire to become a military officer. They forbade it, they said, only to discover the full depth and breadth of the stubborn will of their boy—the same unyielding, unbending personality that would sustain him in the Civil War from its very beginning to its very end. In the end, they, not he, surrendered, and Jacques Toutant-Beauregard called in a political favor to secure an appointment to the U.S. Military Academy at West Point. The boy—and at nearly sixteen he *was* a boy—was enrolled in March 1834.

Despite his plantation background, the continual indoctrination as a member of the aristocracy, his belated acquaintance with the English language, and his own willful pride, young Beauregard got along surprisingly well with his classmates, who found him charming, affable, and doubtless appealingly exotic, if perhaps a trifle aloof. That he converted *Pierre Gustave Toutant* to initials at this time, often dropping the *P* altogether and calling himself "G. T. Beauregard," suggests that he made an effort to fit in. His classmates showered him with affectionate nicknames, including "Little Creole" and "Little Frenchman" (he stood five-foot-seven, not short for the era, but his delicate brown features made him look smaller) and "Little Napoleon." Future Confederate luminaries became close friends, including Jubal Early, Richard Ewell, and Braxton Bragg, but so did such figures of the Union as Irvin McDowell (against whom he would be pitted at First Bull Run), Joseph Hooker, and William Tecumseh Sherman. He excelled in his studies and was a favorite among his teachers, including artillery instructor Robert Anderson, who saw in him the makings of a fine artilleryman. Anderson would be the Fort Sumter commandant whose fate it became, in April 1861, to discover just how capable an artillerist his former student was.

FIRST ASSIGNMENTS

Fellow cadets recalled "G. T. Beauregard" as a very fine horseman and athlete who did very well academically—he would graduate second in the Class of 1838—and a few spoke of something more, a detail befitting the aura of romance that hung about him. It was rumored that he fell in love with Winfield Scott's daughter, Virginia, and that the two even became secretly engaged, only to meet with the general's objection that they were too young to marry. The story goes that they separated but wrote to one another faithfully, yet neither received the other's letters. It was years later that Beauregard discovered that Virginia's mother had intercepted her daughter's outgoing billets-doux as well as his incoming missives. By that time, however, he had married another woman. The story has never been confirmed, but it was told over and over by those who soldiered with Beauregard early in his career.

At the top of his class, Beauregard naturally requested assignment in the Corps of Engineers and was immediately dispatched to work on the most ambitious and important projects the army had in hand, including Fort Adams at Newport, Rhode Island. That a newly minted engineer should have received so coveted an assignment testifies to the early esteem in which he was held. In 1839, promoted to first lieutenant, he was sent to Pensacola, Florida, to build coastal defenses there, and was shipped off next, in 1844, to make improvements at Fort McHenry, Baltimore Harbor. This assignment introduced him to Baltimore high society, and the pro-Southern gentry of that city feted the handsome lieutenant lavishly.

His Baltimore interlude was all too brief. In February 1845, he was sent to his native Louisiana to construct and improve the Mississippi River forts. Here the dark side of the Southern gentleman was revealed. A dispute with a Lieutenant John Henshaw turned ugly, becoming what men of Beauregard's turn of mind liked to call an "affair of honor," and Beauregard challenged the man to a duel. The weapons of choice were shotguns. Fortunately for both men, the local sheriff got wind of the duel and arrived on the "field of honor" just in time to arrest the pair before a shot was fired.

U.S.-MEXICAN WAR, 1846–1848, AND AFTER

Perhaps just as fortunate was the arrival of the U.S.-Mexican War, which took Beauregard out of Louisiana and opened to him a much larger field of honor. He was assigned to Winfield Scott's army as an engineer serving directly under the general's chief engineering officer, Captain Robert E. Lee, and alongside another top-performing West Point graduate, Lieutenant George Brinton McClellan.

Beauregard was in the thick of the action at the Battles of Contreras (August 19–20, 1847) and Churubusco (August 20), his performance in these contests earning him a brevet to captain. With Lee, he was credited for plotting out the path by which Scott's army reached Mexico City. Indeed, the officers gathered with Scott praised young Beauregard's eloquence in persuading the commanding general to change certain aspects of the assault plan against Chapultepec. At the battle for that fortress (September 12–13, 1847), the culminating struggle for the Mexican capital, he was wounded in the shoulder and thigh, received the personal thanks of General Scott ("Young man," Old Fuss and Feathers reportedly said, "if I were not on horseback I would embrace you"), and a brevet to major.

Despite his wound, Beauregard made certain that he was among the very first officers to enter Mexico City on September 15. But he was rankled by the fact that Lee received three brevets—to colonel—to his two for the reconnaissance and tactical planning performed in connection with the assault on Chapultepec. Beauregard made no secret of his opinion that *he* had undertaken far more hazardous and important work than *Lee,* or any other officer, for that matter.

After the war, in 1848, Beauregard took charge of "the Mississippi and Lake defenses in Louisiana" for the U.S. Army Engineer Department—though he often traveled far outside of the area, repairing and expanding forts throughout the South and building new ones. He also supervised dredging and digging projects to improve the shipping channels at the mouth of the Mississippi River and even invented and patented a "self-acting bar excavator," which was an aid for ships in clearing sand and clay bars. Beauregard pursued this engineering work for a dozen years following the war with Mexico. During this time, he also restlessly struggled to gain a foothold in Democratic politics. When his first wife died in 1850, he remarried a planter's daughter named Caroline Deslonde, sister-in-law of Louisiana's powerful senator John Slidell. This connection, largely passionless, gave Beauregard entrée into the party's inner circle, and he plunged into the 1852 presidential campaign of Franklin Pierce, who had been a general in the U.S.-Mexican War. This brought a handsomely paid patronage appointment from President Pierce, who named Beauregard—still a serving U.S. Army officer—superintending engineer of the New Orleans Federal Customs House. It was no sinecure, but a genuine engineering challenge. Built in 1848 on swampy Louisiana soil, the edifice was fast sinking. From 1853 to 1860, while he held the job, Beauregard devised and supervised successful procedures for saving the building.

None of this, however, was sufficient diversion for Beauregard, who, like many other peacetime army officers, became intolerably bored. Toward the end of 1856, he notified the Engineer Department that he intended to travel to Nicaragua to join William Walker, the self-described "gray-eyed man of destiny," who had led a "filibustering" campaign in Central America and managed to seize control of the Nicaraguan government. Walker had dangled before Beauregard an offer to serve as his number two in command of his military forces. General-in-Chief Winfield Scott, among others, managed to talk Beauregard out of his decision to go—which was a good thing, since Walker's reign proved brief. The gray-eyed man of destiny was destined to execution by Honduran firing squad on September 12, 1860.

In 1858, Beauregard took a stab at elective office for himself, making a narrowly unsuccessful run for New Orleans mayor. By this time, as the nation's slide toward civil war accelerated, he made no secret of his Southern sympathies, although he did not actively oppose Abraham Lincoln or campaign for any other candidate in 1860. Perhaps he believed that doing so would damage his prospects for obtaining an appointment as superintendent of West Point. Senator Slidell called in favors, and Beauregard was duly installed at the academy on January 23, 1861.

By this time, secession was in full swing, and his office was quickly overrun with Southern cadets who asked him whether and when they should resign from the academy. "Watch me," Beauregard replied to them, "and when I jump, you jump. What's the use of jumping too soon?"

As it turned out, he was never given the opportunity to jump. Five days into his new job, Louisiana seceded and his own orders to report to West Point were rescinded. He was kicked out, having set a record for the shortest tenure as academy superintendent that, understandably, has yet to be broken. Although historians and others have marveled that Beauregard had been named superintendent in the first place, given his outspoken Southern sympathies, he himself protested that his sense of honor had been offended by the dismissal, which (he wrote to the War Department) had cast "improper reflection upon my reputation" because no hostilities had actually begun. He was further outraged that the War Department refused to reimburse him for the $165 he claimed as travel expenses from West Point back to his home in New Orleans. Even after he resigned his commission, which

he did several weeks after settling back home, he continued to pepper the War Department with demands for reimbursement. In the meantime, he advised local authorities on how to strengthen Forts St. Philip and Jackson, which guarded the Mississippi River approaches to New Orleans.

BATTLE OF FORT SUMTER, APRIL 12–13, 1861

Beauregard had outsized ambitions concerning how he would serve the Confederacy—and how it would serve him. He had designs on being named commander of the Louisiana state army and was crushed when the state legislature appointed Braxton Bragg instead. As a sop to Beauregard, Bragg offered him a colonelcy in the state force, to which Beauregard indignantly responded by enlisting as a private in the Orleans Guards, a private militia battalion made up exclusively of Creole planter-class aristocrats like himself. This, however, was a mere gesture. He assiduously worked his connection with Slidell and, through him, reached President Jefferson Davis in the hope of being given a top command in the projected Confederate States Army. Now it was Bragg's turn to be consumed with envy, as he was assailed by rumors that Beauregard was indeed about to be appointed general-in-chief.

Davis, however, had other plans for Beauregard. Summoning him to Montgomery, Alabama, the initial capital of the Confederacy, he offered him the rank of brigadier general—a satisfying leap from his last U.S. Army rank of major—and assigned him command of Charleston's defenses. Davis was particularly concerned about the presence of the federal forts, especially Fort Sumter, in Charleston harbor, and he saw in Beauregard the kind of engineering background the job required, together with the Creole plantation credentials and aristocratic bearing that would impress the upper crust of Charleston. Officially commissioned in the Provisional Army

Fort Sumter under attack. HARPER'S ILLUSTRATED WEEKLY

of the Confederate States on March 1, 1861, P. G. T. Beauregard became the first general officer of the Confederacy.

He arrived in Charleston on March 3, called on Governor Francis Wilkinson Pickens, then toured the harbor defenses. He saw immediately that a great deal had to be done, especially with regard to the positioning of guns. Gratified by the tumultuous reception the people of Charleston gave him, he was determined to secure their goodwill and took a comradely approach to recruiting local volunteers and enlisting them in the hard work of reorganizing the defenses. Accepting him as one of their kind, the locals cooperated with zeal, deploying guns under Beauregard's direction in batteries at Morris, James, and Sullivan Islands, Mount Pleasant, and Forts Moultrie and Johnson, all drawing a bead on Fort Sumter.

Beauregard also initially approached Major Robert Anderson, his West Point artillery instructor and now commandant of Fort Sumter, with similar courtliness and professional camaraderie, even sending him and his fellow Sumter officers cases of vintage brandy, good whiskey, and fine cigars. Anderson returned them all.

On April 11, 1861, Beauregard put Colonel James Chestnut, a prominent South Carolina politician, and another man in a rowboat and sent them out to the fort under a flag of truce with a personal note to Anderson, again calling for his surrender and promising in return that all "proper facilities will be afforded for the removal of yourself and command, together with company arms and property, and all private property, to any post in the United States which you may select. The flag which you have upheld so long and with so much fortitude, under the most trying circumstances, may be saluted by you on taking it down."

Asking the messengers' indulgence, Anderson composed a careful and courteous reply to his former pupil. The demand, he wrote, was one "with which I regret that my sense of honor, and of my obligations to my government, prevent my compliance." As he handed over the reply, he confided to the envoys: "Gentlemen, if you do not batter us to pieces, we shall be starved out in a few days."

Just before one o'clock on the morning of April 12, 1861, Chestnut, with three other men, again rowed to the fort to advise the commandant that Beauregard would continue to hold his fire on condition that Anderson provide a firm date and time for his withdrawal from Fort Sumter. After a long conversation with his officers, Anderson, at 3:10 a.m., handed Chestnut his written reply. He would evacuate by April 15—unless he received orders to the contrary from "my government." Chestnut, on whom Beauregard had conferred plenipotentiary authority, told Anderson that his conditions were unacceptable, and, right there and then, he scrawled a declaration warning him that the bombardment of Fort Sumter would commence in one hour. With this, he rowed away.

Shortly before 4:30 that morning, Beauregard ordered Captain George S. James to fire a signal gun as the command for the general barrage to begin. A Lieutenant Henry Farley, commanding a two-mortar battery on James Island, fired precisely at 4:30. This was the first shot of the war. For that entire day, the bombardment was unceasing and continued into Saturday, April 13, before Anderson, having decided that duty and honor were amply satisfied, lowered the Stars and Stripes. Beauregard ordered an immediate cease-fire. Fort Sumter had taken some four thousand incoming rounds—astoundingly, without a single casualty.

FIRST BATTLE OF BULL RUN, JULY 21, 1861

Hailed throughout the South as the "Hero of Fort Sumter," Beauregard answered President Davis's summons to the newly established capital of Richmond, Virginia, and was given command of the "Alexandria Line," the defensive forces organized to repel an anticipated attack by West Point classmate Brigadier General Irvin McDowell.

Beauregard took two approaches by way of preparation. The first was to formulate a plan to consolidate the troops commanded by General Joseph E. Johnston in the Shenandoah Valley with his own Alexandria Line. His objective was not merely to defend his position at the Manassas rail junction, but to mount a counteroffensive against McDowell's troops and against Washington, D.C., itself. The second approach was an exercise in what modern armies call psyops—psychological operations. Rising to a height of inflammatory hyperbole, Beauregard published a warning to the people of Virginia that a "restless and unprincipled tyrant has invaded your soil." He accused Abraham Lincoln of abandoning all "constitutional restraints" to throw "his abolition hosts among you, who are murdering and imprisoning your citizens. . . . All rules of civilized warfare are abandoned" by barbaric men whose "war cry is 'Beauty and booty.'"

Both approaches struck fire. Johnston, senior to Beauregard, bowed to his battle plan, and throughout Virginia, the people were roused to defend their "sacred soil." Only Jefferson Davis, it seems, was plagued with doubt. Beauregard's plan appeared to him to be an untenable stretch that ignored logistical realities. (This assessment would prove to be his response to Beauregard's strategic contributions throughout the war.) Nevertheless, on this occasion, Davis, like Johnston, acquiesced in the brigadier general's plan.

The battle began early on July 21. The plans of both McDowell and Beauregard called for envelopment of the enemy, but McDowell got

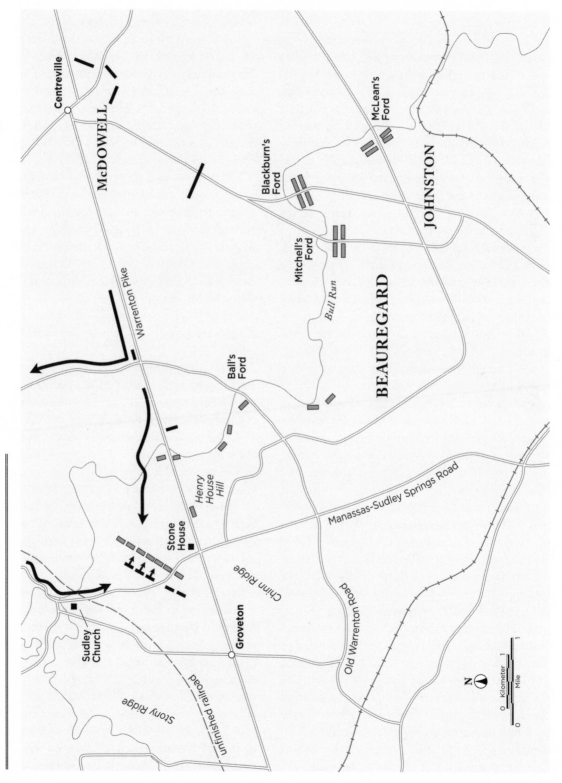

the jump on Beauregard by menacing his left flank. Stubborn as always, Beauregard at first paid little attention to this as he maneuvered to make an attack from his own right flank until the more experienced Johnston persuaded him to devote his attention to his threatened left at Henry House Hill. Thus alerted, Beauregard turned over to Johnston the overall coordination of the battle while he personally rallied the troops at the point of contact. Beauregard rode down to the front lines, exposing himself to enemy fire as he brandished regimental colors and exhorted his men to action. In this way, he managed to hold the line at Henry House Hill, buying time for all of Johnston's troops to arrive from the Shenandoah Valley. Fully reinforced, Beauregard and Johnston launched a counterattack that turned the tables on McDowell, routing the Union forces and sending them into headlong retreat to Washington.

Although Beauregard had drawn up the original plan, he quickly yielded overall direction of the battle to Johnston while he rode off to play the part of the romantic, dashing front-line general. There can be no denying that his display was effective—not only in rallying the troops, but in snatching all the glory for himself—but the battle, as fought, was largely the work of Johnston. For his part, Johnston was extraordinarily generous, recommending on July 23 the promotion of Beauregard to full general. Davis accepted the recommendation but soon regretted his decision as the volume of talk increased touting the hero of Fort Sumter and Manassas as his most desirable rival in the popular election of a Confederate president (Davis's appointment had been provisional) scheduled for November. The friction between the two men increased during the winter lull in combat as Beauregard pushed for an invasion of Maryland to position the army for a rear and flanking attack on Washington. Even as Davis criticized Beauregard for having failed to follow through on his promised attack against Washington after Bull Run,

he rejected the Maryland invasion as impractical. Affronted, Beauregard requested immediate reassignment to New Orleans but was refused. He then fell into dispute with other officers and with the Confederate secretary of war. He carried these arguments into the newspapers, using their pages to charge that the failure to exploit the Bull Run victory had been the result of President Davis's interference.

Davis was in a tough spot. Beauregard had made himself intolerable, but the president dared not fire the hero of two major battles. Instead, he pushed him out west, to Tennessee, where, on March 14, 1862, he was assigned as second-in-command under General Albert Sidney Johnston (no relation to Joseph E. Johnston) in the Army of Mississippi.

BATTLE OF SHILOH, APRIL 6–7, 1862

Albert Sidney Johnston welcomed the arrival of Beauregard. He was in a perilous position, having been forced into retreat to Alabama after Ulysses S. Grant had taken Forts Henry and Donelson. Both Johnston and Beauregard understood that the critical task now was to engage Grant again before he could link up with the forces of Don Carlos Buell and attack Corinth, Mississippi.

Like Joseph E. Johnston, A. S. Johnston was senior to Beauregard, and, also like J. E. Johnston, he yielded to him in planning the surprise attack on Grant's camp at Pittsburg Landing, Tennessee, near a church called Shiloh. Insofar as the plan was daring—a massive frontal assault—it was admirable. But poor organization undermined it. Beauregard threw each corps successively against the whole of Grant's line instead of assigning a portion of the line to each corps. Although the resulting attack was fierce, it was confused and inefficient. On April 6, the Confederates came close to annihilating Grant, but after A. S. Johnston was mortally wounded late in the afternoon, the assault faltered. By nightfall, Beauregard, now in full command, ordered a withdrawal, which gave Grant and William Tecumseh Sherman the time they needed to regroup with reinforcements from the just-arrived Buell. Grant's counterattack on April 7 forced Beauregard to fall back on Corinth, Mississippi. What had begun as a great Confederate victory-in-the-making ended in a costly defeat.

"SIEGE" OF CORINTH, APRIL 29–MAY 30, 1862, AND ITS AFTERMATH

After Shiloh, Major General Henry W. Halleck decided to assume field command from Grant but then moved so slowly against Beauregard's position at Corinth that the Confederate general had plenty of time to withdraw, on May 29, to Tupelo, Mississippi, covering his exit with a clever theatrical ruse—running empty trains back and forth and ordering his men to cheer with each "arrival," thereby giving Halleck the impression that he was being heavily reinforced.

Most historians view the outcome of the "Siege" of Corinth—an assault on an empty town—as a Union humiliation; however, Davis chose to interpret Beauregard's withdrawal as dishonorable because it had happened without a substantial fight, and when Beauregard followed this by taking sick leave without securing permission, the Confederate president replaced him as Army of Mississippi commander with General Braxton Bragg.

BACK TO CHARLESTON

Not to be beaten by Halleck *or* Davis, Beauregard rallied friends in the Confederate Congress to petition Davis to restore his command. "If the whole world were to ask me to restore General Beauregard to the command which I have already given to General Bragg," Davis wrote in reply, "I would refuse it." He then ordered Beauregard back to Charleston to command the coastal defenses of South Carolina, Georgia, and Florida.

Given Beauregard's engineering and artillery qualifications, it was a reasonable personnel decision. Beauregard, however, took it as an insult, nothing more or less than a way of high-handedly depriving him of a field command. But to his credit, he did not waste time pouting and performed brilliantly in defense of Charleston against naval and land assaults in 1863. Accurate and devastating coastal fire repulsed Rear Admiral Samuel Francis Du Pont's bid to retake Fort Sumter on April 7, 1863, and land and sea attacks from July to September 1863 were all beaten off.

Beauregard the engineer embraced innovation, endorsing experiments with torpedoes (naval mines), with torpedo-rams (small ramming vessels fitted with a projecting spar torpedo, intended to blast a hole through the enemy ship's hull below the waterline), and most famously with the submarine *H. L. Hunley*—an ill-fated venture that nevertheless foreshadowed an important future direction in naval warfare.

If Davis hoped that taking Beauregard off the field would quiet him down, he was very much mistaken. The general poured out plans and schemes, including a proposal that the governors of the Confederate states meet with the governors of the Union's Midwestern states—where pro-Confederate (so-called Copperhead) support was strong—and persuade them to make a separate peace. When Davis rejected this out of hand, Beauregard proposed a radical revision of military strategy, which called for shifting a great deal of strength away from Robert E. Lee and the Eastern Theater and putting it in the West, in order to threaten the Union by way of its back door. This grand redistribution of military assets was to be coordinated with action by a fleet of British-built torpedo-rams to be used to recapture New Orleans, thereby threatening the Union from the southwest as well.

BERMUDA HUNDRED CAMPAIGN AND THE DEFENSE OF PETERSBURG, MAY 15 AND JUNE 15–18, 1864

Nothing came of any of Beauregard's grand strategies, which apparently were not even accorded a serious hearing. Instead, he was sent in 1864 to assist Army of Northern Virginia commander Robert E. Lee in the defense of Richmond as it was being menaced by Grant's Overland Campaign. On May 15, he deftly defeated the inept Major General Benjamin Butler at the Battle of Ware Bottom Church, which was followed by construction of the Howlett Line, a fortified defensive line thrown across the town of Bermuda Hundred, thereby bottling up Butler and his Army of the James, effectively neutralizing it for the remainder of the war.

Beauregard followed his feat at Bermuda Hundred with an extraordinary defense at the so-called Second Battle of Petersburg on June 15 to 18. With no more than 2,200 men initially, he held off an assault by some sixteen thousand Union troops. Had Union general William F. "Baldy" Smith acted aggressively at the beginning, Beauregard would surely have been defeated. But thanks to the combination of Smith's delay and Beauregard's bravado, the Confederate commander bought time for the reinforcement of the Petersburg defenses and prevented the Union from scoring a potentially war-winning breakthrough. Beauregard's stand brought about a ten-month Union siege of the city.

MORE GRAND PLANS

Having defeated Butler and saved Petersburg from immediate invasion, P. G. T. Beauregard believed that Lee and Davis would have no choice but to accept his newest proposal: that he lead an all-out offensive against the North, sweeping Butler aside and wiping out Grant, thereby quite tidily winning the war.

Neither Davis nor Lee believed Beauregard's scheme was anything more than so much airy talk. Davis did give him a new assignment in October, however, ordering him to turn his divisions over to Lee's Army of Northern Virginia and assume command of the Military Division of the West. The catch was that he would not have direct responsibility for field operations. He was to oversee them, yet to refrain from intervening in them unless there was a crisis. Intended to keep a popular general in the public eye while denying him ultimate command authority, the arrangement was a blatant example of Davis's mismanagement of the military situation.

When John Bell Hood resigned as commander of the Army of Tennessee (part of the Military Division of the West) in February 1865, Beauregard persuaded Davis to replace him with Joseph E. Johnston. Johnston, in turn, asked Beauregard if he would consent to serve in the field, *under* his command. We do not know what answer Johnston expected. Certainly those who knew Beauregard throughout the war would not have predicted the response he gave, which was a simple and gracious yes. For the good of the cause, he would step down from departmental command and accept, yet again, the number two post in an army.

It was a noble gesture, but by this time the Confederacy lacked the resources even to slow, let alone stop, either Grant or Sherman, and soon after Lee surrendered the Army of Northern Virginia to Grant on April 9 at Appomattox, Beauregard and Johnston united with Secretary of War John C. Breckinridge in reporting to President Davis that the cause was lost and surrender was the only remaining reasonable option. General Johnston formally surrendered the Army of Tennessee to Sherman at the Bennett Place, near Durham, North Carolina, on April 26, 1865.

Beauregard in later life. Wikimedia Commons

After the War

P. G. T. Beauregard did not behave as the diehard Old South reactionary he certainly seemed to be at the start of the war. To be sure, he rejoined the Democratic Party, and he protested against the harsh aspects of Radical Republican Reconstruction, but, at the same time, he spoke out in favor of granting full civil rights, including full voting rights, to the emancipated slaves.

The world had been watching him during the war, and he received offers to command the armies of Romania (1866) and Egypt (1869), but he turned these down to become a Southern railway tycoon and consulting engineer. He served profitably as president of the New Orleans, Jackson & Mississippi Railroad from 1865 to 1870 and also of the New Orleans and Carrollton Street Railway from 1866 to 1876. During his tenure with the latter, the old engineer designed a system of cable-drawn streetcars.

He served as adjutant general for the state militia of Louisiana and as manager of the Louisiana Lottery, a corrupt institution he was charged with reforming. This he proved unable to do. In 1888, he was elected commissioner of public works for New Orleans and held this office until his death on February 20, 1893.

Chapter 2
JOSEPH E. JOHNSTON
RATING: ★ ★ ⋆

Joseph Eggleston Johnston. NATIONAL ARCHIVES AND RECORDS ADMINISTRATION

EVALUATION

Two classes of men were convinced that Joseph E. Johnston was among the greatest generals of the Civil War: those who served under him and those, including Ulysses S. Grant and William T. Sherman, who fought against him. Others, Confederate president Jefferson Davis foremost among them, believed his lack of aggressiveness cost him—and the Confederacy—victory in every campaign he led.

Military historians are divided in opinion. Some hold that, had Johnston received adequate

support instead of criticism and interference from Davis, his careful, prudent approach to war-fighting, which substituted maneuver for battle, might have positioned the South to avoid unconditional surrender. Others condemn him in the harshest way they can: by describing him as the Confederate George McClellan.

Principal Battles

PRE-CIVIL WAR

Nat Turner's Rebellion, 1831
- In Virginia; his unit arrived too late to participate in the manhunt for Turner

Black Hawk War, 1832
- In Illinois; his unit arrived too late to participate in combat

Second Seminole War, 1835–1842
- In Florida; in uniform, he participated in some skirmishes, but saw intense action in the conflict as a civilian civil engineer, sustaining his first combat wound

U.S.-Mexican War, 1846–1848
- Siege of Veracruz, March 9-29, 1847: Twice wounded
- Contreras, August 19-20, 1847
- Churubusco, August 20, 1847
- Molino del Rey, September 8, 1847
- Chapultepec, September 12-13, 1847: Having been brevetted to lieutenant colonel for his earlier exploits, he led a heroic assault in which he was wounded three times

CIVIL WAR
- First Battle of Bull Run, July 21, 1861: In Virginia; acquiescing in P. G. T. Beauregard's battle plan, Johnston was responsible for its overall execution, although Beauregard took the lion's share of credit for the victory
- Seven Pines (Fair Oaks), May 31-June 1, 1862: In Virginia, the Peninsula Campaign; at high cost,

Johnston stopped McClellan's advance just outside of Richmond, but he was seriously wounded and knocked out of the war for six months

- Vicksburg Campaign, December 1862–July 4, 1863: In Mississippi; outnumbered and in conflict with Jefferson Davis and Army of Mississippi commander John C. Pemberton over strategy, Johnston wanted to yield the city to free up military resources
- Jackson, May 14, 1863: In Mississippi; massively outnumbered, Johnston evacuated this vital industrial city and transportation hub, which was destroyed, sealing the doom of Vicksburg
- Atlanta Campaign, May 7–September 2, 1864: In Georgia; after the fall of Chattanooga, Johnston fought a campaign of strategic retreat against Sherman's advance to Atlanta until President Davis replaced him with the more aggressive John Bell Hood
- Kennesaw Mountain, June 27, 1864: In the Atlanta Campaign; Johnston's only victory against Sherman in this campaign, it did nothing to stop his advance against Atlanta
- Bentonville, March 19–21, 1865: In North Carolina; Johnston's final battle before negotiating surrender terms with Sherman

---

Joseph E. Johnston was the only general officer of the United States Army to resign his commission and fight for the Confederacy. Fellow Virginian Robert E. Lee, the next highest-ranking U.S. Army officer to resign, was a colonel when Johnston had been a brigadier general. In theory, therefore, Johnston was the Confederacy's senior ranking officer.

But the Civil War killed theories as prodigally as it killed men. Despite a glorious record of combat, Johnston was U.S. Army quartermaster general—in essence, the chief supply clerk—when he left. It was a fact that President Jefferson Davis used to justify listing him fourth behind the other full generals whose appointments he announced in the autumn of 1861. Samuel Cooper (who would never see combat), Albert Sidney Johnston (no relation to Joseph), and Lee were all senior to him. Thus Joseph E. Johnston entered the Civil War angry and unhappy, feeling the weight of insult and injustice, his working relationship with Davis poisoned from the outset, and his credentials—his very fitness—as a combat commander cast into deep doubt.

A Son of Old Virginia

Like Robert E. Lee, Joseph Eggleston Johnston was born a son of Old Virginia. Lee was the son of "Light-Horse Harry" Lee of Revolutionary War fame, and Johnston the seventh child of Peter Johnston, who had fought under one of Light-Horse Harry's officers, Major Joseph Eggleston, during the revolution. The boy was born on February 3, 1807, in Longwood House, the seat of Peter Johnston's Cherry Grove plantation near Farmville.

A prominent planter and a judge, the husband of Mary Valentine Wood Johnston—herself the niece of Patrick ("Give me liberty or give me death") Henry—Peter Johnston possessed more than enough social prestige and political clout to obtain a nomination for his son's entry into the U.S. Military Academy in 1825. The young man enrolled, having been given the best of the kind of preparation Old Virginia plantation life could provide: plenty of manly outdoor activity, including hunting (which developed horsemanship and marksmanship), a sense of tradition and stewardship, and a combination of home schooling and lessons at Abingdon Academy that were both elegantly steeped in the classics. Young Joe Johnston's classmate Robert E. Lee beat him academically at West Point, placing second in the forty-six-member Class of 1829 while Johnston came in at thirteen, but his showing was sufficiently respectable to get him an appointment as second lieutenant in Company C of the 4th U.S. Artillery. And, once in the army, Johnston's rise was faster than Lee's. Promoted to brigadier general in 1860, he earned the distinction of being the first West Point graduate to make general officer.

UPRISINGS

In 1830, Second Lieutenant Johnston was assigned, with Company C, as a coastal artillerist to garrison duty at Fort Columbus, Governors Island, New York. Here he passed an uneventful year before transferring, in August 1831, to Fort Monroe, in southeastern Virginia. He and his company were assigned to reinforce the garrison so that it could resist what was being called Nat Turner's Rebellion.

Just before sunup on August 22, a slave preacher named Nat Turner led other slaves in an uprising against their master, Joseph Travis, then fanned out into Southampton County, killing every white person unfortunate enough to cross their path. (Among those who narrowly escaped the rampage was fifteen-year-old George Henry Thomas, a Virginian who would fight steadfastly for the Union at Chickamauga, Gettysburg, and elsewhere.) By the time Johnston and Company C arrived at Fort Monroe, Turner had been captured and executed, but his "rebellion" had been the realization of every slave owner's nightmare. Although his family owned slaves, Johnston professed a moral revulsion to slavery, yet he was retained with the rest of Company C at Fort Monroe largely to ensure that any further uprising could be quickly contained and suppressed. The assignment, in any event, proved to be a pleasant interlude, especially since he was reunited with Lee, with whom he renewed and strengthened the friendship begun at West Point.

In May 1832, Johnston and his company were sent to Illinois, where they were committed to service in the Black Hawk War. As in the case of Nat Turner's rampage, the army was tasked with putting the lid on another "uprising," this one led by a Sauk chief, Black Hawk, who refused to accept eviction from his tribe's traditional hunting grounds east of the Mississippi River and had clashed violently with new settlers along its banks. Johnston was excited by the prospect of the mission, which put him under the command of fellow Virginian Major General Winfield Scott, but neither Johnston nor anyone else in Scott's command ever faced Black Hawk and his warriors in battle. The entire force was swept by cholera, which killed about half of Scott's thousand-man command by the time it had gotten as far as Chicago. With only about two hundred "effectives," including Johnston, Scott pressed on to the Mississippi River, only to learn that Black Hawk and his band had been defeated at the Battle of Bad Axe in August. Having traveled some two thousand miles, barely escaping dread disease, Johnston returned to Fort Monroe.

He remained in this pleasant, placid service until 1836, when General Scott personally requested his service on his staff as he fought the Second Seminole War (1835–1842) in Florida. There were heated skirmishes—Johnston's first taste of combat—but most of the campaign consisted of futile tramps through miserable swampland in pursuit of an ever elusive enemy.

CIVILIAN INTERLUDE

In 1837, a treaty was signed with the Seminoles, who agreed to withdraw from their ancestral homes in Florida and resettle in Indian Country (modern Oklahoma and parts of adjacent states). With this, the fighting ended, and Johnston, seeing little future in the peacetime military, resigned his commission in March to start a career as a civilian engineer.

His West Point training stood him in good stead as he studied civil engineering, and by the end of 1837, he was employed as a contract topographic engineer aboard a small U.S. Navy survey craft commanded by Lieutenant William Pope McArthur. The peace brought by the treaty with the Seminoles proved fleeting, and, on January 12, 1838, at Jupiter, Florida, Seminole warriors set upon Johnston and the survey party he led. In the exchange of fire that followed,

Johnston would later claim to have accumulated some thirty bullet holes in his clothing, and one bullet deeply creased his scalp, excavating a scar he would carry for life. One sailor in the survey party later reported that the "coolness, courage, and judgment" Johnston "displayed at the most critical and trying emergency was the theme of praise with everyone who beheld him." Indeed, Johnston seems to have been exhilarated by this close brush with violent death. Although he was earning far more as a civilian engineer than as a military officer, he immediately resolved to return to the army.

In April, Johnston traveled to Washington, D.C., where he was commissioned a first lieutenant of topographic engineers on July 7. On that very day, he received an additional brevet to captain in recognition of his valor—though as a civilian—at Jupiter.

In 1841, Johnston was assigned as an engineer on the Texas–United States boundary survey, then returned to the East as the head of a coastal survey. While surveying near Baltimore, he met Lydia McLane, the daughter of Louis McLane, who had been a congressman and a senator from Delaware and had served in Andrew Jackson's Cabinet as secretary of the treasury and secretary of state. Although she was fifteen years his junior, Johnston courted her, and they married in July 1845.

U.S.-MEXICAN WAR, 1846–1848

At the outbreak of the war with Mexico in April 1846, Johnston wasted no time requesting a combat assignment. General Scott welcomed him to the engineer staff of his Southern Army, which was preparing for its spectacular amphibious landing at Veracruz and an overland march to Mexico City. His fellow engineer officers were P. G. T. Beauregard, George B. McClellan, and the ranking member, Robert E. Lee. Once the Veracruz campaign was under way, Scott assigned Johnston to command a regiment

known by the Napoleonic name of *voltigeurs* (literally "vaulters," called such in Napoleon's armies because they were trained to vault onto the rump of cavalry horses and ride double with cavalrymen in order to move quickly on the battlefield). In Scott's army, the voltigeurs were elite reconnaissance-skirmishers who operated far in advance of the main force. They were tasked with ascertaining enemy troop dispositions and, when possible, engaging and holding the enemy until the main force could arrive. In recognition of their elite status, they were issued special gray uniforms to distinguish them from blue-clad conventional troops.

In the opening phases of the Veracruz campaign, at the head of the voltigeurs, Johnston was wounded twice in combat but recovered in time to participate in the principal battles en route to Mexico City, including Contreras (August 19–20, 1847), Churubusco (August 20), Molino del Rey (September 8), and Chapultepec (September 12–13), where he was wounded by musket fire no fewer than three times as he led his men up the slope of this hill topped by a fortified "castle" on the outskirts of Mexico City. Having already been brevetted to lieutenant colonel for his earlier valor, Johnston was specially cited by General Scott as a "great soldier," the general wryly adding that he had the "unfortunate knack of getting himself shot in nearly every engagement."

THE FIRST GENERAL

His multiple woundings did nothing to sate Johnston's appetite for violent combat, and when, after the war, he returned to military engineering, this time as chief topographical engineer of the Department of Texas from 1848 to 1853, he found the tedium at times intolerable. Seeking more action, he transferred from the engineers to the cavalry in 1855, only to ponder resigning his commission in 1857 as his friend McClellan had done.

But he stuck it out. In 1858, he was transferred to Washington, then served for a time in California, returning to Washington, where, in 1860, he was promoted to brigadier general and named Quartermaster General of the U.S. Army on June 28. His ambition was to use this new position, in which he was responsible for managing much of the military budget, as a springboard to becoming the senior officer of the entire army. With this ambition uppermost in his mind, he did his best to try to ignore the developing secession crisis. Whatever was happening throughout the South, he resolved to do his duty to the United States and its army as long as he wore the uniform. He was hardly what the press at the time called a "fire eater"—a vehement advocate of secession. He despised slavery, and he rejected the argument many Southerners were making, that the right to secede from the Union was implied by the Constitution. In any case, whether it was a right or not, he opposed secession. Yet he came to the conclusion, as did Robert E. Lee and other sons of Old Virginia, that Virginia was his "country" and that he owed his loyalty first and last to it. He determined that he would share the fate of his state, whatever it might be.

Winfield Scott, his old commanding officer, a fellow Virginian, begged Johnston to remain loyal to the U.S. Army. When he saw that he was not getting through, that Johnston did not intend to allow his army loyalty to trump his allegiance to Virginia, Scott turned to Lydia McLane Johnston, who was a Baltimorean, not a Virginian. When she explained to General Scott that her husband would never "stay in an army that is about to invade his native land," Scott took a fallback position, asking her to persuade him to leave the U.S. Army if he must but not to join "theirs." In fact, Lydia Johnston believed that Jefferson Davis would "ruin" her husband, but she knew it was hopeless to try to persuade him not to rally to the defense of his "country," his Virginia. As soon as the state seceded

on April 17, 1861, he presented his resignation to General Scott, leaving behind him in Washington virtually all that he owned, save for the sword his father had carried in the American Revolution.

Harpers Ferry Command, Spring 1861

Johnston arrived in Richmond on April 25 and called on Governor John Letcher to offer his services. Letcher told him that Robert E. Lee had arrived just four days earlier, at which time he appointed him commander of the state's troops. After quickly consulting Lee, he offered Johnston command of state troops in and around Richmond. It was, Johnston recognized, a vital assignment, since Richmond, though not yet the capital of the Confederacy, was the capital of the South's principal state and a key industrial and transportation center. As such, it was sure to be a prime target for Union attack. What is more, the city's defenses were chaotic, and the situation cried out for someone to take charge. Johnston possessed the powerful command presence required to pull everyone into line.

While he threw himself into the work of military organization in Richmond, Johnston waited for the results of the Virginia Convention, which would decide on the final membership of the state army's officer corps. Two weeks after his arrival in Richmond, Johnston was disappointed to learn that the convention had decided that Lee would be the only major general. When Letcher rushed to offer Johnston an appointment as brigadier general, he turned it down. Although he had left the U.S. Army to defend his home state, he now offered his services to the Provisional Confederate Army. It was not a decision based on Confederate nationalism but on a perceived command opportunity. Although the Confederate army offered nothing higher than the brigadier rank, Johnston understood that the Congress was about to pass a resolution elevating all brigadiers to full generals. He accepted the lower rank with the understanding that it would soon be raised.

After Johnston was formally commissioned on May 14, President Davis dispatched him to relieve Thomas J. Jackson as commanding officer at Harpers Ferry. Fifty-four-year-old Joseph E. Johnston was a distinguished and distinguished-looking officer, famed for combining valor with calm dignity and a compelling, charismatic personal presence. Davis hoped that he was just the man to work miracles at Harpers Ferry, but the president was about to learn that Johnston was not in the miracle business. Two days after arriving at his new command, he sent Davis a message declaring his opinion that Harpers Ferry could not be held against an enemy attack, at least not with the relatively small force he had available.

It was hardly what Davis or the Congress wanted to hear.

Johnston's recommendation was to pull back from Harpers Ferry—let the Union have it—and instead use the freed-up resources to defend the Shenandoah Valley whenever and wherever required. Without a shot having been fired, Johnston was already proposing retreat. It rankled. However, in the end, Davis and his War Department agreed to allow him to pull back as far as Winchester, which he did behind a skillfully deployed cavalry screen that prevented Union forces from seeing where he had gone.

The maneuver would prove emblematic of Johnston's strategic thinking. It would also ignite a debate about his fitness for command that would endure throughout the war.

For traditional military thinkers, like Davis, nothing was more important than holding and defending territory. Johnston, in contrast, believed that preserving the ability of an army to maneuver preserved its ability to fight, to do damage to the enemy army. Instead of tying down an army to a particular place, Johnston was willing to trade territory for maneuverability. From the beginning, he believed that defeating the

Union states in straight-up warfare was impossible. The North had more people, more industry, more money. If, however, the South could stay in the fight, bleeding the North, the Confederacy just might outlast the Union will to continue the war. It was the lesson of the American Revolution, his father's war. General Washington had well known that the puny Continental Army could not hope to defeat the military forces of the British nation, but if it could stay in the fight, it stood a chance of stretching the war will of British people and politicians just beyond the breaking point.

The question was this: Did Johnston's vision of the nature of the Civil War demonstrate a truly advanced grasp of big-picture strategy? Or was he just insufficiently aggressive to defend the "sacred soil" of the Confederacy and bring the fight to the enemy?

FIRST BATTLE OF BULL RUN, JULY 21, 1861

Letting go of Harpers Ferry and consolidating in and around Winchester gave Johnston the room he needed to maneuver what was now called the Army of Shenandoah. The very first major battle of the war, at Manassas Junction near Bull Run Creek, would prove the wisdom of Johnston's approach. By regarding territory as something to be occupied and relinquished at will, so that forces could be concentrated wherever and whenever needed, Johnston was able to rush his army to reinforce P. G. T. Beauregard when it became clear that Union general Irvin McDowell was leading an attack against Manassas Junction. Consistent with his practical approach to combat, Johnston, though senior to Beauregard, turned over to him the major responsibility for planning the battle because he reasoned that Beauregard, already on the scene, knew the terrain better than he. When execution of the plan threatened to come apart, however, Beauregard threw overall field command back to Johnston while he concentrated on rallying, guiding, and

Federal cavalry at Sudley Springs after the First Battle of Bull Run. Library of Congress

generally exhorting the troops. In the end, this approach brought a major victory for the Confederacy and an even bigger humiliation for the Union. It also meant, however, that Beauregard grabbed the lion's share of the credit for the victory since he appeared onstage, as it were, while Johnston worked behind the scenes.

Both Beauregard and Johnston resisted pursuing McDowell's routed forces into Washington—and Jefferson Davis held them both responsible for what he deemed their lack of aggressiveness. Both generals would endure strained relations with Davis throughout the rest of the war, but while the conflict between Davis and Beauregard tended to be a matter of personality, that between Davis and Johnston was always over strategy. In both instances, the result was destructive for the Confederate war effort. As for the judgment of history on the First Battle of Bull Run, most historians believe that Beauregard and Johnston did squander an opportunity to do much more damage to McDowell's army and to terrorize Washington in the bargain. There is, however, wide difference in opinion about just how costly aggressive exploitation of the Bull Run victory would have been.

Had he a freer hand, Jefferson Davis would likely have formally censured Johnston rather than merely criticized him for failing to follow up on the result of First Bull Run. But he dared not be too critical of a general who was tremendously popular with the people, his fellow officers, and the men under his command. Thus, in August, as Johnston himself had predicted, he was elevated to full general. That was the work of the Congress, and Davis did nothing to stop it; however, in the promotion list he submitted to Congress, he listed Johnston fourth, behind Samuel Cooper, Albert Sidney Johnston, and Robert E. Lee, and ahead of only Beauregard. As the first senior officer (and only general officer) to resign from the U.S. Army to join the Confederate forces, Johnston believed he should also be ranked as the senior officer in the Confederate army. He never forgave Davis for what he considered a supreme insult, and this added significantly to the ill will that existed between the men.

PENINSULA CAMPAIGN, MARCH–JULY 1862

Early in 1862, Johnston was assigned command of what the Confederates at first called the Army of the Potomac but would soon rename the Army of Northern Virginia. Its mission was to defend Richmond against Major General George B. McClellan's Peninsula Campaign.

Once again, Johnston chose to avoid open battle whenever he could, making a series of strategic withdrawals that sorely tested Davis's patience and nerve. Johnston allowed McClellan to approach within five miles of the capital. At this point, the Confederate president issued an ultimatum to the Army of Northern Virginia commander. "If you will not give battle," he wrote, "I will appoint someone to command who will."

Thus goaded, Johnston counterattacked at the Battle of Seven Pines (Fair Oaks) on May 31 and June 1, 1862. The result was very costly to both sides: 5,031 killed, wounded, captured, or missing among the Union troops, and 6,134 among the Confederates. Johnston halted McClellan's advance but also fell back on the outer defensive works of Richmond. Among the Confederate casualties was Johnston, who, on the battle's second day, was hit by a bullet in the right shoulder and then wounded full-on in the chest by a massive shell fragment, which knocked him off his horse. At first, it seemed certain that the wounds were mortal, as Johnston lapsed into unconsciousness. Surprisingly, he rallied, but it would be six months before he would return to a field command.

Davis, who was present on the field, ministered to the stricken general. Despite their deep disagreement on strategy, he showed genuine concern for the man. Yet he also took the opportunity to appoint Robert E. Lee, a far more aggressive general, in his place. Johnston approved of the appointment, partly because he believed that Lee was extremely capable, but also because he understood that Lee would essentially call for the same strategy he himself had advocated. When Lee asked for reinforcements and Davis eagerly complied, Johnston remarked that his wound had been "fortunate" after all because "concentration" is what he himself had "earnestly recommended, but had not the influence to effect. Lee," he observed, "had made them do for him what they would not do for me."

VICKSBURG CAMPAIGN, DECEMBER 1862–JULY 4, 1863

During Johnston's convalescence from his wounds, he became a close friend of Senator Louis T. Wigfall, a leader of the anti-Davis faction in the Confederate Congress. Clearly, Johnston had decided to work politically against

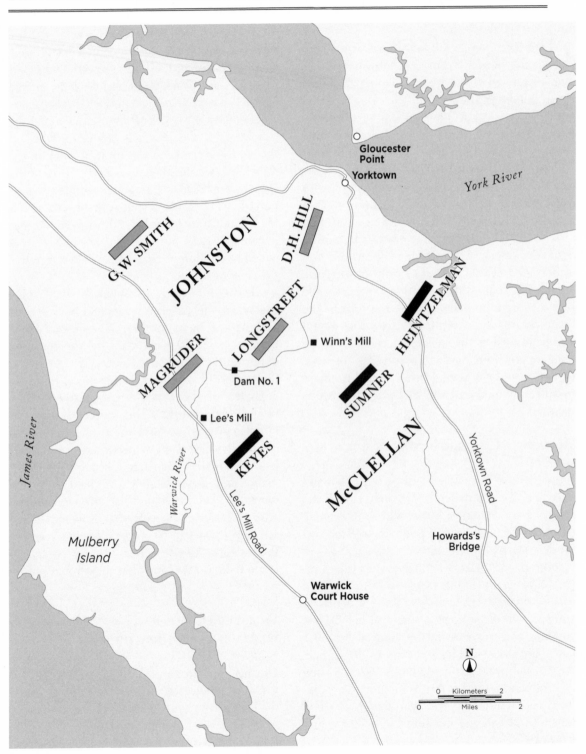

Gloucester
Point

Yorktown

York River

G.W. SMITH

JOHNSTON

D.H. HILL

HEINTZELMAN

LONGSTREET

Winn's Mill

MAGRUDER

Dam No. 1

SUMNER

Lee's Mill

James River

KEYES

McCLELLAN

Warwick River

Yorktown Road

Howards's
Bridge

Lee's Mill Road

Mulberry
Island

Warwick
Court House

N

0   Kilometers   2

0   Miles   2

Davis, and Davis knew this; nevertheless—and even with his grave doubts about Johnston's policy of strategic retreat—he was eager for the general's return to service. Johnston was a popular hero and still highly regarded throughout the army. Davis believed that he could not afford to lose him, and when he was pressured to give Johnston a major command, he complied, assigning him to direct all forces between the Appalachians and the Mississippi River.

Although Johnston reported to his new assignment early in November 1862, he was still weak and would not be fully fit to command for some more months. He established his headquarters in Chattanooga on December 4, but while this put him with Braxton Bragg's Army of Tennessee, the first problem he tackled was Vicksburg, Mississippi. Pointing out to Davis its strategic importance as the fortress by which the Confederacy controlled the Mississippi River, Johnston called for reinforcing Lieutenant General John C. Pemberton's Department of Mississippi and East Louisiana, whose troops held the town. Davis, however, refused to transfer men from Lee's theater. Thus, when Grant commenced his siege of unreinforced Vicksburg, Johnston recommended the abandonment of the city, so that Pemberton's Army of Mississippi could join forces with the Army of Tennessee, outnumber Grant, and drive him off the Vicksburg front. Appalled by the mere suggestion of relinquishing the Confederacy's "Gibraltar of the West" without so much as a fight, Davis did not bother to argue with Johnston. Instead, he bypassed him, ordering Pemberton to remain in Vicksburg and, from within, hold the city at all costs.

For his part, Johnston saw no reason to sacrifice to a forlorn hope those men still directly under his command. When Grant attacked Jackson, Mississippi, on May 14, 1863, Johnston, massively outnumbered, withdrew from this crucial supply link to Vicksburg. Grant's troops overran the town and burned it, destroying an important industrial and rail center. The effect on Confederate logistics in the region was obvious. Perhaps even more devastating, however, was the impact on morale, which widely collapsed beyond even Johnston's ability to rally his troops. Pemberton held on in Vicksburg as long as he could, but the destruction of Jackson made the outcome inevitable. The city fell to Grant on July 4, 1863.

ATLANTA CAMPAIGN, MAY 7–SEPTEMBER 2, 1864

In November 1863, Grant forced Braxton Bragg's Army of Tennessee out of Chattanooga and into Georgia. Bragg was relieved at his own request, whereupon Jefferson Davis offered his command to Lee, who refused. Senator Wigfall led the political pressure on Davis to give Johnston the command. Although Johnston already had jurisdiction over the Western Theater, heading up the Army of Tennessee would be a genuine field command, not a desk job.

Johnston was pleased to be in the field again, and he devoted much of the winter of 1863–1864 to preparing the army to confront Major General William T. Sherman's advance from Chattanooga into Georgia and, in particular, Atlanta. Johnston believed the problem was to devise the most effective way to use his inferior numbers against Sherman's much larger army. As usual, Davis wanted him to make a do-or-die stand, with the objective of keeping Sherman out of Atlanta at all costs. Also as usual, Johnston wanted to retain mobility instead of commit his forces to the static defense of a place. His principal tactic would be to use a portion of his army as a shield to hold Sherman while he counterattacked, whenever and wherever possible, with the rest of the army. In this way, he hoped to grind away at the enemy while wearing down popular will among Northerners to continue the fight. He reasoned that if he could prevent Sherman from taking Atlanta before Lincoln stood for reelection in November 1864, there was a very good chance that the president would be defeated and that the Democrat who entered the White House in his place would offer an acceptable negotiated end to the bloody conflict.

Given the dwindling resources of the Confederacy, it was perhaps a reasonable strategy, but it would require continual strategic retreat toward Atlanta, and this Davis could not accept. He sent Bragg, whom he had appointed his military advisor, to tell Johnston in no uncertain terms that the mission of the Army of Tennessee was to recapture the state whose name the force bore. Johnston replied that the army was too small and too depleted for that. Thus the stage was set for a strategic debate that continues to this day. Was Johnston's policy of strategic retreat the best available approach to an all-but-hopeless situation? Or was he simply afraid to commit to aggressive, decisive battle?

As it happened, strategic retreat failed to have the effect Johnston hoped for. As he fell back toward Atlanta, he repeatedly set up strong defensive positions by which he intended to wear Sherman down. But Sherman proved to be a sophisticated tactician, who did not oblige Johnston by battering his forces against the Confederate defenses. Much as Grant did with Lee's Army of Northern Virginia, Sherman found ways to sideslip and maneuver around the positions Johnston took. To avoid being flanked, Johnston was repeatedly forced to pull up stakes and fall farther back on Atlanta. To be sure, his defensive stands were taking a toll on Sherman, but Johnston was also losing men, and while Sherman could replace his losses, Johnston could not. Moreover, Atlanta, the prize his retreat strategy put at risk, was not, in the end, an expendable piece of "territory." It was a mighty industrial center and the central rail hub of the entire Confederacy. It was one of the engines that drove the war.

Johnston fought defensively at Dalton, Georgia, evacuating it on May 13 and falling back on Resaca, where he established a strong defensive position. Sherman had nearly one hundred thousand men available, Johnston about sixty thousand. He inflicted perhaps as many as five thousand casualties on Sherman's superior forces in a battle spanning May 13 to 15, suffering 2,800 killed, wounded, missing, or captured before withdrawing to Adairsville and fighting a brief battle there on May 17 before falling back again. He turned to fight at Cassville on May 20, then retreated, fighting battles at New Hope Church on May 25, Pickett's Mill on May 27, and Dallas on May 28. Casualties mounted on both sides; then, for the first three weeks of June, the opposing armies maneuvered more than fought.

It was astounding that Johnston had managed to stay in the fight against two-to-one odds. From his point of view, this was an achievement that offered the best hope the Confederacy had for something better than total defeat and unconditional surrender. Davis did not see it this way, however, and Lieutenant General John Bell Hood, one of Johnston's corps commanders, fed the president's discontent with a series of letters complaining that Johnston was a defeatist who was keeping *his* corps from making an impact against Sherman.

Although Johnston won a significant victory against Sherman at the Battle of Kennesaw Mountain on June 27, inflicting three thousand casualties while suffering no more than a thousand himself, his strategic retreat to the mountain had put Sherman just seventeen miles from Atlanta's center, with Union troops menacing the city from the west as well as the north.

Davis once again dispatched Bragg to assess the situation. When he returned to Richmond, he told the president to relieve Johnston without delay. Davis was more than ready, and Hood replaced Johnston on July 17, 1864.

Where Johnston was cagey, always looking to preserve his army so as to remain in the fight, Hood was the bluntest of blunt instruments, impulsive, impatient, aggressive. Sherman was overjoyed when he heard that Hood had replaced Johnston. He knew the fight would be fierce, but he also knew that it would at last be decisive. Hood lost Atlanta to Sherman on September 2, then went on to lose much of the Army of Tennessee fighting at the Battles of Franklin on November 30, 1864, and Nashville on December 15 and 16.

The End

Johnston's departure from the Army of Tennessee had been sorrowful. Two of his subordinate generals, William Joseph "Old Reliable" Hardee and William Whann Mackall, went so far as to request to be relieved. Davis might have been more than ready to give up on Johnston, but most of the army and a majority of the Southern people were not. When Georgia "howled" under the scourge of Sherman's March to the Sea, a popular outcry arose for the return of Joe Johnston. Davis could not bring himself to approach the general personally but instead reinstated him via Robert E. Lee, who personally asked his old friend to assume command of what was now called the Department of South Carolina, Georgia, and Florida, as well as the Department of North Carolina and Southern Virginia.

Johnston accepted, but vast as the new commands sounded, there was really very little to take charge of. Only the Army of Tennessee, depleted as it had been under Hood, remained a considerable military force. Johnston used it at the Battle of Bentonville, North Carolina, on March 19 to 21, 1865, managing to catch part of Sherman's army by surprise before he was overwhelmed by superior numbers—Sherman fielded sixty thousand men, Johnston twenty-one thousand—and retreated first to Raleigh and later to Greensboro, North Carolina, where he planned to make a stand.

But there would be no battle. Instead, word having reached him of Lee's surrender at Appomattox Court House, Johnston met with Davis and his Cabinet in the bedroom of a quiet Greensboro house as the members of the Confederate government paused in their flight from Richmond. P. G. T. Beauregard was present as well. Davis admitted that the situation was "terrible," but he expressed his opinion that "we can whip the enemy if our people turn out."

Johnston held his tongue until Davis prodded him. "My views, sir," Johnston said at last, "are that our people are tired of war, feel themselves whipped, and will not fight." He told the president that the men of his army were "deserting in large numbers" and in the wake of "Lee's surrender . . . regard the war as at an end. . . . My small force is melting away like snow before the sun, and I am hopeless of recruiting it."

Davis solemnly turned to Beauregard. Usually given to rhetorical extravagance, he spoke simply: "I concur in all General Johnston has said."

JOHNSTON AND LEE—A PHOTOGRAPH OF 1866.

Joseph E. Johnston (left) with Robert E. Lee in 1869.

With this, Johnston secured the president's permission to negotiate with Sherman, the two meeting at a farm called the Bennett Place outside of Durham. They held three sessions together, on April 17, 18, and 26, 1865, at the conclusion of which Johnston formally surrendered the Army of Tennessee as well as all Confederate forces still active in North Carolina, South Carolina, Georgia, and Florida. In total, it was a much larger force than what Lee had surrendered at Appomattox, nearly ninety thousand soldiers.

AFTER THE END

With the war over, Johnston moved to Savannah, Georgia, became president of a railroad for a time, then briefly ran an insurance business from 1868 to 1869. In 1874, he published his voluminous *Narrative of Military Operations*, a strategic and tactical analysis of the war that was intensely critical of Jefferson Davis and those generals who did his bidding. Returning to Virginia in 1877, he bought a house in Richmond and served as president of an express company. Two years later, he entered Congress as a Democrat but decided to retire from politics in 1881 after serving a single term. Fellow Democrat Grover Cleveland appointed him a U.S. commissioner of railroads in 1885, and he served until 1891.

The most frequently wounded general of the Civil War, Johnston proved as indestructible as his battered Army of Tennessee. He outlived Sherman, to whom he was ever grateful for the kindness he had shown his beaten army, feeding and caring for it after the surrender at the Bennett Place, and he proudly served as a pallbearer in Sherman's funeral procession through the icy rain of February 19, 1891. Throughout the length of the procession, he walked bareheaded, and when a concerned member of the funeral party advised the old man to put on his hat, lest he take ill, Johnston responded, "If I were in his place and he standing here in mine, he would not put on his hat."

Soon after William Tecumseh Sherman's funeral, Joseph Eggleston Johnston contracted pneumonia. He died on March 21, 1891.

Chapter 3

ROBERT E. LEE

RATING: ★ ★ ★ ⭒

Robert E. Lee. NATIONAL ARCHIVES AND RECORDS ADMINISTRATION

EVALUATION

Perhaps no general in any army at any time has been more universally admired than Robert E. Lee. His character commanded the devotion of his men as well as the people of the South (who, for the most part, idolized him) and won the ungrudging respect of his Union opponents. His ability to hold together the Army of Northern Virginia under conditions of crushing hardship was nearly miraculous. He possessed the topographical understanding of the brilliant engineer that he was; few commanders have so completely grasped the concept of what modern soldiers call battlespace. His approach to tactical problems was innovative and often daring,

as when he deliberately divided his forces in the face of the enemy at the Second Battle of Bull Run and at Chancellorsville. His "big picture" concept of the appropriate Confederate strategy was persuasive, though ultimately unsuccessful. He believed that time was the South's enemy and that the North had to be dealt a series of quick, aggressive offensive blows to break its will to fight and force its leaders to negotiate a peace favorable to the Confederacy. Lee was a commander of great personal courage, who also had an uncanny facility for seeing the battle from his adversary's point of view.

Yet he was far from being a perfect general. His policy of offense, of offering battle at every opportunity, led to his sacrificing the very real advantages of fighting a defensive war on "home soil." Even more critical was the deep flaw in his command style. Without doubt, Lee possessed compelling "command presence," but his habit of couching in the consultative language of gentleman soldiers what should have been emphatic, direct, and absolute orders to subordinates sometimes led to a breakdown in coordination among the elements of his Army of Northern Virginia. At Gettysburg, the results of this command style were notoriously catastrophic. Lee seems often to have lacked the energy as well as the willingness to ride herd on his subordinates and to ensure the proper, prompt, and complete execution of his orders. For this, he and his army sometimes paid a heavy price.

Finally, speed and maximum aggression were the hallmarks of Lee's strategy and tactics, and the foundation of his battlefield success. These, however, required a willingness to spend lives. Ultimately, Lee was unable to produce with this bloody prodigality the results he wanted—and the Confederacy needed—before he had bled his army white. When Ulysses S. Grant turned the Civil War into a contest of attrition, Lee and his force were doomed.

In the end, perhaps Robert E. Lee's greatest contribution to the Civil War was the aura of nobility and honor he generated about himself. Thanks in large part to him, the Civil War definitively ended rather than petered out in the bitter "Bleeding Kansas"-style violence of a prolonged guerrilla resistance. Lee showed his men how to win battles, but, in final defeat, he also showed them how to surrender with a dignity and a humanity that contributed to the healing of the nation.

Principal Battles

PRE-CIVIL WAR

U.S.-Mexican War, 1846–1848

- Siege of Veracruz, March 9–29, 1847: As an engineer officer of Winfield Scott's staff, Lee performed key reconnaissance and was instrumental in laying out the route of advance toward Mexico City
- Cerro Gordo, April 18, 1847
- Contreras, August 19–20, 1847
- Churubusco, August 20, 1847
- Chapultepec, September 12–13, 1847: Throughout General Scott's march from Veracruz to Mexico City, Lee was instrumental in scouting and plotting routes of march and assault, typically at great hazard to himself

Capture of John Brown at Harpers Ferry, October 16–18, 1859

- Commanded militia and U.S. Marines in the swift and efficient suppression of Brown's Harpers Ferry raid

Civil War

- Cheat Mountain, September 11–13, 1861: In western Virginia; Lee's performance was disappointing and brought much criticism in the press
- Seven Days, June 25–July 1, 1862: In Virginia; Lee suffered more casualties than George B. McClellan but forced him into a humiliating retreat from the outskirts of Richmond
- Second Bull Run, August 28–30, 1862: In Virginia; a brilliant victory, in which Lee exhibited his

remarkable facility for imagining the battle from his enemy's point of view
- South Mountain, September 14, 1862: In Maryland; this prelude to Antietam was a clear Union victory
- Antietam, September 17, 1862: In Maryland; the culminating battle in Lee's bold invasion of Maryland; failures of execution led to a narrow Confederate tactical victory, but a decided Union strategic win, in that Lee was forced to withdraw to Virginia
- Fredericksburg, December 11–15, 1862: In Virginia; a smashing victory for Lee, who outgeneraled Ambrose Burnside in every conceivable way
- Chancellorsville, April 30–May 6, 1863: In Virginia; outnumbered two to one, Lee scored another overwhelming—if costly—victory against the Army of the Potomac, this time under Joseph Hooker
- Gettysburg, July 1–3, 1863: In Pennsylvania; the apotheosis of Lee's strategy of offense, the battle resulted in a turning-point defeat for Lee and the Confederate cause
- Overland Campaign, May–June 1864: In Virginia; forced onto the defensive by his defeat at Gettysburg, Lee scored bloody tactical victories at the Wilderness and Spotsylvania Court House, and an overwhelming win at Cold Harbor, yet failed to stop Grant's southward advance
- Siege of Petersburg, June 9, 1864–March 25, 1865: In Virginia; despite Lee's efforts to avoid fighting a war of attrition, the Civil War culminated in a ten-month stalemate, costly to both sides
- Appomattox Campaign, March 29–April 9, 1865: In Virginia; after evacuating Petersburg, Lee sought in vain a means of linking his Army of Northern Virginia with Joseph Johnston's Army of Tennessee in an effort to avoid unconditional surrender; his surrender of the Army of Northern Virginia effectively—though unofficially—ended the Civil War

By the time Robert E. Lee was born on January 19, 1807, at Stratford Hall, the Westmoreland, Virginia, plantation house of Henry "Light-Horse Harry" Lee, his father was desperately juggling dwindling funds in a hopeless effort to satisfy his increasingly restive creditors. The hero of the American Revolution would enter debtors' prison in 1810, when Robert was three, and the family was forced to move out of Stratford and into a tiny house in the old town of Alexandria.

Two years later, when his fifth child was just five years old, on July 27, 1812, the Federalist Lee was severely injured when he came to the aid of his friend Alexander Contee Hanson, a Baltimore newspaper editor who had dared to oppose the War of 1812 and who was now under vicious attack by a Democratic-Republican mob. While struggling to recover—he never would—Lee abandoned his family, settled for a time in the West Indies beginning in 1813, then returned to the United States, taking up residence at Cumberland Island, Georgia, where he died in 1818.

The absentee father had left his family poor, and upon Robert, the youngest, increasingly fell the burden of caring for his mother through her long decline. Bereft of Stratford and all it said of Old Virginia, fortuneless, and having given up his freedom to look after his mother, Robert E. Lee nevertheless worshipped the man he knew far better as a bold figure of history than as a flesh-and-blood father. It was not so much that he idealized Light-Horse Harry's historical memory as that he willingly suppressed the bad judgment, irresponsibility, and squalor that followed. A natural-born idealist, Robert E. Lee saw his father as the quintessential Virginian. Later, as a soldier himself, he would see Virginia as the land of his father, an ennobled place that was far more immediately his country than the United States was. For Lee, duty, honor, and country were supreme concepts, yet they were concepts seen through the narrow prism of his vision of Virginia. This would drive him to a passionate greatness as a general, it would profoundly influence the fate of the Union and the Confederacy during the Civil War, and it would shape the character and destiny of one of America's most universally and deeply revered generals.

WEST POINT AND FIRST ASSIGNMENTS

Animated by the martial ideals exemplified by his father, Robert E. Lee enrolled at West Point in 1825 and compiled an exceptional record over the next four years. He was the first cadet to make sergeant at the end of his first year, he passed through all four years without earning a single demerit, and in the Class of 1829 he was second only to Charles Mason. Like virtually all top-performing cadets, he chose the Corps of Engineers as his branch and was duly commissioned a brevet second lieutenant in it.

His first assignment was seventeen months of supervising foundation work for Fort Pulaski on Cockspur Island, Georgia. This was followed in 1831 by work on Forts Monroe and Calhoun at the tip of the Virginia Peninsula. They were military engineering works in the grand tradition, and Fort Monroe was not unjustly dubbed the "Gibraltar of the Chesapeake."

It was while he was stationed at Fort Monroe that he began a relationship with another paragon of Old Virginia when he courted Mary Anna Randolph Custis, daughter of George Washington Parke Custis, Martha Custis Washington's son, whom George Washington had adopted. Mary's father was not cheered by the prospect of his daughter marrying a landless, semi-impoverished professional soldier, but he recognized in Lee what everyone sooner or later saw in him: a nobility of vision grounded in the practical competence and exuberant imagination of an engineer. There was no getting around it. Robert E. Lee was a remarkable young man, and Mary's father was soon won over. The couple married on June 30, 1831. They would have four daughters and three sons, and although a soldier's life took Lee away from his family for long stretches, he proved the devoted father his own father had failed to be.

In the meantime, peace, the undoing of many young American military careers during the 1820s and 1830s, was just what Lee needed to develop as a remarkably creative engineer. He was based in the chief engineer's office in Washington, D.C., from 1834 to 1837, but during the summer of 1835 worked on the survey of the Ohio-Michigan state line. In 1837, he was sent to St. Louis harbor to solve a problem of massive proportions as the Mississippi River inexorably moved away from the city's levee system. Left unchecked, the consequences would be catastrophic for the economy of this key gateway. Lee devised a practical plan to redirect the river's flow in a way that minimized the deposit of sediment, which had been driving the river from the city. This experience, along with a project to blast a navigation channel through the Des Moines Rapids of the Mississippi River at Keokuk, Iowa, taught Lee a great deal about solving big, complex problems with strategic elegance.

U.S.-MEXICAN WAR, 1846–1848

Promoted to captain in 1842, Lee was assigned as post engineer at Fort Hamilton, in the Bay Ridge section of Brooklyn. His mission was to strengthen and waterproof the defensive works along Verrazano Narrows. Here Lee met Lieutenant Thomas J. Jackson—the future Stonewall Jackson, destined to serve in the Civil War as Lee's right hand through the Battle of Chancellorsville in May 1863.

Lee was posted to Fort Hamilton for four years, until he was called to the service of Major General Winfield Scott in the spring of 1846 to fight in the war with Mexico. Despite his great success as an engineer, Lee identified himself first and foremost as a soldier, and, after more than two decades in the United States Army, he had yet to hear a shot fired in anger. He burned for action.

Although Captain Lee was assigned to Scott's staff, his was hardly a desk job. Lee, along with George B. McClellan and P. G. T. Beauregard, was an engineer officer, which meant that his most important mission was topographical reconnaissance with the object of plotting out the best routes of advance and attack and identifying the most effective emplacement of artillery and fortifications. Such work was often hazardous in the extreme, requiring long-range solitary

Robert E. Lee as a captain in the Corps of Engineers at the time of the U.S.-Mexican War. FROM FRANK MOORE, ED., *PORTRAIT GALLERY OF THE WAR* (1865)

scouting rides, alone and far from the main body of troops. Throughout the march from Veracruz to Mexico City, Lee undertook the prime responsibility for reconnaissance. At the Battles of Cerro Gordo (April 18, 1847) and Chapultepec (September 12–13, 1847), he provided Scott with the intelligence he needed to make devastatingly effective flanking attacks through adverse terrain the Mexican commanders had left undefended. Promoted to brevet major after Cerro Gordo, he fought next at Contreras (August 19–20, 1847) and Churubusco (August 20, 1847), for which he was brevetted to lieutenant colonel. Slightly wounded at Chapultepec, he was subsequently brevetted to colonel.

One of the most dramatic aspects of the U.S.-Mexican War was that it brought together in comradeship so many officers who would take up arms for the opposing sides in the Civil War. Union general-in-chief Winfield Scott, who thought Lee the "very best soldier [he] ever saw in the field," would unsuccessfully seek him for an important Union command in the Civil War. And it was in the conflict with Mexico that Lee met his ultimate adversary, Ulysses S. Grant. Yet Lee gained more from his experience in Mexico than an acquaintance with fellow officers and a taste of combat. As an engineer charged with understanding the connections between topography and battle, he conceived his early notions of the very landscape of war. Mostly, this would prove invaluable to him in the conflict nearly two decades later; however, some military historians have speculated that he may also have received a distorted impression of the sovereign power of frontal attacks. For the U.S. Army in Mexico, such attacks invariably worked well, but they were directed against poorly trained soldiers of low morale who carried weapons charged with notoriously low-performing Mexican gunpowder. Such would not be the case in the Civil War, and while Lee was characteristically an innovative tactician on the battlefield, his resort to the grand frontal assault in "Pickett's Charge" on day three of the Battle of Gettysburg would prove tragic on a vast scale.

FROM ENGINEER TO CAVALRYMAN

Peace was a letdown for Lee, as it was for many other officers. From 1848 to 1852, he was assigned to the garrison at Fort Carroll in Baltimore Harbor with interruptions for various mapping and surveying expeditions, including one to update maps of Florida. Through President Franklin Pierce's secretary of war, Jefferson Davis, he received an offer to assist Cuban rebels in their ongoing struggle for independence from Spain. Lee was not interested in what he considered a foreign adventure.

Nor, however, was he especially pleased with his next assignment, which he received in 1852,

a coveted appointment as superintendent of the U.S. Military Academy at West Point. He preferred active service commanding troops, even in peacetime, to leading the academy, and he also craved an assignment closer to Arlington, the Virginia estate that had become his home after he married into the Custis family. Separation from his wife and children was hard on him, but he undertook his new mission with professional zeal, introducing major improvements in West Point's buildings and facilities and, more important, expanding its academic program, focusing more intensely on military tactics and strategy and generally raising the level of demand placed upon cadets. His ambition was to ensure that West Point would become a center of military excellence, not just a place for well-connected young men to get an education at taxpayer expense. Lee was also hands-on with the cadets and made it his business to get to know them. In the two years he served as superintendent, Lee met many of the younger generation of officers who would play important roles in the Civil War, including the man who would lead the Army of Northern Virginia's cavalry, J. E. B. Stuart. He also had the satisfaction of seeing his eldest son, George Washington Custis Lee, graduate during his tenure, first in the Class of 1854.

The U.S. Congress authorized the creation of four new regiments in March 1853, and in 1855, when the 2nd U.S. Cavalry was actually formed, Lee was thrilled that Secretary of War Davis assigned him as the regiment's second in command, at the rank of brevet lieutenant colonel. (Lee had reverted to his regular army rank of captain after the U.S.-Mexican War.) He willingly left the Corps of Engineers to accept the cavalry post in what was intended as an elite unit assigned to Camp Cooper, Texas, with the mission of protecting settlers against Apache and Comanche raiders. His commanding officer was regimental colonel Albert Sidney Johnston, who would become one of the giants of the Provisional Confederate Army early in the Civil War.

John Brown's Harpers Ferry Raid, October 16-18, 1859

Lee was forced to interrupt his western service with the 2nd Cavalry in 1857 when his father-in-law, George Washington Parke Custis, died, leaving behind a shambles of a will and a large estate encumbered with massive debts. Taking on the burden of executor, Lee also committed himself to reforming management of the Arlington plantation and took a series of protracted leaves of absence from active duty. He was also concerned about the deteriorating health of his wife, Mary, who was becoming increasingly disabled by arthritis. Poorly paid in the military and often forced to live apart from his needy family, Lee contemplated resigning his commission. In the end, however, he could not bring himself to do so.

On October 16, 1859, John Brown, who had earned a national reputation in "Bleeding Kansas" as a ruthlessly militant abolitionist, led a party of sixteen white men and five black men in a nighttime raid on the federal arsenal and armory at Harpers Ferry, Virginia. To ensure that he could hold his prize, Brown took about sixty townspeople hostage, among them the great-grandnephew of George Washington. Hunkered down in an arsenal building, Brown sent two of his raiders to rally local slaves. Brown was confident that a slave army of thousands would soon rally to his command.

By daybreak of October 17, however, no such army materialized, and local residents had surrounded Brown, his raiders, and their hostages and began to exchange fire with them. By the afternoon, after two of Brown's sons had been killed, the surviving raiders hauled their hostages to a firehouse adjacent to the armory building and holed up there.

Lee, immersed in the tangled affairs of Arlington, was the nearest available field-grade officer when he was summoned to command an ad hoc assemblage of Maryland and Virginia militiamen and a Washington-based detachment of U.S. Marines to recover control of the armory and arsenal. His second in command was Lieutenant James Ewell Brown "Jeb" Stuart. If it was unusual to put marines under army officers, it was perhaps even stranger that Lee had not even found the time to change out of the civilian clothes he was wearing when he was ordered to Harpers Ferry.

On his arrival, he found the locals frantic to free their fellow citizens, friends, and family members. Lee, the military professional, explained to them that launching an immediate attack in what was then the failing light of the end of the day risked killing many of the hostages. He let the night pass, then, at sunup on the 18th, sent out Jeb Stuart with a flag of truce to call on Brown to surrender.

If Lee's calm and deliberation were characteristic of the engineer, his orders to Stuart foreshadowed the wily tactician of the Civil War to come. Battles, he knew, are not won by doing what is expected. Before he sent Stuart to Brown, he instructed Stuart to wave his hat if the man refused to surrender.

As Stuart emerged from the firehouse, he held his broad-brimmed cavalry hat by its crown, then waved it in a broad arc above his head. Lee launched his militia and marines. They targeted the firehouse door, smashed it down, poured in, and instantly ran bayonets through the first two raiders they encountered. Lee had instructed them to save what hostages they could. When it was over just three minutes after it had begun, *all* but four townsfolk were still alive. As for Brown and his men, *only* four escaped death, including Brown himself, deeply gashed by a marine saber.

The Fateful Decision

Judging from his official report on Harpers Ferry to Colonel Samuel Cooper, U.S. Army adjutant general, Lee did not regard Brown's raid as a prelude to civil war, but merely as the "attempt of a fanatic or madman." The five African Americans in Brown's party, Lee believed, had been pressed into service against their will, "forced from their homes in this neighborhood." After he returned to Texas, however, Lee became part of an action whose significance he could not minimize, let alone deny.

Soon after the secession of Texas on February 1, 1861, Brevet Major General David E. Twiggs, commanding the Department of Texas, surrendered—without authorization and without firing a shot—his entire command to Confederate authorities, resigned his commission (though not before he was dismissed from the U.S. Army on charges of treason), and became a general officer in the Confederacy. Lee immediately returned to Washington, where he was promoted to colonel and assigned to command the 1st Cavalry on March 28, 1861.

His colonelcy was among the first the newly inaugurated president, Abraham Lincoln, signed, having been urged to do so by U.S. Army general-in-chief Winfield Scott, who told the president that he intended to put Lee in a major army command. But when he was offered the rank of major general in the U.S. Army on April 18, 1861—at the time, it was the highest rank in the army—Lee declined. Fellow Virginian Scott was appalled. He knew that, privately, Lee had not only denounced secession but had even heaped scorn and ridicule on the very idea of a "Confederacy." Scott may or may not have known, however, that, earlier, in response to a subordinate's question about whether he intended to fight for the Confederacy or remain with the Union, Lee had replied both ambivalently and ambiguously, "I shall never bear arms against the Union, but it may be necessary for me to carry a musket in the defense of my native state, Virginia, in which case I shall not prove recreant to my duty," even as he refrained from responding to an offer of a commission from Confederate authorities. Scott made a last-ditch effort to talk Lee out of defecting, but when Lee resigned on April 20, all Scott

could say to him was that he had "made the greatest mistake of [his] life."

On April 23, Lee accepted command of Virginia state forces but was soon transferred to the Provisional Army of the Confederate States as one of its first five full generals. His first field command, in western Virginia—present-day West Virginia—hardly proved auspicious. He was saddled with insubordinate militia officers and was operating among a hostile local population. On September 11, 1861, he decided to attack Cheat Mountain, high ground controlling a major turnpike and several mountain passes. Federal troops his men had captured earlier persuaded Lee that some four thousand Union soldiers held the Cheat summit, far outnumbering his own force. Actually, a mere three hundred bluecoats occupied the summit, but the disinformation was sufficient to prompt Lee to hesitate, and he thereby lost the element of surprise. Because of this, when he finally attacked, he found himself facing all-too-genuine Union reinforcements. After a two-day skirmish, Lee withdrew. Although his casualties were light, the Richmond press mocked him as "Granny Lee" and "Evacuating Lee."

Having come up short in his maiden Civil War battle, Lee was removed from field command and assigned to organize the coastal defenses in the Carolinas and Georgia. Without a credible Confederate navy, however, the assignment was hopeless, and, once again, the press was critical. President Jefferson Davis took him on as his personal military advisor and also tasked him with overseeing the fortification of Richmond—another unglamorous job.

THE SEVEN DAYS, JUNE 25–JULY 1, 1862

On June 1, 1862, Joseph E. Johnston was severely wounded at the Battle of Seven Pines. Although the press was unkind to Lee, his fellow officers were confident that he had the makings of a great commander. President Davis chose him to replace

Johnston as commanding officer of the Army of Northern Virginia—a move the stricken Johnston praised in the highest possible terms.

Johnston had responded to Union general George B. McClellan's Peninsula Campaign with his customary tactic of the strategic retreat. In sharp contrast, Lee gave fierce battle in the so-called Seven Days (June 25–July 1, 1862). Essentially, a series of attacks on the Army of the Potomac, the Seven Days Battles took a heavy toll on the Army of Northern Virginia, but they broke McClellan down in mind and spirit. Although he substantially outnumbered Lee, McClellan was always convinced that the Union had the lesser numbers, and instead of advancing toward Richmond, he steadily retreated from it. "No captain that ever lived," the *Richmond Dispatch* now crowed, "could have planned or executed a better plan." In fact, Lee's tactics and execution were far from perfect, but his willingness to be unremittingly aggressive was precisely the element required to defeat a man like McClellan.

SECOND BATTLE OF BULL RUN, AUGUST 28–30, 1862

After driving McClellan away from Richmond, Lee continued his aggressive approach to the war by targeting Major General John Pope's Army of Virginia while it was near Manassas— site of the First Battle of Bull Run (July 21, 1861)—isolated from the Army of the Potomac, which was withdrawing at a snail's pace to link up with Pope. Lee possessed a keen appreciation of the dynamic nature of opportunity in combat. Give Pope time to unite with McClellan, and the resulting force would be virtually unbeatable. Act now, however, before the Army of Virginia could consolidate with the Army of the Potomac, and Pope was vulnerable to defeat in detail.

At the Second Battle of Bull Run, Lee deliberately violated one of the most basic tenets of battle tactics by dividing his army in the presence of the enemy, assigning one "wing" to Stonewall Jackson and the other to James Longstreet. Jackson went into action with his wing on August 28, and by the next day Pope was convinced that he had trapped him and that victory was within easy grasp. What he failed to understand was that Jackson held *him* and continued to do so as Longstreet counterattacked with his wing on August 30, catching Pope entirely by surprise. His attack simultaneously brought to bear all twenty-five thousand men of his wing and was the greatest mass assault of the Civil War. Overwhelming, the attack collapsed Pope's left flank, driving his army into retreat and defeat that were narrowly redeemed from total rout by heroic rear-guard action.

BATTLE OF ANTIETAM, SEPTEMBER 17, 1862

The combination of the Seven Days and the Second Bull Run moved the battle lines in Virginia back from a position no more than a half-dozen miles outside of Richmond to just twenty miles outside of Washington. This Lee achieved in a span of three months. Such speed would prove to be the hallmark of his strategy. He believed that time was not on the side of the South because the Union possessed the resources to outlast the Confederacy in any prolonged war of attrition. Lee therefore concluded that the best strategy was to act aggressively, inflicting so much damage on Union forces that the people of the North would lose their will to fight and would demand a favorable negotiated peace. Having dealt the Union two severe blows on Southern soil, he decided next to invade the North, in Maryland, on September 5, 1862.

In one of the most incredible episodes of the war, a Union soldier discovered a detailed copy of Lee's invasion plan, "Special Order No. 191," which had been lost or discarded on the site of an abandoned Confederate encampment. When Major General George B. McClellan read it, he remarked gleefully, "Here is a paper with which, if I cannot whip Bobby Lee, I will be willing to go home." Nevertheless, McClellan's attempt to strike at both of Lee's flanks at Antietam Creek and then attack the center with his reserves faltered in the execution, and the Battle of Antietam became a bloodbath of unprecedented volume and horror. Of 75,500 Union troops engaged, 12,401 were killed, wounded, captured, or missing. Of 38,000 Confederates, 10,316 became casualties. These figures meant that the battle was a tactical victory for Lee, but a strategic victory for McClellan, since he forced Lee to withdraw from Maryland.

BATTLE OF FREDERICKSBURG, DECEMBER 11–15, 1862

Fortunately for Lee, McClellan was insufficiently aggressive to pursue his retreat. This prompted President Lincoln to relieve McClellan as commander of the Army of the Potomac and replace him with Ambrose Burnside, who, though reluctant to accept the command, was eager to strike a decisive blow once he had taken the position. His plan was to advance through Fredericksburg, Virginia, in a headlong move against Richmond. In this, speed was of the essence—yet it was speed that Burnside seemed utterly incapable of achieving. Delays, especially in throwing bridges across the Rappahannock River, gave Lee, the veteran engineer, the time he needed to create extremely strong defenses, including artillery positions, along Marye's Heights, the high ground behind the town of Fredericksburg. By the time Burnside attacked on December 13, 1862, he was up against an enemy established in virtually impregnable positions. The outcome was catastrophic for the Army of the Potomac, which suffered 12,653 killed, wounded, captured, or missing out of some 114,000 engaged, while Lee's Army of Northern Virginia, with some 72,500 engaged, lost 5,377 killed, wounded, captured, or missing.

BATTLE OF CHANCELLORSVILLE, APRIL 30–MAY 6, 1863

Defeat at Fredericksburg moved Lincoln to replace Burnside with Joseph Hooker, who worked vigorously to restore the battered Army of the Potomac both materially and in spirit, then set out to renew the advance against Richmond via a fresh attack on Lee. Instead of simply throwing the whole of his army against the formidable Fredericksburg defenses as Burnside had done, Hooker planned to send a third of his forces under John Sedgwick in a diversionary attack across the Rappahannock above Lee's Fredericksburg entrenchments. At the same time, Hooker would lead another third in a swing up the Rappahannock so that he could descend upon Lee against his vulnerable left flank and rear. Except for about ten thousand cavalry troopers under George Stoneman, who were tasked with disrupting Lee's lines of communication to Richmond, the rest of the army would be held in reserve at Chancellorsville, prepared to reinforce either Sedgwick or Hooker as needed.

It was a *good* plan, but Lee was a *great* general. He soon grasped Hooker's intentions. Lee dispatched cavalry under Jeb Stuart to take control of the roads in and out of Chancellorsville. This prevented Hooker from sending out his own cavalry patrols, thereby depriving him of vital reconnaissance. Thrown into blind confusion, Hooker set up defenses at Chancellorsville instead of advancing to the battlefield he had selected some twelve miles east of town. Thus Lee had forced him to relinquish the initiative and play by *his* rules.

After sending Jubal Early with some ten thousand men to delay the Union troops at Fredericksburg, Lee led the rest of his army against Hooker's main position at Chancellorsville. Much as he had done against Pope at the Second Battle of Bull Run, Lee boldly divided his army. He allocated twenty-six thousand men

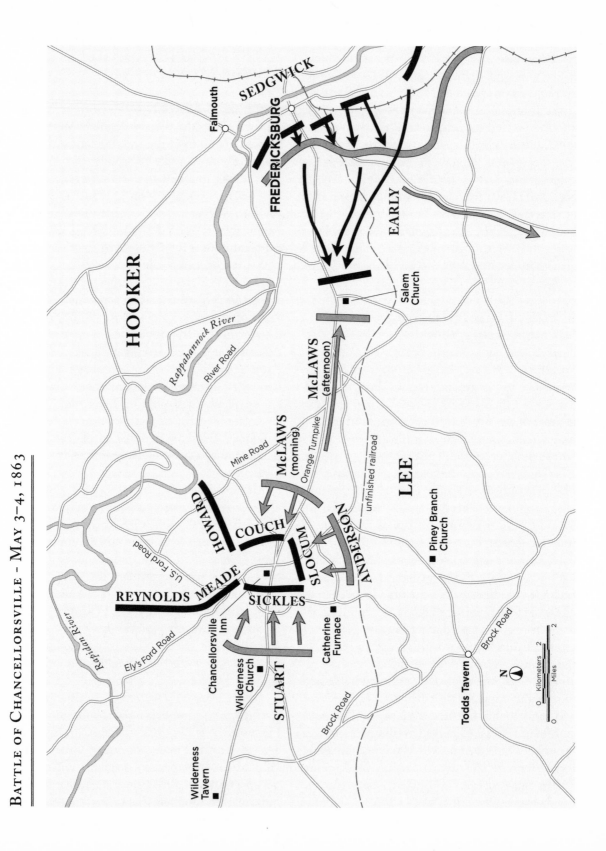

BATTLE OF CHANCELLORSVILLE – MAY 3–4, 1863

to Stonewall Jackson to make a surprise attack against Hooker's flank. Lee would use seventeen thousand men to attack against Hooker's front while Early employed the rest of the troops to continue to hold the Union forces at Fredericksburg.

Two hours before dusk on May 2—an unusual time for an attack—Jackson hit Hooker's right flank so unexpectedly that one Union soldier likened it to "a clap of thunderstorm from a cloudless sky." The blow routed one entire corps and knocked Hooker's main force out of its prepared defensive positions. By May 4, the Army of the Potomac, twice the size of the Army of Northern Virginia, was in full retreat.

Of nearly 134,000 men engaged, Hooker suffered 17,197 killed, wounded, captured, or missing. Lee fielded almost 61,000 men, losing 13,303 killed, wounded, captured, or missing. Among the fallen was "Stonewall" Jackson, mortally wounded by friendly fire. The Union would recover from its losses, terrible as they were, but the Confederacy could never replace all that it had lost, especially Jackson.

BATTLE OF GETTYSBURG, JULY 1–3, 1863

Costly as it was, Lee's victory at Chancellorsville heartened Richmond, but Davis's top advisors, concerned about the deteriorating situation in the war's Western Theater, wanted to draw resources from Lee to be used to hold Vicksburg against Grant's siege. Lee persuaded Davis to keep the focus on the Eastern Theater. He proposed another invasion of the North, again designed to sap the Union's will to continue the fight. By invading Pennsylvania this time, Lee intended to achieve three objectives. First, he would plunder provisions from the fertile farmlands. Second, he intended to demonstrate Southern military might, which would not only erode Northern morale but could also win allies in France and England. Third, he wanted to open up an avenue of attack against Washington.

Achieving all of these objectives, Lee believed, would influence the elections that were coming in November 1864, perhaps costing Lincoln reelection and ushering into the White House a Democratic candidate far more likely to negotiate an immediate end to the war with terms favorable to the Confederacy.

The Army of the Potomac that Lee would face at the point of encounter, a Pennsylvania crossroads town called Gettysburg, was now under the command of Major General George Gordon Meade, a conventional but competent commander whom Lee respected far more than he had McClellan, Pope, Burnside, or Hooker. As the opposing armies maneuvered prior to battle, they knew little or nothing of one another's whereabouts. Jeb Stuart was leading the cavalry in a roundabout raid that accomplished little and deprived Lee of critically important intelligence precisely when he needed it most. Nevertheless, at first contact on July 1, 1863, the Confederates had the advantage of numbers and carried the day, forcing the elements of the Army of the Potomac present in Gettysburg to give up the town. Lee's subordinate, General Richard Stoddert Ewell, was insufficiently aggressive and yielded important high-ground positions at Cemetery Hill and Cemetery Ridge. Possession of these would prove to be the key to Union victory.

Day two of the battle, July 2, saw intense combat that failed to dislodge the Union from its high-ground positions and that bought time for the arrival of the main part of the Army of the Potomac. Lee, however, was persuaded that victory could still be achieved by an overwhelming attack against what must surely be an exhausted enemy. Against the earnest counsel of his chief lieutenant, James Longstreet, Lee mounted on July 3 the twelve-thousand-man "Pickett's Charge" in a frontal assault against the Union high-ground positions and suffered a defeat comparable to what he had dealt Burnside at Fredericksburg.

In the end, casualties from the three-day battle were the highest in the war on both sides. Of 93,921 engaged, the Union lost 23,055 killed, wounded, captured, or missing. Lee, who fielded 71,699 men, lost 23,231 killed, wounded, captured, or missing. Had Meade made the difficult decision to pursue Lee after the collapse of Pickett's Charge, he might have substantially wiped out the Army of Northern Virginia before it had withdrawn below the Virginia border. But he did not, and Lee escaped with his army much reduced but still intact.

That Lee managed to hold the army together is a powerful testament to his command presence. Yet his defeat at Gettysburg exposed two weaknesses in even this extraordinary commander. The most glaring was the tragic lapse in judgment that moved him to order Pickett's Charge in the first place. As Longstreet and others saw, it had virtually no prospect of success. The product of a strange spasm of unrealistic optimism, Pickett's Charge was a suicide mission. But even before this, Gettysburg threw into relief the danger inherent in Lee's style of command. He did not so much issue orders to key subordinates as he made gentlemanly requests of them. In the case of Stuart and Ewell, Lee's choice to avoid absolute and urgent commands invited fatal consequences: Stuart's absence from battle at a critical time and Ewell's failure to secure terrain that the engineer Lee must have understood was essential to victory.

THE OVERLAND CAMPAIGN, MAY–JUNE 1864

Robert E. Lee accepted full responsibility for the defeat at Gettysburg and tendered his resignation, which Jefferson Davis refused to accept.

Lee reluctantly adopted a defensive strategy aimed at preventing Ulysses S. Grant, now the Union's general-in-chief, from capturing Richmond. The Union effort to do just this was the Overland Campaign, which was conducted by Grant and Meade in May and June 1864 and included major battles at the Wilderness (May 5–7, 1864), Spotsylvania Court House (May 8–21) and Cold Harbor (May 31–June 12). In each of these, Lee dealt Grant a tactical defeat, inflicting on the Union more casualties than Grant inflicted on him. Yet, as both Grant and Lee well knew, the Union could make up its losses, while the Confederacy, short on manpower, short on supplies, short on matériel, short on everything needful, could not. What is more, unlike ordinary commanders, who retreated in defeat, Grant merely sidestepped Lee after each blow and advanced farther south, inexorably drawing closer to Richmond.

SIEGE OF PETERSBURG, JUNE 9, 1864– MARCH 25, 1865

Late in the spring of 1864, Grant suddenly shifted his advance from Richmond to Petersburg, the crucial rail link that supplied Richmond. The inept leadership of Union general William F. "Baldy" Smith cost him a very real opportunity to take Petersburg before it was reinforced and, once that opportunity had passed, Lee did not let it return. Drawing on all his engineering skill, he improved the already elaborate system of trenches and other works that defended Petersburg and conducted a fierce campaign of static trench warfare that anticipated World War I's Western Front by a half-century.

Lee sent Jubal A. Early through the Shenandoah Valley to raid Washington, D.C., hoping that this would force Grant to abandon the Siege of Petersburg to defend the capital. Instead, Grant sent Philip Sheridan into the Shenandoah Valley to counter Early, and thus the siege continued unabated, steadily grinding away at the poorly supplied Army of Northern Virginia.

APPOMATTOX CAMPAIGN, MARCH 29–APRIL 9, 1865

On January 31, 1865, Jefferson Davis named Lee general-in-chief of the Confederate armies—but

Lee on his beloved horse Traveller, shortly after the war. Wikimedia Commons

there was now precious little left to command. All Lee could do was focus on leading his Army of Northern Virginia in a desperate breakout from the Petersburg entrenchments at the end of March. He knew that giving up Petersburg meant the loss of Richmond, but he also believed that if he could keep his greatly reduced army intact and find a way to link it up with Joseph E. Johnston's Army of Tennessee in the Carolinas, the fight could go on, and there would be a chance to achieve something better than unconditional surrender.

But the effort was hopeless. From one battle to another—the most important were at Five Forks (April 1) and Sayler's Creek (April 6)—Lee led his ever-dwindling army in retreat, finally falling back upon Appomattox Court House on April 9, the day he sent to Grant for surrender terms.

The circumstances of the surrender are narrated in Chapter 18 of this book. By this time, Lee's chief concern was to prevent starvation among those who had survived battle and to obtain some guarantee that the war would indeed end and the national healing begin. The terms he drew up with Grant allowed his army, having laid down its arms, to go home, "not to be disturbed by United States authority so long as they observe their paroles." To ensure that this promised generosity would actually be practiced, Lee steadfastly resisted the call from some of his subordinates to continue the war as guerrillas. That no guerrilla or insurgent phase of combat began was not only exceptional in a civil war,

Robert E. Lee. NATIONAL ARCHIVES AND RECORDS ADMINISTRATION

it was due in no small measure to Lee's still-commanding influence. As great a general as he was in battle, his most important achievement may well have been the example he set in surrender after battle. Hardly abject, his capitulation was dignified, inviting rather than begging for the generosity of the victors even as it renounced the bitterness and hunger for vengeance that so often accompanies defeat.

POSTWAR ACTIVITY

The war had aged Lee prodigiously, and he looked far older than his fifty-eight years in 1865. He accepted the presidency of little Washington College in Lexington, Virginia, in October 1865 and transformed this obscure Southern institution into a school that boasted a national identity. (After Lee's death, it was renamed Washington and Lee College.) He remained at the helm of the college until his death on October 12, 1870, from the pneumonia that had followed a stroke suffered two weeks earlier. No general, Northern or Southern, is more universally revered, although a few have both merited and received higher praise as tacticians and strategists.

Chapter 4

THOMAS J. "STONEWALL" JACKSON
RATING: ★ ★ ★ ★

Thomas J. "Stonewall" Jackson. LIBRARY OF CONGRESS

EVALUATION

Eccentric, driven by what some would deem a profound religious faith and others might call fanatic zeal, Thomas J. "Stonewall" Jackson was a tactical genius. As a subordinate commander (except during the Valley Campaign), he was never responsible for big-picture strategy, but he was the greatest field commander on either side, and his combat practices had a great impact on tactics, while his tactics had a highly significant effect on strategy.

Jackson drilled his soldiers relentlessly, preparing them for the extraordinary demands he made on their endurance. His approach to combat, which was to leverage small numbers against much superior forces, required ceaseless maneuvering, often through long forced marches at great speed. Early on, he arrived at a formula for victory—deceive and surprise the enemy, defeat larger forces in detail, follow up victory with ruthless, annihilating pursuit—and, to a remarkable degree, he consistently followed through on it. His performance at the First Battle of Bull Run, the Valley Campaign, the Second Battle of Bull Run, Antietam, Fredericksburg, and Chancellorsville showed him to be a war-winning general, while his disappointing performance in the Seven Days Battles was an aberration that was almost certainly the product of personal fatigue as well as the exhaustion of his command. His death, as a result of a friendly-fire incident, at Chancellorsville very nearly amounted to a decapitating blow from which the Confederate military could never and would never recover.

Principal Battles

PRE-CIVIL WAR

U.S.-Mexican War, 1846–1848

- Contreras, August 19–20, 1847
- Churubusco, August 20, 1847
- Chapultepec, September 12-13, 1847: Jackson defied orders to withdraw from an exposed artillery position on the grounds that continuing to fight was less risky than retreating—he was proved right; Jackson received three brevets and one regular promotion during the war, the most of any soldier in the conflict

CIVIL WAR

- First Battle of Bull Run, July 21, 1861: In Virginia; his timely arrival turned the tide of battle and earned him the most famous sobriquet of the war: Stonewall

- Valley Campaign, March 23–June 9, 1862: In Virginia, consisting of the Battles of Kernstown, March 23; McDowell, May 8; Front Royal, May 23; Winchester, May 25; Cross Keys, June 8; and Port Republic, June 9; tactically, the most brilliant campaign of the Civil War; with some seventeen thousand men, Jackson neutralized some sixty thousand Union troops

- Seven Days, June 25–July 1, 1862: In Virginia; with he and his men exhausted from continuous combat in the Shenandoah Valley and forced marches, Jackson's performance in these battles proved highly disappointing

- Second Battle of Bull Run, August 28–30, 1862: In Virginia; commanding the left wing of Lee's army, Jackson made a remarkable flanking maneuver that held Pope's army in place as Longstreet's right wing smashed into and defeated it

- Antietam, September 17, 1862: In western Virginia and Maryland; captured Harpers Ferry and absorbed much of McClellan's offensive at Sharpsburg

- Fredericksburg, December 11–15, 1862: In Virginia; held off the brunt of Burnside's repeated frontal attacks

- Chancellorsville, April 30–May 6, 1863: In Virginia; his surprise flanking assault on the Union XI Corps was one of the most devastating attacks of the Civil War—a masterpiece

When the Battle of Gettysburg was lost, Robert E. Lee offered comfort to General Cadmus Wilcox, whose brigade had been decimated in Pickett's Charge. "Never mind, general," he said, "all this has been my fault—it is I who lost this fight. . . ." And Lee thereafter never sought to shift the burden of failure onto anyone else's shoulders—with one possible exception. Years later, he reportedly observed, "If I had had Jackson at Gettysburg, I should have won the battle, and a complete victory there would have resulted in the establishment of Southern independence."

Although some question the authenticity of the remark about Jackson, Lee nevertheless saw him as what George Washington biographer James Thomas Flexner later famously called his subject: the indispensable man. Intuitively, all the Confederate South seems to have felt this

as well. After Jackson succumbed to pneumonia following a friendly-fire wounding at the Battle of Chancellorsville, he was accorded a funeral of the kind normally reserved for monarchs and presidents. He lay in state at the Executive Mansion in Richmond, then was moved by an escort of general officers to the Confederate House of Representatives, where his remains were viewed by more than twenty thousand awestruck and grief-stricken mourners. "The affections of every household in the nation were twined about this great and unselfish warrior," a Richmond paper observed. His death deeply marred the Confederate triumph at Chancellorsville. A tragic coda to that victory, it seemed to many the end of all hope for the Southern cause.

AN ORPHAN'S LIFE

The circumstances of his birth, humble and remote, much like those of Abraham Lincoln, were hardly calculated to produce a cultural icon and military celebrity in whom an entire people so deeply invested their aspirations. Thomas Jonathan Jackson could trace his ancestry to a pair of felons, great-grandparents John Jackson and Elizabeth Cummins, who had both been sentenced to periods of indentured servitude and transported from England to America after separate convictions for larceny. The two met aboard the ship that took them to Annapolis, Maryland. They would eventually establish themselves in western Virginia and fight as Patriots in the American Revolution, producing a large family that would remain in the region. Son Edward Jackson sired Jonathan Jackson, who married Julia Beckwith Neale. Their third son was Thomas.

He was born in Clarksburg, Virginia—now West Virginia—on January 21, 1824. His father was a lawyer, but struggling and poor, his mother a schoolteacher, pale, frail, and sickly. Two years after Thomas came into the world, his father died of typhoid, days after that disease had taken his six-year-old sister Elizabeth. A day after her husband died, Thomas's mother gave birth to another girl, named Laura Ann. A widow at twenty-eight, Julia proudly turned away all offers of charity and instead sold off the family's meager possessions to pay the debts Jonathan had left her. She moved herself and her three surviving children into a rented one-room house and did her best to feed her family by teaching school and taking in sewing. She found a new husband in 1830, attorney Blake Woodson, fifteen years her senior. A widower with eight children of his own, he brought a modicum of improvement in the family's finances, though not much. In 1831, after giving birth to Woodson's child, Julia died. By this time, however, her three children from her first marriage had been parceled out to relatives. Thomas and Laura Ann lived with their uncle, Cummins Jackson, owner of a gristmill at Jackson's Mill in what is today West Virginia.

For the four years he and his sister lived with their uncle, Thomas thrived in the affection and cheerful warmth Cummins provided, but in 1834 he and his sister were separated, Laura Ann going to live with her mother's family, and Thomas with his father's sister and her husband, one Isaac Brake, who treated him like an unwelcome stranger. Thomas ran away in 1836, walking the eighteen miles through tangled woods back to Jackson's Mill and the welcoming arms of his Uncle Cummins, with whom he lived for the next seven years. During this time, he labored on the family's farm and cobbled together a rudimentary education, some of it at school, most of it at home on his own. Again like Lincoln, Jackson read borrowed books by firelight—though (it was said) he produced his fire by burning pine knots, which his uncle's slaves brought him in exchange for his teaching them to read (in violation of Virginia law).

WEST POINT

As a teenager, Thomas Jackson used what little education he had to teach school; he also found employment as a town constable and what has been described as an engineering assistant. He earned sufficient local renown in these professions to move others to encourage his taking a competitive examination for admission to West Point in 1842. He failed, but just barely, and when the candidate who had edged him quickly dropped out of the Class of 1846, Jackson was invited to take his place.

He struggled mightily to stay afloat in the bottom third of his class during his first year, and while he displayed no particular aptitude for learning, he possessed a spectacular capacity for hard work. He made it his practice in the fall and winter to pile the grate in his room with coal just before lights out, and, lying on the floor before the grate, he read by the glow of the coals late into the night. Through dint of such dogged application, he clawed his way up academically, ultimately graduating seventeenth out of fifty-nine cadets in what some military historians have called the greatest class in the academy's history. His effort was an object of wonder and admiration among his peers, who remarked that, if he had remained just one more year, he would have graduated number one.

What Cadet Jackson demonstrated above all at West Point was his unconquerable will. But he also eagerly absorbed all lessons offered in the military art, particularly those of Professor Dennis Hart Mahan (1802–1871), the academy's leading tactical and strategic theorist. Mahan was a keen student of the campaigns of Napoleon, and he taught his cadets that the common thread uniting these remarkable campaigns was speed of maneuver and boldness of attack—tempered with judgment born of reason. Jackson adopted this cluster of concepts as a veritable tactical mantra, which he would apply in virtually every battle he fought in the Civil War.

U.S.-MEXICAN WAR, 1846–1848

The Class of 1846 had what its members all deemed the great good fortune to graduate directly into the war with Mexico. Jackson's standing was good enough to warrant a second lieutenant's commission in the 1st U.S. Artillery Regiment, which was quickly packed off to combat under Major General Winfield Scott.

Jackson served with Scott at the Siege of Veracruz and the advance to Mexico City, distinguishing himself particularly at the Battles of Contreras (August 19–20, 1847) and Churubusco (August 20, 1847). At the Battle of Chapultepec (September 12–13, 1847), the culminating struggle for the conquest of Mexico City, Jackson commanded a highly exposed artillery position, refusing an order to withdraw in the face of superior enemy numbers and instead directing fire against the attackers, whom he decimated. When his commanding officer demanded that he justify his insubordination, Jackson explained

Jackson as a young U.S. Army officer.
VIRGINIA MILITARY INSTITUTE

his judgment that it would have been more hazardous to withdraw than it was to continue firing. In the end, the officer agreed with him, and the episode became one of the legends of the war. By war's end, Jackson earned three brevet promotions (up to brevet major) in addition to promotion to the regular army rank of first lieutenant. None other than Winfield Scott himself held a banquet in Mexico City with First Lieutenant Jackson the guest of honor.

Jackson remained in Mexico with occupation forces and used his ample spare time to study religion (in which he was becoming increasingly and ever more deeply interested), to teach himself Spanish, and to read history. While living in this Catholic country, he found himself strongly drawn to Catholicism and stunned his fellow officers by taking up residence for some weeks in a monastery, where he had the opportunity to converse on religious matters with the archbishop of Mexico. In the end, however, he turned from Catholicism to the Episcopal Church, in which he was subsequently baptized. By the 1850s, he would leave that church for the more austerely demanding tenets of Presbyterianism.

VMI PROFESSOR

Jackson returned to the United States late in 1848 and was stationed with the garrison at Fort Hamilton in Brooklyn, moving in 1850 to Fort Meade, near Tampa, Florida. Both assignments were dull. He filled his time with religious study and, according to many who served with him, a morbidly growing preoccupation with the state of his health. He ascribed the chronic indigestion from which he suffered to some mysterious disorder that was insidiously gnawing at his vitals. To combat it, he adopted an austere diet void of seasoning and consisting mostly of vegetables and fruit. He also began a rigorous regimen of general-knowledge reading, committing himself to digesting fifty pages a day every day, in English, Spanish, and other languages.

With all of this, Jackson somehow also found time to investigate a rumor of sexual impropriety alleged to have been committed by the commanding officer of Fort Meade, Brevet Major William H. French. When French demanded that he drop the impertinent investigation, Jackson refused, whereupon French had him arrested for insubordination. In due time, French's arrest order was reversed without court-martial, but, eager to put distance between French and himself, Jackson accepted in March 1851 an invitation from the superintendent of the Virginia Military Institute (VMI) in Lexington, Virginia, to become the school's professor of natural and experimental philosophy (that is, physics) and instructor of artillery.

Jackson proved woefully inept in the classroom. He knew nothing about physics coming into the position, and he struggled to keep a day or two ahead of his students. At that, his physics classes were conducted as rote lectures, essentially verbatim regurgitations of what Jackson had read in the textbook the night before. Excruciatingly bored, his students were unruly, and Professor Jackson seemed wholly incapable of instilling any discipline in them. As an artillery instructor, he was, however, considerably more successful. Combining what he had learned from Mahan with his own battlefield experience, he taught his cadets that mobility tempered by discipline was key to victory and that a successful commander is one capable of probing an enemy's intentions and his strength without revealing his own. Doctrinally, Jackson preached the gospel of a combined arms approach to combat, using the deadly efficiency of artillery to prepare the way for infantry assault.

Popular with neither his physics nor his artillery students was Jackson's insistent religious proselytizing, which became so egregious that in 1856 an alumni group petitioned for his dismissal. The petition was ignored.

Professor Jackson managed to find a kindred spirit in Elinor "Ellie" Junkin, the daughter of the president of Washington College, the other institution of higher learning in Lexington. He married her in 1853; on October 22, 1854, she gave birth to a stillborn son, began hemorrhaging uncontrollably, and died. Prostrated by grief, Jackson turned yet more deeply to his faith, becoming a Presbyterian deacon and founding a Sunday school for slaves. He took time out for a European tour, then was remarried in 1857, this time to Mary Anna Morrison, the daughter of the first president of Davidson College.

CIVIL WAR OUTBREAK

The quiet routine of academia was shattered in December 1859, when Jackson was assigned to command twenty-one VMI cadets manning a pair of howitzers as part of the military contingent assigned to provide security at the hanging of John Brown following his trial and conviction for the raid on the arsenal at Harpers Ferry.

The Brown hanging must have reminded Jackson, if he needed any such reminder, that the nation was in deep crisis. Although he believed that states possessed the inherent right of secession, Jackson was opposed to fighting over it, and he organized a citizens committee in Lexington to discuss alternatives to war. He also convened a public prayer meeting to beseech the Lord for peace. He said that his combat experience in Mexico had taught him that war was "the sum of all evils." Nevertheless, he felt about Virginia much the same way as Lee did. It was his "country," and he would defend it. But he added a dimension that went beyond Lee. Virginians, he believed, were more godly than Northerners, and in this fight, God would surely be on the side of the righteous.

When the war commenced in April with the fall of Fort Sumter, Jackson resigned his U.S. Army commission and offered his services to his state. Appointed a colonel of Virginia troops, his first assignment was the training of recruits, but on April 27, 1861, Governor John Letcher ordered him to assume command at Harpers Ferry—the federal arsenal had been commandeered by the state—and to assemble a brigade for the defense of this strategically crucial town at the border of the North.

Waiting for him at Harpers Ferry was a ragtag contingent of 2,500 militiamen and volunteers, earnest but untrained. Jackson drilled them mercilessly, as much as seven hours a day, even as he set about recruiting more soldiers, until he had built up a brigade of 4,500 comprising the 2nd, 4th, 5th, 27th, and 33rd Virginia Infantry regiments, all from the Shenandoah Valley.

FIRST BATTLE OF BULL RUN, JULY 21, 1861

On May 23, 1861, Joseph E. Johnston arrived to assume overall command at Harpers Ferry and assigned Jackson to command the brigade he had created, now designated as the First Brigade. On June 17, political allies in Richmond ensured Jackson's promotion to brigadier general. In the meantime, Johnston, who now commanded some ten thousand men in and around Harpers Ferry, made the strategic decision to relinquish the town to assume what he deemed a more readily defensible position that would not tie his troops down to any one place. The move was made in time for Jackson to play a crucial role in the First Battle of Bull Run.

P. G. T. Beauregard's forces, in place at Manassas Junction on the morning of July 21, 1861, were giving way under a heavy Union assault and had fallen back upon a position known as Henry House Hill. Just as the brigade commanded by Brigadier General Barnard Elliott Bee Jr. was about to crumble, Jackson appeared with his 1st Brigade. The story goes that he rode back and forth under heavy fire, marshaling and rallying his men to stand against the Union onslaught while periodically raising his left hand to heaven, as if to exhort the Lord himself to battle.

Bee, desperately trying to stem the panic in his disintegrating line, called out to his men: "There is Jackson standing like a stone wall. Let us determine to die here, and we will conquer. Rally behind the Virginians!"

Stereopticon view of "Stonewall Jackson's Entrenched Lines" at the First Battle of Bull Run.

NEW YORK PUBLIC LIBRARY DIGITAL LIBRARY

And so—the story goes—they did. With this, the tide of battle began to turn. By the end of the day, it was the Union army under Irvin McDowell that melted away in headlong retreat, Jackson's 1st Brigade became known thereafter as the "Stonewall Brigade," and Jackson himself as "Stonewall." It would be the most famous sobriquet to emerge from the war, and nothing will change that, although some historians have cited witnesses who claimed that General Bee had actually expressed himself more mundanely, to the effect of "Yonder stands Jackson like a stone wall; let's go to his assistance." Still others reported that Bee did not intend the "stone wall" comparison as a rallying cry, but as a complaint. He wanted Jackson to get moving instead of just standing "like a damned stone wall." The truth of Bee's intended meaning will never be known, since he died in combat before the day ended.

Although the arrival of Jackson and the Stonewall Brigade saved the day for the Confederates, it was the shift from a defensive posture to an offensive one late in the afternoon that brought victory. At this point, Jackson called to his men to "yell like furies" as they charged, and, for the first time on any battlefield, friend and foe alike heard the "rebel yell." It has been described as a high-pitched keening that seemed to come from the same otherworldly place as another attribute of Jackson: the eerie light of his deep blue eyes. For while the world would come to know him as Stonewall, his men knew him even better as "Old Blue Light."

The effect of the rebel yell was both electric and primal. The Federal lines broke, and panic-stricken soldiers fled. Union losses at Bull Run would tally up at 2,896 killed, wounded, captured, or missing, while total Confederate losses were 1,982. But Stonewall Jackson was hardly satisfied with this result. President Jefferson Davis, who was on scene to micromanage the battle—something he would often do, much to the consternation of his generals—agreed with

P. G. T. Beauregard and Joseph Johnston that McDowell's men should be allowed to flee back to Washington. The day belonged to the Confederacy, and, for them, this was enough. Jackson, however, pleaded with Davis: "We have whipped them! They ran like sheep! Give me 5,000 fresh men, and I will be in Washington City tomorrow morning." Although Davis, a habitual blamer, criticized both Beauregard and Johnston for failing to pursue McDowell, he neither ordered nor urged them to do so. As a result, who can say what opportunity the Confederacy lost in the midst of victory?

THE VALLEY CAMPAIGN, MARCH 23–JUNE 9, 1862

Instead of seizing the offensive initiative as Jackson urged, the leaders of the Confederate army, after Bull Run, deployed their forces defensively across a broad swath of Virginia to await the anticipated Union assault. Promoted to major general on October 7, 1861, Jackson was assigned command of the so-called Valley District, headquartered in Winchester. His mission was to defend the Shenandoah Valley, the lush garden and breadbasket of the South and, equally important, a prime avenue of attack against Washington and Baltimore. In the spring of 1862, when the Union's "Young Napoleon," Major General George B. McClellan, led the Army of the Potomac in its roundabout advance on Richmond in his Peninsula Campaign, Jackson was tasked with operating in the Shenandoah Valley to oppose and defeat two Union divisions under Major General Nathaniel P. Banks, which were assigned to keep Jackson from reinforcing Richmond. At the same time, Jackson was also supposed to act against McDowell's large corps, which was positioned to strike at Richmond from the north and to reinforce the rest of McClellan's army as needed.

Jackson's first stroke came at the Battle of Kernstown on March 23, 1862. Relying on poor

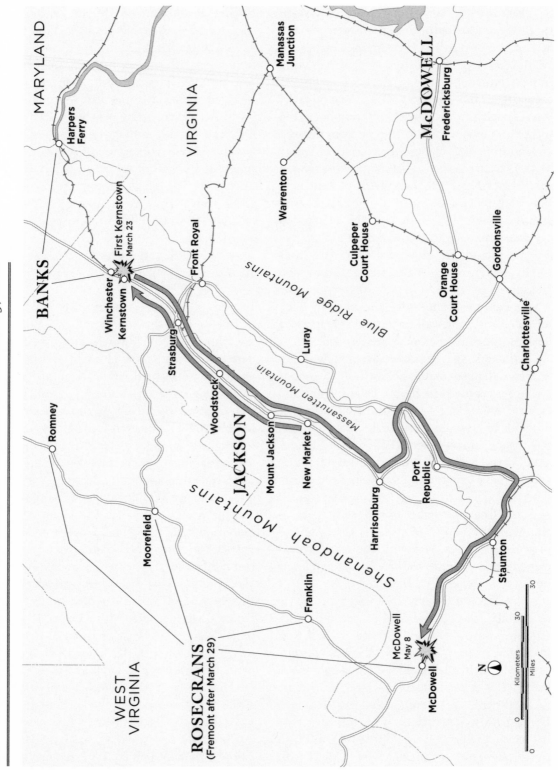

reconnaissance, Jackson believed he was going up against a small detachment only to discover that he was substantially outnumbered. The result of this error was a tactical defeat for Jackson, yet also a significant strategic triumph. Although overmatched—the Union commander, Nathan Kimball, had about 8,500 men, while Jackson led just 3,800—Jackson continued to fight so aggressively that Abraham Lincoln himself, eager to protect Washington, ordered Banks's troops to remain in the Shenandoah Valley and McDowell's corps to hold a position near Fredericksburg. This meant that a total of some fifty thousand Union soldiers were unavailable to McClellan's main invasion force. In sum, Jackson had used 3,800 men to tie down fifty thousand. It was a spectacular instance of strategic leverage, which exemplified Jackson's combat doctrine—always to "mystify, mislead, and surprise the enemy."

But deception was not the sum total of Jackson's tactical philosophy. He also believed that winning a battle was never a sufficient objective. When an enemy was overcome, he held, the next step was pursuit. "If hotly pursued," Jackson wrote, a retreating force "becomes panic-stricken and can then be destroyed by half their number." Jackson stood his assigned Valley mission on its head. Instead of defending the Shenandoah Valley, he resolved to use it as a vast field for offensive action. When possible, he would pursue. He would also maneuver in such ways as to attack whenever the opportunity presented itself. The great thing, however, was timing. The attacks had to come before the enemy could concentrate and consolidate his forces. If he could hit isolated elements hard, Jackson believed that he could defeat the enemy in detail, even if its combined forces far outnumbered his.

Jackson acquired two divisions, one under Major General Richard S. Ewell and another commanded by Major General Edward "Allegheny" Johnson, which gave him an army of seventeen thousand to go up against combined Union forces of some sixty-two thousand. Adhering to his doctrine of maneuver and attack, Jackson was able to render these odds meaningless.

After Kernstown, he managed to deceive Banks into believing that he had abandoned the Valley, which prompted the withdrawal of all but a single Union division from the region. This presented Jackson with an opportunity to attack some six thousand Union troops under Brigadier Generals Robert H. Milroy and Robert C. Schenck at the Battle of McDowell on May 8, 1862. Victory here was followed by the Battles of Front Royal (May 23) and Winchester (May 25), in which Jackson was able to bring superior numbers against isolated Union forces and defeat them in detail. At Winchester, he outnumbered Nathaniel P. Banks 16,000 to 6,500 and took a devastating toll, inflicting more than two thousand Union casualties, killed, wounded, captured, or missing, for a loss to his forces of no more than four hundred men. With this, Banks was driven from the Valley.

The Battle of Winchester convinced President Lincoln that defeating Stonewall Jackson had to take top priority. Generals McDowell and John C. Frémont were sent to converge at Strasburg to interdict Jackson's escape route up the Shenandoah Valley. Even when pursued, however, Jackson continued to outmaneuver the Union forces. He drove his men mercilessly in forced marches that frustrated Union efforts to consolidate its attacks successfully. At Cross Keys on June 8, Jackson defeated Frémont, and at Port Republic the next day he soundly beat 3,500 men under Erastus B. Tyler.

Union commanders were simply dazzled. Jackson moved so fast—646 miles in forty-eight days, winning five important battles during this span—that his small army was dubbed the "foot cavalry." In all, the Valley Campaign was a military masterpiece, certainly the greatest tactical and strategic achievement of the Confederacy. All told, it deprived the Union offensive of some sixty thousand soldiers, it lifted Southern morale while dashing that of the North, it continued to

Jackson in an undated engraving. LIBRARY OF CONGRESS

even as the sounds of battle were clearly audible to everyone. At Gaines's Mill (June 27) and Savage's Station (June 29), he was again late, and at White Oak Swamp (June 30) he stumbled badly by wasting many hours in rebuilding a bridge across White Oak Swamp Creek instead of simply fording the stream. His contribution at the Battle of Malvern Hill (July 1) was unexceptional and costly.

Having created about himself an aura of invincibility during the Valley Campaign, Jackson's subpar performance at the Seven Days came as a shock and a disappointment. Some military historians, taking their cue from James Longstreet's assessment, believe that his genius was incompatible with subordinate command and could be given full rein only when he operated independently. Perhaps. The more probable explanation, however, is simple exhaustion. Nearly two months of forced marches alternating with pitched battle had drained him and his men.

hold the all-important Confederate breadbasket, and it kept alive the threat to Washington. Most immediately, the defeat of the Union in the Valley freed up Jackson and his men to reinforce Robert E. Lee against George McClellan in the Seven Days Battles.

THE SEVEN DAYS, JUNE 25–JULY 1, 1862

Jackson emerged from the Valley Campaign as a full-fledged military celebrity, a star among Confederate generals. His entrance into the Peninsula Campaign should have been suitably spectacular. Using a railway tunnel through the Blue Ridge, then hopping the Virginia Central Railroad, he materialized at Mechanicsville on June 26, 1862, for the second of the Seven Days battles (the Battle of Mechanicsville is also known as Beaver Dam Creek). Yet instead of capitalizing on the surprise he had achieved, Jackson inexplicably bivouacked for the night,

SECOND BATTLE OF BULL RUN, AUGUST 28–30, 1862

Whatever the cause or causes of Jackson's failure in the Seven Days, he more than redeemed himself at the Second Battle of Bull Run when Lee put him in command of the left wing of the army as Longstreet commanded the right wing.

Exhibiting his flair for rapid movement, Jackson swept his wing into position at the rear of Major General John Pope's Army of Virginia. Here, at Manassas Junction, he captured and destroyed the main supply depot of the Union army. This done, he withdrew to a defensive position that lured Pope into repeated assaults, convincing him that he had Jackson on the ropes. In fact, Jackson was holding Pope for Longstreet's right wing to make a smashing impact on the Army of Virginia's left with more than twenty-five thousand men. The magnitude of Pope's defeat dwarfed the result of the First Battle of Bull Run.

BATTLE OF ANTIETAM, SEPTEMBER 17, 1862

When Lee decided to follow up the victory at Second Bull Run with an invasion of Maryland, he split his army (over the protests of Jackson and Longstreet), assigning Jackson to capture Harpers Ferry so that his rear would not be threatened when he attacked Sharpsburg (at Antietam Creek) in Maryland. Jackson quickly overwhelmed the Union forces holding Harpers Ferry—some eleven thousand men—then rushed to join Lee and Longstreet at Sharpsburg.

Had McClellan been more aggressive, the Battle of Antietam, on September 17, would have been catastrophic for the Army of Northern Virginia. Fighting a desperate defense, Jackson's corps absorbed the full force of the Union assaults on the northern end of the line, but it managed to hold and to withdraw, with heavy losses but in good order, along with the rest of Lee's army, back across the Potomac and into Virginia.

BATTLES OF FREDERICKSBURG AND CHANCELLORSVILLE, DECEMBER 11–15, 1862 AND APRIL 30–MAY 6, 1863

Jackson received promotion to lieutenant general, and his command was redesignated as II Corps. He commanded the right wing of the Army of Northern Virginia at Fredericksburg, holding off Ambrose Burnside's strongest assault here and thereby contributing to a costly but major Confederate victory.

The Union defeat at Fredericksburg cost Burnside command of the Army of the Potomac, and his replacement, Joseph Hooker, decided on a new assault. Lee resolved to counter this threat by depriving Hooker of the initiative instead of obliging him by playing the expected defensive role. Once again, Lee boldly violated basic tactical doctrine by dividing his already outnumbered army in the face of the enemy, sending Jackson and II Corps to make a flanking attack on Hooker's right.

Risky as the maneuver was, Lee knew his man. He was employing Jackson to do precisely what he did best. Jackson led his infantry in a wide movement south and west of Hooker's line, all the time using Major General Fitzhugh Lee's cavalry to approach Hooker more closely, so that he could precisely ascertain the position of the Union right flank and rear. Seeing the vulnerability of the Union right, Jackson pounced, forming up his divisions into a line of battle and stealthily advancing into position for attack. All of II Corps was within a few hundred feet of the unsuspecting Union forces when, suddenly, the unearthly rebel yell was raised, and the Confederates unleashed a fierce assault that captured many (some without a shot having been exchanged) and routed the rest. True to his battle doctrine, Jackson called to his troops to "Press on! Press on!" against Hooker's XI Corps, driving it into the very center of the Federal line until the failing light of dusk called a halt.

"AND REST UNDER THE SHADE OF THE TREES"

If anything marred Jackson's devastating assault it was that he had begun too late to finish it in a single day—at least finish it to his satisfaction, which meant pursuing the enemy to annihilation. Thus, on the night of May 2, he and his staff rode quietly through the Wilderness, scouting for avenues for a possible night assault. A nervous picket of a North Carolina regiment, never suspecting that the commanding general would be riding about at night, heard noises and called out the *Who goes there?* Without waiting for a response, he opened fire. His commanding officer, suspecting a "damned Yankee trick," ordered a full volley, even after Jackson's party had answered the picket.

Thomas J. "Stonewall" Jackson was shot in the right hand, left wrist and hand, and left arm. The wounds were bad, but they could have been much worse. No head wound. No gut shot. Nothing vital had been hit. (Several of his staff had been killed outright in the fusillade of friendly fire.) In the darkness, however, Jackson's evacuation took time, and his wounds were not treated for some hours. When brigade surgeon Dr. Hunter McGuire finally saw him, he told Jackson that his left arm required amputation lest blood poisoning set in.

Stonewall Jackson in 1862. LIBRARY OF CONGRESS

"Do for me whatever you think is right," Jackson calmly replied.

Under the circumstances, in the field and during a primitive medical era, the amputation was indeed the correct course of action, and Jackson improved over the next few days. But then pneumonia set in—the result of infection, blood loss, and perhaps the effects of chloroform anesthesia—and the general gradually slipped away. "His mind . . . began to . . . wander," McGuire later wrote, "and he frequently talked as if in command upon the field. . . ."

> *About half-past one he was told that he had but two hours to live, and he answered . . . feebly but firmly, "Very good; it is all right."*
>
> *A few moments before he died he cried out in his delirium, "Order A. P. Hill to prepare for action! Pass the infantry to the front rapidly. Tell Major Hawks—" then stopped, leaving the sentence unfinished.*
>
> *Presently a smile . . . spread itself over his pale face, and he said quietly, and with an expression as if of relief, "Let us cross over the river and rest under the shade of the trees."*

The very day of Jackson's death, on May 10, 1863, Jefferson Davis addressed his fellow countrymen: "Our loss was much less killed and wounded than that of the enemy, but of the number was one, a host in himself, Lieutenant General Jackson . . . war has seldom shown his equal." More humbly, speaking to his camp cook, Robert E. Lee quietly moaned, "William, I have lost my right arm."

Chapter 5

ALBERT SIDNEY JOHNSTON
RATING: INCOMPLETE

Albert Sidney Johnston. WIKIMEDIA COMMONS

EVALUATION

Jefferson Davis judged him the Confederacy's greatest general before the emergence of Robert E. Lee. Ulysses S. Grant believed him overrated. Through the years, Johnston's reputation has seesawed, so that it is at least safe to say he is the single most controversial major Confederate commander to emerge from the Civil War.

Much of the controversy can be attributed to the unfinished nature of his career. He died in the middle of his one great battle, but that he died attempting what others would have considered impossible, mounting a bold offensive amid the collapse of an entire theater of war, hints at greatness. On the other hand, his willingness to entrust the execution of his bold and daring plans to others suggests a fatally flawed style of command.

Principal Battles

PRE-CIVIL WAR

Black Hawk War, 1832
- In Wisconsin; his first up-close experience of war, but without direct participation in combat

Texas Revolution and Aftermath, 1836–1840
- Mounted a campaign against hostile Indians and organized border defenses

U.S.-Mexican War, 1846–1848
- Monterrey, September 21–24, 1846: Acting on his own initiative, reversed a rout and routed a charge of Mexican lancers
- Buena Vista, February 22–23, 1847

Utah (Mormon) War, 1857–1858
- Led a 2,500-man federal force to suppress a Mormon "uprising" and install a non-Mormon government in disputed Utah territory

CIVIL WAR

Battle of Shiloh, April 6–7, 1862
- In Tennessee; with his undermanned theater threatening to collapse, Johnston launched a daring surprise attack against Grant's encampment at Pittsburg Landing, nearly dealing the Army of the Tennessee a lethal blow

---

The three saddest words in the English language, it is often said, are "might have been." As with all momentous events of great consequence, the Civil War is filled with might-have-beens, especially with regard to the outcome of the war for the South. Two Confederate commanders have long endured as subjects of intense might-have-been speculation: Thomas "Stonewall" Jackson and Albert Sidney Johnston.

Some years after the war, Robert E. Lee himself reportedly voiced his belief that if he "had had Jackson at Gettysburg," he would "have won the battle, and a complete victory there would have resulted in the establishment of Southern independence." Jefferson Davis was even more emphatic about what the loss of A. S. Johnston meant. "It was," he said, "the turning point of our fate; for we had no other hand to take up his work in the West."

Yet there is a very important difference between Jackson and Johnston. When he fell at Chancellorsville, Stonewall Jackson had proven the potency of his genius, while Johnston, struggling to cover the vast Western Theater with an undermanned, under-equipped army, had just begun to reveal his powers. Davis, as well as many who served under Johnston, were convinced of his sovereign value to the cause, but Ulysses S. Grant, whom Johnston targeted for destruction at Shiloh, wrote in his *Personal Memoirs* of 1885: "I do not question the personal courage of General Johnston, or his ability, but . . . as a general he was over-estimated."

Concerning Albert Sidney Johnston at least three facts are beyond dispute. He was assigned a vast and critical mission: to hold for the South the Mississippi Valley and beyond. He died with this mission unfulfilled. And, after his death, his reputation became one of the great speculative controversies of the war.

FROM THE KENTUCKY FRONTIER TO WEST POINT

Albert Sidney Johnston was the son of Kentucky's ragged frontier. When he was born on February 2, 1803, the Mason County village of Washington had yet to evolve into even a hard-scrabble farming community. It was as yet a wilderness cluster of cabins huddling around a stockade fort raised to defend against the Shawnee and other hostiles determined to resist the incursion of white settlement. Men fed their families not with the produce of the earth, but with game on paw, wing, and hoof. It was a place that demanded wit, muscle, courage, will, and a talent for getting by on very little. This made it the ideal environment for breeding the leader of a hard-pressed army of rebellion.

Of course, Albert Sidney's parents had no intention of raising a family of rebels. John Johnston was a skilled physician, whose own father had distinguished himself fighting in the American Revolution. The doctor was a New Englander by birth, hailing from Salisbury, Connecticut, and was among the many who saw in the West a way of twining his family's future with the future of the nation. He quickly became prominent in Washington, Kentucky, developing a large practice and earning a seat on the local governing body, the board of trustees.

In this hard place, it proved beyond his medical ability to save his first wife, who succumbed to sickness in 1793. He remarried the following year, to another transplanted New Englander, Abigail Harris, who bore him four children before the birth of her last, Albert Sidney. But it was a hard place, and in the boy's third year of life, his mother died.

Without a mother, it was his father and his oldest sister who raised him up, kept him safe, and saw to it that he received an education well above the frontier standard. While he attended private school through the college preparatory stage, he was also encouraged to indulge an intensely competitive love of riding and hunting, as well as athletic contests with local boys. He grew into a strapping young man of over six feet in height and was the object of admiration throughout the district. John Johnston sent him off to Transylvania College in Lexington, hoping that he would follow in his footsteps and become a physician. There he met fellow student Jefferson Davis, and there he also grew restless in the study of medicine and asked his father to help him obtain an appointment to West Point.

He enrolled in 1822 (Davis would follow two years later) and earned a reputation for satisfactory if not exceptional academic performance. Far more outstanding was his soldierly bearing, the warmth of the friendships he formed, and the sense he created among the other cadets that he was a natural and irresistible leader. He possessed, as if inborn, what soldiers call "command presence," and while a few others overtook him academically (he would graduate eighth in the forty-one-cadet Class of 1826), it was he who was selected as adjutant in his fourth year, the highest honor a cadet can attain.

BLACK HAWK WAR, 1832

Even before he had entered West Point, Johnston excelled at mathematics, and this, coupled with his high class standing, should have propelled him into an assignment in the artillery, second only to the Corps of Engineers in attracting the top academy graduates. But he chose the infantry instead, believing this branch would give him wider scope as a tactician—another of his classroom passions—and, even more important, would offer greater opportunity for higher and more rapid advancement. So strong was this belief that he even turned down an invitation to join Winfield Scott's personal staff.

Having made his decision, he was commissioned a brevet second lieutenant in the 2nd U.S. Infantry. To his chagrin, for the next eight years he did not budge from his initial commissioned rank. Such was the nature of the diminutive U.S. Army at peace.

Johnston served in New York for a time before being transferred to Jefferson Barracks at St. Louis, Missouri. He soon met Henrietta Preston, a Louisville belle and the daughter of William Preston, veteran of the American Revolution and prominent in Louisville society and politics; his son, also named William, would become a general in the Confederate forces. The couple married on January 20, 1829, which must

have brought some relief to the monotony of garrison life, but it was not until the outbreak of the Black Hawk War in 1832 that a genuine career breakthrough seemed to be in the offing.

Assigned as chief of staff, aide-de-camp, and assistant adjutant general to Brevet Brigadier General Henry Atkinson, commander of a regiment sent to put down Black Hawk's "uprising," Johnston yearned for combat. As the general and the regiment prepared for transportation by steamboat up the Mississippi, the young staff officer gained valuable hands-on experience in support and logistics. The trip itself, however, was uneventful, and neither Johnston nor the rest of the regiment would participate in active combat. They arrived at the confluence of the Bad Axe and Mississippi Rivers in time to observe elements of the U.S. Army and local militia massacre members of Black Hawk's "British Band" who sought nothing more than to surrender. For Johnston, it was a disheartening, disturbing, and depressing maiden battle.

TEXAS REPUBLIC, 1836–1840

Discouraged with army life, deeply in debt, seeing no realistic hope for promotion, and learning that his wife had fallen ill with consumption, Johnston resigned his commission in 1834 to return to Kentucky and look after her. It proved to be a prolonged death watch. Henrietta Preston succumbed to her disease in 1836. Their son, William Preston Johnston, would come of age in time to serve as a colonel in the Confederate Army.

To the widower, debt ridden and devoid of prospects, life looked bleak. He sought escape in revolutionary Texas, enlisting later in the year as a private in the Texas army. The Texas Revolution had been won with Santa Anna's defeat at the Battle of San Jacinto on April 21, 1836, but the Mexican government repudiated the treaty signed under duress and made noises about its intention to reconquer the Lone Star Republic. Within a month of his arrival in Texas, Johnston was embraced by President Sam Houston, who jumped him in rank from private to major and appointed him his personal aide-de-camp. On August 5, 1836, he was promoted to colonel and named adjutant general of the Republic of Texas Army, and on January 31, 1837, Houston named him the army's senior brigadier general, with overall command of the entire force.

The promotion vaulted Johnston over Brigadier General Felix Huston, who accused him of attempting to "ruin his reputation" by accepting the appointment. Honor and duty were uppermost in Johnston's hierarchy of values, but he did not believe in fighting duels to defend the former, yet, in this case, he believed that the latter—duty—dictated that he accept the challenge. Failing to do so, he feared, would sacrifice credibility with his troops and, with it, his authority to command. The two men met with pistols on the "field of honor" at dawn on February 7, 1837. Accounts vary as to precisely what happened. According to some, Johnston refused to fire on Huston, who, having no such scruples himself, aimed, shot, and hit Johnston in the right hip. Others insist that both men fired repeatedly, exchanging as many as four shots without any finding its mark. On the fifth shot, Johnston was hit in the right hip (some accounts describe it as the pelvis), the round apparently passing through and through without striking bone. It is unclear whether Johnston recovered sufficiently and in time to assume active command as senior brigadier general, but on December 22, 1838, the second president of the Republic of Texas, Mirabeau B. Lamar, appointed him secretary of war.

The appointment thrilled Johnston. It looked certain that Mexico was about to make good on its threat to invade Texas with the object of reclaiming it, and some five thousand Mexican troops had assembled on the border at Matamoros and Saltillo. After leading a campaign against hostile Indians in northern Texas in 1839, Johnston organized the border defenses.

But early in 1840, the Mexican government recalled its troops from the border, and President Lamar indicated his unwillingness to further press any Texas grievance against Mexico. Frustrated, bored, and seeing as little opportunity in the Texas army as he had had in the U.S. Army, Johnston resigned as secretary of war in February 1840 and was back in Kentucky by May.

U.S.-MEXICAN WAR, 1846–1848

Johnston had managed to put together a small amount of money during his time in Texas, which he now used to finance a Kentucky land speculation scheme. It quickly blew up in his face, and, once again, he found himself heavily burdened by debt. His cares were somewhat relieved by a budding romance with Eliza Griffin, the twenty-three-year-old cousin of his late wife, "a dazzling beauty of the Spanish type," according to a friend of Johnston's, and an accomplished singer and painter. They married in October 1843.

The couple struggled, living mostly on Eliza's funds, with Johnston growing increasingly desperate until, once again, war offered a way out. When Mexican forces attacked Zachary Taylor's army on the Texas border in April 1846, Johnston's first thought was to renew his commission in the Army of the Republic of Texas. Discovering that it had been voided with the annexation of Texas to the United States, he sought a new commission in the regular U.S. Army. Unable to obtain this, he secured a commission as colonel of the 1st Texas Rifle Volunteers, which were subsequently attached to Taylor's forces.

He assumed command in time to see action in the Battle of Monterrey (September 21–24, 1846), but the six-month enlistments of his short-term volunteers were set to expire just before then. Although he persuaded a handful of his men to remain and fight under him, he was essentially a colonel without a command. At the last minute, he wrangled an appointment as inspector general of volunteers and, in this capacity, saw action at Monterrey and at Buena Vista (February 22–23, 1847). At Monterrey, he distinguished himself in spectacular fashion. Without a command of his own, save for the handful of volunteers who had chosen to fight by his side, Johnston was free to employ himself on the field wherever he saw fit. Noting that an Ohio regiment was in danger of being routed by Mexican lancers, Johnston rallied many of the retreating men, who had taken refuge in a cornfield. Re-forming them into an effective line of fire, he personally led a counterattack against the pursuing lancers, driving them back. Joseph Hooker, a captain in the war with Mexico and destined to be a Union general, gave Johnston credit for saving "our division . . . from a cruel slaughter. . . . The coolness and magnificent

presence . . . displayed . . . left an impression on my mind that I have never forgotten." Jefferson Davis, commanding the Mississippi Rifles at Monterrey, praised Johnston's "quick perception and decision" and called them the characteristics of "military genius."

THE UTAH (MORMON) WAR, 1857–1858

Despite his brilliance at Monterrey and, later, at Buena Vista, Johnston was not commissioned in the regular army, and he left Mexico when his term of service in the volunteers expired. He settled with his wife in Brazoria County, Texas, on a plantation he called China Grove, which he struggled to coax into profitable productivity. Once again, however, penury and despair encroached, so that when his former commanding

Battle of Buena Vista during the U.S.-Mexican War as painted by Carl Nebel and published in The War between the United States and Mexico, Illustrated *(1851).*

officer, Zachary Taylor, having been elected president of the United States in November 1848, offered him a regular U.S. Army commission as a major in December 1849, he took it. He took it, even though the position—paymaster—was hardly one he relished. His assignment was to service the far-flung military outposts on the Indian frontier of Texas. It was dangerous work, and it was grueling. During each of the five years he held the post of paymaster, he traveled more than four thousand miles, transporting, accounting for, and distributing pay.

In 1855, Jefferson Davis, serving as secretary of war under President Franklin Pierce, arranged for Johnston to be named commanding colonel of the newly authorized 2nd U.S. Cavalry with Robert E. Lee as his second in command. Indeed, for this elite regiment, Davis cherry-picked Southern officers he believed would break with the U.S. Army in the event of a civil war. In effect, Davis was laying the foundation on which an army of rebellion might be quickly raised.

In 1856, Johnston was also named commanding officer of the Department of Texas, and the following year he was tasked with leading a contingent of 2,500 troops from Texas to suppress a Mormon uprising in Utah after the so-called Mountain Meadows Massacre, in which Mormon zealots had killed 123 non-Mormon settlers. Against all expectation, Johnston proved to be a model of restraint in dealing with the Mormons and, without further bloodshed, was instrumental in establishing, pursuant to President James Buchanan's orders, a non-Mormon government that restored federal authority in the territory. In recognition of his service, he received a brevet promotion to brigadier general late in 1857. Some even believed his display of diplomacy warranted something more, and his name was bandied about as a possible nominee for president on the Democratic ticket for 1860. Protesting that others were "more capable and more fit" for the office, he put a quick end to the talk.

OUTBREAK OF THE CIVIL WAR

Johnston commanded the Department of Utah from 1858 to 1860, returned briefly to Kentucky, and then, on December 21, 1860, sailed to California to assume his new command as head of the Department of the Pacific. As war clouds gathered, he sorted out his loyalties. Opposed to secession, he was nevertheless a believer in the rightness of slavery, and he decided that any attempt to end the "peculiar institution" by federal force constituted tyranny and invasion. Still, when Southern sympathizers called on him at his San Francisco headquarters to ask for his cooperation in capturing strategic facilities if and when war erupted, Johnston replied that he intended to "defend the property of the United States with every resource at my command, and with the last drop of blood in my body." Similarly, when Governor John Downey of California questioned him about his intentions, Johnston replied that he had "spent the greater part of his life" in service to his country and "while I hold her commission I shall serve her honorably and faithfully. I shall protect her public property, and not a cartridge or percussion-cap shall pass to any enemy while I am here as her representative."

In the end, it was General-in-Chief Winfield Scott who made the first move to sever Johnston from the army. Although he believed Johnston was an honorable man, he knew which way his cultural and political allegiances leaned, and he sent Brigadier General Edwin Sumner to relieve Johnston as commander of the Department of the Pacific, ordering him to leave California and to report to Washington. Instead of following that order, however, Johnston resigned his commission shortly after news reached him that Texas had seceded from the Union on February 1, 1861. He moved to Los Angeles and took up residence with some relatives. Remaining there until May, when the War Department officially accepted his resignation, Johnston fled likely arrest by local Union officials, enlisted as a private in the pro-Confederate Los Angeles Mounted Rifles, and rode with them to Texas and the Confederate Territory of Arizona, which he reached on July 4, 1861. From here, he set out on the long journey east to Richmond, Virginia, arriving about September 1, 1861.

Welcoming Johnston to the capital, President Davis informed him that he had been named one of the first five full generals in the Provisional Army of the Confederacy and held rank second only to Samuel Cooper. His assignment, Davis told him, was to command Military Department Number 2—the Western Department—which encompassed Kentucky, Tennessee, Missouri, Kansas, Arkansas, and western Mississippi.

The daunting mission that faced him was to raise, organize, and command the Army of Mississippi, which was charged with the defense of Confederate territory stretching from the Mississippi River to Kentucky and the Allegheny Mountains. To do this, he was allotted no more than twenty thousand troops, about half of whom lacked weapons, save for whatever rifles and shotguns they might themselves own. As one of his aides put it, Johnston "had no army." After pressing President Davis for support, he received reinforcements led by Braxton Bragg, but the total number of troops available to Johnston never exceeded fifty thousand. When he asked for more, Davis instructed an aide to reply that nothing could be done for him and that he had to "rely on his own resources."

As if a shortage of manpower and equipment were not a sufficient handicap to performing what was, in fact, a hopeless mission, Johnston was instructed not to openly violate Kentucky's avowed neutrality. This meant that all-important river defenses had to be placed within Tennessee, so that the two key forts, Henry (on the Tennessee River) and Donelson (on the Cumberland) were far from ideally sited. Vulnerable, the forts were lost in February 1862—Fort Henry on the 6th and Fort Donelson on the 16th. Although Johnston had had

little choice about placement of the forts and was also compelled to build them hastily, he was showered with blame for their fall and for the consequences of their fall—the withdrawal of Confederate forces from Kentucky and middle Tennessee, and the loss of Nashville to Union occupation on February 25.

To demands from the press and some politicians that he fire Johnston, Jefferson Davis replied, "If he is not a general, we had better give up the war, for we have no generals." For his part, Johnston accepted the blame for the reversals in the West, writing to the president that the "test of merit in my profession with the people is success. It is a hard rule, but I think it is right."

BATTLE OF SHILOH, APRIL 6–7, 1862

Johnston accepted blame for the fall of the river forts, but he refused to concede that his theater had been lost. His plan was to rapidly consolidate as much of his forces from around the theater as he possibly could, to accomplish this before the enemy could consolidate his own, and to make a surprise attack on whatever portion of the Union forces presented itself as vulnerable. At this point he was joined by P. G. T. Beauregard, with whom he concentrated his forces at Corinth, Mississippi. Ascertaining that Grant was camped at Pittsburg Landing on the west bank of the Tennessee River near a place called Shiloh, Johnston resolved to mount a massive surprise attack before Grant's Army of the Tennessee could be joined by Don Carlos Buell's Army of the Ohio.

It was a bold, even brilliant idea, and its prospects for success were multiplied by Grant's unsuspecting assumption that Johnston's forces were in no shape to launch an offensive. If the very idea of the attack at Shiloh vindicates Jefferson Davis's lofty appraisal of Johnston, the manner in which Johnston executed it reveals his greatest flaw as a commander. It was a failing he shared with no less a figure than Robert E.

Lee. Like Lee, Johnston saw his role as strategic, and he accordingly left the tactical execution of his strategy to his subordinates. Like Lee, he avoided issuing direct, detailed orders and instead drew up a strategic outline. He relied on Beauregard to fill in the operational details and make it work.

Beauregard, it turned out, was not up to the assignment.

Ordered to advance on April 2, Beauregard should have executed a swift and stealthy movement that would ensure the preservation of surprise. Instead, lack of detailed planning and follow-through supervision resulted in lines of march that crossed and recrossed one another, creating a snarl of confusion and delay. The attack was supposed to be made on April 4, but the army was not in position until April 5. Both of Johnston's subordinates, Beauregard and Braxton Bragg, advised their commanding officer to call off the operation. They were convinced that the snags, the noise, the delays had surely been more than enough to alert the Union forces in the area to the army's presence. Although they calculated that the opposing forces were evenly matched at about fifty thousand men each (Grant actually fielded about forty-two thousand), Beauregard and Bragg assumed that Grant, expecting the attack, had entrenched his forces "to their eyes," making for an impregnable objective. Moreover, undisciplined troops had consumed five days' rations in just three. They were hungry and probably in no condition to give their best.

Johnston listened, hearing his generals out, then calmly replied: "I would fight them if they were a million."

It was not bravado or arbitrary obstinacy that motivated the remark, but a cool, calculated military assessment. This attack, Johnston had concluded, no matter how risky, was the only opportunity he had to save the army and hold on to the Western Department theater.

The attack on Shiloh, April 6, 1862, began with breathtaking success. Grant had taken

no defensive precautions whatsoever, and his encampment was soon overrun. Johnston, who had left the detailed planning and execution to Beauregard in the run-up to battle, now appeared everywhere on the battlefield, personally rallying, forming up, and leading troops.

By midday, victory seemed clearly within grasp. That is when Johnston's troops encountered a pocket of intense, unyielding Union resistance they dubbed the "Hornets' Nest." In the initial attack, the Union soldiers had seemed to melt away. Now, at the Hornets' Nest, wave after Confederate wave broke and fell. Seeing his troops retreat from this redoubt, Johnston dispatched an aide to General John C. Breckinridge to re-form his men and get them to return to the attack. Breckinridge personally rode back to Johnston to tell him that, try as he might, he could not get one of his regiments forward.

"Then I will help you," Johnston quietly replied.

In company with Breckinridge, he rode up to the reluctant regiment and cantered along the line. As he rode slowly by—oblivious to the fire around him—he touched each soldier's bayonet, as if to anoint their blades. "These," he said in a voice just loud enough to be heard, "will do the work. . . . Men, they are stubborn; we must use the bayonet." Reaching the end of the line, he turned in his saddle. "I will lead you," he said.

And so they all swept forward, fired up, pressing forward behind their general—who, suddenly, reeled in his saddle.

Johnston's aide, Isham G. Harris, galloped up, catching the general's shoulder to keep him from falling. *Are you wounded?* he asked.

"Yes, and I fear seriously."

Harris and others nearby lowered Albert Sidney Johnston from his horse. Harris frantically felt of his commander, searching for a wound, but he could find none. And yet the general slipped rapidly away. Only after he had died was it discovered that a bullet had entered behind his right knee, severing his popliteal

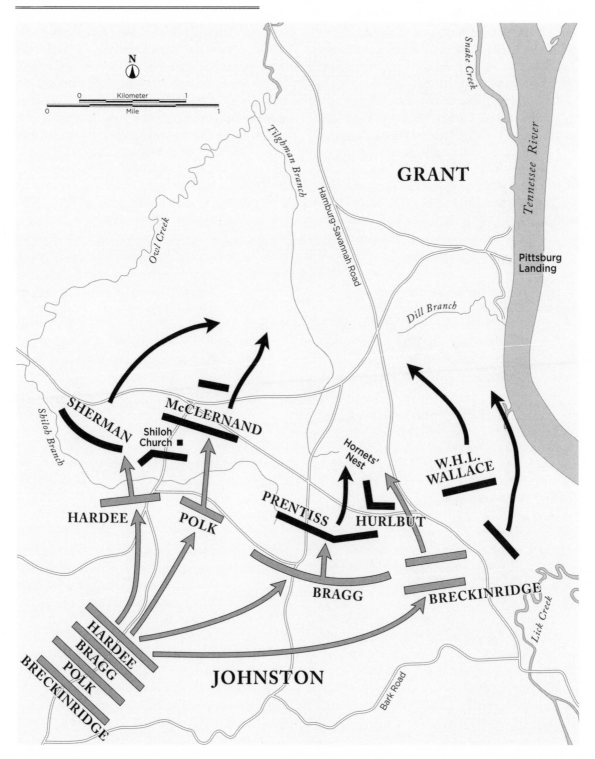

artery. He bled out rapidly into his high cavalry boot, which concealed the wound and the volume of blood it produced. More than likely, given the location of the wound and his position when it was sustained, Johnston had been the victim of friendly fire.

P. G. T. Beauregard was so confident at the end of the day on April 6, 1862, that he reported to Richmond a great victory that had come, tragically, at the loss of the commanding general. In fact, without Johnston to lead, the battle was lost the following day. At the time of his death, Davis considered Albert Sidney Johnston the best general he had. Even after the emergence of Robert E. Lee some two months later in the war, Davis continued to rate Johnston as indispensable. He would attribute the collapse of the Confederate West to his loss.

Chapter 6

BRAXTON BRAGG

RATING: ★

Braxton Bragg. LIBRARY OF CONGRESS

EVALUATION

There were flashes of brilliance, as when, after Shiloh, he put his army on a train to ride the long way round to Chattanooga to checkmate Don Carlos Buell, and there were spasms of ferocity, as when his II Corps went up against the Hornets' Nest at Shiloh. Many of his contemporaries believed that he was a fine trainer of soldiers and that the harsh discipline he meted out was just the tonic for the unruly, ill-educated Confederate enlisted boy and man. More typically, however, Braxton Bragg showed himself to be pathologically disputatious, unimaginative,

indecisive, hesitant, insufficiently aggressive, unwilling to exploit his few victories, and generally contemptuous of others. Perhaps the only major figure in the Confederate military hierarchy who had faith in him was Jefferson Davis. Of course, that counted for a great deal.

Principal Battles

PRE-CIVIL WAR

Second Seminole War, 1835–1842

- Although an artillerist, operated as an infantry officer in what was essentially a police action

U.S.-Mexican War, 1846–1848

- Battle of Fort Brown, May 3–9, 1846: Brevetted to captain for gallantry; subsequently promoted to regular army captain
- Monterrey, September 21–24, 1846: Brevetted to major; rescued elements of Jefferson Davis's Mississippi Rifles
- Buena Vista, February 22–23, 1847: Brevetted to lieutenant colonel

CIVIL WAR

- Shiloh, April 6–7, 1862: In Tennessee; led determined but unsuccessful assault on the Hornets' Nest
- Perryville, October 8, 1862: In Kentucky; after boldly invading Kentucky, failed to follow up on his tactical victory at Perryville and thereby suffered a strategic defeat that relinquished Kentucky
- Stones River, December 31, 1862–January 2, 1863: Near Murfreesboro, Tennessee; sought to redeem himself with a decisive victory against William Rosecrans, but, after a very promising start, withdrew when counterattacked
- Chickamauga, September 19–20, 1863: In Georgia; was instrumental in this bloody Confederate victory, but his failure to follow up allowed the battered Army of the Cumberland to withdraw intact, bringing some of Bragg's subordinates to the verge of mutiny
- Lookout Mountain and Missionary Ridge, November 24–25, 1863: Outside Chattanooga, Tennessee;

his forces laying siege to the Army of the Cumberland in Chattanooga were routed and pursued into Georgia; Jefferson Davis accepted Bragg's request for relief from command

- Second Battle of Fort Fisher, January 13–15, 1865: Near Wilmington, North Carolina; Bragg's failure to reinforce the garrison resulted in the loss of the fort and Wilmington, the last Confederate port open to blockade runners
- Bentonville, March 19–21, 1865: In North Carolina; gamely served as J. E. Johnston's subordinate in this final major battle of the Civil War

Great generals are often hard men. Braxton Bragg was a hard man, but no one would call him a great general. Sometimes, however, he came close to being just good enough.

Did his men love him?

During the U.S.-Mexican War (1846–1848), it is believed that he was twice the target of what today would be called attempted "fragging"—deliberate assassination by friendly fire. One attempt involved the detonation of a twelve-pound explosive artillery shell under his sleeping cot. The cot was a total loss. Bragg escaped unscathed.

Was he a fighter?

Absolutely. But not always with the enemy. In his *Private Memoirs*, U. S. Grant related an "old army" (that is, pre–Civil War) anecdote he called "very characteristic of Bragg." Assigned to a typically undermanned western outpost during the early 1840s, Bragg was both a company commander and the post quartermaster. Grant related that Bragg once submitted a requisition to supply his company, but that, as quartermaster, he rejected his own request. In his capacity as company CO, he resubmitted the document, complete with justification for the expense, only, as quartermaster, to reject it again. Seeing no means of resolution, he appealed to an understandably incredulous post commandant. "My God, Mr. Bragg," he sputtered in exasperation, "you have quarreled with every officer in the army, and now you are quarreling with yourself!"

That virtually all military historians believe the story is the stuff of fantasy and legend does nothing to diminish what it says about how contemporaries perceived Braxton Bragg. Alternately on the verge of success or breakdown, he was an enigma whose "military capabilities," historian Ezra J. Warner observed in 1959, began an argument "during the war [that] has not ceased to this day."

EARLY YEARS

Braxton Bragg's mother had to be released from prison to give birth to him, on March 22, 1817, in Warrenton, North Carolina. That fact alone may have laid on his shoulder a chip he would never allow anyone to knock off. Awaiting trial for having murdered a freed slave, Mrs. Bragg never denied killing the man, but she claimed it was self-defense because he had "disrespected" her. Although she was finally let go without the matter ever coming to trial, neighborhood boys would not let young Braxton forget the circumstances under which he came into the world, and, from then on, it seemed to one and all that he'd been born with what Grant called an "irascible temper" that made him "naturally disputatious." That his father's success in business failed to win him and his family acceptance among the local old-money "aristocracy" doubtless added to the boy's freight of resentment, but it was the senior Bragg's idea that Braxton should acquire the social imprimatur of a West Point education. Mr. Bragg's eldest son, Thomas, was in the North Carolina state legislature and was able to call in a political favor that secured his younger son an appointment to the academy.

Enrolling in 1833, Braxton Bragg was, not unexpectedly, an unpopular cadet, but he nevertheless earned an enviable reputation as bright, hardworking, and "efficient." He graduated in 1837, fifth in a class of fifty, and chose the artillery as his service branch. Commissioned a second lieutenant in the 3rd U.S. Artillery, he was sent to Florida, where he saw light action in the Second Seminole War (1835–1842). He then served in various posts, including on the western frontier, seeing no significant action but enduring much tedium before the outbreak of the U.S.-Mexican War.

U.S.-MEXICAN WAR, 1846–1848

Given the glacial pace of promotion in the nineteenth-century peacetime army, Bragg's entry into the war at the regular army rank of first lieutenant under Major General Zachary Taylor suggests that his commanding officers rated him highly. This could have owed absolutely nothing to his personality. In 1843, while stationed at Fort Moultrie, South Carolina, Bragg responded to a social invitation from his commanding officer, Lieutenant Colonel William Gates, with rudeness bordering on insubordination: "If you order me to drink a glass of wine, I shall have to do it." On another occasion he was even hauled before a court-martial for publicly criticizing Major General Winfield Scott.

He proved to be a valiant and energetic light artillery battery commander in the war with Mexico, earning three brevet promotions and one permanent promotion. The first brevet, for valor at the Battle of Fort Brown (May 3–9, 1846), was to captain, which was made permanent in the regular army the next month. His second brevet, to major, came after the Battle of Monterrey (September 21–24, 1846), and the third, to lieutenant colonel, was the result of his conduct at the Battle of Buena Vista (February 22–23, 1847). Zachary Taylor took notice, as did Colonel Jefferson Davis, after Bragg's timely artillery support extricated a part of Davis's Mississippi Rifles from a particularly tight spot at Monterrey. Bragg and Davis forged a bond of personal and professional friendship that would become critically important during the Civil War.

BETWEEN THE WARS

Bragg received enough press coverage to emerge from the U.S.-Mexican War with a national reputation as a military hero, and when he returned to his hometown of Warrenton, no one dared cast aspersions on him or on his father's "new money" pretensions. Universally feted, he was freely invited into parlors formerly closed to him. The war with Mexico had done nothing to improve Bragg's looks—"sickly, cadaverous, haggard," the British military diarist Lieutenant Colonel James A. L. Fremantle described him, with "bushy black eye-brows which united in a tuff on top of his nose"—but it had nevertheless made him infinitely more attractive, and in 1849 he married Eliza Brooks, a comely Louisiana heiress.

Bragg quietly carried out routine peacetime assignments until December 1855, when a dispute with his friend Jefferson Davis, now secretary of war in the Cabinet of Franklin Pierce, erupted into a major breach. Davis proposed to station artillery units in various western frontier posts. Artillerist Bragg objected to what he deemed the absurdity of "chas[ing] Indians with six-pounders" and called on Davis in Washington to tell him so personally. When the secretary refused to back down, Bragg tendered his resignation. Possibly to Bragg's surprise, Davis jumped on it, accepting it without argument. It may also have been that Bragg deliberately used the dispute as an excuse to leave the army, which he did in January 1856, dipping into his wife's money to finance a sugar plantation outside of Thibodaux, Louisiana.

CIVIL WAR OUTBREAK

While operating his sugar plantation, Bragg obtained two state appointments, one a lucrative position as state commissioner of public works and the other as colonel of the Louisiana Militia. On February 20, 1861, after Louisiana seceded from the Union, he was promoted to major general of the militia and was put in command of forces defending New Orleans. On March 7, 1861, his commission was transferred to the Provisional Army of the Confederate States, and on April 16 he was sent to Pensacola, Florida, to command coastal defenses as well as the Department of West Florida. Promoted to major general on September 12, 1861, his authority was extended the following month to include Alabama and the Gulf Coast, as well as the diminutive Army of Pensacola.

Bragg worked diligently to build up coastal defenses but warned Jefferson Davis that "our strength consists in the enemy's weakness." In other words, given the poverty of Southern military resources, the major ports of New Orleans and Mobile could not be expected to resist a sustained effort against them. Bragg did endeavor to do the best with what he had, and he transformed his small army into the best-trained, most highly disciplined force in the Confederacy. Recognizing his own talent for training troops—a "talent" that was built mainly on his willingness to impose draconian disciplinary penalties—Bragg offered to send his best four regiments to Virginia, where the action was hottest, in exchange for green Virginia recruits, whom he would whip into shape. It was a genuinely valuable and entirely unselfish contribution to the cause.

BATTLE OF SHILOH, APRIL 6–7, 1862

In February 1862, Davis ordered Bragg to reinforce Albert Sidney Johnston's imperiled western command in Kentucky and Tennessee. He went to work training the combined forces, which were soon joined by a contingent under P. G. T. Beauregard, recruits (according to Bragg) who showed "more enthusiasm than discipline, more capacity than knowledge, and more valor than instructions." He applied himself to these men as well, driven by a combination of genuine passion for instilling efficient discipline and

his own ill temper, which was aggravated by a battery of ailments ranging from dyspepsia and migraine headaches to periodic nervous collapse.

Johnston directed Beauregard and Bragg to concentrate all available forces at Corinth, Mississippi, in preparation for a massive assault against Ulysses S. Grant's Army of the Tennessee before it could be reinforced by Don Carlos Buell's Army of the Ohio. By the start of April 1862, the Confederates had mustered some fifty thousand men at Corinth. Grant was vulnerable, encamped at Pittsburg Landing, Tennessee, with forty-two thousand men (Johnston, Beauregard, and Bragg thought he had more). Johnston illadvisedly entrusted the detailed execution of his planned surprise assault entirely to Beauregard, who sufficiently botched the advance on Pittsburg Landing to delay the possibility of attack by two days. Convinced that the element of surprise had been lost, both Bragg and Beauregard advised Johnston to call off the attack, but he insisted that it go forward.

Largely because Grant had dropped his guard, leaving his encampment around Shiloh Church almost entirely undefended, the attack, launched on April 6, began extremely well and looked so promising that victory seemed certain. By midday, however, Confederate forces encountered a pocket of Union resistance so fierce that they dubbed the redoubt the "Hornets' Nest." Bragg led his II Corps strongly against the position, ordering his men to "drive the enemy into the river," but after a half hour of continuous, bloody combat at the Hornets' Nest, Beauregard ordered Bragg and the others to withdraw. To his credit, Bragg vehemently protested that it was essential to complete the attack before nightfall and that it was fatal to let up, but Beauregard pointed out that the men were exhausted, the fight drained out of them. He was confident, he said, that the Yankees could be finished off the next morning.

In the meantime, Albert Sidney Johnston had been mortally wounded, and Beauregard assumed full command. By the time Beauregard resumed the attack on April 7, Buell's army had arrived to reinforce Grant, and, now outnumbered, the Confederates were driven into retreat. The opportunity was forever lost, both sides having spilled more blood than in any other battle so far: 10,699 killed, wounded, captured, or missing among the Confederates, and 13,047 among the Union forces.

INVASION OF KENTUCKY AND BATTLE OF MUNFORDVILLE, SEPTEMBER 14–17, 1862

On the very day that the Battle of Shiloh began, April 6, 1862, Bragg learned that he had been promoted to full general and named to command the Army of Mississippi. Having fallen back on Corinth on April 7, Beauregard decided to evacuate the town, leaving it to Union forces even though he had earlier claimed that to lose Corinth would be to "lose the whole Mississippi Valley and probably the cause." Appalled, Davis seized on Beauregard's decision to take an unauthorized medical leave of absence (his doctor had advised taking a water cure at Bladon Springs, Alabama) to cashier Beauregard and replace him with Bragg as commanding general of the Army of Tennessee.

The new commander believed it essential to rehabilitate a force that Beauregard had left a largely undisciplined mob. Through a combination of stern fatherly concern and harsh regulations—in which many transgressions, such as the unauthorized discharge of a firearm, were punishable by firing squad—he whipped the army into shape. Having put spine into his men, he decided that the next step was to use the army to check the advance of Buell's Army of the Ohio to Chattanooga.

But how? Buell was two hundred miles away. How could he beat the Yankee to Chattanooga?

Bragg's solution was brilliant. Instead of marching overland the two hundred miles to Chattanooga, he put the Army of Tennessee on trains for a nearly eight-hundred-mile round-about rail journey *south* to Mobile, then northeast to Atlanta, and from Atlanta to Chattanooga. In this way, he made the trip in just two weeks, taking up defensive positions in Chattanooga well before Buell arrived. From his base in Chattanooga, Bragg next decided to invade Kentucky, a slaveholding border state that had not seceded from the Union but that had declared itself neutral in the Civil War. Bragg believed that a majority of Kentuckians would regard his entrance into their state as "liberation" from Northern oppression and would flock to the cause. He therefore led his army out of Chattanooga into Kentucky in August and, now pursued by Buell, easily captured the town of Munfordville, taking the entire Union garrison of 4,148 prisoner. From here, Bragg advanced to Bardstown and, on October 4, 1862, paraded his army through Frankfort, the state capital, to show support for the inauguration of Richard Hawes as the provisional Confederate governor.

BATTLE OF PERRYVILLE, OCTOBER 8, 1862

Despite the installation of a Confederate governor, few people in Kentucky rallied to Bragg's army and the cause it represented. As a result, Bragg grew increasingly nervous, especially as Buell's Army of the Ohio had been reinforced to a strength of some seventy-seven thousand men.

On October 1, Buell sent two divisions toward Frankfort, as if intending to attack it. He led the rest of his army in continued pursuit of Bragg. Leading a wing of Bragg's army, Major General Leonidas Polk clashed with Buell at Perryville on October 8 and scored a tactical victory, inflicting 4,276 casualties—killed, wounded, captured, or missing—for a loss of 3,401. General Edmund Kirby Smith, who had linked up with Bragg in the Kentucky invasion, implored him to exploit Polk's initial gain: "For God's sake, general," he pleaded, "let us fight Buell here."

"I will do it, sir," Bragg replied. But he did no such thing. Instead, he issued an order to retreat out of Kentucky via the Cumberland Gap to Knoxville, Tennessee. In dispatches to Richmond, he described the retreat as a "strategic withdrawal" after a great "raid" into Kentucky.

Smith and Bragg's other subordinates were not convinced. They condemned the so-called withdrawal as nothing more or less than a retreat, the product of a failure of nerve, and Bragg's action has been the subject of debate ever since. Some believe Bragg's justification that, with the defeat of Earl Van Dorn and Sterling Price at Corinth, Mississippi, and Lee's withdrawal from Maryland after the Battle of Antietam, an isolated victory at Perryville would have actually cut off what Bragg described in a letter to his wife

as his "noble little army," leaving it surrounded by hostile forces, useless and subject to starvation. Others, however, interpret the retreat as a capitulation, the loss of yet another opportunity and the cancellation of a tactical victory by a self-inflicted strategic defeat.

BATTLE OF STONES RIVER, DECEMBER 31, 1862–JANUARY 2, 1863

Following his withdrawal from Perryville, Bragg's star was in decline with the Southern press, the Confederate people, and most of his fellow commanders. Only his friend President Davis remained a steadfast supporter. On New Year's Eve 1862, the general had an opportunity to redeem himself at the Battle of Stones

The Battle of Stones River. KURZ & ALLISON LITHOGRAPH, CA. 1891

River, near Murfreesboro, Tennessee, against William S. Rosecrans, whom President Lincoln had tapped to relieve the hesitant Buell as commander of the Army of the Ohio (now known as the Army of the Cumberland). Bragg attacked Rosecrans's right and made considerable progress until Major General George Thomas rallied his men and pushed back. Bragg ordered up his reserves, who, however, failed to make a coordinated response and were defeated in detail. Nevertheless, Bragg wired President Davis his belief that "God has granted us a Happy New Year."

The joy did not last long. On January 2, Rosecrans counterattacked with an infantry assault supported by an artillery bombardment so intense that it "opened the door of hell" upon the Army of Tennessee, driving it back to where it had started from. Instead of regrouping and launching a new assault, Bragg, fearing that Rosecrans was about to be reinforced, withdrew. He did not withdraw his *claim* of victory, but few took that claim seriously as he yielded central Tennessee. A joke began to circulate through the ranks of the Confederate army: *Braxton Bragg would never get to heaven because the moment he was invited to enter, he would fall back.*

For the Army of Tennessee, it was a winter of discontent. Virtually every one of Bragg's subordinate commanders expressed their loss of faith in him, and his top two generals, William J. Hardee and Leonidas Polk, wrote to Jefferson Davis to ask that Joseph E. Johnston be ordered to replace Bragg. Ill-tempered and emotionally inept as ever, Bragg retaliated with court-martials and threats of court-martial, but he also wrote to Davis to suggest that he comply and order his relief. With Bragg's army on the verge of mutiny, Davis responded by authorizing Johnston, as commander of the Western Theater, to relieve Bragg of command if he thought fit to do so. Never one to act impulsively, Johnston personally visited Bragg and the army. He found that many generals were indeed hostile to their commander, but, to his surprise, he judged that

morale among the army as a whole was intact, the army was well fed, reasonably well equipped, and certainly well disciplined. He concluded that it would do more harm than good to replace Bragg.

BATTLE OF CHICKAMAUGA, SEPTEMBER 19–20, 1863

But Bragg was exhausted. In his celebrated Tullahoma Campaign of June 1863, Rosecrans had pushed the Army of Tennessee from one position to another, driving it from Tullahoma to Chattanooga and then into Georgia.

From Rosecrans's point of view, he had Bragg on the run. Bragg, however, considered his withdrawal into Georgia a move in a "game of wits," intended to dupe Rosecrans into believing he had been defeated when, in fact, he was continually taking on reinforcements. At last, on September 19, he turned on his pursuer just west of Chickamauga Creek, in Georgia. That first day, Bragg concentrated on holding the high ground until James Longstreet arrived with an entire corps to reinforce him. Bragg prepared his anxious men by telling them that they were being "held ready for an immediate move against the enemy," and he exhorted them to trust "God and the justice of our cause," which, together with "the love of the dear ones at home" made "failure . . . impossible," so that "victory must be ours."

On September 20, reinforced by Longstreet and three more divisions as well as a number of brigades, Bragg struck at the Union's left flank, which broke, largely because, in the confusion of battle, Rosecrans, believing he was *closing* a gap in his line, actually *opened* one. Most of the Army of the Cumberland fell back in confusion on Chattanooga. Only George H. Thomas, the "Rock of Chickamauga," stood fast, thereby preventing a rout that would have annihilated the Union army. Nevertheless, it was clear to Bragg that he had scored a great victory—albeit at a

CHATTANOOGA FROM THE NORTH BANK OF THE TENNESSEE.

"Chattanooga from the North Bank of the Tennessee." HARPER'S ILLUSTRATED WEEKLY

tremendous price (18,454 killed, wounded, captured, or missing versus 16,170 on the Union side). Mindful of the carnage, Bragg ordered his troops to stand down. There would be time enough to finish the battle the following day. Longstreet and Nathan Bedford Forrest, the generals who had led the reinforcements, raised vehement objection. Failing to persuade Bragg to press the army's hard-won advantage, Longstreet fell silent. The fiery Forrest, however, railed at Bragg: "You have played the part of a damn scoundrel. . . . If you ever again try to interfere with me or cross my path, it will be at the peril of your life."

BATTLES OF LOOKOUT MOUNTAIN AND MISSIONARY RIDGE, NOVEMBER 24–25, 1863

After Chickamauga, Bragg deployed his forces on Lookout Mountain and Missionary Ridge to lay siege to the Army of the Cumberland in Chattanooga below. Ulysses S. Grant arrived on November 24 and, in coordination with the besieged army, swept Bragg from both positions over the next two days. Exhaustion and poorly placed artillery—a surprising error on Bragg's part—contributed to what was very nearly a rout as the Army of Tennessee fled into Georgia.

Usually modest on the subject of his victories, Grant positively crowed that "an army never was whipped so badly as Bragg's was." No one would have agreed with this assessment more

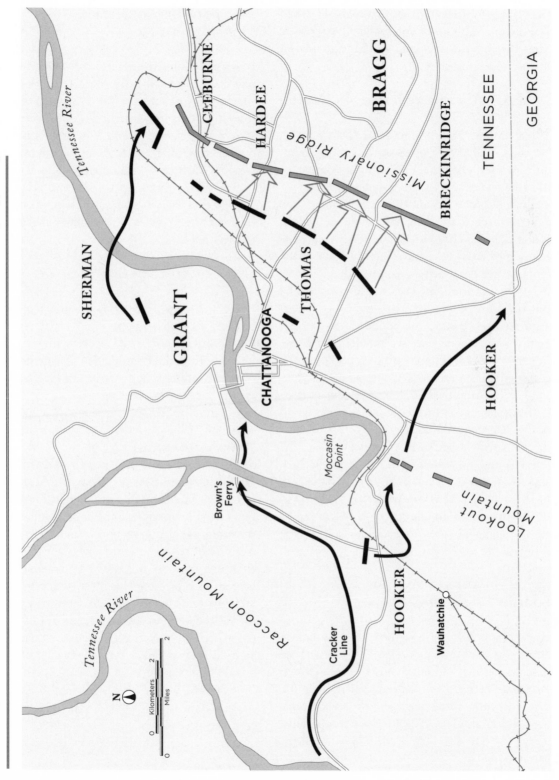

than Bragg himself who, on November 28, asked Davis to relieve him of command. Those orders came through two days later, and he was replaced by Joseph E. Johnston.

MILITARY ADVISOR TO JEFFERSON DAVIS

Three months after his relief at Chattanooga, Braxton Bragg was posted to Richmond, with official orders charging him "with the conduct of military operations of the Confederate States." Technically, this made him something like general-in-chief of the Confederate armies. In actuality, he had been kicked upstairs to serve as President Davis's personal military advisor without any direct authority of command.

If he was humiliated or even discouraged by this dubious "promotion," Bragg did not betray such feelings. Instead, he applied himself diligently to improving massive problems of logistics and supply and to plugging loopholes in the conscription system of a Confederate military starved for manpower. In short order, his portfolio was expanded to include successive command of the defenses of Wilmington, North Carolina, the Department of North Carolina and Southern Virginia, the defenses of Augusta, Georgia, and the defenses of Savannah and Charleston. In January 1865, he was returned to command of the defenses of Wilmington, the only Confederate port not yet completely closed to blockade runners.

SECOND BATTLE OF FORT FISHER, JANUARY 13–15, 1865

From January 13 to 15, 1865, a joint Union army and navy assault on Fort Fisher, sometimes called the "Gibraltar of the South," which guarded Wilmington, succeeded in taking the fort and, with it, the town and its port. Bragg, who had delayed sending in more troops until it was too late, was able to withdraw the fort's garrison intact.

BATTLE OF BENTONVILLE, MARCH 19–21, 1865

Bragg now offered his services as a corps commander (in actuality the depleted "corps" was smaller than a normal division) in what was now Joseph E. Johnston's Army of Tennessee. Johnston accepted, and Bragg fought against William T. Sherman at the Battle of Bentonville, North Carolina. Outnumbered sixty thousand to twenty-one thousand, the Army of Tennessee struggled to what was largely a foregone conclusion: surrender. It was the last major engagement of the Civil War.

END AND AFTERMATH

Bragg and his wife accompanied Jefferson Davis in flight from Richmond. They separated from the president and, in May, were picked up by Union forces, the commander of which immediately accepted Bragg's parole and released him to find his way home. On reaching his Louisiana plantation, Bragg learned that it had been seized and sold at auction by federal authorities. Worse, he discovered that he now had a multitude of creditors but a dearth of friends. He hired himself out on a variety of jobs, ranging from civil engineer to insurance salesman, but his naturally disagreeable ways bounced him from one employment to another. Positions as New Orleans waterworks superintendent and chief engineer for the state of Alabama finally helped him do more than just scrape by, and a lucrative offer to become chief railroad inspector for the state of Texas lured him to Galveston, where, on September 27, 1876, while out for a stroll, he was felled by a massive stroke that killed him instantly.

Chapter 7

JOHN HUNT MORGAN

RATING: ★ ★

John Hunt Morgan. LIBRARY OF CONGRESS

EVALUATION

A self-taught tactical innovator of great courage, John Hunt Morgan brought the hit-and-run cavalry raid to its height in the Civil War and used it as an instrument of what today would be called asymmetric warfare—the effective application of a significantly smaller power against an enemy's larger force. He went on to develop the long-distance raid as a vehicle of insurgency and as a means of logistical disruption and the dissemination of terror among a civilian population. Morgan was far less successful in developing his raiding tactics for strategic effect, however, and, in the end, his operations had no discernible impact on the outcome of the war in his theater. Worse, his ambitious raid into Kentucky, Indiana, and Ohio squandered the most

effective light cavalry in the Confederate army, frittering it away piecemeal and without real strategic effect. In the end, Morgan had more import as a proud icon of the "Lost Cause of the Confederacy" than as an active general in the Confederate forces.

Principal Battles

PRE–CIVIL WAR

U.S.-Mexican War, 1846–1848

- Buena Vista, February 22–23, 1847: Performed splendidly as an officer in the Kentucky Cavalry

CIVIL WAR

- Shiloh, April 6–7, 1862: In Tennessee; dismounted his cavalry raiders and participated vigorously in this bloody battle
- Hartsville, December 7, 1862: In Tennessee; during the Stones River Campaign, made a surprise attack against Thirty-ninth Brigade, XIV Corps of the Army of the Cumberland, taking 1,844 prisoners out of 2,106 engaged
- Morgan's Raid, June 11–July 26, 1863: In Tennessee, Kentucky, Indiana, and Ohio; a brilliant one-thousand-mile raid deep into Union territory—the deepest penetration by uniformed Confederate forces during the war—that caused considerable disruption, terror, and destruction but had no significant strategic effect

In our own age, a soldier like John Hunt Morgan would be called a practitioner of asymmetric warfare, an expert in the effective employment of small forces against much larger military formations. In his own day, he was dubbed a cavalry raider by the Confederates who adored him and a common criminal by the Union officials under whose saddles he was a perpetual burr.

Morgan was a remarkable warrior. Without the benefit—or the handicap—of formal military training, he used cavalry as it had never been used before, in a manner that anticipated certain aspects of partisan or insurgent warfare in the mid-twentieth century and beyond. His was a force of deep penetration and disruption, partly logistical in its impact, partly psychological. He was a nineteenth-century insurgent. Had any significant number of other Confederates followed his example, the Civil War would have been very different in its character, a guerrilla affair with few "set" battles.

EARLY LIFE

John Hunt Morgan was born in Huntsville, Alabama, on June 1, 1825, the first of ten (some sources report eight) children of Calvin Morgan and the woman Calvin had brought back to Huntsville from Lexington, Kentucky, Henrietta Hunt, a celebrated beauty. Although John Hunt Morgan's maternal grandfather, John Wesley Hunt, was a founding father of Lexington and reputedly the first millionaire in Kentucky, Calvin lost his own house in Huntsville in 1831 when the failure of his pharmacy left him unable to pay his property taxes. This brought the Morgans back to Lexington, where John Wesley Hunt employed Calvin Morgan as an overseer on one of his large plantations.

The change from Huntsville to Lexington had a profoundly formative effect on John. From his wealthy grandfather and his associates in the world of the Kentucky plantation, the boy imbibed the quasi-feudal values of the Old South to a far greater degree than if he had known only the world of his pharmacist father. By the age of sixteen, when he enrolled in Lexington's celebrated Transylvania College, John Hunt Morgan was already a courtly, soft-spoken Southern gentleman, a handsome horseman who exuded both a quiet self-confidence and a powerful sense of entitlement. Indeed, he soon chafed under the discipline of the classroom, whose intellectual demands held no allure for

him. His parents as well as his grandfather did not withhold their criticism from the youth, who became increasingly restless and even ungovernable. Responding to a perceived insult from a classmate, young Morgan challenged him to a duel. This resulted in Morgan's suspension from the college in June 1844 after two years in attendance. He would never return.

U.S.-MEXICAN WAR, 1846–1848

Morgan frittered away the next two years until the outbreak of the war with Mexico moved him to enlist as a private in the 1st Kentucky Cavalry. The combination of his horsemanship and family connections quickly earned him a first lieutenant's commission in the regiment, which he retained when the unit was mustered into the federal service. He reached the front early in 1847, in time to participate in the Battle of Buena Vista (February 22–23, 1847), in which the Kentucky Cavalry performed magnificently.

BETWEEN THE WARS

Buena Vista was the last big battle in northern Mexico and the final battle for Major General Zachary Taylor's army. Morgan and the other Kentuckians were mustered out of the service on July 8, 1847. Surprisingly, perhaps, Morgan showed no interest in remaining in the U.S. Army. He had enjoyed combat, but the experience seems to have exorcised his restless demons, and when he returned to Kentucky, he used some of his grandfather's money to purchase a hemp manufactory and subsequently added to this a woolen mill as well as a mercantile concern his grandfather bequeathed to him on his death in 1849. The year before, Morgan, twenty-three, married Rebecca Grantz Bruce, his business partner's eighteen-year-old sister.

John Hunt Morgan became a Southern capitalist, comfortable, confident, and a surprisingly prudent manager. He dipped deeply into the marketing of slaves, and he also became active in local politics and community affairs. This extended, in 1852, to his sponsorship of a militia artillery battery, but his interest in it soon flagged, and the outfit disbanded by 1854. In the meantime, although Morgan prospered, tragedy struck his wife, Rebecca, who developed a disorder diagnosed as septic thrombophlebitis—an infected blood clot—after delivering a stillborn son in 1853. Her condition worsened, eventually necessitating the amputation of her leg. Increasingly an invalid, she grew totally dependent on the continual ministrations of her husband, something he resented but suffered in silence. ·What he could not remain silent about was her family's strident antislavery views, which conflicted with both his own beliefs and his business. Partly in an effort to get away from home whenever possible, Morgan raised a new independent militia unit in 1857, this one a company of cavalry, which he christened the "Lexington Rifles." To occupy his time and in earnest preparation for what he believed was a coming civil war, Morgan dedicated himself to drilling his men, transforming them into a crack unit.

The War Begins

Although Morgan believed in the rightness of slavery, he was, like most of his fellow Kentuckians, a Union loyalist. He took President-elect Lincoln at his word, that he believed the Constitution protected slavery and that he did not intend to interfere with it, and he wrote to his younger brother Tom that he hoped Kentucky would not secede. "Lincoln," he wrote, "will make a good President" and is at least entitled to "a fair trial & then if he commits some overt act all the South will be a unit."

Tom Morgan agreed with his brother on the undesirability of secession; however, in the early summer of 1861, he enlisted in the Kentucky State Guard, which fought for the Confederacy. John Hunt Morgan did not feel that he

could leave his wife, but when she died on July 21, 1861, there was nothing to hold him in Lexington any longer. He settled his business affairs and, in September, led his Lexington Rifles to Confederate Tennessee and presented them to the Provisional Army of the Confederate States.

In November 1861, with Kentucky now a battleground, Albert Sidney Johnston ordered Morgan and his Lexington Rifles to Bowling Green. They operated in the rear of Don Carlos Buell's Federal lines, taking prisoners and disrupting supplies and communications. Hit-and-run tactics were their calling card, and they proved highly effective. From the end of 1861 to the early spring of 1862, the Lexington Rifles conducted one raid after another, sometimes disguised in Union uniforms to disrupt rear echelon operations. Morgan became a popular local figure and earned the admiration of Johnston and other officers.

Battle of Shiloh and the First Kentucky Raid, April 6–7 and July 1862

On April 4, 1862, Morgan was promoted to full colonel and given command of the 2nd Kentucky Cavalry Regiment, of which the Lexington Rifles formed the nucleus. Days later, he and his new command were committed to something bigger than a hit-and-run raid when they were sent to fight at Shiloh. Quickly finding that the tangled terrain was not suited to cavalry, Morgan ordered his men to dismount, and they fought as infantry. It was a valuable lesson that proved to the commander just how flexible his regiment could be.

After Shiloh, in May, Morgan swept variously throughout Tennessee and Kentucky, perfecting the doctrine and tactics of the hit-and-run cavalry raid. The key elements were attacking isolated elements of big units; avoiding becoming outnumbered; striking with great speed; inflicting maximum damage in minimum

Morgan's Raid - July 1863

INDIANA

OHIO

Salineville
July 26

Steubenville

Columbus

Zanesville

Indianapolis

Dayton

Nelsonville

Vernon

Cincinnati

Parkersburg

Buffington Island
July 19

Salem

Vienna

Ohio River

Louisville

Frankfort

Huntington

WEST
VIRGINIA

Corydon
July 9

Lexington

Brandenburg

Bardstown

Lebanon

KENTUCKY

VIRGINIA

Burksville

NORTH
CAROLINA

TENNESSEE

N

Knoxville

Sparta

0   Kilometers   60

0   Miles   60

time; splitting up to confuse the enemy; and vanishing as quickly as you appeared. With these raids, Morgan earned the sobriquet by which he would become famous: the "Thunderbolt of the Confederacy."

On July 4, 1862, Morgan left Knoxville with nearly nine hundred men for the First Kentucky Raid, which terrorized the region for the next three weeks. Again operating in the rear of Buell's army, the raiders took some twelve hundred Federal prisoners (who were instantly paroled, because their presence would overburden the raiders), stole hundreds of horses, and appropriated or destroyed large quantities of Union supplies. All of this was bad enough for Buell's lumbering Army of the Ohio, but it was the effect on military and civilian morale, as well as on the tenuous Union government of this border state, that constituted the heaviest damage.

The effect on Confederate morale was nothing short of miraculous—and, in the end, misleading. Morgan generated excitement in Kentucky, and he also attracted volunteers. He had begun his First Kentucky Raid with nine hundred men. He ended it with 1,200. The success of the raid, the excitement it created, and the growth of Morgan's command contributed to Braxton Bragg's perception that Kentucky was ripe for rebellion and that he was the one to "liberate" it by means of a risky invasion. Morgan's experience had prompted Bragg's assumption that Kentuckians were eager to rally to the Confederate cause. As it turned out, they were not. Insofar as Morgan's raids drove Bragg to act rashly, they did at least as much harm as good.

BATTLE OF HARTSVILLE, DECEMBER 7, 1862

Although Morgan was becoming famous as a raider, he was actually most successful when he coordinated his unique hit-and-run cavalry tactics with the actions of larger forces, as he did during the Stones River Campaign in Tennessee.

While the major armies of Braxton Bragg and William S. Rosecrans sparred with one another ahead of the Battle of Stones River (December 31, 1862–January 2, 1863), Morgan led his raiders in a lightning attack against the Thirty-ninth Brigade, XIV Corps of Rosecrans's Army of the Cumberland on December 7 at Hartsville, Tennessee. Hitting the Union encampment early in the morning, Morgan's men wore a mixture of blue uniforms and civilian clothing, which deceived the Union pickets. Surprise was total, and with just 1,400 men, Morgan defeated 2,106, killing 58, wounding 204, and capturing 1,844. Joseph E. Johnston, the Confederate theater commander, hailed this as a "brilliant" victory and recommended Morgan's immediate promotion to brigadier general, which came through on December 11, just four days after the battle. He felt himself ready to undertake even more ambitious operations.

"MORGAN'S RAID," JUNE 11–JULY 26, 1863

Spectacular as they were, Morgan's early raids drew some criticism for having minimal strategic effect. In June 1863, the new brigadier general sought to answer his critics by mounting what he conceived as a genuinely strategic raid. Its object would not only be the usual disruption of Union rear-echelon operations and interdiction of supply and communication lines, but, even more important, it would serve to force Union commanders to divert resources from Vicksburg in Mississippi and from the Mississippi Valley generally, thereby relieving pressure on Braxton Bragg's beleaguered Army of Tennessee.

This would be no small-unit raid. Morgan led 2,460 cavalrymen—the finest in the Confederate service, which meant the best on the North American continent—out of Sparta, Tennessee, on June 11, 1863. From the outset, however, he departed from the strategic plan he had drawn up with Bragg, who had command authority in the region. Bragg ordered Morgan to limit his activities to Tennessee and Kentucky, so as to provoke the desired Union troop diversions in the region. On his own, however, Morgan decided to extend the raid into Indiana and Ohio for the explicit purpose of terrorizing the North.

Morgan crossed into Kentucky on July 2 and engaged outnumbered elements of the 25th Michigan Infantry at the Battle of Tebbs Bend on July 4. Outgunned though they were, the Union troops deflected the attack and avoided capture (inflicting eighty casualties on Morgan while suffering twenty-nine), but Morgan continued northward, surprising a Union garrison at Lebanon on July 5. In an intense six-hour battle, General Morgan's brother Tom was killed, but the raiders captured the garrison (unable to accommodate prisoners, Morgan ordered their immediate parole) and burned most of Lebanon's public buildings.

Grief-stricken by the loss of his brother, Morgan nevertheless pressed on due north to Bardstown, engaging small Federal units along the way. At Bardstown, he took a turn both unexpected and unauthorized. Instead of continuing north to Louisville, he veered northwest to Brandenburg on the Ohio River. Before he crossed the river into Indiana, he split up his command to create confusion, but this dodge succeeded only in getting the detached portion captured near New Pekin, Indiana. Morgan was more successful using another deceptive tactic, tapping into telegraph lines and faking Union messages replete with disinformation and greatly inflated estimates of his numbers. This manipulation of a key Civil War–era technology was typical of Morgan at his most inventive.

Although Morgan's venture into Indiana was unauthorized, it was not impulsive. He had sent his spy, Captain Thomas Hines, into Indiana the month before to determine if local Copperheads (Confederate sympathizers) would likely rise up in support of a rebellion. Hines reunited with Morgan at Brandenburg on July 8, and although

his news was discouraging—there would be no Copperhead uprising—Hines joined the raiders in commandeering a pair of steamers, the *John B. McCombs* and the *Alice Dean*, to cross the river into Indiana with the 1,800 men left in Morgan's command. At their landing place, Mauckport, they were met by a unit of Indiana home guardsmen, which they easily drove off. The fleeing Indianans left behind some valuable artillery, which Morgan appropriated. He put the *Alice Dean* to the torch and sent the *John B. McCombs* downriver, charging its skipper to warn away all would-be pursuers. Panic now rippled through Indiana, and its governor, Oliver P. Morton, put out a call for militia volunteers while Major General Ambrose Burnside, commanding the Department of the Ohio, dispatched Union forces as well as militia to interdict Morgan's routes back to the South.

But this was no hit-and-run raid. Instead of turning back south, Morgan continued north and, on July 9, a mile south of Corydon, he encountered more militia, which he readily outflanked, routing the outnumbered force of perhaps 400 to 450 men. It was after this Battle of Corydon that Morgan's raiders began taking a toll on civilians, killing a toll taker and a Lutheran farmer-minister and stealing horses and cattle. Popular sentiment, even among Copperheads, began to turn against the raiders.

Morgan swung northeast, sowing terror through the region's small towns. In a skirmish on July 11, a number of his men were captured. This setback seems only to have hardened Morgan's attitude, and, riding into Salem, Indiana, on July 12, he set fire to railroad cars, a depot, and railway bridges, looted merchants, and demanded what he called "taxes" from local flour and gristmill operators before setting out east to the Ohio border.

Morgan crossed the Indiana-Ohio line on July 13, along the way wrecking whatever seemed to him of military value and deftly evading the forces Burnside had organized mainly to defend

"Morgan's Raiders Enter Washington, Ohio," as reported in Harper's Weekly *on August 15, 1863.*
HARPER'S ILLUSTRATED WEEKLY

Cincinnati. Burnside, however, studied his maps carefully, and he correctly surmised that Morgan would seek to return to the South via West Virginia. The only convenient means of crossing the Ohio into that recently created state was at Buffington Island, which had a lightly defended Union fort. Burnside dispatched Union troops and gunboats to the scene, while also ordering a militia regiment to hold the fort.

It was a close race. Morgan arrived opposite Buffington Island at dusk on July 18, and while he saw that the fort was garrisoned only by the militia, he decided that it was too hazardous to attack at night. His delay proved fatal.

The cavalry and gunboats Burnside had sent arrived on the morning of July 19, and the Battle of Buffington Island that day pitted 14,000 Union troops against just 1,700 raiders, killing 52 of them, wounding 100, and capturing some 750, including another of the Morgan brothers, Richard, and Morgan's top lieutenant, Colonel Basil W. Duke.

Morgan and the remaining raiders were blocked on the south, so they continued northeast deeper into Ohio. Some three hundred raiders subsequently managed to slip into West Virginia, but Morgan continued to raid in Ohio, losing troopers at each skirmish along the way as he probed for a place to cross the Ohio River. His pursuers never let up, and on July 26, Union cavalry under Brigadier General James M. Shackelford ran to ground Morgan and the four hundred or so men who were still with him at the Battle of Salineville.

Morgan and his officers were not treated as prisoners of war, but, in a calculated insult, were labeled common criminals and accordingly remanded to the Ohio Penitentiary in Columbus. (Most of the enlisted men were shipped off to Camp Douglas, a vast and squalid prisoner-of-war stockade outside of Chicago.) Astoundingly, the penitentiary proved unable to hold them. On November 27, 1863, Morgan and six officers, including the spy Thomas Hines,

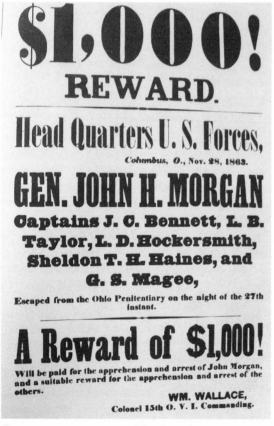

Poster announcing a reward for the capture of John Hunt Morgan, escaped from the Ohio Penitentiary. WIKIMEDIA COMMONS

tunneled out of their cells, into the prison yard, and to the wall, which they climbed to freedom. Two were subsequently recaptured, but Morgan and four others returned to Confederate territory, where they were feted as heroes.

In forty-six days they had ridden over one thousand miles, had taken some six thousand Union soldiers and militiamen prisoner (all were immediately paroled), had destroyed many bridges, and had torn up miles of railroad track. Hundreds of thousands of dollars in military supplies and civilian goods were looted or destroyed. In Ohio, some 2,500 horses were stolen and approximately 4,375 private homes and businesses were ransacked and robbed. Yet while it did draw some thousands of Union troops away from other duties, the raid had negligible strategic impact, especially in the shadow of the great Union victories at Gettysburg (July 3) and Vicksburg (July 4).

MORGAN'S END

For the Confederacy, the net result of Morgan's Raid was worse than strategic ineffectiveness. In exchange for inflicting a certain amount of terror, looting, and destruction, Morgan frittered away the best light cavalry the Confederacy had. Bragg complained that this cavalry would have been of much greater value to him and his hard-pressed western command in direct battle against the enemy army, and while he did not dare to court-martial or cashier the popular Morgan, he urged General Johnston to assign him, on August 22, 1864, to command the relatively small Trans-Allegheny Department, which encompassed eastern Tennessee and southwestern Virginia.

Morgan mounted more raids, but the men he commanded were nothing like his original handpicked elite. The new raids into Kentucky were little more than pillaging sprees, so wildly unmilitary that they prompted a Confederate War Department investigation, which charged Morgan with allowing the equivalent of banditry. Clearly, Bragg and others were setting up the "Confederate Thunderbolt" for removal from command. Before this could happen, however, he was killed.

Around five o'clock in the morning on September 4, 1864, Federal cavalry surprised Morgan as he woke in the appropriated bedroom of an appropriated house in Greeneville, Tennessee. Pulling on his britches and boots, Morgan hid in some bushes near the house. The official Union report of what happened next was that Morgan refused an order to halt and was therefore shot. Morgan's men, however, told the story very differently. They claimed that the unarmed general came out of his hiding place, hands up, and called out, "Don't shoot. I surrender." A Union trooper replied, "Surrender and be God damned—I know you." With that, he leveled his carbine and shot John Hunt Morgan down, crowing to his fellow troopers that he had "killed the damned horse thief." Confederate authorities never wavered from their assertion that General Morgan had been murdered for fear that, if captured, he would make good another escape highly embarrassing to Union authorities.

The Union troopers could kill John Hunt Morgan, but they could not snuff out his legend. By the time of his death, however, that legend did less to inspire militarily useful action than it

A romantic picture of the raider Morgan, engraved after an 1862 photograph. HARPER'S ILLUSTRATED WEEKLY

added grist to the mythological mill that would grind out the postwar literary, political, and popular culture movement known as the "Lost Cause of the Confederacy"—the idea that the Southern cause, noble, chivalrous, and ultimately right, had been defeated only by the North's superior numbers and economic power.

Chapter 8

NATHAN BEDFORD FORREST

RATING: ✸ ✸ ✸

Nathan Bedford Forrest. LIBRARY OF CONGRESS

EVALUATION

Like John Hunt Morgan (Chapter 7), Nathan Bedford Forrest was brilliantly self-taught in the military art. Both were remarkably inventive practitioners of asymmetric warfare, leveraging meager resources to great effect against superior forces. Yet, while Morgan saw himself as a latter-day knight without armor, Forrest regarded himself as a soldier and a leader of soldiers. He was not a knight or a crusader, but a man of war,

and "war," he said, "means fighting, and fighting means killing." Such was his stock in trade.

Adversaries such as Ulysses S. Grant and William T. Sherman thought Forrest the most dangerous man west of the Blue Ridge and Alleghenies. Sherman, whose approach to war at times more closely resembled than differed from Forrest's, called him a "devil." The word may not have been tossed off casually. Like the devil, Forrest knew how to sow chaos and destruction with consummate craft, and his method relied as heavily on intimidation, bluff, and deception as it did on saber's edge and gunpowder. All that kept him from joining the ranks of the very greatest generals of the Civil War was his subordinate position, which confined him to a wholly tactical role, albeit one that sometimes had a strategic impact. Sherman was accorded independent command and thus had a larger, far more strategically significant field in which to practice his own sometimes calculatedly cruel version of warfare.

Principal Battles

Civil War

- Sacramento, December 28, 1861: In Kentucky; a skirmish in which Forrest expertly used the element of surprise to rout his adversary, Major Eli H. Murray

- Fort Donelson, February 11–16, 1862: In Tennessee; refusing to follow his commander in capitulation, Forrest preserved his forces

- Shiloh, April 6–7, 1862: In Tennessee; fought a brilliant rear-guard action on the second day of battle

- First Battle of Murfreesboro, July 13, 1862: In Tennessee; wreaked havoc in Grant's rear echelons

- Cedar Bluff, May 3, 1863: In Alabama; using bluff and deception, Forrest prompted the surrender of a Union force more than twice his size

- Chickamauga, September 19–20, 1863: In Georgia; was frustrated by Braxton Bragg's failure to support his vigorous pursuit of the retreating Army of the Cumberland

- Okolona, February 22, 1864: In Mississippi; once again Forrest defeated a Union force twice his size
- Fort Pillow Massacre, April 12, 1864: In Tennessee; Forrest's possible complicity in the execution of African-American prisoners of war remains a dark stain on his reputation
- Brice's Crossroads, June 10, 1864: In Mississippi; remarkable victory against a force more than twice the size of Forrest's own
- Tupelo, July 14–15, 1864: In Mississippi; Forrest's outnumbered forces were driven from the field
- Second Battle of Memphis, August 21, 1864: In Tennessee; an audacious but ineffective raid on the city
- Third Battle of Murfreesboro, December 5–7, 1864: In Tennessee; a brief action preparatory to the Battle of Nashville
- Nashville, December 15–16, 1864: In Tennessee; although his failure to prevent John M. Schofield's withdrawal from Franklin contributed to the defeat of John Bell Hood at Nashville, Forrest's brilliant rearguard action prevented the total defeat of Hood's Army of Tennessee
- Wilson's Raid, March–April 1865: In Alabama and Georgia; outnumbered, Forrest unsuccessfully opposed Union brigadier general James H. Wilson's destructive cavalry raid against various manufactories in Alabama and Georgia at the end of the war

For many Americans, both in the 1860s and afterward, the Civil War has been thoroughly steeped in romance. For many Southerners in particular, this attitude was defined and amplified by the concept of "the Lost Cause," the idea that the Confederate cause was noble and right, and that Southern soldiers and their leaders had possessed the skill and courage to achieve a righteous and deserved victory, but were deprived of it by dint of Northern demographic, economic, and industrial dominance. Nor have Northerners been immune to the romantic vision of the war. For some it was a great crusade, a holy struggle to save the Union and a contest to end the evil of slavery.

For many on both sides, the war seemed a hallowed adventure, and men of achieved distinction, aspiration to distinction, or the pretension to distinction clamored for high command, the honor of leading other men into romantically desperate battle.

But a select few, including some of the most strikingly successful generals of the Civil War, wanted no part of the supposed "romance" of war. William T. Sherman put his conception of war very simply—not in the most often quoted sentence "War is hell," but in what he told the mayor of Atlanta: "War is cruelty." And the general Sherman most feared and hated, Nathan Bedford Forrest, the man he called a "devil" and the commander he considered more dangerous than any other in the South, had his own single-sentence definition of war: "War means fighting, and fighting means killing."

LIFE BEFORE THE WAR

Nathan Bedford Forrest was born on July 13, 1821, in a cabin near Chapel Hill, Tennessee. His father eked out a living as a blacksmith and would sire eleven more children before he died in 1838, leaving Nathan to support them and their widowed mother. Maybe it was this hard circumstance that, early in life, knocked notions of romance and glory out of the young man's head.

His hardscrabble circumstances left no time for school—he spent a total of six months in a classroom—before his uncle Jonathan Forrest took him into his business in Hernando, Mississippi, in 1841. Four years later, Jonathan Forrest got into a heated argument with some business rivals, the Matlock brothers, which escalated into a violent brawl in which he was killed. Nathan Forrest responded by shooting and killing two of the brothers. After he emptied his double-barreled (two-shot) pistol in the process, a bystander tossed him a knife, which Forrest used to slash the two other Matlocks, wounding both. (One would later freely serve under Forrest during the Civil War.) There was nothing of blood vengeance about the killings, merely the evening of a score. As Nathan Bedford Forrest saw it, a man did not allow his kinsman's killers to go unkilled. It was that simple.

As for young Forrest, he discovered in himself a business sense as natural as it was aggressive. He rapidly acquired a pair of cotton plantations in the Tennessee Delta country, holdings amounting to about three thousand acres by 1860, and he owned at least forty-two slaves. Before long, he came to realize that even more money was to be made in the buying and selling of slaves than in the raising of cotton, and so he opened a slave-trading business in Memphis. His apologists among historians point to evidence that Forrest treated his slaves well, perhaps not so much out of fellow feeling for them as human beings but out of good common business sense. His inventory was valuable, and as a good businessman he did everything he had to do to protect it.

However Forrest felt about slaves and slavery, the trade made him rich. Not only did he easily support his mother and siblings—even financing college educations for all of his brothers—Forrest became a local politician, gaining election in 1858 as a Memphis alderman. By the start of the Civil War, he held a fortune well in excess of a million dollars. Forrest pursued a course of self-education and became a voracious reader and a careful writer. During the Civil War, he would labor intensively over critical orders, concerned to strike just the right "pitch," as he called it. Throughout his life, he would express embarrassment over his educational deficiencies, especially (he freely admitted) when he was in the company of well-educated men. Despite this, he seems never to have sought admittance to genteel Southern society. He was a notorious—and mostly winning—gambler, but (as his obituary put it) he was always "known to his acquaintances as a man of obscure origin and low associations . . . a man of great energy and brute courage." Even ensconced in wealth, Forrest seems to have reveled in and traded on his reputation as a dangerous and unpredictable man.

THE WAR BEGINS

When Tennessee seceded from the Union in June 1861, the thirty-nine-year-old Forrest and his fifteen-year-old son presented themselves for enlistment as privates in the Provisional Army of the Confederate States. After training at Fort Wright in Randolph, Tennessee, they were mustered into Company E of the Tennessee Mounted Rifles on July 14. Forrest was shocked by the impoverished condition of the unit and offered to purchase sufficient horses, uniforms, and weapons to fit out a volunteer regiment. As a planter, Forrest was exempt from service under Confederate law, and those planters who did choose to serve always joined as officers. In response to his offer to finance a regiment, Governor Isham G. Harris commissioned Private Forrest a lieutenant colonel and asked him to recruit and train a battalion of volunteer Confederate Mounted Rangers. The officers of the Tennessee Mounted Rifles enthusiastically endorsed the governor's commission because they recognized in Forrest, who had no training in the military art, a born fighter and a leader of fighting men. Forrest personally raised and trained the battalion, and by October was given command of an entire regiment, which was named for him.

It was not uncommon for wealthy Southerners to raise and finance individual companies during the Civil War, but it was almost unheard of for them to create entire battalions, let alone regiments. Moreover, from the beginning, Forrest molded his outfit into a unique fighting unit. He handpicked his troopers for their agility, horsemanship, daring, and, most of all, for their willingness to kill. After Shiloh (April 6–7, 1862), he would run a recruiting ad in the *Memphis Appeal* that called out, "Come on, boys, if you want a heap of fun and to kill some Yankees."

While he thought of his entire regiment as an elite fighting force, he selected from it the best of the best to serve as his "Escort Company," a shock-troop unit of forty to ninety men, which, at one point, included eight of Forrest's slaves. In addition to their fighting skill, the troops of the Escort Company were big men and, like Forrest himself (six-foot-two, 210 pounds), intimidating men. Forrest made it his practice to personally sharpen *both* edges of his cavalry saber before each battle.

Historians would make much of the fact that Forrest joined the Confederate army as a private and emerged as a general. Yet, as a general officer, he never personally gave up what he saw as the only important duty of an *enlisted* soldier: killing. The modern estimate is that Forrest killed at least thirty-three men in combat, using his pistol, his double-edge saber, or a shotgun.

SKIRMISH AT SACRAMENTO, KENTUCKY, DECEMBER 28, 1861

Forrest's first engagement occurred at the backwoods Kentucky village of Sacramento. Learning that a Union detachment of five hundred men was moving through the area, Forrest led just two hundred men in stealthy pursuit. Splitting this small force into three parts, he dismounted one portion to make a frontal attack while the two other elements, mounted, attacked the left and right flanks of the Union detachment. It was a classic envelopment—holding the enemy by its nose while unexpectedly hitting it from the two flanks—and it gave the impression of overwhelming strength. Key to Forrest's tactics was deception. An inveterate gambler, he was also a natural bluffer—but the essence of the bluff was always

intense and violent activity. "Forward, men," he would order, "and mix with them!" In this first engagement of two hundred against more than twice that number, Forrest and his men killed or captured every one of the enemy.

BATTLE OF FORT DONELSON, FEBRUARY 11–16, 1862

Ordered to take his regiment to beleaguered Fort Donelson in February 1862, Forrest found himself being asked to surrender—not by the enemy, but by the Confederate command at the fort. Ulysses Grant had just taken Fort Henry (February 6), leaving Donelson cut off. On February 14, Union gunboats began to shell Fort Donelson. Confederate commander John Floyd decided to attempt a breakout through Grant's siege lines and attacked early the next day. In this action, Forrest's cavalry captured a Union artillery battery and cleared Grant's troops from the three roads leading to the fort. Confident that he had given Floyd just what he needed to break out, Forrest was stunned when the general announced his decision to surrender both the fort and his command.

Battle of Fort Donelson. KURZ & ALLISON LITHOGRAPH, CA. 1891

"I did not come here for the purpose of surrendering my command," Forrest boomed. Pointing out the breakthrough he had made, he offered to use his cavalry as a rear guard to protect Floyd's command. When the general remained adamant in his decision to give up, Forrest addressed the men of his own command: "Boys, these people are talking about surrendering, and I am going out of this place before they do or bust hell wide open." With that, he probed the siege lines, found an opening, and decamped, leaving Floyd to surrender some twelve thousand men.

Forrest marched to Nashville. Recognizing that the fall of Forts Henry and Donelson meant that the Tennessee capital would soon be captured, he took it upon himself to impose martial law on the city. Inventorying everything of military value, especially the machinery in a local arms factory, he hurriedly arranged for its evacuation, thereby saving the Confederacy millions of dollars in scant war production funds.

BATTLE OF SHILOH, APRIL 6–7, 1862

Forrest and his regiment reached the Shiloh battlefield on the second day of combat, just in time to fight a rear-guard action that saved many Confederate soldiers. At Fallen Timbers he charged through General Sherman's skirmish line only to realize that his men had stopped following him when they came up against the main body of an entire Union brigade. Undaunted, Forrest—mounted and alone—charged the front of the brigade. Blue-coated soldiers swarmed him. After emptying both of the Colt revolvers he carried, he drew his double-edged saber and began slashing. As he turned in the saddle to bring down his blade, a musket ball lodged in his spine, almost knocking him off his horse. Quickly recovering and despite his wound, Forrest seized the collar of the soldier who had fired at him and lifted him onto his horse. Using him as a human shield, he rode back to his own lines.

FIRST BATTLE OF MURFREESBORO, JULY 13, 1862

A full week passed before Forrest was able to get to a surgeon, who successfully extracted the musket ball in a procedure performed without anesthesia. Forrest spent more than a month recuperating in Memphis, then took command of a new and untested cavalry brigade cobbled together from an assortment of regiments that included citizen volunteers as well as slaves. On July 13, 1862, using a combination of bluff and violence, Forrest forced the surrender of the Union garrison at Murfreesboro.

The action earned him promotion to brigadier general, but in December 1862, the brigade he had led against Murfreesboro and molded into a crack unit was reassigned. Forrest was instructed to raise a new brigade of two thousand. Ordered to raid Union lines of supply and communications in western Tennessee in order to disrupt Grant's siege of Vicksburg, Forrest protested that he needed time to train his recruits, few of whom were even armed. When Braxton Bragg refused to withdraw his order, Forrest became grimly determined to do his best. He decided that his best chance was to avoid any pitched battles and instead lure Grant's troops into as many fruitless pursuits as possible, creating distractions and forcing Grant's commanders to exhaust their men and to dilute and divert them from the siege.

Forrest led his inexperienced troopers in a series of hard rides and lightning raids, all hit-and-run, never lingering long enough to engage enemy soldiers. He pushed into Kentucky; unlike the raider John Hunt Morgan, however, he stopped at the Ohio River. Along the way, Forrest accumulated a stock of Union weapons and a good many more recruits than he had started off with. While Morgan's raids would have little strategic impact, Forrest's vigorous rampage certainly interfered with and delayed Grant at Vicksburg.

BATTLE OF CEDAR BLUFF, MAY 3, 1863

Disgusted with being the victim of Forrest's raids, Grant retaliated by sending a brigade of 1,500 Union cavalry under Colonel Abel Streight to counterraid Confederate positions in north Alabama and west Georgia. One of Streight's objectives was to sever the railroad south of Chattanooga, Tennessee, thereby cutting Bragg's lines of supply. Mustering no more than six hundred men, Forrest pursued Streight's much larger force, never letting up for more than sixteen days until he had run Streight to ground at Cedar Bluff, Alabama, on May 3.

Forrest was no fool, and he knew that six hundred versus more than twice that number presented poor odds. Once again, he resorted to bluff and deception, parading some of his troopers around the top of a hill over and over, thereby giving the impression that he had about five thousand men. After doing this for a while, he sent a trooper under a flag of truce to demand Streight's surrender. The Union commander consented to a meeting with Forrest, and when he inquired point-blank as to the size of his command, Forrest replied that he had "enough to whip you out of your boots." When Streight refused to surrender, Forrest turned to his bugler. "Sound to mount," he ordered. At this, Streight changed his mind and gave up without a fight.

BATTLE OF CHICKAMAUGA, SEPTEMBER 19–20, 1863

At the Battle of Chickamauga, Forrest predictably chafed under Bragg's command. His cavalrymen vigorously pursued William Rosecrans's retreating Army of the Cumberland, taking large numbers of prisoners. He was not alone among Bragg's subordinates in his belief that following up on the Confederate victory at Chickamauga would not only retake Chattanooga, but badly cut up the Union forces. When Bragg refused to exploit the victory, Forrest thundered at him, calling him a "damned scoundrel" and "coward" and declaring that if Bragg were "any part of a man" he would "slap his jaw"—that is, challenge him to a duel. Instead, he warned Bragg that if he ever again tried to "interfere with" him or "cross [his] path," it would be at the peril of his life. With this, he demanded a transfer. Two weeks later, Forrest was assigned to an independent command in Mississippi and, on December 4, 1863, he was promoted to major general.

BATTLE OF OKOLONA, MISSISSIPPI, FEBRUARY 22, 1864

Both Grant and Sherman regarded Forrest as a high-priority target, and Sherman repeatedly sent cavalry units in search of him. One such detachment, seven thousand men under Brigadier General William Sooy Smith, caught up with him at Okolona, Mississippi, only to find themselves in an exhausting running battle, in which Forrest maneuvered so as to attack them in the rear. Although Smith significantly outnumbered Forrest, the relentless nature of the Confederate attacks demoralized his command, which withdrew to Memphis. "Smith's command was nearly double that of Forrest," General Grant observed candidly, "but not equal man to man."

FORT PILLOW MASSACRE, APRIL 12, 1864

On April 12, 1864, Forrest sent a Confederate division under Brigadier General James R. Chalmers to Fort Pillow, an earthwork fort on a high bluff overlooking the Mississippi River. Originally built by Confederate general Gideon Pillow, it had been captured by the Union and was occupied by a garrison consisting of 262 African-American soldiers and 295 whites. The mission of Fort Pillow was to cover Union supply lines. Forrest's mission was to disrupt those very lines, and he understood that retaking Fort Pillow was essential to his mission. After Chalmers had succeeded in driving in the fort's pickets

BATTLE OF CHICKAMAUGA.

Battle of Chickamauga. KURZ & ALLISON LITHOGRAPH, CA. 1891

and encircling the garrison, Forrest arrived and assumed personal command. He sent a surrender demand. When the garrison commander refused, he ordered an attack.

Southern and Northern accounts differ sharply as to what happened next. The only points beyond dispute are that 231 Union troops were killed, and about 100 were wounded; in addition, 168 whites and 58 blacks were captured. (Forrest lost just 14 killed and 86 wounded.) According to Forrest, the heavy Union losses were the result of a refusal to surrender. According to Union survivors of what they called a "massacre," the garrison surrendered as soon as the fort had been breached, but Forrest's men shouted, "No quarter! No quarter! Kill the damned niggers; shoot them down!" And so they did.

The congressional Joint Committee on the Conduct of the War, hardly an impartial body, concluded that Forrest and his troops were indeed guilty of atrocities. They had cut down most of the garrison *after* it had surrendered, and they had even buried some black soldiers alive. They also burned down tents that sheltered the Federal wounded.

BATTLE OF BRICE'S CROSSROADS, JUNE 10, 1864

The controversy concerning the full extent of Forrest's role in the Fort Pillow Massacre is ongoing among historians, but most agree that it was and remains a bloody stain on the general's record. More immediately, the event galvanized

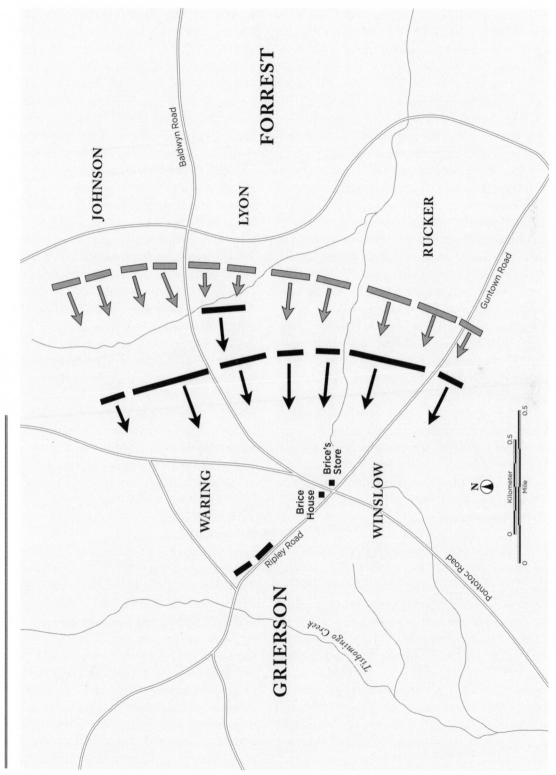

BATTLE OF BRICE'S CROSSROADS – JUNE 10, 1864

FORREST

JOHNSON

Baldwyn Road

LYON

RUCKER

Guntown Road

WARING

Brice's
Store

Brice
House

Ripley Road

WINSLOW

Pontotoc Road

GRIERSON

Tishomingo Creek

N

Kilometer   0.5

Mile   0.5

0

0

Northern resolve to stop Nathan Bedford Forrest. Yet when his 3,500 men went up against 8,500 under Union brigadier general Samuel D. Sturgis at the Battle of Brice's Crossroads, Mississippi, on June 10, 1864, it was once again Forrest who emerged the victor.

After leading Sturgis and his command in a long pursuit calculated to exhaust them, Forrest deployed his troopers at the crossroads, poised to make a violent counterattack. When Sturgis's infantry collided with Forrest's cavalry, the worn-out Union soldiers were simply not up to resisting the counterattack. It came swiftly, viciously, and with maximum energy. The Union skirmish lines dissolved, sending retreating soldiers crashing into one another. Seizing on the chaos and panic, Forrest ordered a full cavalry charge into the retreating army. He wreaked havoc on Sturgis's command, capturing 16 cannon, 176 wagons, and some 1,500 stands of small arms while killing 223 and wounding 394. A staggering 1,623 Union troops simply went missing, presumably having fled. Forrest's casualties were 96 killed and 396 wounded. Particularly humiliating to the Union was the poor performance of the African-American regiment under Sturgis's command.

TUPELO, MEMPHIS, AND JOHNSONVILLE, JULY 14–15, AUGUST 21, AND NOVEMBER 4-5, 1864

Sherman had greater success against Forrest at the Battle of Tupelo, Mississippi, on July 14 and 15, 1864. Union forces under Major General Andrew J. Smith not only succeeded in driving him from the field, but they also inflicted a wound on Forrest's foot. Yet the "Wizard of the Saddle" (as the Southern press called him) continued his disruptive raids, including a daring but ultimately ineffective strike against the Memphis business district in August 1864 and an extremely destructive assault on Sherman's supply depot at Johnsonville, Tennessee, on November 4-5, 1864.

FRANKLIN AND NASHVILLE CAMPAIGN, DECEMBER 1864

Driven out of Atlanta by Sherman, John Bell Hood led his Army of Tennessee in losing battles against Union forces at Franklin and Nashville, Tennessee. Forrest participated in these, but he clashed with Hood over the latter's refusal to allow him to block Union major general John M. Schofield's route of retreat from Franklin. Forrest finally prevailed—over Hood, but not over Schofield, who defeated him. Union troops under the redoubtable George H. Thomas hit Hood hard, dealing out a bloody defeat and forcing him to fall back on Nashville.

Withdrawing from Franklin to Nashville, Hood left Forrest to fight Union forces near Murfreesboro on December 5, 1864. This so-called Third Battle of Murfreesboro went badly for Forrest, even as Hood suffered a decisive defeat at Nashville. Forrest extricated himself from Murfreesboro and reached Nashville in time to conduct a valiant rear-guard action, which prevented the Army of Tennessee from being completely destroyed. Nevertheless, it was finished as a significant military force for the rest of the war. In February, Forrest was promoted to lieutenant general.

THE END

Forrest engaged Brigadier General James H. Wilson at the Battle of Selma, Alabama, on April 2, 1865, during Wilson's Raid through Alabama and Georgia in March and April, but he was defeated by Wilson's overwhelmingly superior numbers and received a severe saber wound in the battle. The following month, on May 4, General Richard Taylor, commanding the Confederate Department of Alabama and Mississippi, surrendered. Although the capitulation of the department was binding on Forrest, many on both sides expected him to fight on. But Forrest knew that the war had been lost, and on May 9,

1865, he officially surrendered, publishing to his troops a farewell address that echoed Robert E. Lee's own farewell to the soldiers of the Army of Northern Virginia. If any principal Confederate commander could have been expected to assume leadership of a guerrilla movement, Forrest was the most likely candidate. Instead, he told his soldiers that "it is our duty to divest ourselves of all . . . feelings of animosity, hatred, and revenge." Insofar as "it is in our power to do so," he advised cultivating "friendly feelings towards those with whom we have so long contended. . . . Neighborhood feuds, personal animosities, and private differences should be blotted out; and, when you return home, a manly, straightforward course of conduct will secure the respect of your enemies. Whatever your responsibilities may be to Government, to society, or to individuals meet them like men." His address continued:

I have never, on the field of battle, sent you where I was unwilling to go myself; nor would I now advise you to a course which I felt myself unwilling to pursue. You have been good soldiers, you can be good citizens. Obey the laws, preserve your honor, and the Government to which you have surrendered can afford to be, and will be, magnanimous.

AFTER THE WAR

Nathan Bedford Forrest commanded none of the great "set piece" battles of the Civil War, and his victories, though remarkable and costly to his Union adversaries, had no decisive strategic effect. Yet he is widely regarded as one of the most important and influential commanders in the war. He was a leading exponent of guerrilla-style tactics in modern warfare, and, equally important, was among the first to create and practice the doctrine and tactics of mobile warfare. The quotation often attributed to him, that victory was a matter of "gittin thar fustest with the mostest," is apocryphal (especially in its mock dialect form), yet *getting there first with the most* does express the essence of Forrest's combat policy, the doctrine of mobility and maneuver, and it has formed the kernel of United States war-fighting practice from World War II onward.

Forrest set about trying to rebuild his business ventures and his fortune after the war. He settled in Memphis and became president of the Marion & Memphis Railroad, which, however, sank into bankruptcy under his leadership. He never recovered financially and scraped by at the end of his life as the warden of a state prison farm. For many, his postwar legacy is irredeemably tarnished by his involvement in the Ku Klux Klan (KKK), which was founded in Pulaski, Tennessee, in 1866 and evolved into a violent shadow government in opposition to the military state governments imposed during Reconstruction. It is widely but erroneously believed that Forrest was instrumental in founding the KKK. He was not; it is, however, highly likely (though not certain) that he was the organization's first grand wizard, its official leader. During the late 1860s and early 1870s, Forrest himself approved of the KKK but publicly denied any direct association with it, and when he came to believe that the KKK had become ungovernable and merely vicious, he disavowed the organization completely. Nor did he advocate segregation or the doctrine of black inferiority. On the contrary, his avowed position was extraordinarily progressive on matters of race, especially for a man of his background, time, and place. He called for racial equality and racial harmony and believed that all professions should be open to all people, black or white.

Nathan Bedford Forrest died in Memphis on October 29, 1877, from complications of diabetes.

Chapter 9

J. E. B. Stuart

RATING: ★ ★ ⚝

James Ewell Brown Stuart. National Archives and Records Administration

Evaluation

Jeb Stuart was an exuberant warrior and a great cavalryman, whose magnificent exploits did much to promote the development of the cavalry's preeminence among the service branches of the Confederate army. He elevated the cavalry raid to the status of an art, and, at his best, he carried out the more traditional cavalry functions of reconnaissance and force screening more effectively than any other cavalry commander on either side.

But the key phrase is *at his best*. Image and self-image were important to Stuart—not just personally, but as the cornerstones of his charisma and command presence—and these sometimes got in the way of his mission objectives. At Gettysburg, this had the catastrophic effect of depriving Robert E. Lee of critical reconnaissance and intelligence when they were needed most. Part of the blame belongs to Lee, who wrote Stuart's orders very poorly; however, Stuart showed poor tactical and strategic judgment at the time of Gettysburg and contributed to the defeat of the Army of Northern Virginia and, ultimately, the demise of the Confederacy.

Principal Battles

PRE–CIVIL WAR

Early Indian Wars, 1855–1859

- In Texas and Kansas; he was wounded by Cheyenne raiders at Solomon River, Kansas, on July 29, 1857

"Bleeding Kansas," 1854–1860

- In Kansas; participated in the policing of violence between proslavery and antislavery factions

John Brown's Raid on Harpers Ferry, October 16–18, 1859

- In western Virginia; as Robert E. Lee's aide, Stuart bore the surrender demand to Brown

CIVIL WAR

- First Battle of Bull Run, July 21, 1861: In Virginia; led a saber charge some witnesses believe precipitated the general rout of Union forces
- "Ride around McClellan," June 12–July 15, 1862: In Virginia; Stuart led a spectacular cavalry reconnaissance around the entire Army of the Potomac, gaining much intelligence while humiliating Union commander George B. McClellan
- Catlett's Station Raid, August 22, 1862: In Virginia; in a second raid against the Union army, Stuart purloined General Pope's best uniform, a wealth of

supplies, and important military papers

- Second Battle of Bull Run, August 28–30, 1862: In Virginia; Stuart led his cavalry with spectacular success in this Confederate victory, seamlessly coordinating with Lee's infantry

- Maryland invasion and Battle of Antietam, September 17, 1862: In Maryland; Stuart performed disappointingly both in his reconnaissance role before Antietam and in combat during the battle

- Chambersburg Raid, October 10, 1862: In Pennsylvania; Stuart performed another spectacular "ride around" the Army of the Potomac but accomplished nothing of strategic importance

- Fredericksburg, December 11–15, 1862: In Virginia; Stuart's reconnaissance was key in positioning James Longstreet's forces on the heights overlooking Fredericksburg

- Chancellorsville, April 30–May 6, 1863: In Virginia; Stuart spearheaded Stonewall Jackson's famed flanking attack against Joseph Hooker, then assumed temporary command of II Corps after the wounding of Jackson and A. P. Hill

- Brandy Station, June 9, 1863: In Virginia; Alfred Pleasonton's cavalry attack surprised Stuart, and although Pleasonton was forced to withdraw, the audacity and competence of the attack eroded Confederate confidence in Stuart's invulnerability

- Stuart's Ride at Gettysburg, June 25–July 2, 1863: In Pennsylvania; through a combination of Lee's poorly written orders and a lapse in Stuart's judgment, the Army of Northern Virginia cavalry was out of touch with Lee during the most critical phase of the Battle of Gettysburg; this was the nadir of Stuart's career

- Overland Campaign, May–June 1864: In Virginia; Stuart was tireless in providing screening, delaying, and rear-guard actions during Lee's defense against Grant's advance

- Yellow Tavern, May 11, 1864: In Virginia; outnumbered more than two to one by Philip Sheridan's cavalry, Stuart led a desperate stand before he was cut down by Private John A. Huff, a former sharpshooter

Among the icons of the Civil War is the *warrior on horseback*, and no mounted warrior was and remains more gloriously iconic than James Ewell Brown Stuart. He makes a highly appealing picture, arrayed in his trademark scarlet-lined cloak and plumed cavalier hat, a red rose adorning his broad lapel. Yet the reality of Jeb Stuart was far too complex to capture in any iconic image.

Like Stuart, the cavalry itself is for many an emblem of the Civil War. But the reality behind the role of cavalry in that conflict was, like the reality of Stuart, more complex. Even the casual Civil War buff knows that the Confederate cavalry was superior to that of the Union—at least until Philip Sheridan's Shenandoah Valley Campaign of August 7 to October 19, 1864—but the truth is that cavalry did not come easily to either side. In both the North and the South, the first top commanders thought almost exclusively in terms of infantry, artillery, and engineering. It was thanks largely to Jeb Stuart that cavalry took root in the Confederate army at all, and its development in that army owes much to the magnificent example he set.

Stuart made cavalry an indispensable branch for the Confederacy. Therein lay his great contribution to the Southern war effort, yet also his greatest failing.

FROM PLANTATION TO WEST POINT

James Ewell Brown Stuart—known by his first three initials, combined phonetically into the familiar "Jeb"—was born on February 6, 1833, at Laurel Hill Farm, his family's plantation in the Blue Ridge country of Virginia, near the North Carolina line. Though not of the Tidewater, his was nevertheless a distinguished family, his great-grandfather, Major Alexander Stuart, having fought at the Battle of Guilford Court House during the American Revolution and his father, Archibald, having served in the War of 1812. Archibald Stuart went on to become a prominent attorney and politician, who served in the Virginia General Assembly and, briefly, in the U.S. Congress.

Jeb Stuart received his early education from his mother, who also imparted to him a strong belief in God and the Methodist religion. Her lessons were supplemented by those of local tutors until the boy was twelve years old, when he was sent off to school at Wytheville, Virginia, then to Danville, where he was tutored by his paternal aunt. In 1848, at fifteen, he gained admission to Emory & Henry College after being turned down for enlistment in the U.S. Army because he was too young. He did reasonably well in college but acquired a reputation for fighting, always over some issue of honor, whether actual or perceived.

Honor, of course, was not Stuart's idiosyncrasy. His world revolved around it. When his father failed to win reelection to Congress in 1848, young Stuart assumed that any chance of his getting nominated to West Point—for the fighting lad still wanted to be a soldier—had evaporated. Yet, not entirely to his surprise, the man who had defeated the senior Stuart, Representative Thomas Hamlet Averett, nominated Jeb in 1850. The gesture, gracious as it was, was also simply the honorable thing to do.

Stuart thrived at the academy, where he was very popular. His best friends became Fitzhugh and George Washington Custis Lee, respectively the nephew and son of Robert E. Lee, who was appointed superintendent of West Point in 1852. Soon, Jeb Stuart became an intimate of the entire Lee family. He graduated with the Class of 1854, standing thirteenth out of forty-six. He achieved the rank of second captain of the Corps and was named an honorary cavalry officer because of his easy expertise in the saddle. Legend has it that, as he approached his final year, Stuart felt himself in danger of excelling so highly in academics that he would be pushed into the Corps of Engineers, which he considered a dull assignment. In truth, his grades—especially in engineering—were simply not good enough to have admitted him into the engineers, even if he had wanted such an appointment. Instead, he was commissioned on graduation a brevet second lieutenant in the United States Mounted Rifles, a cavalry unit based in Texas.

EARLY INDIAN WARS AND "BLEEDING KANSAS"

Stuart was assigned to Fort Davis in what is today Jeff Davis County, Texas, and from the end of January 1855 through much of April he led scouting missions along the San Antonio–El Paso Road. Late in the spring of 1855, he was transferred to the newly created 1st Cavalry Regiment at Fort Leavenworth, Kansas Territory, where he served as regimental quartermaster and commissary officer under Colonel Edwin V. "Bull" Sumner.

Promoted to first lieutenant soon after his transfer to Fort Leavenworth, he also met that year Flora Cooke, whose father, Lieutenant Colonel Philip St. George Cooke, commanded the 2nd U.S. Dragoon Regiment. Within two months of meeting, Stuart and Flora were engaged, and on November 14 they were married.

While stationed at Fort Leavenworth, Stuart saw frequent action pursuing and skirmishing with Indians and policing the guerrilla violence between proslavery and antislavery factions in "Bleeding Kansas." On July 29, 1857, in a skirmish with Cheyenne raiders at Solomon River, Kansas, Stuart was wounded in a saber charge. Scattering a party of Indians, Stuart chased down one warrior, shooting him in the thigh with his cavalry pistol. The Indian spun around and fired back with his own pistol. Although the round struck Stuart full-on in the chest, the Indian's weapon was old, and the wound was superficial. Over the years, popular lore, however, inflated this incident, portraying the wound as life-threatening and also suggesting that Stuart was in command of a cavalry unit, which, though gravely injured, he led back to the fort some two hundred miles away. In fact, Stuart was part of a detachment personally led by Colonel Sumner.

JOHN BROWN'S RAID, OCTOBER 16–18, 1859

Shortly after Flora Stuart gave birth to a daughter—also named Flora—on November 14, 1857, Stuart was transferred to Fort Riley, where he remained until the outbreak of the Civil War. In 1859, he devised a special saber hook for fastening the cavalry saber to one's belt. He received a patent and secured a government contract to produce the hardware. While he was in Washington, D.C., concluding the purchase agreement and pursuing an application for a position in the army's quartermaster department, Stuart volunteered to serve as aide-de-camp to Colonel Robert E. Lee, who had just been ordered to command a company of Washington-based marines and four companies of Maryland militia to retake the U.S. Arsenal at Harpers Ferry, which the militant abolitionist John Brown had seized.

At seven o'clock on the morning of October 18, Lee gave Stuart the hazardous mission of riding to the Engine House, where Brown and his band were holed up with his hostages, to deliver a surrender demand. Lee had instructed Stuart to wave his cavalry hat if Brown (as expected) rejected the demand. That would be the signal for the marines and militia to storm the Engine House. Stuart carried out his assignment with calm deliberation, delivered the message, turned from Brown, casually waved his hat, then deftly stepped out of the line of attack and fire. The operation was over within three minutes, and Brown, wounded by a deep saber blow to the back of his neck, was in custody.

OUTBREAK OF WAR

As civil war loomed, First Lieutenant Jeb Stuart had no need to agonize, as many others did, over what side he would take. "I go with Virginia" is how he explained his intentions should his native state secede. The state seceded on April 17, 1861, but Stuart nevertheless accepted his promotion to U.S. Army captain on April 22. It was not until May 3 that he resigned his commission to join the Provisional Army of the Confederate States. That his own father-in-law, Lieutenant Colonel Philip St. George Cooke, chose to remain loyal to the Union and the U.S. Army although he was likewise a Virginian, gave Stuart no pause. On the subject of loyalty, he was an absolutist, and he insisted on changing the name of his son, who had been born on June 26, 1860, from Philip St. George Cooke Stuart to James Ewell Brown Stuart Jr.

FIRST BATTLE OF BULL RUN, JULY 21, 1861

Commissioned a lieutenant colonel of Virginia Infantry in the Confederate Army on May 10, 1861, Stuart reported to Colonel Thomas J. Jackson, soon to become known as Stonewall Jackson, who was in command at Harpers Ferry of what had been designated the Army of Shenandoah. Stuart persuaded Jackson to overlook his designation as an infantry officer and allow him instead to command the Shenandoah army's cavalry companies. Jackson agreed, and Stuart quickly consolidated these units into the 1st Virginia Cavalry Regiment. Robert E. Lee approved, and Stuart was promoted to full colonel on July 16, 1861. Thus Stuart had made himself instrumental in the very inception of the Confederate cavalry, which, for most of the war, would prove to be the preeminent mounted force on the continent.

Stuart led his cavalry in a mission to screen the advance of the Army of Shenandoah (now under the command of Joseph E. Johnston) from Winchester to Manassas during the First Battle of Bull Run. Once in the battle, he led a spectacular saber charge against a regiment of New York Zouaves, sending them into a panicked rout. Some witnesses believe that this was the action that precipitated the general Union retreat. Johnston was full of praise for Stuart's action at First Bull Run, calling him "wonderfully endowed by nature with the qualities necessary for an officer of light cavalry. Calm, firm, active, and enterprising." Stuart was rewarded with a promotion to brigadier general on September 24, 1861, and given command of the cavalry brigade for what became the Army of Northern Virginia.

THE "RIDE AROUND MCCLELLAN," JUNE 12–JULY 15, 1862

In the spring of 1862, during Union general George B. McClellan's Peninsula Campaign targeting Richmond, Stuart led his cavalry in rearguard actions covering the withdrawal of the Army of Northern Virginia up the peninsula in the face of McClellan's advance. When Johnston was badly wounded at the Battle of Seven Pines on June 1, Robert E. Lee was given command of

the army, which he instantly put on an offensive footing.

Lee tasked Stuart with making an intensive reconnaissance of the right flank of McClellan's Army of the Potomac to determine its vulnerability to attack. At the head of 1,200 cavalrymen, Stuart rode out on the morning of June 12, quickly concluded that the flank was indeed exposed, then proceeded to "ride around" the entire Union army, a circumnavigation of 150 miles. He returned to Lee and the Army of Northern Virginia on July 15, with 165 Union prisoners of war, 260 horses and mules, and a wealth of supplies in tow. Not only did he deliver to Lee precisely the intelligence he needed, he elevated Confederate morale while lowering that of the Union in inverse proportion. McClellan, the vaunted "Young Napoleon," was humiliated. Chronically hesitant and unsure of himself, McClellan was even more profoundly shaken

"Stuart's Cavalry on their Way to the Potomac—Sketched Near Poolesville, Maryland, by Mr. A. R. Waud."
HARPER'S ILLUSTRATED WEEKLY

by the "ride around." On a more personal note, Stuart had the pleasure of defeating the Army of the Potomac's cavalry, which was commanded by none other than his father-in-law, Colonel Cooke.

CATLETT'S STATION RAID, AUGUST 22, 1862

The "Ride around McClellan" earned Stuart promotion to major general on July 25, 1862, his cavalry brigade was expanded to divisional status, and he was personally elevated in the Confederate public eye to a position roughly equal to that of Stonewall Jackson. His triumph, however, was nearly doomed to a very short life.

On August 21, Stuart became the target of a Union raid in retaliation for the "ride around." Narrowly escaping capture, Stuart fled without his trademark plumed hat and scarlet-lined cloak, which were eagerly appropriated by the Federal raiding party. Not to be trifled with, Stuart mounted a bigger raid the next day against Catlett's Station, headquarters of the commander of the newly created Army of Virginia, the insufferably pompous Major General John Pope. Stuart purloined the general's dress uniform, together with a Union payroll, and Pope's papers, which included intelligence concerning reinforcements for the Army of Virginia. This material would prove invaluable in the coming Second Battle of Bull Run. Always ready to twist the knife, Stuart sent Pope a message: "You have my hat and plume. I have your best coat. I have the honor to propose a cartel for the fair exchange of the prisoners." Resolutely humorless, Pope did not respond.

SECOND BATTLE OF BULL RUN, AUGUST 28–30, 1862

Stuart's cavalry played three roles at the Second Battle of Bull Run. It scouted out the route by which James Longstreet's "wing" of the divided

Army of Northern Virginia delivered the smashing twenty-five-thousand-man assault against Pope's flank while the Union general's attention was riveted on Jackson's "wing." The second role was acting as a screen for Longstreet's infantry assault while protecting his flank with artillery batteries. Stuart's third role in the battle was the pursuit of the retreating Federals after Longstreet's assault. His men captured three hundred of Brigadier General John Buford's cavalry brigade troopers. At Second Bull Run, Stuart made more, and more effective, use of cavalry than perhaps in any other battle of the Civil War.

MARYLAND INVASION AND BATTLE OF ANTIETAM, SEPTEMBER 17, 1862

When Lee followed up on his triumph at Second Bull Run by invading Maryland in September 1862, Stuart's cavalry screened the northward advance of the Army of Northern Virginia. For the first time, however, Stuart was guilty of a lapse in performing reconnaissance. During a full five days of Lee's invasion, Stuart rested his men and even threw a celebratory party for Confederate sympathizers at Urbana, Maryland. Stuart seems to have lost his "grip" on the strategic situation, which led to a Confederate defeat at the Battle of South Mountain (September 14, 1862).

Hard on the heels of the South Mountain exchange came the Battle of Antietam, in which Stuart used his horse artillery to attack the Union flank just as McClellan began the opening attack of the battle. Stonewall Jackson directed Stuart to lead his cavalry in a drive to turn the Union right flank and rear, to expose it to a follow-up infantry attack from the West Woods. Stuart launched probing attacks against the Union lines, but this time his artillery barrages were more than answered by Union counterbattery fire. In fact, Stuart's probing attacks unleashed a massive reply, which actually prevented Jackson from executing the turning movement and follow-up he had planned. It was only McClellan's inherent reluctance to follow through on his own success that saved the Army of Northern Virginia from something approaching annihilation.

THE CHAMBERSBURG RAID, OCTOBER 10, 1862

On October 10, 1862, Lee, having withdrawn into Virginia, sent Stuart to demolish a railway bridge near Chambersburg, Pennsylvania, while also performing reconnaissance on Federal troop dispositions in the area and capturing civilian hostages to be used in exchange for certain Virginians being held by the Union.

Stuart expanded his brief ambitiously, performing another "ride around" of the Army of the Potomac, a cavalry dash of 120 miles performed in less than sixty hours, extending from Leesburg, Virginia, to Chambersburg, Pennsylvania, and back. Once again, the Union army suffered humiliation but little of strategic advantage was gained by this ride, which brought both rider and beast beyond the edge of exhaustion.

BATTLE OF FREDERICKSBURG, DECEMBER 11–15, 1862

At the end of October, McClellan commenced a desultory pursuit of Lee. Stuart responded by screening the movements of Longstreet's corps, in the process clashing with Union cavalry as well as infantry in skirmishes near Mountville and Aldie (October 28) and at Upperville (October 29). He was crushed on November 6, not by the forces of McClellan, but by a telegram informing him that his daughter, Flora, had died three days earlier of typhoid. She was not yet five years old.

Suppressing his grief, Stuart next performed extensive reconnaissance that allowed Lee to plan the defense of Fredericksburg from the high ground overlooking the town. This put Longstreet's corps in a virtually impregnable position when Ambrose Burnside, who had replaced McClellan as commander of the Army of Northern Virginia, launched his disastrous frontal assaults on December 13, 1862. During this phase of the battle, Stuart and his cavalry operated to cover Stonewall Jackson's flank at Hamilton's Crossing. His horse artillery was especially devastating against Burnside's hapless charges.

BATTLE OF CHANCELLORSVILLE, APRIL 30–MAY 6, 1863

After Fredericksburg, Stuart conducted a major raid to within a dozen miles of Washington, D.C., capturing a significant number of Union prisoners of war and supplies and destroying railway track and a bridge. Come spring 1863, he and his cavalry division were instrumental in Stonewall Jackson's great flanking march in the Battle of Chancellorsville. On May 1, Stuart's reconnaissance discovered that the right flank of the Army of the Potomac (now under the command of Joseph Hooker) was exposed and vulnerable. On May 2, Stuart's cavalry led Jackson's II Corps against that flank, thereby routing the entire XI Corps. Stuart was leading the pursuit of the retreating Federals when word caught up with him that Jackson and A. P. Hill, Jackson's senior division commander, had been seriously wounded and were out of action. Although Brigadier General Robert E. Rodes was next in seniority among infantry commanders, he passed command to Stuart, whose reputation among the soldiers of II Corps was so high that Rodes believed the transition to Stuart at this critical moment would be more successful.

The loss of Jackson and Hill was potentially devastating, but Stuart performed well as an ad hoc infantry corps commander, following through on the flanking attack with another assault against the Union right flank on May 3. When Hill recovered sufficiently to return to duty on May 6, Stuart relinquished command to him. General Lee would have been amply justified in giving Stuart a full corps command, but he believed that his ability with cavalry was too valuable an asset and so retained him in his position.

BATTLE OF BRANDY STATION, JUNE 9, 1863

On June 5, with Lee and a pair of his infantry corps camped near Culpeper, Virginia, Stuart requested that the commanding general witness a grand field review of his troops, some nine thousand cavalrymen and four batteries of horse artillery, near Brandy Station. Lee agreed, but because he was unable to attend the June 5 review, the display was repeated on June 8. When the Southern press published stories decrying this waste of resources on vain demonstrations, Lee ordered Stuart to cross the Rappahannock on June 9 to conduct raids on advanced Union positions.

Taking note of the activity near Culpeper and Brandy Station, Major General Joseph Hooker ordered the Army of the Potomac cavalry commander, Major General Alfred Pleasonton, to attack Stuart's cavalry. Stuart was caught by surprise, and a spectacular ten-hour cavalry fight, the biggest of the war, ensued. In the end, Pleasonton withdrew, thereby allowing Stuart to declare victory, although he had gained nothing and had allowed himself to be surprised. On balance, the Battle of Brandy Station hinted at Stuart's vulnerability to the growing spirit and competence of the Union cavalry. The Southern press in particular took note, and Confederate morale suffered accordingly.

STUART'S RIDE AT GETTYSBURG, JUNE 25–JULY 2, 1863

As Lee maneuvered to engage the Army of the Potomac in Pennsylvania, Stuart was eager to repair the damage his reputation had suffered as a result of Brandy Station. Lee ordered Stuart to

perform reconnaissance and make raids, judging (Lee wrote) "whether you can pass around [the Army of the Potomac] without hindrance" and, in the process, doing to "them all the damage you can." He also instructed Stuart to guard the mountain passes and to screen the right flank of Richard S. Ewell's II Corps. Poorly written and even self-contradictory, the orders left a great deal to Stuart's interpretation and discretion. He interpreted them to provide the widest latitude possible for a *third* "ride around" the Army of the Potomac. In this, most military historians fault Stuart for a lapse of judgment motivated by vainglory; others fault Lee's orders, which were framed more in the nature of suggestions than straightforward directions. In truth, what happened next was a blend of Stuart's poor judgment and Lee's command style.

Beginning on June 25, Stuart advanced well east of the Army of the Potomac, doing much damage to railroads and terrorizing citizens in the vicinity of Washington and Baltimore. Along the way, he found himself blocked by Federal infantry columns and was compelled to move ever farther east. Ultimately, he went so far out of his intended way that he not only failed to make contact with Ewell, but he also remained out of communication with Lee during the first two days of what had developed as the Battle of Gettysburg. In the days leading up to the single most consequential battle of the Civil War, the commander of the Army of Northern Virginia was effectively blind and deaf while traversing enemy territory. It was a catastrophe of war-losing proportions.

When Stuart arrived at Gettysburg late in the day on July 2, Lee viewed the booty he brought with him—captured Union supply wagons that had served only to slow him down yet more—with disgust. No one overheard what Lee said to Stuart, except for "Well, general, you are here at last," which Stuart himself took as a sharp rebuke. With the failure of Pickett's Charge on July 3, all that was left for Stuart to

Stuart's Ride at Gettysburg - June–July 1863

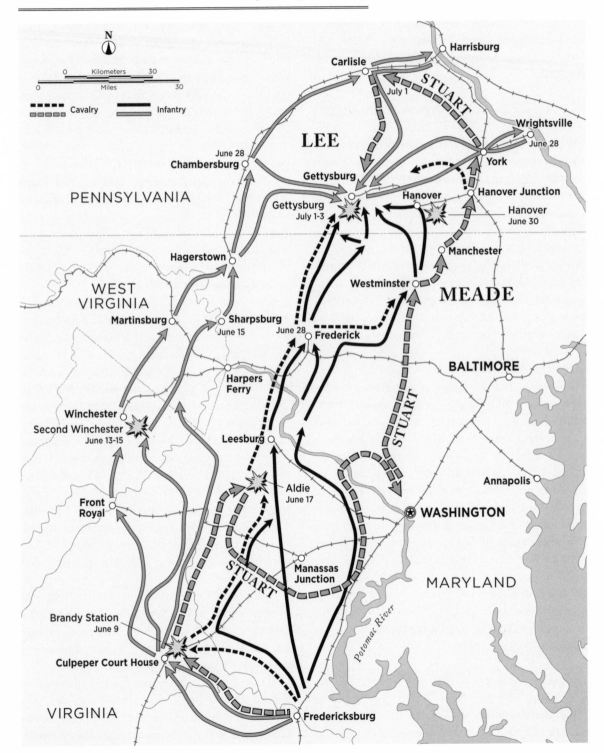

N

Kilometers
0   30
Miles
0   30

- - - - Cavalry   ▬▬▬ Infantry

Harrisburg

Carlisle

STUART
July 1

Wrightsville
June 28

York

LEE

Chambersburg
June 28

Gettysburg

Gettysburg
July 1-3

Hanover

Hanover Junction

Hanover
June 30

PENNSYLVANIA

Hagerstown

Manchester

WEST
VIRGINIA

Westminster

MEADE

Martinsburg

Sharpsburg
June 15

Frederick
June 28

BALTIMORE

Harpers
Ferry

Winchester
Second Winchester
June 13-15

Leesburg

STUART

Annapolis

Front
Royal

Aldie
June 17

WASHINGTON

Brandy Station
June 9

STUART

Manassas
Junction

MARYLAND

Culpeper Court House

Potomac River

VIRGINIA

Fredericksburg

do was to screen Lee's retreat, which he did with great vigor and heroism. His men were the last to cross the Potomac into Virginia.

In the immediate aftermath of the Battle of Gettysburg, Lee was unambiguous in accepting full responsibility for the defeat. Others, however, unwilling to believe in Lee's fallibility, blamed it all on Stuart—more precisely on Stuart's absence—and, to a lesser extent, on James Longstreet's lack of aggression. A balanced analysis requires taking into account Lee's judgment and his poorly written orders as well as Stuart's judgment and his interpretation of those orders. Had Lee been more direct in telling Stuart what he wanted or had Stuart more effectively prioritized his objectives—setting reconnaissance above all else—the outcome at Gettysburg (or wherever else in Pennsylvania the showdown battle might have been fought) could well have been very different.

A Southern icon during the war, Jeb Stuart was the inspiration for poems, stories, and popular songs. LIBRARY OF CONGRESS

OVERLAND CAMPAIGN, MAY–JUNE 1864

The Battle of Gettysburg marked Lee's irreversible shift from an offensive posture to a defensive one. Stuart tangled with elements of the Army of the Potomac during Grant's Overland Campaign, the bloody advance toward Richmond, but was forced to function mostly in bitter—though quite effective—rear-guard actions, as Grant, even after suffering defeat, continued his relentless advance.

At the Battle of the Wilderness (May 5–7, 1864), Stuart suffered significant casualties inflicted by George Armstrong Custer's Michigan Brigade but was subsequently able to delay the main Federal infantry advance to Spotsylvania Court House, giving Lee critical time to set up strong defensive positions.

BATTLE OF YELLOW TAVERN, MAY 11, 1864

Ulysses S. Grant had appointed Major General Philip Sheridan commander of the Army of the Potomac's Cavalry Corps, only to find that the army's commander, George Meade, continually argued with him over just how the cavalry was to be used. Sheridan sought to claim an aggressive strategic role for his command, while Meade wanted cavalry to perform the conventional functions of screening and reconnaissance. When Sheridan impudently defied Meade, asserting that he could concentrate his cavalry and whip Stuart once and for all, the Army of the Potomac commander reported the conversation to General Grant, seeking Grant's support to threaten Sheridan with a charge of insubordination. Instead, Grant replied that Sheridan "generally knows what he is talking about," and he instructed Meade to let him launch his operation against Stuart.

Sheridan's first move was against the Beaver Dam Station of the Virginia Central Railroad. His troopers attacked a train transporting three thousand Union prisoners and liberated them.

They then destroyed a huge cargo of rations and medical supplies Lee could ill afford to lose. Stuart, desperate, sent some three thousand of his cavalry to attack Sheridan, who had in his command nearly twelve thousand troopers.

On May 11, the forces clashed near an abandoned inn called Yellow Tavern six miles north of Richmond. Despite Sheridan's two-to-one advantage over Stuart, it was a very close-run fight. After some three hours of combat, the 1st Virginia Cavalry charged head-on into a Union advance, pushing it back. Positioned on the top of a small hill, Stuart personally led the battle. He could hardly have made himself a more conspicuous figure, and a dismounted 5th Michigan Cavalry private, John A. Huff, a former sharpshooter, saw him, recognized him, leveled his .44-caliber revolver at him, and fired.

The round entered Stuart's left side, penetrating his stomach before exiting his back. Few survived gut shots in the Civil War. Taken to the home of Dr. Charles Brewer, his brother-in-law, Stuart lingered until 7:38 p.m. on May 12, the day after the battle. He died before his wife could reach his bedside. Notified of Stuart's death, Lee broke the news to his staff, remarking, as if by way of epitaph, "He never brought me a piece of false information."

Chapter 10

JAMES LONGSTREET

RATING: ★ ★ ⁄

James Longstreet. LIBRARY OF CONGRESS

EVALUATION

James Longstreet, widely considered the finest corps commander on either side of the Civil War, may also fairly be judged one of the war's most profound and perceptive strategic and tactical thinkers. In sharp contrast with the resolutely aggressive and offensively oriented Robert E. Lee, whose chief lieutenant he was, Longstreet advocated what he called "tactical defense," a policy of enticing the enemy to attack one's own strongly defended positions. This approach was based largely on Longstreet's understanding of the nature of the weapons technology of the era, which enabled long arms and cannon to be fired continually and in mass, a circumstance (Longstreet understood) that invariably favored the defender.

The downside of Longstreet's allegiance to "tactical defense" was inflexibility when it came to accommodating offensively oriented plans and orders with which he disagreed. His response was sometimes passive-aggressive and sometimes more frankly defiant. In either case, the result was damaging to outcomes. For this reason, he must be rated in the upper middle rather than the top rank of the conflict's commanders.

Principal Battles

PRE–CIVIL WAR

U.S.-Mexican War, 1846–1848

- Palo Alto, May 8, 1846: Participated in this first major battle of the war
- Resaca de la Palma, May 9, 1846: His first experience of combat at full intensity
- Monterrey, September 21–24, 1846: The last battle Longstreet fought under Zachary Taylor's command
- Contreras, August 19–20, 1847
- Churubusco, August 20, 1847: His performance in these two battles gained Longstreet a brevet to captain
- Molino del Rey, September 8, 1847: Brevetted to major for gallantry
- Chapultepec, September 12–13, 1847: Bore the regimental colors up to the castle, where he was wounded in the thigh

CIVIL WAR

- Blackburn's Ford, July 18, 1861: In Virginia; Longstreet's brigade repulsed a Union reconnaissance force

- First Battle of Bull Run, July 21, 1861: In Virginia; although not heavily engaged in this battle, Longstreet was among those who pleaded in vain with P. G. T. Beauregard and Joseph E. Johnston to pursue the beaten Federals to Washington

- Peninsula Campaign, March-July 1862: In Virginia; at Yorktown, May 4, and Williamsburg, May 5, he dogged George B. McClellan's Army of the Potomac, slowing its advance on Richmond, but at the much bigger Battle of Seven Pines, May 31–June 1, he badly fumbled the main attack through a misunderstanding of orders

- Seven Days, June 25–July 1, 1862: In Virginia; Longstreet more than redeemed himself by driving McClellan relentlessly back down the peninsula

- Second Battle of Bull Run, August 28–30, 1862: In Virginia; Longstreet's stunning twenty-five-thousand-man flanking attack against John Pope brought Confederate victory

- South Mountain, September 14, 1862: In Maryland; Longstreet delayed McClellan's advance to Antietam long enough to give Robert E. Lee valuable time to create a strong defensive position

- Antietam, September 17, 1862: In Maryland; Longstreet's mastery of what he called "tactical defense" saved the Army of Northern Virginia from annihilation

- Fredericksburg, December 11–15, 1862: In Virginia; Longstreet was the architect of a powerful defense that brought Lee a lopsided victory against Ambrose Burnside

- Tidewater operations, April 11–May 4, 1863: In Virginia; Longstreet's operations against Union coastal access were intended to remove a seaborne threat to Lee's army, but they meant that he was absent from the crucial Battle of Chancellorsville

- Gettysburg, July 1–3, 1863: In Pennsylvania; Longstreet's fundamental tactical differences with Lee created problems of execution that, some believe, contributed to Lee's defeat in this turning-point battle

- Chickamauga, September 19–20, 1863: In Georgia; Longstreet's smashing attack through a gap in the Union line sent most of the Army of the Cumberland in retreat to Chattanooga

- Chattanooga and Knoxville Campaigns, October–December 1863: In Tennessee; Longstreet's innovative approach to preventing Ulysses S. Grant from breaking the siege of Chattanooga was overruled by Braxton Bragg, and Longstreet subsequently advanced on Knoxville too late to prevent its fall

- Wilderness, May 5–7, 1864: In Virginia; rejoining the Army of the Potomac, Longstreet led a devastating attack against Winfield Scott Hancock's II Corps but was severely wounded

- Siege of Petersburg, June 9, 1864–March 25, 1865: In Virginia; after recovering from a wound, Longstreet mainly commanded the defenses around Richmond

- Appomattox Campaign, March 29–April 9, 1865: In Virginia; Longstreet accompanied Lee on the retreat that culminated in the surrender of the Army of Northern Virginia

---

As a boy, he dreamed of martial glory and devoured books about Washington, Napoleon, Caesar, Alexander, all of history's "great captains," those credited in the collective human memory with war-winning victory and conquest. As an adult, James Longstreet would begin to live his dream, becoming the senior lieutenant general of the Confederacy and winning acclaim as a master battlefield tactician. Yet the dream was shattered at Gettysburg, and the remainder of Longstreet's long and mostly successful life was shadowed by accusation and recrimination. The boy who would be conqueror became the favorite scapegoat of those Southerners who reveled in mourning the valiant "Lost Cause."

FROM PLANTATION TO WEST POINT

James Longstreet was born on January 8, 1821, in the heart of the plantation South, the Edgefield District of South Carolina. On his father's side, the family traced its American roots to the Dutch New Netherland colony of the mid-seventeenth century. James, his father, had grown up in New Jersey, and his mother, Mary Ann Dent, in Maryland. They were, therefore, Northern immigrants to the Southern way of life.

The senior Longstreet encouraged his son's early dreams of a military career, and for that reason sent him to Augusta, Georgia, when he was nine, so that he could attend the Richmond County Academy, which offered (Mr. Longstreet believed) the level of academic preparation necessary to get him a place at West Point. In Augusta, the boy lived with his aunt and uncle, a warm and kindly couple with considerable influence in the community. Uncle Augustus Baldwin Longstreet, owner of a plantation called Westover on the edge of the city, was not only a newspaper editor, teacher, and Methodist minister, but he had also served in the state legislature and on the state supreme court. In 1833, James's father died during a cholera epidemic. His mother and siblings moved to Somerville, Alabama, but young James remained in Augusta with his aunt and uncle.

Although James disdained study and often produced disappointing results at the Richmond County Academy, Augustus flexed his considerable political muscle in 1837 to obtain for him an appointment to West Point. When he discovered that Georgia's quota of cadets had been filled, he wrote to Mrs. Longstreet, who prevailed on her relative, Reuben Chapman, congressman for Alabama's First District. It was he who secured the appointment, and Cadet James Longstreet passed through the academy's gates in June 1838 as a nominee from Alabama.

Athletic and eager to learn the rudiments of tactics, strategy, and the military art, Longstreet turned in no more than a marginal academic performance. He was popular, but his popularity was founded in part on his willingness to get himself into trouble. Close friends included classmates Daniel Harvey Hill, George Pickett, and John Bell Hood—all destined to become prominent Confederate generals—but also such Union luminaries as William S. Rosecrans, John Pope, and George Henry Thomas. Another classmate, Ulysses S. Grant, would become his friend for life and, after the war, a political benefactor. The

combination of mediocre academics and a multitude of demerits put him at the bottom of his Class of 1842, number fifty-four out of fifty-six cadets.

U.S.-MEXICAN WAR, 1846–1848

Commissioned a brevet second lieutenant in the 4th U.S. Infantry, Longstreet was posted to Jefferson Barracks, at St. Louis, Missouri, from 1842 to 1844. He was delighted when Grant was subsequently posted to the barracks as well, and he introduced his best friend to his fourth cousin, Julia Boggs Dent, whom Grant married in 1848—with Longstreet serving as best man. While stationed at Jefferson Barracks, Longstreet also met his future wife, Maria Louisa (Louise) Garland, daughter of Lieutenant Colonel John Garland, commander of Longstreet's regiment. They would be married the same year that Grant and Julia wed.

In the fall of 1844, Longstreet left St. Louis for stints in Louisiana and in Florida, which was followed in 1846 by a transfer to the 8th U.S. Infantry on the Texas-Mexico border as the two nations hurtled toward war.

Longstreet began his service in the war with Zachary Taylor's Northern Army, fighting at Palo Alto (May 8, 1846), Resaca de la Palma (May 9, 1846), and Monterrey (September 21–24, 1846). Casualties were heavy, especially at Resaca de la Palma, and badly depleted units were repeatedly reorganized; thus, after Monterrey, Longstreet was transferred to the Southern Army of Winfield Scott and fought at the Battles of Contreras (August 19–20, 1847) and Churubusco (August 20, 1847), for which he was brevetted to captain. For his gallantry at Molino del Rey (September 8, 1847), he received another brevet promotion, to major.

Longstreet played a prominent role in the Battle of Chapultepec (September 12–13, 1847), when he had the honor of bearing the regimental colors up the steep slope to the castle. As he was approaching the wall surrounding the stronghold, he took a bullet in the thigh and began to fall. As he fell, he handed the colors to his friend and West Point classmate Lieutenant George E. Pickett, who carried them over the wall.

BETWEEN THE WARS

After a prolonged and painful recovery from his wound, Longstreet was briefly posted again at Jefferson Barracks, and then, in May 1849, traveled with his wife and newborn son to San Antonio, Texas, where he served as 8th Regiment adjutant. Over the next twelve years, he and his family moved from one frontier post to another, mostly in Texas, including Fort Martin Scott near Fredericksburg and Fort Bliss in El Paso. His duties were uneventful, even when he led scouting missions along a frontier that was often torn by white-Indian violence.

In July 1858, Longstreet was promoted to the regular army rank of major and was assigned as the 8th Infantry paymaster. During this period he may have been active in a scheme to annex the Mexican state of Chihuahua and bring it into the Union as a slave state. The evidence for this is not definitive, however. There can be no doubt that he supported slavery and shared his Uncle Augustus's belief in the doctrine of states' rights, but he was never an enthusiastic advocate of secession, which he thought impractical, even though he believed that it was within a state's rights to leave the Union. Unlike many others who would resign their U.S. Army commissions to fight for the South, Longstreet did not closely identify with his birth state, South Carolina, nor with Georgia, the state in which he had come of age. It was only after the fall of Fort Sumter in April 1861 that he decided to cast his lot with the Confederacy, and he did so by resigning his commission on May 9, 1861, and offering his military services to Alabama, mainly because that state had sent him to West Point and his mother lived there.

BLACKBURN'S FORD AND THE FIRST BATTLE OF BULL RUN, JULY 18 AND 21, 1861

Almost immediately after presenting himself to Governor Andrew Moore of Alabama, Longstreet was commissioned a lieutenant colonel, not, however, in the state forces, but in the Provisional Army of the Confederate States. He was sent to Richmond to meet with President Jefferson Davis, who, on June 22, 1861, told him that, as of June 17, he had been commissioned a brigadier general. On June 25, the day on which he formally accepted the commission, he was ordered to report to Brigadier General P. G. T. Beauregard at Manassas, Virginia. That officer assigned him command of a brigade consisting of the 1st, 11th, and 17th Virginia Infantry regiments.

Anticipating imminent combat, Longstreet subjected his brigade to an accelerated regimen of drill. Contact with the enemy came on July 18, 1861, at Blackburn's Ford on Bull Run Creek in Prince William and Fairfax Counties. Longstreet's brigade easily repulsed a Union reconnaissance force in this prelude to the major battle of July 21.

Although Longstreet and his brigade had had the honor of first contact, they were not heavily committed in the First Battle of Bull Run proper. This was not for lack of trying. Longstreet was among those who pleaded with Beauregard and Joseph E. Johnston to pursue the beaten Union army, to dog it all the way to Washington. When his entreaties fell on deaf ears, he exclaimed to his aide Moxley Sorrel, "Retreat! Hell, the Federal army has broken to pieces," then dissolved into a wordless fury over the great opportunity that was being squandered.

Throughout his Civil War career, Longstreet would find himself drawing criticism as overly cautious, deliberate, and methodical. He would emerge as a master of defensive rather than offensive warfare. Yet he certainly recognized an opportunity to expand on a victory when he saw it, and at Manassas he burned with futile desperation to make something more of what had been accomplished in the Confederate army's first major clash with the Union—on Washington's back doorstep, no less.

PENINSULA CAMPAIGN, MARCH–JULY 1862

Although Longstreet, like others subordinate to Beauregard and Johnston at Bull Run, was frustrated by the failure to pursue Irvin McDowell's Union troops, his performance before and during the First Battle of Bull Run went neither unnoticed nor unrewarded. On October 7, Longstreet was promoted to major general and was assigned command of a division of Johnston's Army of Northern Virginia.

Longstreet was known to his family and close friends by the nickname Pete (it had come about through his father's admiration of his son's steadfast bearing, which he thought resembled Peter, the "rock" on whom Jesus built his church). Before the Civil War was over, he would often be known as "Gloomy Pete," but as the army went into winter quarters in the fall of 1861, he was nothing if not jovial, and he was well known to relieve the tedium of camp routine with comradely conversation, convivial drinking, and friendly rounds of card playing. All of this came to a terrible end in January 1862 when an epidemic of scarlet fever swept through Richmond, killing the Longstreets' year-old daughter and their four- and six-year-old sons within the space of a week. Garland, his thirteen-year-old, barely recovered from the disease. From this point forward, Longstreet was a changed man, subdued in manner and increasingly devout in his practice of the Episcopal faith.

He clearly lacked much of his characteristic energy and acuteness of mind in resisting McClellan's Peninsula Campaign during the spring of 1862. He was effective in the defensive role of rear-guard commander at Yorktown (May 4, 1862) and Williamsburg (May 5, 1862), doggedly striking at McClellan's Army of the Potomac and bogging it down as it advanced on Richmond. But when he was called on to conduct the principal attack at the Battle of Seven Pines on May 31, he seemed to get everything wrong. Badly misunderstanding General Johnston's verbal orders, he ended up sending his men the wrong way down the wrong road. They ran into other Confederate units, causing confusion and delay, which blunted what Johnston had intended as an overpowering counterattack against McClellan.

After the battle, Longstreet revealed an unattractive side of himself as a commander. Refusing to accept blame for errors that were clearly his fault, he wrote an after-action report that shamelessly scapegoated Major General Benjamin Huger.

THE SEVEN DAYS, JUNE 25–JULY 1, 1862

As far as Longstreet was concerned, the only good to come out of the Battle of Seven Pines was the replacement of the wounded Joseph E. Johnston as Army of Northern Virginia commander with Robert E. Lee. The men trusted each other completely, and Lee gave Longstreet operational command of fifteen brigades, almost half of the Army of Northern Virginia.

Having fumbled at Seven Pines, Longstreet was masterful in the Seven Days Battles as he relentlessly pushed McClellan's Army of the Potomac back down the Virginia Peninsula, forcing him farther and farther from Richmond. At the Battle of Gaines's Mill (June 27, 1862), the largest of the Seven Days battles, Longstreet was especially aggressive. Indeed, throughout all the battles, he was the standout among Lee's lieutenants, notably outperforming Stonewall Jackson.

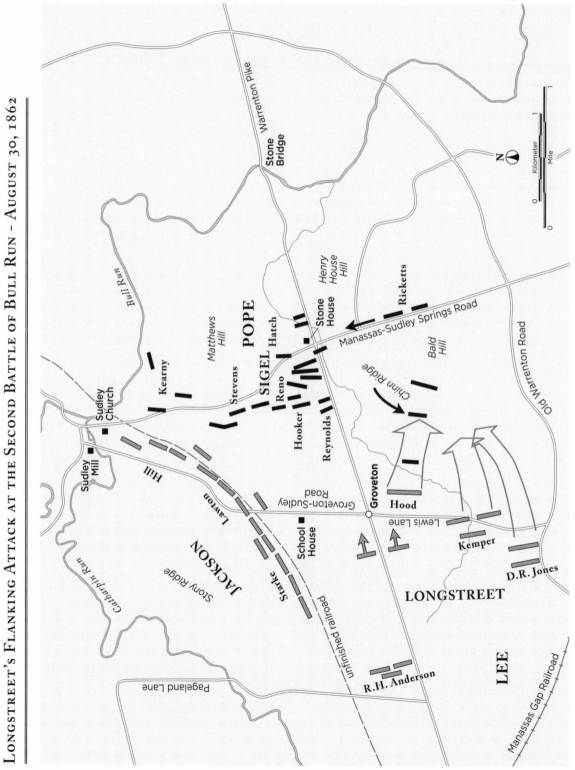

SECOND BATTLE OF BULL RUN, AUGUST 28–30, 1862

After the failure of McClellan's Peninsula Campaign, Lee turned his attention toward John Pope's new army, the Army of Virginia, in what he hoped would be a successful bid to defeat it in detail before Pope could be reinforced by McClellan's Army of the Potomac. As he prepared to do battle with Pope at Manassas, site of the First Battle of Bull Run, Lee's audacious strategy was to divide his army in the face of the enemy, assigning Stonewall Jackson to command its left wing and Longstreet its right wing.

Jackson made a broadly arcing advance that sent his wing against the rear of Pope's Army of Virginia. Then, uncharacteristically, he changed from offensive to defensive mode and took up a position that virtually demanded an attack against him. Pope obliged on August 28 and 29. Confident that he was destroying the Army of Northern Virginia, the Union general was oblivious to the maneuvers of Longstreet's right wing, which, on August 29, pounded into him.

Among military historians, Longstreet's admirers applaud his ability to carry out a stunning surprise flanking attack with an entire corps. His critics, however, fault his habitual caution and deliberation. They argue that he should not have allowed Jackson to absorb punishment for two full days before making a decisive move. Indeed, Longstreet's early postwar critics—those who heaped blame upon him for Lee's defeat at the Battle of Gettysburg—point to what they call his "reluctance" to attack at Second Bull Run as a prelude to his similar hesitation at Gettysburg.

Even if we grant the criticism some validity, it is hard to overlook the major victory Longstreet brought Lee. Exploiting Pope's belief that Jackson was in retreat, Longstreet mustered twenty-five thousand men against the Union flank. Even conceding Longstreet's slow initial approach, the actual attack, once launched, was a masterpiece of field tactics. No commander in the Civil War handled so many men so effectively in achieving a single objective.

BATTLES OF SOUTH MOUNTAIN AND ANTIETAM, SEPTEMBER 14 AND 17, 1862

Longstreet excelled at defensive strategy, which made him (sometimes for the better, sometimes for the worse) the perfect foil to Lee, who adopted a strategy of offense in the belief that the Confederacy could not afford to risk the slow death of attrition a defensive policy might bring. Lee's invasion of Maryland in September 1862 was, of course, offensive in nature, but he ended up having to take a defensive stance at South Mountain (September 14) and at the Battle of Antietam (September 17).

At South Mountain, Longstreet's defensive tactics delayed the Union forces effectively as Lee prepared a strong position at Antietam. During that battle, Longstreet's corps was outnumbered by Union units two to one but nevertheless held the line. He made an ally of the terrain, which effectively evened the odds. Those who ascribe Longstreet's embrace of tactical defense to a deficiency of bold aggressiveness do him a disservice. Longstreet believed that the massed firepower, both from shoulder weapons and artillery, available to both sides in the Civil War naturally favored those who occupied a strong defensive position. The greater power of the available weapons was defensive—repulsing attacks—not offensive, and Longstreet's understanding of this put him ahead of his time.

Lee greatly appreciated Longstreet's performance at Antietam, and, on October 9, pursuant to his recommendation, he was promoted to lieutenant general—the Confederate army's senior general officer of that rank. The following month, Longstreet was formally assigned command of the Army of Northern Virginia's I Corps, a force of some forty-one thousand men.

BATTLE OF FREDERICKSBURG, DECEMBER 11–15, 1862

When, after bloody Antietam, Lee withdrew back to Virginia from Maryland and George B. McClellan declined to pursue his retreat, Abraham Lincoln relieved McClellan as commanding general of the Army of the Potomac and replaced him with Ambrose Burnside. Reluctant to accept the command, Burnside was nevertheless eager to prove himself and decided on an immediate advance to Richmond via Fredericksburg.

As Lee's I Corps commander, Longstreet took the lead in setting up the defense of Fredericksburg. This he did masterfully, creating elaborate defensive works and taking special advantage of Marye's Heights behind the town. At the foot of this high ground was a long stone wall, behind which Longstreet deployed troops and artillery with very deadly results. Longstreet approached the deployment of all his artillery with exquisite deliberation, ensuring that the field any Union advance would have to traverse would be thoroughly swept by deadly fire.

The battle, when it came, was one of the deadliest and most lopsided of the war. Of some 114,000 engaged, Burnside lost 12,653 killed, wounded, captured, or missing. Lee suffered 5,377 casualties out of some 72,500 engaged. The disparity in casualties was thanks to Longstreet, against whose superbly defended positions Burnside tragically hurled wave after wave.

ABSENCE FROM THE BATTLE OF CHANCELLORSVILLE, APRIL 30–MAY 6, 1863

From April 11 to May 4, 1863, Longstreet's corps was engaged in operations along the Virginia seaboard, which culminated in the Battle of Suffolk (also known as the Battle of Fort Huger), intended to retake Fort Huger from Union forces. Repossession of this fort would return control of the Nansemond River to the Confederacy and remove the threat of Union

Stereopticon view of the stone wall at Marye's Heights, Fredericksburg, behind which Longstreet placed riflemen and artillery to deadly effect. NEW YORK PUBLIC LIBRARY DIGITAL LIBRARY

seaborne operations against the Army of Northern Virginia. On April 29, however, General Lee ordered Longstreet to break off the engagement so that he could participate in what would become the Battle of Chancellorsville. By the time Longstreet arrived, however, the battle was over and won.

By any measure, Lee had achieved a brilliant victory at Chancellorsville, though at a high cost, and Longstreet's critics, both in 1863 and today, fault him for having failed to return from Suffolk more expeditiously. They point to this as evidence of his unwillingness to give Lee his full cooperation and suggest that this foreshadowed his lapses at Gettysburg.

BATTLE OF GETTYSBURG, JULY 1–3, 1863

The Battle of Chancellorsville brought both an important victory for Lee—which he hoped to expand into a turning point of the war—and a terrible loss: the death of Stonewall Jackson. Without Jackson, Longstreet was now unquestionably Lee's top lieutenant, and the two debated what to do next.

Longstreet wanted Lee to detach his corps from the Army of Northern Virginia and let him lead it to Tennessee to reinforce Braxton Bragg against William Rosecrans, defeating him and thereby compelling Grant to divert forces from his Vicksburg siege. Lee rejected this essentially defensive strategy and insisted that the Army of Northern Virginia remain concentrated in the east for a major offensive, an invasion of the Union via Pennsylvania.

Longstreet was not happy, but he offered no protest. His only request was that the invasion, by definition an offensive action, should rely on defensive tactics, which he defined as tactics intended to "force the enemy to attack us, in such good position as we might find in our own country." This, Longstreet argued, "might assure us of a grand triumph." According to Longstreet's postwar memoirs, Lee "readily assented" to defensive tactics as "an important and material adjunct to his general plan." Nothing in the records Lee left, however, corroborates such an assent, and in 1868 Lee directly disavowed having ever made Longstreet "any such promise." On the other hand, immediately after the Battle of Gettysburg, Lee reported that he had not intended to "fight a general battle at such a distance from our base, unless attacked by the enemy," which suggests that he intended to pursue the policy Longstreet proposed. If there *was* an understanding between Lee and Longstreet concerning tactical defense, then Longstreet's conduct at Gettysburg must be considered beyond reproach. If there *was not* such an understanding, then Longstreet's critics gain ground for their assertion that his failure to embrace the aggressive spirit of the battle contributed to the Confederate defeat.

After Chancellorsville, Lee had reorganized the Army of Northern Virginia into three corps, assigning Richard S. Ewell command of II Corps and A. P. Hill command of a newly created III Corps. The four divisions of Longstreet's original I Corps were reduced to three, commanded by Lafayette McLaws, George Pickett, and John Bell Hood. Leading I Corps, Longstreet trailed II Corps through the Shenandoah Valley. He arrived at Gettysburg too late on July 1 to participate in the first day of battle; however, he accompanied Lee in surveying the situation that had been created on that first day. With his eye for defensive positions, Longstreet judged that the high ground onto which the Union had been driven east and south of Gettysburg gave them a formidable position. Longstreet counseled Lee to avoid a direct assault on it and instead march around the left flank of the Union position to set up a defensive line between the Army of the Potomac and Washington, D.C. This, Longstreet argued, would lure the Union army down from its formidable heights to engage a force that would be perceived as a direct threat against Washington.

Lee protested that this would effectively put him in the position of withdrawing from a fight that had gone so well the first day. He believed that such a "retreat" would be demoralizing, and he insisted on immediately attacking the Union high-ground positions. He believed that the Army of the Potomac was depleted and exhausted by the battering of the first day and that it was ready to break.

Longstreet seems to have been incapable of accepting Lee's order, and Lee, in turn, seems to have been unable to elicit from Longstreet full, unquestioning, and cheerful obedience. Repeatedly, Longstreet reiterated his case for a flanking movement. Repeatedly, Lee rejected it and on July 2 ordered direct coordinated assaults on the left and right flanks of the Union army. Longstreet stalled in the execution, perhaps hoping that Lee would change his mind. When he finally—and belatedly—commenced the ordered attack, he suddenly, even perversely, insisted on following Lee's orders to the letter. He rejected John Bell Hood's very sound suggestion that his division be allowed to attack from the rear, and instead led a blunt frontal assault, which, since his delay had given the Union forces more time to prepare defenses, was doomed to fail.

At the end of day two, the Union was still in possession of the high ground, and on day three, July 3, Lee ordered Longstreet to mount the massive assault against the center of the Union line that history remembers as Pickett's Charge. Longstreet replied flatly to Lee that he did not want to make the attack. To his subordinate commanders Longstreet remarked, "I do not see how it can succeed." To him it looked as if the Union troops were in a position precisely analogous to what he had occupied at Fredericksburg, and he had no desire to play the part of Ambrose Burnside. "I have been a soldier all my life," he pleaded with Lee. "There are no fifteen thousand men in the world that can go across that ground." But Lee was adamant. Instead of disputing the issue, he simply gestured toward the Union line. "There," he told Longstreet, "is the enemy, and there I mean to attack him."

Longstreet was so overcome that when General Pickett asked him for the order—"Shall I lead my division forward, sir?"—according to his own recollection, he could not say a word but "only indicated it by an affirmative bow." Before it was over, Pickett's Charge would cost the Army of Northern Virginia some 6,555 men killed, wounded, or captured.

BATTLE OF CHICKAMAUGA, SEPTEMBER 19–20, 1863

After the catastrophe of Pickett's Charge and the loss at Gettysburg, Longstreet once again sought transfer to the Western Theater and out from under the shadow of Robert E. Lee. On September 5, Jefferson Davis finally ordered Longstreet to lead the I Corps divisions of McLaws and Hood, together with one brigade from Pickett's division and an artillery battalion under Porter Alexander, 775 miles to link up with Braxton Bragg in Georgia. No fewer than sixteen railroad transfers were required, and the entire operation consumed three weeks, with Longstreet and the advance elements of I Corps arriving on September 17, 1863, and the bulk of the corps following just in time for the Battle of Chickamauga, which was under way.

Bragg assigned Longstreet command of the left wing of his army and gave the right to Leonidas Polk. On September 20, the second day of the battle, Longstreet massed an attack against a narrow front, which exploited a gap that Rosecrans, confused by battle and the tangled terrain, inadvertently opened up in his line. Longstreet sent the entire Union right in a panicked retreat. Major General George H. Thomas was able to rally some of the retreating elements and form them into a defensive line on Snodgrass Hill. Lacking support from Polk's right wing, Longstreet beat against Thomas—the "Rock of Chickamauga"—in vain, and with nightfall,

Thomas was able to withdraw in good order, thereby preventing a total rout. Had Bragg possessed a greater grip on the overall situation, he would have ordered Polk to reinforce Longstreet, and the Confederate victory, impressive though it was (thanks in large measure to Longstreet), would have been devastating.

Keenly aware of Bragg's inadequacies, Longstreet agitated for his removal and pleaded his case before Jefferson Davis during a field visit. Davis, personally loyal to Bragg since the two had fought together as comrades during the U.S.-Mexican War, sided with Bragg, who punished Longstreet by reducing the number of troops under his command.

CHATTANOOGA AND KNOXVILLE CAMPAIGNS, OCTOBER–DECEMBER 1863

Longstreet struggled against domination by someone he considered a losing general. While Bragg laid siege against the Army of the Cumberland, which had withdrawn from Chickamauga and holed up in Chattanooga, Longstreet proposed a more innovative and active plan to foil Grant's attempt to break the siege—by gaining control of the rail network and by threatening the Union reinforcements that were arriving to augment the siege. Although Davis approved of Longstreet's plan, Bragg rejected it—and, once again, Davis backed him. Bragg sent Longstreet and his corps east to check an advance by Ambrose Burnside and occupy Knoxville. He moved so slowly, however, that the city fell before he reached it.

When Bragg's siege of Chattanooga finally collapsed on November 25, 1863, Longstreet was initially ordered back west to join the Army of Tennessee in its withdrawal through northern Georgia. Instead, he continued on his way eastward, at times pursued by Major General William Tecumseh Sherman, before he linked up with the Army of Northern Virginia in the spring of 1864.

BATTLE OF THE WILDERNESS, MAY 5–7, 1864

Despite their differences at Gettysburg, Lee was overjoyed to have his "Old War Horse" back with him. At the Battle of the Wilderness, Longstreet immediately demonstrated his worth by pounding into the Army of the Potomac's II Corps along the Orange Plank Road, taking a terrible toll and almost sending it from the field. The II Corps commander, Winfield Scott Hancock, remarked to Longstreet after the war that he, Longstreet, had "rolled [him] up like a wet blanket."

When Longstreet was wounded by friendly fire—shot through his shoulder, the round destroying the nerves to his right arm (rendering it useless for much of the rest of his life), then grazing his throat—his attack flagged, giving the Union commanders the time they needed to re-form, thereby blunting the Confederate victory. As for Longstreet, his injuries kept him out of the war throughout the remainder of the spring and summer of 1864.

SIEGE OF PETERSBURG AND APPOMATTOX CAMPAIGN, JUNE 9, 1864–APRIL 9, 1865

Longstreet rejoined the Army of Northern Virginia in October, as the Siege of Petersburg dragged on. His role was primarily to command the Richmond defenses until the Appomattox Campaign, in which he accompanied Lee as I Corps commander and (after the death of A. P. Hill on April 2) as III Corps commander as well. When Lee discussed surrender with him, Longstreet, who never forgot his friendship with Grant, assured him that the Union general-in-chief would negotiate fairly—though, at the last minute, as he rode with Lee to the McLean House surrender conference at Appomattox Court House on April 9, 1865, Longstreet declared, "General, if he does not give us good terms, come back and let us fight it out."

AFTER THE WAR

Longstreet was intensely active after the war. Settling his family in New Orleans, he became a partner in a cotton brokerage as well as president of the Great Southern and Western Fire, Marine and Accident Insurance Company. Determined to return his life to some degree of normality, he applied to President Andrew Johnson for a pardon, but even though Grant endorsed the application, Johnson turned him down. Congress overrode the president in 1868, restoring Longstreet to the full rights of citizenship.

A Mathew Brady photograph of Longstreet after the war.
LIBRARY OF CONGRESS

Far more controversially, Longstreet joined the Republican Party, supported Reconstruction, and campaigned for Grant for president in 1868. His grateful friend rewarded him with an appointment as surveyor of customs in New Orleans, and the Republican governor of Louisiana named him adjutant general of the state militia. Later, Longstreet also held command of the state police within New Orleans. Many fellow Southerners considered him a traitor to the Lost Cause, and in 1875, fearing for their safety, the Longstreets moved from New Orleans to Gainesville, Georgia. President Rutherford B. Hayes appointed him ambassador to the Ottoman Empire in 1880, and under Presidents William McKinley and Theodore Roosevelt, he served as U.S. commissioner of railroads from 1897 to 1904.

Longstreet survived a fire on April 9, 1889, that destroyed his Gainesville house and, with it, his trove of Civil War documents and souvenirs. His wife, Louise Longstreet, never recovered from the trauma of the fire and died before the year was out. Eight years later, in 1897, seventy-six-year-old Longstreet married thirty-four-year-old Helen Dortch, having published the year before *From Manassas to Appomattox*, his wartime memoir, much of which was taken up with a defense of his war record. At the start of the twentieth century, Longstreet's health went into steep decline, and he died on January 2, 1904, of pneumonia and the complications of cancer.

Chapter 11

JOHN BELL HOOD

RATING: ★ ⭒

John Bell Hood. LIBRARY OF CONGRESS

EVALUATION

John Bell Hood was a tough, charismatic combat leader, a fierce warrior whose early battlefield successes launched him from lieutenant to general in less than a year. Promoted to independent command, he failed disastrously. His great qualities—courage, command presence, and the ability to inspire deeds of valor—were not sufficient to cover his lack of tactical brilliance and strategic savvy. The editor who wrote his obituary in Kentucky's *Clark County Democrat* described him succinctly as "an excellent soldier but such a poor general."

Principal Battles

PRE–CIVIL WAR

Texas-Comanche frontier violence, 1856–1858

- Hood received his first battle wound in an ambush by Comanche warriors

CIVIL WAR

- Eltham's Landing, May 7, 1862: In Virginia; exceeding his orders, Hood repulsed a Federal unit here during the Peninsula Campaign
- Gaines's Mill, June 27, 1862: In Virginia, during the Seven Days; Hood's Texas Brigade blasted through the Union lines in the highlight Confederate victory of the Seven Days Battles
- Second Battle of Bull Run, August 28–30, 1862: In Virginia; promoted to division commander, Hood spearheaded James Longstreet's massive flanking attack that sent John Pope's army reeling
- Antietam, September 17, 1862: In Maryland; Hood sacrificed much of his division to protect Stonewall Jackson's corps
- Fredericksburg, December 11–15, 1862: In Virginia; occupying a position between Longstreet's main line and Jackson's corps, Hood's division saw relatively little action in the battle
- Operations at Suffolk, April 11–May 4, 1863: In Virginia; operated as part of Longstreet's corps against Union threats to the Army of Northern Virginia
- Battle of Gettysburg, July 1–3, 1863: In Pennsylvania; protested Lee and Longstreet's ordered frontal assault on Little Round Top and proposed that his division attack from the rear—a good idea that Longstreet rejected
- Battle of Chickamauga, September 19–20, 1863: In Georgia; first battle Hood fought after recovering from severe wounds at Gettysburg; fought fiercely and was frustrated by Braxton Bragg's refusal to pursue the retreating Army of the Cumberland
- Atlanta Campaign, May 7–September 2, 1864: In Georgia; reversing Joseph E. Johnston's policy of tactical defense, Hood launched four fruitless and costly counterattacks on William T. Sherman, losing Atlanta and many of his soldiers

- Franklin-Nashville Campaign, September–December 1864: In Tennessee; hoping to draw Sherman away from Georgia, Hood marched west to link up with Nathan Bedford Forrest; his battles against Generals John M. Schofield and George H. Thomas at Franklin and Nashville decimated the Army of Tennessee, effectively removing it as a strategic force for the remainder of the war; Nashville was lost to the Union; Hood was relieved at his own request

The Civil War has been called the "American Iliad" because of its epic nature. At times, however, the epic verged on out and out melodrama. Such was the case with the meteoric rise and precipitous fall of John Bell Hood, who made an undistinguished start at West Point—charitably tutored by top cadet James McPherson, whom one of Hood's soldiers would kill at Atlanta—fought valiantly against Comanche warriors in Texas, entered the Confederate service as a lieutenant, was a brigadier general within eleven months, and rose to lieutenant general and temporary general before the end of the war. He would earn a reputation as a fierce and fearless fighter, a wildly inspiring leader, who repeatedly endured grievous wounds for the Confederate cause. Rewarded with an independent command, he lost Atlanta and Nashville and left the Army of Tennessee a shell of no strategic value.

From Kentucky Aristocrat to West Point Cadet

John Bell Hood was born in Owingsville, Kentucky, on June 29, 1831, the son of physician John W. Hood and Theodosia French Hood. They were the cream of Kentucky society, who lived on a six-hundred-acre plantation, were served by slaves, and generally comported themselves as minor aristocrats. Young Hood shared his parents' values, differing with his father only on the subject of vocation. John W. wanted his boy to study medicine; John Bell never wanted to be anything other than a soldier. Reluctantly, the senior Hood allowed his wife's brother, U.S.

Representative Richard French, to nominate John Bell to West Point in 1849 and, when the appointment came through, Dr. Hood suppressed his doubts, objections, and regrets and gave his consent for his underage boy to enroll.

Cadet Hood had imagined the United States Military Academy as a glorious field on which young knights errant serve their apprenticeship. Instead, he found himself beset with rules, drill, classroom tedium, more drill, more rules, and fellow cadets who mercilessly mocked his thick Kentucky accent and the slow, heavy manners of what was, aristocratic pretensions notwithstanding, a rawboned provincial boy. He found academics a grind and racked up 196 demerits for poor conduct and other infractions, just four shy of mandatory dismissal. He managed to claw his way to cadet lieutenant by September of his fourth year, only to be busted back to cadet private in December after being found guilty of absence without leave. Hood nevertheless graduated with the rest of his Class of 1853, albeit in forty-fourth place among fifty-two. His weakest subject area was ethics, in which he ranked dead last.

Fellow 1853 graduates that year included McPherson and another Union general with whom Hood was destined to do decisive battle, John M. Schofield. His artillery instructor was no less than George H. Thomas, the "Rock of Chickamauga" whom he would also beat during the Civil War.

Comanche War in Texas

Commissioned a second lieutenant upon graduation, Hood was assigned to the 4th U.S. Infantry in California, where he found his routine duties, carried out in frontier isolation, almost unendurably tedious. In 1855, he was grateful for transfer to the 2nd U.S. Cavalry, which Secretary of War Jefferson Davis had just created and staffed with the most promising Southern officers, covertly fashioning the elite nucleus around which a

Confederate army could be formed in the event of secession and civil war. Headquartered at Fort Mason, Texas, a rugged and remote place made exciting by the proximity of hostile Comanche, the 2nd was commanded by Colonel Albert Sidney Johnston, with Lieutenant Colonel Robert E. Lee—West Point superintendent when Hood attended—as second in command.

Not only did Hood fall in love with Texas and the Texans, he embraced the hazards of patrol in Comanche country. For him, pursuit, combat, and the prospect of killing or being killed were the soldier's stock in trade. After the dreary disappointments of West Point and California, he believed himself in his element at last.

During the summer of 1857, while on patrol along Devil's River, he and his unit were ambushed by Comanche warriors, whom he managed to drive off, but not without taking an arrow through his left hand. He did not let the wound disable him. Pulling the shaft out of his flesh, he fought on, killing two Indians before the others withdrew and dispersed. In recognition of his courage and skill, he was promoted to first lieutenant.

CIVIL WAR OUTBREAK

And at the rank of first lieutenant was where he remained. The offer of the post of chief instructor of cavalry at West Point, made in 1860, might have gotten him a bump up to captain, but he declined the offer, explaining that he wanted to stay in service with a field regiment. In part that was surely true, but it was also the case that, with civil war imminent, Hood was more comfortable among his fellow Southerners in the 2nd Cavalry than in a teaching post on New York's Hudson River.

Unlike many Southern officers, who resigned only after their home state seceded, Hood turned in his resignation in April 1861, almost immediately after the fall of Fort Sumter. He returned to Kentucky, intending to offer the state militia his services, but finding that the state government

did not intend to secede, he hopped a train for Montgomery, Alabama, at the time the capital of the Confederacy. After securing a commission as first lieutenant in the Provisional Army of the Confederate States, he was packed off to Richmond, Virginia, and instructed to report to Robert E. Lee.

Lee welcomed his former student and subordinate but did not detain him long. Hood was dispatched to Yorktown under the command of Colonel John Magruder, who was desperate for experienced officers to resist anticipated Federal attacks. Embracing the newcomer, Magruder assigned him command of all his cavalry companies, promoting him to captain and then almost immediately to major. Recognizing the value of Hood's experience, Magruder wanted to ensure that he was senior to all other company commanders.

Hood led patrols up and down the Yorktown peninsula before he was called back to Richmond, to which Texas had sent troops for service in the Eastern Theater. These companies were consolidated into the 4th Texas Infantry Regiment and, on September 30, 1861, Hood was promoted to colonel and given command of the unit. On February 20, 1862, the 4th Texas Infantry was upgraded to brigade strength and became known as Hood's Texas Brigade, attached to what was at the time the Confederate Army of the Potomac, but which would soon be designated the Army of Northern Virginia. On March 3, 1862, in recognition of his status as a brigade commander, Hood was promoted to brigadier general.

BATTLE OF ELTHAM'S LANDING, MAY 7, 1862

He really hadn't done much to warrant this blur of promotions from lowly first lieutenant to lofty brigadier general, but he had benefited from the Confederacy's acute shortage of experienced officers, his own reputation as a fearless fighter (based on his brush with the Comanches), his instant rapport with the Texans, and what today would be called his "command presence"—his charisma as a general. The rapid promotions might not have been entirely rational, but they undoubtedly *seemed* right.

He led his Texas Brigade against elements of George B. McClellan's Army of the Potomac at the Battle of Eltham's Landing in New Kent County, Virginia, on May 7, 1862, during the Peninsula Campaign. Hood pushed back a Union brigade under Brigadier General John Newton in the thick woods lining either side of the road leading to the landing. Concerned that poor visibility in the tangled countryside would cause friendly fire accidents among inexperienced troops, Hood ordered his men to advance with rifles unloaded. Suddenly, he encountered a Union corporal, rifle leveled at him, just fifteen paces off. Luckily, Private John Deal of the Texas Brigade, having disobeyed Hood's orders, shot the corporal before he could fire on Hood. The incident was typical of the loose relationship Hood maintained with his Texans—he gave orders but didn't always expect them to be obeyed—and typical as well of Hood's leadership style in combat: always leading from the front, sharing fully in the dangers to which he subjected his men.

The Battle of Eltham's Landing was essentially a skirmish, not a full-scale battle, but it laid the foundation of Hood's reputation as an aggressive hands-on commander. Not everyone was thrilled, however. Army of Northern Virginia commander Joseph E. Johnston, who had ordered Hood to avoid a major engagement, demanded to know why he had deliberately led his Texans into the teeth of battle. Was Eltham's Landing, he asked, "an illustration of the Texan idea of feeling an enemy gently and falling back?" He continued: "What would your Texans have done, sir, if I had ordered them to charge and drive back the enemy?" Hood was not about to apologize. "I suppose, general," he replied, "they would have

driven them into the river, and tried to swim out and capture their gunboats." Now it was Johnston's turn to make a strategic retreat. Smiling, he advised Hood to "teach your Texans that the first duty of a soldier is literally to obey orders."

It was a pleasant exchange with a light touch, yet it clearly revealed the flaws in Hood's ideas of command and subordination.

BATTLE OF GAINES'S MILL, JUNE 27, 1862

During the Seven Days (June 25–July 1, 1862), Hood and his Texas Brigade acted boldly at the Battle of Gaines's Mill (June 27, 1862). Positioning himself at the head of his brigade, Hood led a powerful charge that tore through the Union line. The spectacle of his howling Texans charging into the lines of blue was thrilling to fellow Confederates and horrifying to Union commanders. It was the most spectacular Confederate achievement in the entire Seven Days, and although Hood—in the forefront and thick of the battle—emerged unscathed, every other officer among his Texans was killed or wounded.

"These men are soldiers indeed!" the characteristically taciturn Stonewall Jackson exclaimed admiringly, and Hood was promoted to command a division in Major General James Longstreet's I Corps of the Army of Northern Virginia.

SECOND BATTLE OF BULL RUN, AUGUST 28–30, 1862

Hood was becoming a celebrity among Confederate commanders, and he played the part to the hilt. He acquired a reputation as a gallant and irresistible lady's man as well as a high-stakes gambler, known to break losing streaks by doubling down, especially when the odds were against him. Whatever he might lack in high cards, he made up with bluffs bold enough to cause almost anyone to fold.

Jefferson Davis was delighted with Hood's growing reputation for gallantry on and off the field. He saw Hood not only as a winning commander, but also as an uplifting icon of the Confederacy. Others, especially Joseph E. Johnston, were far more wary, deeming Hood ambitious to a fault, a man whose principal objective was his own advancement and whose grasp of strategy was unproven and doubtful. Still, he and his Texans became the go-to unit when Longstreet wanted the sharpest possible point on his spear. It was Hood who led Longstreet's twenty-five-thousand-man strike against the Union army's left flank at the Second Battle of Bull Run (August 28–30, 1862), which sent John Pope reeling into retreat and nearly brought the annihilation of the Army of the Potomac.

Thrilled with what he had achieved at Second Bull Run, Hood called the flanking attack the "most beautiful battle scene I have ever beheld," yet his subsequent behavior marred what should have been for him a flawless victory. On the final day of the battle, Hood's men captured some badly needed Union ambulances, which Nathan George "Shanks" Evans, an officer senior to him, ordered to be turned over to him. Hood refused, provoking Evans to order his arrest for gross insubordination. Robert E. Lee, who had assumed command of the Army of Northern Virginia after Johnston had been gravely wounded at the Battle of Seven Pines on May 31, was anxious to preserve the chain of command, but he also wanted to retain Hood as a combat officer as he followed up the victory at Second Bull Run with a planned offensive into Maryland. Seeking to give Hood a means of ending his arrest and exile from active leadership, Lee asked him to apologize to Evans, after which he would call the matter settled. Stubbornly, Hood refused, insisting that he was right and Evans was wrong.

Unwilling to leave Hood behind, Lee ordered him to accompany his Texans in the advance into Maryland—directing him to march in the rear rather than lead the division. Hood obeyed, but when his men saw him, they chanted within earshot of Lee, "Give us Hood! Give us Hood!" In response, Lee again asked Hood to apologize. Again Hood refused. Stymied, Lee declared that he was "suspending" Hood's arrest, and he invited the general to lead the now-cheering Texans. Lee knew when he had a powerful weapon at hand, and he was not about to relinquish it.

BATTLE OF ANTIETAM, SEPTEMBER 17, 1862, AND AFTER

Lee would need it. At Antietam, Hood commanded a small division, which was kept in reserve behind Stonewall Jackson's corps. When Jackson suddenly came under attack, Hood led his division to Jackson's relief. Although vastly outnumbered, Hood refused to withdraw from the rescue, even as his ranks withered under fire, the bodies piling so high and thick that Hood later wrote that he feared his horse would trample the wounded. In vain, he cried out, "For God's sake, more troops!" but there were none.

Hood was outraged that Lee had put him in a position to lose more than two thousand men killed or wounded. When the commanding general inquired as to the condition of his troops, Hood looked Lee in the eyes and replied: "They're all dead on the field where you sent them." Jackson, both grateful and impressed, recommended Hood's immediate promotion to major general, which followed on October 10, 1862. Yet despite his ambition and the gratification the promotion gave him, Hood never shook off the bitterness of the losses he had suffered, and he never forgave Lee.

Hood went on to participate in the Battle of Fredericksburg (December 11–15, 1862), but his position in the center, between those lines under Longstreet's direct command at Marye's Heights and those under Jackson, meant that he and his division saw relatively little action. From the Battle of Chancellorsville (April 30–May 6, 1863), he was totally absent, since he was with the rest of Longstreet's I Corps in and about Suffolk, Virginia, interdicting Union attempts to gain a landing place for seaborne action against the Army of Northern Virginia. Yet Chancellorsville had a profound effect on his future. The death of Stonewall Jackson, mortally wounded by friendly fire, prompted Lee to reorganize the Army of Northern Virginia. Hood advised him to reduce the size of the army's corps and increase their number. Lee, who could clearly tell that Hood expected to be given command of one of the new corps, told him that he "must so inspire and lead [his] brave division as it may accomplish the work of a corps." Although Hood took this exhortation to heart, he also resented Lee's unwillingness to promote him to higher command. Lee's response embodied his understanding that Hood, although he was an inspiring combat leader, was not equipped to command the largest formations, whether a corps or an army. There is no evidence, however, that Hood read this message between the lines.

BATTLE OF GETTYSBURG, JULY 1–3, 1863

Operating as part of Longstreet's I Corps, Hood's division arrived too late on day one (July 1, 1863) of the Battle of Gettysburg to participate in the fighting. On day two, he protested to Longstreet Lee's order to attack the Union position on Little Round Top frontally and sought permission instead to advance around the left flank of the Union army, beyond Big Round Top to a position from which he could attack the Union rear. It was a sound plan, but Longstreet, though unhappy himself with Lee's orders, insisted that they be followed to the letter. Reluctantly, Hood commenced the frontal assault late in the afternoon, but early in the attack, an artillery round exploded over his head, sending iron fragments tearing into his left arm. He had to be evacuated from the field, and although he would keep his arm, the nerves were so badly damaged that he was unable to use it for

the rest of his life. In his absence, Brigadier General Evander M. Law assumed command of the division but proved unable to create the necessary momentum to overcome the extraordinary resistance offered by Colonel Joshua Chamberlain on Little Round Top. The attack failed, leading Lee to make the fateful decision on day three to hurl nearly fifteen thousand men against the Union high ground in Pickett's Charge.

BATTLE OF CHICKAMAUGA, SEPTEMBER 19–20, 1863

For more than two months, Hood convalesced from his wounds. By the time Hood was ready to return to duty, Lee had detached Longstreet's corps from the Army of Northern Virginia and sent it to Tennessee to reinforce Braxton Bragg's Army of Tennessee. Hood caught up with his division in Longstreet's corps on September 18, 1863, just in time for the Battle of Chickamauga.

On September 19, a confused William Rosecrans, believing that a gap existed in the Army of the Cumberland's line, moved troops to plug it. In fact, moving the troops created a gap where none had existed, and Longstreet, perceiving this, organized a massive attack against it. As usual, Hood and his division were the leading edge of the assault. He and his men broke through, but Hood was wounded by a minié ball in the thigh, necessitating amputation of his right leg just four inches below the hip. No one expected him to live, and Longstreet rushed a recommendation for his promotion to lieutenant general effective September 20.

HOOD, JOHNSTON, AND DAVIS

Hood recovered, albeit slowly. While convalescing in Richmond, he met frequently with Jefferson Davis, who admired his courage and aggressive spirit all the more. For his part, Hood manipulated Davis, presenting himself as one who would (in his words to the president) "follow you to the death." Promoted to lieutenant general on Longstreet's recommendation (when Longstreet doubted he would live to accept the promotion), Hood was now eligible for the corps command Lee had refused him. Davis did not share Lee's perception of Hood's limitations, and, withdrawing an earlier recommendation that a corps be assigned to the very able Daniel Harvey Hill, Davis awarded a corps to Hood.

The Army of Tennessee, of which that corps was a part, was now under the command of Joseph E. Johnston, who had replaced Braxton Bragg after Bragg's defeat at Chattanooga. On arriving at his new command, Hood believed his first task was the rehabilitation of the men of the corps, who had been thoroughly demoralized by the retreat from Chattanooga. He set about this very effectively, parading, reviewing, and generally building his troops' self-esteem. The toll on him, however, was heavy. His wounded arm and the stump of his leg gave him continual agony, which he sought to dull with laudanum, an opiate that almost certainly impeded his judgment—to what degree, we cannot know.

Atlanta Campaign, May 7–September 2, 1864

As Hood worked to build up the fighting spirit of his corps, he found himself increasingly disappointed by Johnston's reliance on defensive strategy and tactics in his long strategic withdrawal from William Tecumseh Sherman, who was advancing on Atlanta. Secretly, Hood began writing reports to President Davis, chronicling Johnston's long retreat and criticizing him for it. Finally, on July 17, 1864, after receiving a corroborating recommendation from Braxton Bragg, who had become Davis's military advisor, the Confederate president removed Johnston as commander of the Army of Tennessee and replaced him with Hood, who also assumed the rank of temporary general. Davis did consult Lee before appointing Hood, and had Lee frankly expressed his reservations about Hood's fitness for independent command, perhaps the president would have reconsidered. Instead, Lee was evasive, remarking only that Hood was "a bold fighter, very industrious on the battlefield, careless off."

Hood's first battle was at Peachtree Creek, at the time on the outskirts of Atlanta (today well within the city limits). Reversing Johnston's policy of strategic retreat, he launched an attack on July 20. It was the first of four in the Atlanta Campaign, all of which failed and none of which gained anything. Of 65,000 Army of Tennessee soldiers engaged, 34,979 became casualties, killed, wounded, missing, or captured. Union losses, of the 112,000 engaged, were 31,687 killed, wounded, missing, or captured. On September 2, 1864, as Sherman cut the rail lines into Atlanta, Hood withdrew from the city, leaving it to the Union.

Franklin-Nashville Campaign, September–December 1864

Hood withdrew from Atlanta to the west with the intention of linking up with the army of Nathan Bedford Forrest and retaking Tennessee, from which he might then invade Kentucky. Hood believed that attacking Union forces in the Western Theater would force Sherman to abandon his eastward "March to the Sea" to come to the rescue of the units in the West. This would not only relieve the pressure on the people of Georgia, but also remove a threat to the rear of Lee's Army of Northern Virginia.

The chief problem with Hood's plan—which, given the depleted state of his army, was never very feasible in any event—was that Sherman declined to pursue Hood. Instead, he detached Major General George H. Thomas to assume command of Union forces in Tennessee while he continued the March to the Sea as planned.

From September to December 1864, Hood fought a series of battles in an effort to envelop

Battle of Nashville - December 15-16, 1864

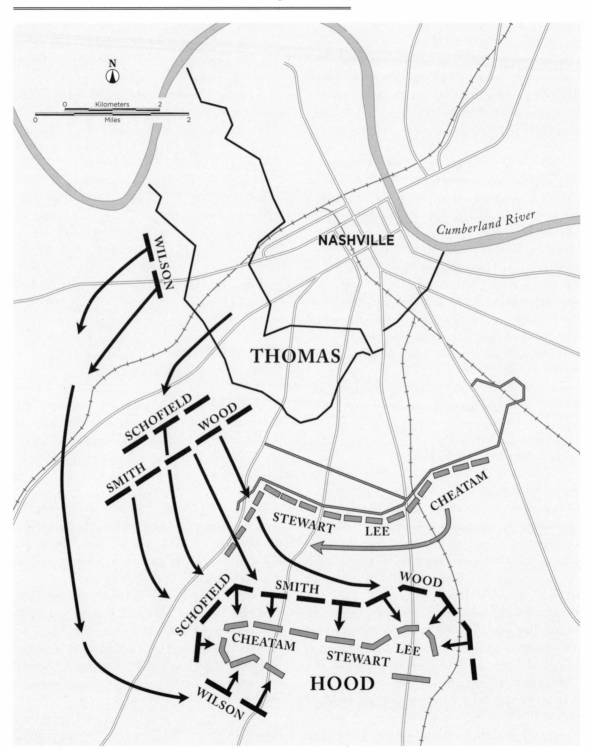

N

Kilometers
Miles

NASHVILLE

Cumberland River

WILSON

THOMAS

SCHOFIELD

WOOD

SMITH

STEWART

LEE

CHEATAM

SCHOFIELD

SMITH

WOOD

CHEATAM

STEWART

LEE

HOOD

WILSON

a portion of the Army of the Ohio under Major General John M. Schofield and prevent it from linking up with General Thomas at Nashville. On November 29, Hood missed an opportunity to trap Schofield at Spring Hill, allowing him to slip out and establish a strong defensive position at Franklin. On November 30, a frustrated Hood hurled his men against Schofield in a foolish and self-destructive action sometimes called "Pickett's Charge of the West," sending his troops across some two miles of exposed ground, where they were slaughtered. Of about 27,000 Confederates engaged, 6,252 were killed, wounded, captured, or went missing.

From Franklin, Schofield marched to Nashville, where he joined forces with Thomas, creating an army of fifty-five thousand to fight the thirty-thousand men under Hood. In a forlorn

Federal out line at Nashville, December 16, 1864. Library of Congress

John Bell Hood. NATIONAL ARCHIVES AND RECORDS ADMINISTRATION

hope, Hood attempted to lay siege against Thomas's and Schofield's superior numbers. During the Battle of Nashville on December 15 and 16, 1864, Hood's Army of Tennessee was decisively defeated, with six thousand killed, wounded, captured, or gone missing. Although Joseph E. Johnston would later re-form the army to fight Sherman in the Carolinas, it would never recover from the Battles of Franklin and Nashville and was essentially neutralized as a strategically significant fighting force.

THE END AND AFTER

The youngest full general of the Civil War at thirty-three (the temporary appointment was never confirmed by the Confederate Senate), Hood was nevertheless described by one eyewitness at the end of 1864 as "feeble and decrepit" in appearance. Following the Battle of Nashville,

he asked President Davis to relieve him of command. Davis obliged, replacing him with Johnston. Confederate (and former U.S.) senator Louis T. Wigfall of Texas remarked that Hood "had a fine career before him until Davis undertook to make him what the good Lord had not done—to make a great general of him." In a final gesture of desperation, the Confederate president sent Hood to Texas with orders to raise a new army. By the time he got there, however, Lieutenant General Edmund Kirby Smith had surrendered the Texas forces he commanded. There was no point in continuing the fight, and Hood gave himself up to Federal forces at Natchez, Mississippi, on May 31, 1865. He was immediately paroled.

Battered and beaten, Hood was still chronologically a young man. He set up after the war as a cotton factor and commission merchant in New Orleans, and when he failed to prosper in these undertakings, became president of the Life Association of America insurance company. He married a New Orleans woman, Anna Marie Hennen, in 1868 and sired upon her eleven children by 1878, among them a remarkable three sets of twins. His insurance business collapsed amid a yellow fever epidemic that year, and he scrambled to remain afloat financially, even offering to sell to the United States government a trove of letters and historic documents he had collected for his memoirs. The next year, however, the yellow fever returned, claiming in cruelly rapid succession his wife, his eldest child, and, on August 30, 1879, himself. His ten surviving orphaned children were immediately rendered destitute, saved only by P. G. T. Beauregard, who organized the Hood Orphan Memorial Publication Fund, which financed the posthumous publication of Hood's memoir, the combative *Advance and Retreat*, ensuring that the proceeds of publication would go to the orphans, who were adopted by families in Louisiana, Mississippi, Georgia, and Kentucky, as well as New York.

Chapter 12

JUBAL EARLY

RATING: ★ ★

Jubal Early. LIBRARY OF CONGRESS

EVALUATION

"My bad old man," Robert E. Lee called him. He intended it as high praise. Jubal Early had no religious faith, few friends, didn't care whom he offended, fathered four illegitimate children, was often insubordinate, had opposed secession, and cared little for the usual Confederate ideologies, but he refused either to admit or accept defeat, and to his considerable tactical skill, he added a sheer and ornery will to prevail. In the major battles, Early was the defensive stalwart on whom the commanding generals, especially Lee, knew they could rely. By the Shenandoah

Valley Campaign of 1864 and his daring raid to the very doorstep of Washington, he extended the war by six months or more. After the war, he kept fighting—on paper and in the press, creating and disseminating the powerful mythology of the Lost Cause of the Confederacy.

Although he was a remarkable battlefield commander, Early was never entrusted with a large, permanent independent command. He was no strategist, and although he imposed effective discipline on the men of his commands, he inspired no affection, let alone devotion. He was a *battle* leader, but not a leader for *war*. There was about him too much of the angry individualist to be a general of the very first rank. In the end, he kept the cause alive, long after it had been lost. Whether in 1864 or during the years following the war, this was an enterprise of dubious value.

Principal Battles

PRE-CIVIL WAR

Second Seminole War, 1835–1842
- Locha-Hatchie Ford, January 24, 1838: Early's maiden battle, in which he fired and was fired upon, but confessed that the enemy remained invisible throughout

U.S.-Mexican War, 1846–1848
- Early did not participate in combat but earned praise as military governor of Monterrey

CIVIL WAR
- Blackburn's Ford, July 18, 1861: In Virginia; Early reinforced units that turned back a Federal reconnaissance in force, impressing his commanding officers
- First Battle of Bull Run, July 21, 1861: In Virginia; Early led his regiment in the attack that turned the battle into a Union rout; promoted to brigadier general
- Williamsburg, May 5, 1862: In Virginia; led his brigade with energy and tactical skill that again drew

the attention of his superiors, but a wound put him out of action for nearly two months

- Seven Days, June 25–July 1, 1862: In Virginia; at the final battle of the Seven Days, Malvern Hill, July 1, 1862, Early got lost in the woods and arrived too late to get into the fight
- Cedar Mountain, August 9, 1862: In Virginia; won Stonewall Jackson's gratitude for holding his right flank "with great firmness"
- Second Battle of Bull Run, August 28–30, 1862: In Virginia; with tactical expertise and resolute calm, reinforced A. P. Hill at a critical juncture
- Antietam, September 17, 1862: In Maryland; with just 1,400 men, Early held the West Woods against elements of three Union corps until the arrival of reinforcements
- Fredericksburg, December 11–15, 1862: In Virginia; saved the day for Robert E. Lee by plugging a gap in Jackson's line before it broke; promoted to major general
- Chancellorsville, April 30–May 6, 1863: In Virginia; with five thousand men, held Marye's Heights against two Union corps at Fredericksburg while the main battle was fought at Chancellorsville
- Gettysburg, July 1–3, 1863: In Pennsylvania; fought extensively in the battle and was especially successful in the run-up to the engagement and during day one of the battle proper
- Overland Campaign, May–June 1864: In Virginia; participated in the Wilderness, May 5–7, Spotsylvania Court House, May 8–21, and Cold Harbor, May 31–June 12; assumed command of III Corps after A. P. Hill fell ill, and, promoted to temporary lieutenant general, replaced Richard Ewell as corps commander at Cold Harbor, May 31–June 12
- Shenandoah Valley Operations, June 13–October 19, 1864: In Virginia; Lee detached Early for independent command in the Valley, tasked with defeating Union general David Hunter there and menacing Baltimore and Washington to take the pressure off Petersburg and Richmond; Early performed brilliantly
- Lynchburg, June 17–18, 1864: In Virginia; drove Hunter out of the Shenandoah Valley
- Monocacy, July 9, 1864: In Maryland; scored a tactical victory against Major General Lew Wallace, who, however, gained the strategic advantage of delaying Early's raid on Washington
- Battle of Fort Stevens, July 11–12, 1864: Outside Washington, D.C. Early's attack on the outer defenses of the capital—personally witnessed by President Lincoln—created fear and forced Ulysses Grant to devote some of his front-line troops to Washington's defense
- Third Battle of Winchester, September 19, 1864: In Virginia; Early suffered defeat at the hands of Philip Sheridan's superior numbers
- Fisher's Hill, September 22, 1864: In Virginia; another battle with Sheridan, and another defeat
- Cedar Creek, October 19, 1864: In Virginia; in a daring surprise attack, Early nearly routed Union forces, which, however, Sheridan successfully rallied in a counterattack
- Waynesboro, March 2, 1865: In Virginia; vastly outnumbered by Union cavalry under Brigadier General George Armstrong Custer, Early's command was all but annihilated; the defeat prompted Lee to relieve Early

---

If Jubal Early had had his way, the Civil War would never have begun, but, once begun, it would never have ended. A reluctant rebel, he was also the most stubborn rebel, to the day he died in 1894, a thoroughly unreconstructed champion of the cult of the Lost Cause.

Yet he may also have been the least popular officer in the Confederate army. Virtually no one, save Robert E. Lee himself, liked Early. Little wonder. Though born and bred in plantation Virginia, he was the antithesis of the "Southern gentleman": gruff, deliberately offensive, insulting, profane, and an atheist among fundamentalist believers. A harsh disciplinarian to subordinates, he was often insubordinate to superiors. But it was he, of all Confederate generals, who brought soldiers closest to Washington, brought them very nearly face to face with Abraham Lincoln himself.

A CADET FROM VIRGINIA

Born on November 3, 1816, in Franklin County, Virginia, Jubal Early was the third of ten children of Joab and Ruth Hairston Early, a prominent southwestern Virginia family. Joab owned a thousand-acre plantation, held the title of colonel in the county militia, and was a member of the Virginia legislature. During the first third of the nineteenth century, even children of the most prosperous families west of the Tidewater were often poorly educated, but Joab insisted that his sons and daughters be lifted above the prevailing ignorance. After elementary education in the local one-room schoolhouse, Jubal was sent to academies in Lynchburg and Danville.

In 1833, a year after his mother died, Jubal Early obtained an appointment to the U.S. Military Academy. A restless cadet, he was indifferent to his studies and cared so little about graduating that, in 1835, he sought his father's permission to leave West Point to join the Texas war for independence from Mexico. It galled him that the Texans' pleas for aid from the United States fell on deaf ears, and he explained to his father that simple "humanity" demanded his participation in the war. Only Joab Early's adamant refusal to grant permission kept Cadet Early at his studies, so that he did manage to graduate with the Class of 1837, doing so at a respectably ranked eighteenth out of fifty.

Second Seminole War and U.S.-Mexican War, 1835–1842 and 1846–1848

Commissioned a second lieutenant upon graduation, Early was assigned to the 3rd U.S. Artillery Regiment and sent to Fort Monroe, Virginia, where he was tasked with training the incoming recruits of Company E in preparation for assignment to Florida to fight in the ongoing Second Seminole War. He quickly earned a reputation for instilling strict discipline, and his commanding officers judged him to be a highly efficient trainer of troops.

When Company E shipped out to Florida, Second Lieutenant Early was assigned temporary company command and led the troops into the Everglades in pursuit of Seminoles who resisted "removal" to Indian Territory west of the Mississippi. He fought his maiden battle on January 24, 1838, at Locha-Hatchie Ford. It was typical of the army's long and frustrating pursuit of the Seminole. There was shooting, but the enemy remained largely invisible in the swampland.

Later in 1838, Early was sent west to patrol the frontier of Indian Territory in anticipation of a Cherokee uprising. No fighting materialized and, on July 31, 1838, fed up with army life, Early resigned his commission—only to learn days later that he had been promoted to first lieutenant. He later remarked that the promotion might well have kept him in the army had he known about it, but he never expressed regret over leaving. It gave him an opportunity to return to his native Franklin County, Virginia, where he apprenticed to attorney N. M. Taliaferro and by 1840 gained admission to the bar.

The naturally disputatious Early relished the practice of law, and in 1841 he parlayed his legal experience into a successful run for the Virginia House of Delegates. But come 1846 and the outbreak of the war with Mexico, Early sought readmission to the military. He reentered the U.S. Army by way of the Virginia militia as the governor commissioned him a major in the 1st Virginia Volunteers. The unit was federalized, and Early was again assigned to Fort Monroe as a trainer of troops.

Early's regiment did not ship out for Mexico until March 1847. Assigned to Zachary Taylor's Northern Army, the unit saw no combat but was assigned to occupation duty, and in April Early was named military governor of Monterrey. He proved well suited to the position, imposing strict but fair military order on the civilian population as well as the occupation forces and earning the admiration of Jefferson Davis, colonel of the Mississippi Rifles. The two men developed a mutual admiration.

Unfortunately for Early, he fell ill with flu-like symptoms in the fall of 1847. The sickness developed into general rheumatism, which was severe enough to warrant his being invalided back to the States. Recovering sufficiently to return to duty in 1848, he was sent back to occupation duty until April 1848, when he again returned home. His rheumatic condition would return to plague him repeatedly throughout his life, sometimes with disabling effect.

A confirmed bachelor, Early nevertheless began seeing late in 1848 a seventeen-year-old girl named Julia McNealey. The two would conduct an intimate relationship until McNealey married another man twenty-three years later, in 1871. During their long affair, she bore four children, for whose care Jubal Early always provided. While some may have been shocked, there was no career-wrecking scandal. Indeed, the relationship seems generally to have met with quiet acceptance.

CIVIL WAR OUTBREAK

Early's domestic arrangements were not the only unconventional aspects of his life as a Southerner. As mentioned, he was an atheist—although he often argued that slavery was a condition imposed by "the Creator"—and, as a liberal-minded Whig, he was opposed to secession, even though he conceded that the North sought unfairly to dominate the South economically and sometimes impinged on the rights of the states of the region. He believed that compromise between the extremes of states' rights in the South and abolitionism in the North was not only possible, but urgently necessary to avoid the dissolution of the nation. When Early was elected to the Virginia convention debating secession in 1861, he made impassioned speeches defending the promise of President Lincoln in his first inaugural address—that he had no intention of interfering with slavery where it existed and would protect the constitutional property rights of slave owners. Even after the capture of Fort Sumter in April 1861, Early continued to argue against the secession of Virginia. When it finally came to a vote, he voted against secession.

Early never changed his convictions on the subject of the sanctity of the Union; however, when the convention decided to take Virginia out of that Union, he vowed to defend his native soil against any invasion from the North. With this decision, the anti-secessionist became one of the Confederacy's most passionate and dogged warriors.

BATTLE OF BLACKBURN'S FORD AND FIRST BULL RUN, JULY 18 AND 21, 1861

Offering his military services to Governor John Letcher, Jubal Early was commissioned a colonel of the Virginia Militia and was dispatched to Lynchburg to recruit three regiments and to assume command of one of them. Designated the 24th Virginia Infantry, Early's regiment was attached to the Provisional Army of the Confederate States and his colonelcy was transferred from the state to the Confederate service.

In the lead-up to the First Battle of Bull Run (July 21, 1861), Early assumed command of the 6th Brigade under P. G. T. Beauregard, leading it in a skirmish at Blackburn's Ford (July 18) that added firepower to the Confederate forces arrayed there against a Union reconnaissance in force. Minor in itself, the encounter nevertheless impressed General Beauregard, who welcomed the brigade into the action at Bull Run three days later, in which Early participated in the attack that turned the Federal right and precipitated Irvin McDowell's humiliating rout.

BATTLE OF WILLIAMSBURG, MAY 5, 1862

His performance at Blackburn's Ford and the First Battle of Bull Run earned Early a promotion to brigadier general, and his brigade was attached to what was now called the Army of Northern Virginia under Joseph E. Johnston.

At the Battle of Williamsburg (May 5, 1862) during the Peninsula Campaign, Early showed great tactical skill against superior Union forces.

He was wounded twice in the course of the fight: A ball hit him in the neck, doing relatively minor damage, but was followed by another that entered through one shoulder, traversed his back, and exited the other shoulder. Astoundingly, though seriously injured, Early continued to command until blood loss brought him close to death.

SEVEN DAYS, JUNE 25–JULY 1, 1862

Early took nearly two months to recover from his wounds, and even after this period his doctors tried in vain to dissuade him from returning to combat. It was the end of June when he rejoined the Army of Northern Virginia, now under the command of Robert E. Lee, during the Seven Days Battles. His assignment to take over a brigade that had been under the command of Arnold Elzey, disabled by wounds, put him directly under Stonewall Jackson, who came to admire Early's aggressive spirit.

Early led his brigade in the final battle of the Seven Days, at Malvern Hill (July 1, 1862), where he was supposed to reinforce D. H. Hill on Lee's right; however, after getting lost in thick woods, he was unable to get the brigade into position in time to actively fight in the battle.

CEDAR MOUNTAIN AND SECOND BULL RUN, AUGUST 9 AND AUGUST 28–30, 1862

Early and his brigade acquitted themselves splendidly, however, at Cedar Mountain, where he held Jackson's right flank with what Stonewall characterized as "great firmness," repulsing attack after attack.

At the end of the month, in the Second Battle of Bull Run, Early arrived just in time to reinforce A. P. Hill, who was struggling to hold Jackson's left at Stony Ridge. His absolute calm under fire was a marvel to those who witnessed it—and it was critical to maintaining the resolve of his brigade. Praise was universal, and there was much buzz, following Second Bull Run, about

a promotion to major general. Yet his superiors remained reluctant to take that step.

BATTLE OF ANTIETAM, SEPTEMBER 17, 1862

By the time of Antietam, Lee and Jackson recognized Early as a commander on whom they could rely to provide the most resolute of defenses. Early in the battle, he was assigned to take a stand with his brigade—now numbering just 1,400 men—in the West Woods until the position could be reinforced. Early was beleaguered by elements from three Union corps, and though he was vastly outnumbered, he did hold until reinforcements arrived.

Next, when his division commander, Alexander Lawton, was critically wounded, Early assumed divisional command and managed the battlefield transition so seamlessly that Lee gave him permanent command of the division—yet he and Richmond withheld the promotion to major general that should have gone with the increased command responsibility. Bitterly disappointed, Early was too proud to protest and instead soldiered on as a brigadier doing a major general's job.

BATTLES OF FREDERICKSBURG AND CHANCELLORSVILLE, DECEMBER 11–15, 1862 AND APRIL 30–MAY 6, 1863

Early once again demonstrated his value when he brought his division to the aid of Jackson at Fredericksburg just as Major General George Gordon Meade was attacking a gap in Stonewall's line. Had Early failed to materialize in time or had he handled his division with anything less than calm perfection, Meade might well have achieved the breakthrough that eluded the Army of the Potomac on that terrible day.

Unable to ignore the very real fact that Early had saved the day at Fredericksburg and was instrumental in delivering to the Confederacy a smashing victory, the Richmond government finally authorized his promotion to major general on January 17, 1863. Lee, who never had doubts about Early, assigned him five thousand men to defend Fredericksburg at Marye's Heights during the Battle of Chancellorsville (April 30–May 6, 1863).

Both Lee and Early well knew that General Joseph Hooker was sending against him two full corps under Major General John Sedgwick and that the assignment involved extreme hazard. Moreover, the mission was the equivalent of an independent command, since Early was isolated from the main body of the Army of Northern Virginia. In some ways, the ensuing battle went badly, since Early was overrun by Sedgwick's superior numbers. Yet Early himself remained unshaken and transformed his mission into a highly effective delaying action, which occupied

Sedgwick while Lee and Jackson concentrated on the main battle at Chancellorsville, dealing Hooker a defeat as lopsided as it was horrific (17,197 Union casualties versus 13,303 for the Confederacy). Lee was able to turn from his victory at Chancellorsville and relieve the pressure on Early, forcing Sedgwick to withdraw.

ADVANCE INTO PENNSYLVANIA AND THE BATTLE OF GETTYSBURG, JULY 1–3, 1863

After the mortal wounding of Stonewall Jackson at Chancellorsville, Early was assigned to command a division in the corps of Lieutenant General Richard S. Ewell. Early's division effectively plowed the road for the advance, engaging and defeating Union forces at Winchester, Virginia, and clearing a route through the Shenandoah Valley through which the main body of

Early's charge on east Cemetery Hill at the Battle of Gettysburg, July 2, 1863. CENTURY MAGAZINE

the Army of Northern Virginia advanced. Early marched into Gettysburg, Pennsylvania, on June 26, demanding, as Confederate raiders often did, a ransom to spare the town from burning. Although the ransom went unpaid, Early did not put Gettysburg to the torch, but instead marched on, seizing York, Pennsylvania. Not only was this the biggest Union town the Confederates ever captured, the town fathers yielded to his demand for ransom, paying a cash sum of $28,000. By June 28, advance elements of Early's division were on the banks of the Susquehanna River but were recalled to Gettysburg on June 30 as Lee consolidated the Army of Northern Virginia for engagement with the Army of the Potomac.

Early's division, constituting the left flank of the Confederate line, closed on Gettysburg from the northeast on July 1. Clashing with a Union division under Brigadier General Francis Barlow, Early delivered a devastating blow that drove the Union forces through Gettysburg and forced them to fall back on Cemetery Hill and Cemetery Ridge south of town. Although Early had inflicted three times the casualties he incurred and had captured many prisoners of war, the Union's possession of the high ground would prove critical to the course of the battle.

On day two of Gettysburg, July 2, Early led assaults on east Cemetery Hill in an attempt to toll up the Union's right flank. At first, he made significant progress, but he could not complete the operation before Union reinforcements arrived to drive back the two brigades he led.

On day three, July 3, Early participated in an unsuccessful assault on Union positions at Culp's Hill, east of east Cemetery Hill, and after the catastrophic failure of Pickett's Charge later in the day, Early positioned his division to act as a rear guard as the Army of Northern Virginia withdrew from Gettysburg on July 4 and 5.

Early was bitter over what he considered Ewell's weak performance at Gettysburg—his failure to act more aggressively to take Cemetery Hill and Culp's Hill—and he sometimes deliberately overstepped his command authority as Ewell's corps served in the Shenandoah Valley during the winter of 1863–1864. On at least one occasion, Ewell was sufficiently provoked to order Early's arrest for insubordination. Lee, however, persuaded of Early's capacity for higher command, intervened.

OVERLAND CAMPAIGN, MAY–JUNE 1864

Lee summoned Ewell and, with him, Early, back from the Shenandoah Valley in the spring of 1864 to resist Ulysses S. Grant's advance against Richmond in the Overland Campaign. Early fought in the Battle of the Wilderness (May 5–7, 1864) and at Spotsylvania Court House (May 8–21), assuming command of III Corps when A. P. Hill was stricken with illness. During the battle, Early, who held the right flank of the front known as Mule Shoe, was not positioned for the hottest action. Nevertheless, at Cold Harbor (May 31–June 12), Lee had sufficient confidence in Early to promote him to temporary lieutenant general on May 31, remove the faltering Ewell from II Corps command, and install Early in his place.

SHENANDOAH VALLEY OPERATIONS, JUNE 13–OCTOBER 19, 1864

After the Battle of Cold Harbor and as the Siege of Petersburg began, Lee sent Early on his most important mission of the war. He dispatched him and his corps into the Shenandoah Valley to drive Union major general David Hunter out and to menace Baltimore and Washington in order to force Grant to divert troops from Richmond and the developing Petersburg siege.

Early tangled with Hunter at the Battle of Lynchburg (June 17–18, 1864), driving him westward out of the Valley. At the same time, Early and his men destroyed track and bridges of the Baltimore and Ohio Railroad, then advanced

Combat artist Alfred R. Waud sketched "Destruction of the R. R. bridge, over the Monocacy River near Frederick, Md." on July 9, 1864. It illustrates the damage caused by one of Early's raids.

into Maryland. On July 9, Union general Lew Wallace attempted to block Early's advance on Washington at the Battle of Monocacy near Frederick. Wallace had a force of 5,800 men against 14,000 under Early, and although Early scored a tactical victory—inflicting nearly 1,300 casualties—Wallace achieved the strategic advantage by delaying Early's advance, thereby buying time for the reinforcement of Washington's defenses.

After Monocacy, Early menaced Baltimore with a brigade of cavalry as he marched with the main body of his army on Washington. Grant rushed units from the Petersburg front to defend the capital, which also called on administrative troops and civilians to pitch in. Lincoln asked Grant to consider coming to Washington to direct its defense personally, but the commander persuaded the president that his presence at Petersburg was more important.

On July 11, Early reached the forts defending Washington itself. As the Confederates approached, the War Department cobbled together all available forces, including elderly veterans from the Soldiers' Home and disabled troops from the Invalid Corps. On July 11 and 12, President and Mrs. Lincoln, accompanied by political dignitaries, visited Fort Stevens, then on the city's northwest perimeter. An exchange with Early's sharpshooters broke out, and Lincoln mounted a firing step to peer over the parapet for a view of the action, exposing his head and chest to the enemy fire. A surgeon standing beside Lincoln was wounded, and a young officer shouted to the president, whom he did not recognize: "Get down, you damn fool!" That officer was Captain Oliver Wendell Holmes Jr., who would later become the most eloquent and celebrated associate justice ever to sit on the U.S. Supreme Court.

On the verge of ordering a general attack, Early was apparently dismayed by the sudden appearance of the VI Corps, a veteran Union unit, and withdrew during the night of July 12–13. He backtracked through the Shenandoah Valley, continuing his destructive raid against the B&O Railroad, and through the first week of August, he harried Union units in the Valley, prompting Grant to send Philip Sheridan with about forty-eight thousand men to defeat Early and carry out his own raid through the Shenandoah, closing it as a backdoor to Washington and ending its usefulness as the bountiful "breadbasket of the Confederacy."

With his superior forces, Sheridan chased Early up the Shenandoah Valley while burning barns, burning crops, and destroying cattle. Sheridan won a major victory against Early at the Third Battle of Winchester on September 19, and another at Fisher's Hill on September 22. But Early was far from finished. At dawn on October 19, he launched a surprise attack on the Federal position at Cedar Creek, Virginia, sending panic-stricken troops into a disordered

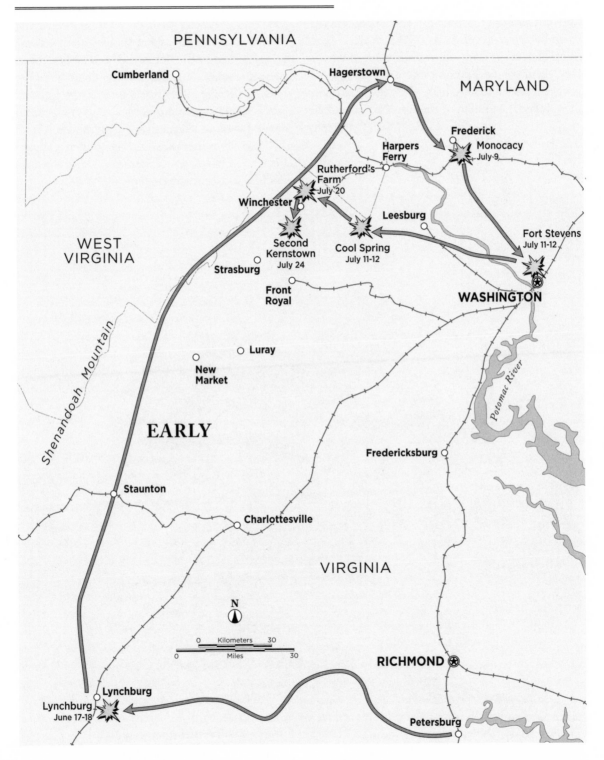

PENNSYLVANIA

MARYLAND

Cumberland

Hagerstown

Frederick
Monocacy
July 9

Harpers
Ferry

Rutherford's
Farm
July 20

Winchester

Leesburg

Fort Stevens
July 11-12

WEST
VIRGINIA

Second
Kernstown
July 24

Cool Spring
July 11-12

Strasburg

WASHINGTON

Front
Royal

Luray

Potomac River

New
Market

EARLY

Fredericksburg

Staunton

Charlottesville

VIRGINIA

N

0   Kilometers   30

0   Miles   30

RICHMOND

Lynchburg

Lynchburg
June 17-18

Petersburg

retreat. Sheridan, who was at Winchester en route to Washington, galloped to the battlefield, rallied the troops, restored fighting order, and led them back into combat. By 4:00 that afternoon, Sheridan's command staged a furious counterattack, turning a Federal rout into a victory against Jubal Early. At Cedar Creek, Sheridan lost 5,665 men, killed, wounded, or missing, out of 30,829 engaged, and Early lost 2,910, killed, wounded, or missing, out of 18,410.

BATTLE OF WAYNESBORO, MARCH 2, 1865, AND AFTER

By December 1864, most of Early's corps had rejoined Lee in the defense of Petersburg. Early himself remained in the Shenandoah Valley to command what amounted to a rump force of some 1,600 men, which was virtually wiped out at the Battle of Waynesboro, Virginia, on March 2, 1865, by Sheridan and Brigadier General George Armstrong Custer. Early managed to evade capture—though just barely.

"Officers and men of Company F, 3rd Massachusetts Heavy Artillery, in Fort Stevens," on the northwest perimeter of Washington, D.C. The fort was the object of Early's attack on July 11-12, 1864. NATIONAL PARK SERVICE

Following this defeat, Robert E. Lee relieved Early. While his confidence in his "ability, zeal, and devotion to the cause [was] unimpaired," Lee explained, it was clear that other commanders and the troops had lost their belief in Early. Lee therefore felt compelled, he wrote to Early, "to endeavor to find a commander who would be more likely to develop the strength and resources of the country, and inspire the soldiers with confidence."

A little more than a month after Early's defeat at Waynesboro, Robert E. Lee surrendered at Appomattox and gave himself up to Grant. Early, however, fled to Texas on horseback with the hope of joining forces with Lieutenant General Edmund Kirby Smith. In concert with him, he intended to recruit a new army and continue the fight. Discovering on his arrival, however, that Smith had surrendered, Early continued to ride, crossing the border into Mexico. In May of the following year, he took a ship to Canada by way of Cuba and settled in Toronto, which had become a haven for a small colony of Confederate refugees. Here he wrote *A Memoir of the Last Year of the War for Independence, in the Confederate States of America* (1867), which detailed his exploits in the Shenandoah Valley.

In 1868 President Andrew Johnson pardoned Jubal Early and other top Confederate generals. Early returned to Virginia in 1869, settling in Lynchburg and taking up again the practice of law. In 1877 he was appointed commissioner of the Louisiana Lottery. But neither the law nor the lottery was Early's chief postwar passion. He became a vocal critic of James Longstreet, blaming him for turning what should have been *Lee's* war-winning victory at Gettysburg into *Longstreet's* defeat and the defeat of the Confederate cause. More than any other individual in the immediate postwar period, Jubal Early was responsible for creating the myth of the "Lost Cause," around which a durable Southern cult developed, united in the belief that the war aims of the Confederacy had been good, noble, and just, and that Southern generals and fighting men, though clearly superior to those of the Union, were nevertheless doomed to ultimate defeat by the North's greater population, industrial might, and raw wealth.

On February 15, 1894, the seventy-seven-year-old Early stumbled and fell down a long flight of stairs. Shaking off the incident, he denied that he had been hurt, much as he denied that the South had been truly beaten. Two weeks after his fall, on March 2, he was dead.

PART TWO

GENERALS NORTH

Chapter 13

WINFIELD SCOTT

RATING: ★ ★ ★

"Old Fuss and Feathers": General-in-chief Winfield Scott at the start of the Civil War. NATIONAL ARCHIVES AND RECORDS ADMINISTRATION

EVALUATION

Hero of the War of 1812 and prime architect of victory in the U.S.-Mexican War, Winfield Scott was general-in-chief of the Union army at the outbreak of the Civil War. Old, obese, and unwell, he retired seven months into the war, having drawn up a grand plan of blockade that was universally mocked but ultimately adopted.

It is all too easy to see in the doddering three-hundred-pound general derisively dubbed "Old Fuss and Feathers" a parody of military command and a symbol of the Union army's initial unpreparedness to effectively fight the Civil War; however, Scott entered the war as the nation's most distinguished and longest-serving commander, and he contributed to the war effort its most comprehensive and coherent strategic program.

Principal Battles

PRE-CIVIL WAR

War of 1812

- Queenston Heights, October 13, 1812: In Ontario; British victory in which Scott performed gallantly but was captured

- Chippawa, July 5, 1814: In Ontario; U.S. victory in which Scott's "Camp of Instruction" was instrumental in professionalizing the fledgling U.S. Army

- Lundy's Lane, July 25, 1814: In Ontario; a tactical draw but a British strategic victory, in which Scott led a heroic attack but was severely wounded

U.S.-Mexican War

- Veracruz, March 9-29, 1847: In Mexico; commencement of Scott's daring amphibious invasion of Mexico

- Cerro Gordo, April 18, 1847: Between Veracruz and Jalapa, Mexico; en route to Mexico City but significantly outnumbered, Scott nevertheless flanked the enemy and drove them from a strong defensive position

- Contreras, August 19-20, 1847: Near Mexico City; en route to the capital, Scott routed the Mexican defenders

- Churubusco, August 20, 1847: Near Mexico City; Scott's victory here brought U.S. forces to within five miles of the Mexican capital

- Chapultepec, September 12-13, 1847: Outside of Mexico City; the bloody culminating battle of the war with Mexico

Civil War

- Anaconda Plan, 1861: Scott's much derided plan of naval blockade and Mississippi River domination, which ultimately guided Union strategy throughout most of the war

Winfield Scott (1786–1866) suffered the misfortune of having lived the handsome years of his life, when he was a strapping young officer, before the invention and subsequent popularization of photography. The daguerreotypes that have come down to us show a scowling three-hundred-pound rotundity whose flaccid jowls ooze from between the wings of his starched collar. By the time of these images, the years just before the Civil War and the first months of that conflict, he was the army's senior general, universally known as "Old Fuss and Feathers," a nickname that he had acquired long before on account of his uncompromising insistence that the soldiers of the U.S. Army actually *look* like soldiers but that was applied in his later years because he was old, waddled when he walked, and had a fondness for uniforms refulgent in gold lace and outsized epaulets. Even worse for his historical reputation, most modern Americans first encounter him at the outbreak of the Civil War, when his old age and corpulence seem fitting symbols for just how ill-prepared the U.S. Army was to fight for the preservation of the Union.

But at the height of his fame and achievement, in the U.S.-Mexican War (1846–1848), after Scott had won the Battles of Cerro Gordo, Contreras, Churubusco, and Chapultepec, then occupied Mexico City and ended the war in triumph, no less a figure than the Duke of Wellington—victor of Waterloo, the vanquisher of Napoleon—proclaimed Scott the world's "greatest living soldier." Too old, too gouty, too fat even to ride a horse at the outbreak of the Civil War, Scott turned over command to young George B. McClellan on November 1, 1861, barely seven months into the conflict, but he had already

exercised a profound influence on the course of the war. When the nation dissolved back in April of that year, he formulated for a beleaguered President Abraham Lincoln the first cogent, cohesive, realistic, and effective long-term strategy for fighting the conflict. Widely mocked at the time, it is a strategy that still startles by its comprehensive modernity, and it turned out to be the key to winning the war—once it was adopted and adapted by Generals Ulysses S. Grant and William Tecumseh Sherman three years after Scott had proposed it. Moreover, during the War of 1812 and up to the outbreak of the U.S.-Mexican War, Winfield Scott did more than any other military or civilian official to transform an ill-equipped, ill-trained, dispirited federal police force into a genuine and credible United States Army. During the war with Mexico, he not only led that army to triumph, but he also commanded more than one hundred of the men, Northerners and Southerners, who would serve as generals during the Civil War, including Grant, Sherman, Robert E. Lee, and Thomas J. Jackson—not to mention the president of the Confederacy, Jefferson Davis.

FROM LAWYER TO SOLDIER

Born on a modest plantation in Dinwiddie County, near Petersburg, Virginia, on June 13, 1786, just three years after the Treaty of Paris ended the American Revolution, Winfield Scott was six years old when his father died, leaving the boy's mother with half a dozen children to raise. She tutored Winfield at home, imparting to him a passion for honesty and a love of reading. The owner of a neighboring plantation took delight in lending him books from his library, especially the classics of history that most interested him. At twelve, Winfield enrolled in a boarding school and, two years later, attended a Richmond academy. He was seventeen in 1803 when his mother died. Until this point, he later confessed, he had been content to achieve a comfortable mediocrity in his studies. Now he was determined to honor the memory of his mother by buckling down. He left the academy and enrolled at the College of William and Mary in Williamsburg, staying just long enough—a year—to discover a tolerable interest in the law. At the time, it was common for aspiring lawyers to forgo an academic degree and instead apprentice with an established attorney to gain admission to the bar. Scott returned to Petersburg, where he entered the office of David Robinson.

Petersburg was hardly a bustling urban area and, as Abraham Lincoln would do years later in Illinois, Scott rode the circuit of outlying country courthouses. But while the young Lincoln would revel in the life of an itinerant attorney, Scott grew doubtful about his vocation. He began to feel himself adrift until, like much of the rest of the country, he was shocked by what the papers called the "*Chesapeake* affair." On June 22, 1807, the U.S. Navy frigate *Chesapeake*, off the coast of Norfolk, Virginia, was hailed by the captain of HMS *Leopard*, who demanded to board the ship to search it for deserters from the Royal Navy. Commodore James Barron, the commander of the American vessel, refused, whereupon the *Leopard* opened fire, killing three and wounding eighteen, including Barron, who, after returning a single shot, surrendered his ship. The British skipper spurned the surrender, but he did board, seizing four deserters, three of whom were U.S. citizens. "Never since the Battle of Lexington have I seen this country in such a state of exasperation," President Thomas Jefferson said of the incident and ushered through Congress the Embargo of 1807 as what he hoped would be an alternative to the war for which many clamored. At the same time, Jefferson also authorized an eight-regiment expansion of the puny U.S. Army. Scott suddenly found himself answering the call for volunteers.

The rank of corporal was immediately conferred on him, probably because he was a large and imposing figure at six-foot-four and 230 pounds, and although his service ended in short order as the immediate threat of war died down, Scott was hooked. He briefly resumed the practice of law but also prevailed on a friend who—in an era when federal officialdom was a very small community—knew President Jefferson and thereby secured a commission as captain of light artillery in one of the eight new regiments. Scott had occupied the interval between asking his friend for help and getting the commission in poring over every military manual and strategic treatise he could lay his hands on. By the time he set about recruiting a hundred men to form his company, he was about as well versed in military theory as most professional American soldiers—though, at the time, this wasn't saying much.

A CAREER BEGINS AND—ALMOST—ENDS

In the fall of 1808, Scott was sent at the head of his company to New Orleans, where the earnest young captain got a rude lesson in the pitiful state of United States arms. He had trained his handpicked company by the book only to find that he had joined an army wholly without discipline, with abysmal morale, and wallowing in inefficiency and outright corruption. It didn't take long for lawyer Scott to lay the blame for it all at the feet of his commanding officer, Brigadier General James Wilkinson. The man in charge of army forces in the South, Wilkinson was an officer destined to compile a record of malfeasance and misfeasance nearly exuberant in its volume and invention, culminating in an infamous conspiracy with Aaron Burr to create a private empire in Mexico and the territory of the Louisiana Purchase.

Scott would never be a politically savvy figure. His beloved mother, he said, had taught him to be honest, even ruthlessly frank. And so he made no secret of his opinion of Wilkinson and his leadership, prompting the general to court-martial the upstart. Without doubt, Wilkinson was guilty of everything Scott charged him with.

But Scott was equally guilty of insubordination and was suspended, with neither rank nor pay, for a full year. If this was intended as a test of his commitment to the army, he passed. Without giving word to any thought of resignation, he served his suspension and returned to duty—in plenty of time to fight in the War of 1812.

WAR OF 1812: BATTLE OF QUEENSTON HEIGHTS, OCTOBER 13, 1812

The War Hawks in Congress propelled the nation into war against Britain with scarcely a thought about the unpreparedness of the U.S. military, especially the army. In this climate, Scott, so recently an insubordinate young captain, was jumped to the rank of lieutenant colonel and given command of a brand-new artillery regiment. War was declared on June 18, 1812, and in October Scott was dispatched with two of his regiment's companies to join an invasion force bound for Canada. The ill-conceived operation, under the command of Stephen Van Rensselaer, a "political" general—that is, an officer commissioned for his connections rather than his military experience—was doomed from the start. Among other things, it was a mix of regular army troops and militiamen, who, at the last minute, balked at crossing the international border into Canada, arguing (quite rightly, in fact) that, as militia troops, they were obligated to fight only on domestic soil. The trouble was that, on the night of October 13, Scott and his men had already rowed across the Niagara River to capture the British fort at Queenston Heights. They found themselves outnumbered and outgunned—without the militia support on which they had counted. Right then and there, Scott conceived a contempt for the militia system and a determination to do all he could to encourage and promote the creation of a full-time professional army. But his more immediate concern was fighting the Battle of Queenston Heights against impossible odds. He did all he could,

held out far longer than anyone had a right to expect, then surrendered only when his force was overrun and he himself was taken prisoner.

Released in an 1813 prisoner exchange, Scott, though defeated, was hailed a hero, promoted to colonel, and assigned to Major General Henry Dearborn as his adjutant general. Unlike Van Rensselaer, Dearborn had sufficient military experience to recognize and enough character to acknowledge his own deficiencies as a commander. Unabashedly, he turned over to Scott the task of organizing his army. The new colonel did not fail him. After hammering Dearborn's four thousand men into a well-organized unit, Scott personally led an assault force on May 27 against Fort George on the Niagara Peninsula. Although wounded, Scott continued to lead the assault until the fort was taken. After Scott had been invalided from the field, however, Dearborn declined to capitalize on what he had gained. Instead of pressing the invasion forward, Dearborn chose merely to occupy the Canadian side of the Niagara. An exasperated President James Madison subsequently relieved Dearborn, promoted Scott to brigadier general—at twenty-seven he was by far the youngest general officer in the U.S. Army—and, when he was sufficiently recovered from his wounds, sent him back to the Niagara front.

WAR OF 1812: BATTLES OF CHIPPAWA AND LUNDY'S LANE, JULY 5 AND JULY 25, 1814

Scott led a brigade of New York militia in the Battle of Chippawa on July 5, 1814. For the first time in the war, an American unit defeated a British force in straight-up combat. The New Yorkers wore gray uniforms, instead of the U.S. Army blue, prompting the stunned redcoats to attribute their loss to having gone up against "regulars." As militiamen, they were anything but "regulars," of course; however, under Scott, they fought as if they were—better, actually, because they fought not like American regulars but British ones. The achievement of the New York "Grays" is memorialized in the gray uniforms still worn by West Point cadets. As many see it, the true birth of the United States Army may be dated from Scott's victory.

Scott went on to fight in the Battle of Lundy's Lane on July 25, 1814, perhaps the bloodiest single combat of the War of 1812. Early in the fighting, a musket ball shattered his collarbone, knocking him unconscious and sidelining him for the rest of the war. Taking him out of the action, his wound ceded center stage to Andrew Jackson at the Battle of New Orleans—though Scott's achievement was by no means forgotten. He received both the thanks of Congress and a brevet promotion to major general, a wartime rank he retained after the Treaty of Ghent ended the war.

IN THE SERVICE OF PRESIDENT JACKSON

In peace, Scott did not let up in his efforts to create a strong, permanent, professional national army. From 1818 to 1821, he undertook, single-handedly, the wholesale rewriting of the army's manual of regulations. This completed, he did what he could to personally train the small force and, in 1831, answered President Andrew Jackson's call to prepare federal troops to march against the state of South Carolina in the Nullification Crisis, when the militant leaders of that state refused to enforce federal tariff regulations and even threatened secession.

The following year, as commanding general of the army's Eastern Division, he led a thousand men to Fort Dearborn (modern Chicago) to fight in the Black Hawk War, only to be stymied by an outbreak of cholera at the fort, which delayed his arrival at the front until most of the fighting against the "renegade" Sauk chief was over. He did, however, play a central role in negotiating the Treaty of Fort Armstrong with the Sauk and Fox in September 1832, then immediately set out for South Carolina on orders from President Jackson to observe the activities of the

"Nullifiers." It was an exquisitely delicate mission: Scott had to reinforce the federal garrisons around Charleston without unduly enflaming public passions in the state. He performed the work masterfully.

After passage of a compromise tariff defused the Nullification Crisis, Scott's next assignment, in February 1836, was to effect the "removal" of the Seminoles from Florida to Indian Territory in the West, as mandated by the Indian Removal Act of 1830. In this assignment, Scott was plagued by insubordinate subordinates, green troops, and a chronic dearth of supplies; most of all, however, he was the victim of his own inflexible military thinking. Bitter experience in the War of 1812 had taught him to accept nothing less than total discipline from his troops, and that translated into strict adherence to conventional—that is, "European"— training, tactics, and formations. Although these were unsuited to the circumstances of the Seminole War, which was essentially a police action in a swampy wilderness, Scott refused to consider, let alone adopt and adapt, the kind of guerrilla tactics the Seminole warriors themselves employed. The result was a drawn-out, inconclusive, and costly campaign, which did not succeed in "removing" the Seminoles.

In 1838, Scott organized the removal of the Cherokees to Indian Territory, which he planned to carry out as humanely as possible. The removal, however, proved so infamous in its cruelty that the route of the march is known today by the name the Cherokees gave it: the Trail of Tears. In fairness to Scott, he was not present to enforce the execution of his operational plans because he was urgently recalled to Washington after he had taken the Cherokees only as far as Nashville, Tennessee. His new assignment was to deal with a border dispute between Maine and New Brunswick, Canada. Thanks to his calm skill as a negotiator, the so-called Aroostook War remained bloodless and was quickly resolved.

U.S.-MEXICAN WAR

In 1841, Scott was appointed general-in-chief of the U.S. Army. Over the next several years, looking toward 1848, this, combined with his demonstrated diplomatic skills, made him appear to the Whigs as an appealing choice for a run at the White House. In 1846, however, the United States went to war against Mexico, and Scott could think only of his duties as the senior commander of the army. Understandably, he believed that he was the man to lead that army into war, but he was also convinced that time was needed to prepare it for the task of fighting a foreign power whose military was much larger than that of the United States and, by reputation at least, was better trained and better equipped. President James Polk, however, would brook no delay, and when Scott balked, he simply asked Congress to authorize two new major generals to lead the army in an immediate invasion. Scott wrote to the president, protesting that "I do not deserve to place myself in the most perilous of all positions—a fire upon my rear from Washington, and the fire, in front, from the Mexicans."

Hailed as the "Great Pacificator" after he peacefully resolved the Aroostook War, Scott succeeded only in antagonizing President Polk, who kept him in Washington as he sent Major General Zachary Taylor to lead forces against Mexico. Taylor did well—so well that Polk feared his newly minted status as a military hero would make him an unbeatable rival for the presidency in 1848. Polk decided, therefore, to swallow his anger and dilute Taylor's fame by sending a second invasion force into Mexico under Scott, whom he considered less formidable as a future political rival. Besides, although Taylor was producing victories, he was insufficiently aggressive, having repeatedly failed to capitalize on his combat gains by pressing the war to a triumphant conclusion. Scott promised bigger results.

And he got them. Commanding the force designated the Southern Army, he rapidly eclipsed Taylor, the Northern Army commander. As aggressive as Taylor was cautious, Scott led the first amphibious landing in U.S. Army history, at Veracruz, Mexico, and fought a brilliant and dashing campaign to the very gates of Mexico City, moving so far and so fast that the Duke of Wellington pronounced the doom of the American army, which was operating far ahead of its lines of communication and supply. Scott's bold advance was, however, unstoppable, and he inflicted on the Mexican forces at the culminating Battle of Chapultepec (September 12–13, 1847) more than 2,600 casualties before going on to occupy Mexico City. Ulysses S. Grant, a captain serving in Scott's army, remarked that the general never had "a force equal to one-half of that opposed to him . . . yet he won every battle, he captured the capital, and conquered the government."

Scott urged a quick negotiation to conclude a treaty, since he feared that the imminent collapse of the Mexican government would delay an end to the war and perhaps suspend its resolution in limbo. Working with a junior State Department official, Nicholas Trist, Scott assumed a degree of plenipotentiary authority not only beyond anything President Polk had granted him, but of a kind and scope that would not be seen again until the likes of Dwight D. Eisenhower and Omar Bradley in World War II.

THE CIVIL WAR BEGINS

As President Polk had predicted, Zachary Taylor was the more formidable political candidate than Scott, who lost the Whig nomination for the presidency to him in 1848. Scott won the nomination in 1852 but lost the general election to Democrat Franklin Pierce. The chief problem was that while the Whigs supported the Constitutional status of slavery, Scott opposed it even though he was a Southerner. Thus, in the end, he suffered a loss of Northern votes (on account of his party's proslavery stance) as well as the

THE GAME-COCK & THE GOOSE.

Trading on his brilliant record in the U.S.–Mexican War, Winfield Scott ran for president as a Whig against Democrat Franklin Pierce. This political cartoon shows candidate Scott pulling ahead of Pierce, who was also a war hero. "What's the matter, Pierce? feel Faint?" Scott asks, referring to an incident in which Pierce collapsed on the field during the Battle of Churubusco. "Ha! ha! ha!" he continues, "lord what a Goose! don't you wish you had my Cock? Well good bye, Pierce, good bye." In fact, Pierce won the election to become the nation's fourteenth president. LIBRARY OF CONGRESS

loss of Southern votes (because of his personal antislavery position). Nevertheless, he remained the senior commander of the U.S. Army and was Union general-in-chief when the attack on Fort Sumter opened the Civil War on April 12 and 13, 1861.

There was great fear throughout the North that Scott, a Virginian, would resign his commission and throw in with the Confederacy. But if such a thought had ever occurred to him, he never expressed it. Although he had been defeated for the presidency, Scott went into the Civil War a national hero. Yet he knew better than anyone else that he had grown too old, too fat, and too infirm even to ride to the front, let alone into battle. A realist and a patriot, he offered a major command to the officer he wanted to put in line to take over for himself, Colonel Robert E. Lee, who had served him heroically and effectively in Mexico and whom he judged "the very best soldier [he] ever saw in the field."

Like Scott, Lee was a Virginian; unlike Scott, he believed his duty to Virginia trumped his duty to the United States and, like many other Southern officers, he resigned his commission, asking, "How can I draw my sword upon Virginia, my native state?" Hoping to persuade him, Scott met with Lee, and when he realized that there would be no changing his mind, he spoke with his customarily brutal frankness: "Lee, you have made the greatest mistake of your life. . . ."

SCOTT'S "ANACONDA"

Northerners and Southerners alike deluded themselves into believing the war would be sharp and short. Scott, the realist, told the politicians and the people what they did not want to hear: that the war would be hard and long. While his countrymen clamored for the kind of lightning campaign he had conducted in Mexico, Scott insisted that it was necessary to buy time to prepare the army for a full-scale invasion of the South. He proposed a strategy that would gain the time needed to build up the army even as it embodied the elements of a long-range plan to defeat the Confederacy. He identified as the key strategic objectives taking control of the Mississippi River and the major Atlantic and Gulf ports; once these had been seized, he called for moving against Atlanta, the overland transportation hub of the South, arguing that this was a far more important objective than Richmond, Virginia, the Confederate capital. Just as the Mississippi River and the seaports were the vital water courses of the South, Atlanta was the nexus of its rail network. Render all of these avenues of movement and supply unusable, he reasoned, and the South would be strangled. Moreover, victory would be achieved with a minimum of destruction and loss of life. Although the people and the politicians demanded an immediate and glorious overland invasion, Scott called for a massive and lusterless naval blockade with

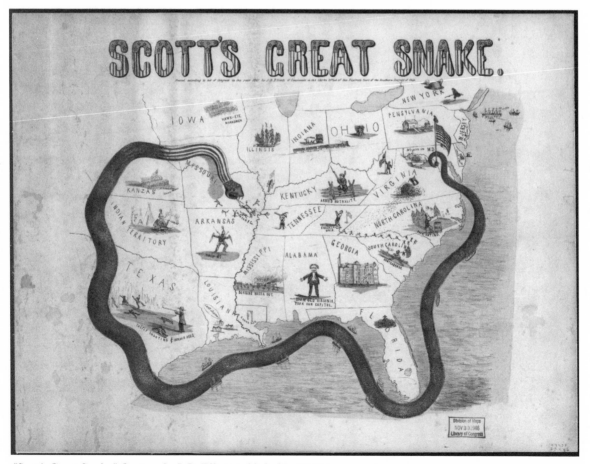

"Scott's Great Snake." Cartoon by J. B. Elliott published in 1861. LIBRARY OF CONGRESS

which he intended to constrict the Confederacy as an anaconda throttles its prey.

It was by no means a thoroughly realistic plan. The U.S. Navy, after all, was far too small to impose an adequate blockade against the entire Southern coast. But even acknowledging this, Scott insisted that the blockade would become increasingly effective as the navy built more ships. In any case, it was a plan more realistic than the pipe dream of ending the war with a single decisive battle. Although Scott was an admirer of Napoleon—whose military pronouncements he translated for the benefit of West Point cadets—and rigorously introduced Napoleonic tactics to the U.S. Army, he understood that such tactics were outmoded and unsuited to a civil war fought by large armies using more advanced weapons than Napoleon had. The "Anaconda

Plan," in contrast, was a very modern program for something akin to "total war," war against the very lifeblood of the South, yet without resorting to the full measure of human loss total war usually implies.

The press, politicians, the public, and even his fellow officers did not see it this way. They scorned the Anaconda Plan as dishonorable, even cowardly because it lacked the pomp, glory, and gore that befit gentlemen fighting a struggle over nationhood. We know now that, in its broadest outline and objectives, something very like the Anaconda Plan proved in the end to be the most effective overall strategy the Union adopted. By the time Ulysses S. Grant became the Union's general-in-chief on March 12, 1864, the South was struggling under an ever-expanding ocean blockade. Grant himself had been instrumental in seizing control of the Mississippi River, and he would soon send William T. Sherman on a campaign to seize and occupy Atlanta. Scott, however, resigned toward the end of the first year of the war, on November 1, 1861, turning over command (as ordered by President Lincoln) to George B. McClellan, whom the press hailed as the "Young Napoleon" but whose dilatory ineptitude would lengthen the war by years (Chapter 14). Nevertheless, the aged, ailing, and infirm Scott lived to 1866, long enough to witness the Union victory and to understand the role his plan had played in achieving it.

A hybrid of steam and sail, the USS Monongahela *was typical of U.S. Navy ships that served in Scott's "Anaconda" blockade.* FROM *THE PHOTOGRAPHIC HISTORY OF THE CIVIL WAR* (1911)

GEORGE B. MCCLELLAN

RATING: ⭐

Mathew Brady portrait of George B. McClellan. Dubbed the "Young Napoleon" by a hopeful Northern press, McClellan's hand in blouse may have been intended to emphasize the comparison; however, it was also a conventional pose in military portraits of the period.

NATIONAL ARCHIVES AND RECORDS ADMINISTRATION

EVALUATION

Extraordinarily intelligent, number two in his West Point class, universally praised as a brilliant organizer, beloved by his troops, and impressive to the public, George B. McClellan was nevertheless unsuited to large-unit combat command. Personally courageous, he was nevertheless chronically and pathologically inclined to magnify the challenges and obstacles he faced, to believe that those above him wished to see him fail, and, most of all, to wildly overestimate the strength of the enemy. These psychological defects prevented him from committing his troops to battle in a timely manner, which repeatedly resulted in tragically missed opportunities for decisive victories that would likely have shortened if not ended the Civil War before the close of its second year. A talented, earnest, humane officer, McClellan, evaluated in terms of the results he produced and did not produce, was the single most notable failure among the Union's high command.

Principal Battles

PRE–CIVIL WAR

U.S.-Mexican War, 1846–1848

- Contreras, August 19–20, 1847: Served as an engineer and was frequently under fire

- Churubusco, August 20, 1847: As at Contreras, McClellan served as an engineer; his gallantry here and at Contreras earned him a brevet promotion to first lieutenant

- Chapultepec, September 12–13, 1847: His hazardous reconnaissance mission for General Winfield Scott earned him a brevet to captain

Civil War

- Philippi, June 3, 1861: In present-day West Virginia; the first organized land action of the war, this skirmish was a victory for McClellan, who tended to exaggerate both its scope and significance

- Rich Mountain, July 11, 1861: In present-day West Virginia; a two-hour fight that soundly defeated a small Confederate force and brought McClellan to President Lincoln's attention

- Peninsula Campaign, March–July 1862: In Virginia; included the Siege of Yorktown, the Battles of Williamsburg, Eltham's Landing, Norfolk, Drewry's Bluff, Hanover Court House, and Seven Pines (aka Fair Oaks); this roundabout alternative to a direct assault on Richmond lost the Army of the Potomac valuable strategic initiative and certainly prolonged the war

- The Seven Days, June 25–July 1, 1862: In Virginia; in this set of battles ending the Peninsula Campaign—Oak Grove, Beaver Dam Creek (aka Mechanicsville), Gaines's Mill, Garnett's and Golding's Farm, Savage's Station, Glendale (aka Frayser's Farm), White Oak Swamp, and Malvern Hill—McClellan allowed Lee to drive his Army of the Potomac away from Richmond in a humiliating retreat down the Virginia Peninsula

- South Mountain, September 14, 1862: In Maryland; McClellan pursued Lee in an effort to drive him out of Maryland

- Antietam, September 17, 1862: In Maryland; in this, the bloodiest single-day battle in U.S. history, McClellan drove Lee out of Maryland but at great cost and without inflicting decisive damage on the Army of Northern Virginia

After the fall of Fort Sumter on April 13, 1861, the people of the North rallied behind such newspaper titans as *New York Daily Tribune* publisher Horace Greeley in demanding a single great stroke that would avenge the surrender and smash the Confederacy. Old Fuss and Feathers—some were now deriding him even more stridently as "Old Fuss and Feeble"—General Winfield Scott dared to push back against the clamor, arguing that the army was hardly big enough or fit enough to strike a decisive blow and warning that the war would be longer and bloodier than anyone imagined. No one wanted to hear this, and so Brigadier General Irvin McDowell was called on to do what Scott said could not be done.

McDowell was not an entirely unreasonable nominee for the job. Educated in France and at West Point (he graduated in the Class of 1836 alongside Pierre Gustave Toutant Beauregard, whom he was about to face in battle), McDowell was better trained than most U.S. Army officers and had seen combat in the U.S.-Mexican War, though not as a commander of troops in battle. Nevertheless, his climb up the officer

ranks, while not totally undeserved, had been due at least as much to his bosom friendship with Salmon P. Chase, Lincoln's powerful secretary of the treasury, as it was to any demonstration of actual military prowess. When he took charge of what the Union was calling its Army of Northeastern Virginia, McDowell was savvy enough to see that he had been given command of summer soldiers, green men and callow boys who had enlisted as if for a lark. In his private moments, he must have agreed with Scott: *They weren't ready*. But he could not stand up to the pressure of the politicians, who in turn could not resist the crush of their constituents, who called for a single bloody blow that would teach the rebels a lesson and finish the rebellion once and for all. What is more, as most Northerners saw it, this really wasn't asking for much.

THE SHOCK OF BULL RUN

McDowell the studious West Pointer drew up a brightly burnished plan of attack against the Confederate forces massed in northern Virginia, a stone's throw from Washington, at Manassas, along the Bull Run. It looked very good on paper but was burdened by classroom complexities far beyond the ability of his untutored troops and their scarcely better-prepared commanders to execute in the field. Still, by the third week in July 1861, McDowell had assembled at Alexandria, Virginia, the largest field army ever to muster on the North American continent to that time, thirty-five thousand men in blue. With numbers like these, how could they fail?

They could. They did. Bull Run ended in a humiliating Union rout on July 21, 1861.

McDowell's men had marched to battle at the leisurely pace that suited a soft summer day, many pausing to pick blackberries along the road, which was lined with fashionable Washingtonians, who had brought picnic lunches to enjoy while taking in the show that was about to begin. Now, the battle ended, the survivors—tired, frightened, demoralized troops—elbowed past the picnickers, who dropped baskets and jugs as they joined their defeated army in flight back to a capital that suddenly seemed under siege.

On July 22, the day after Bull Run, news came of two victories in western Virginia, at Philippi and Rich Mountain, won by a young, handsome Union general named George Brinton McClellan. Skirmishes rather than full-out battles, these wins paled in comparison to the catastrophe in northern Virginia—McClellan had inflicted perhaps ten casualties on the Confederates at Philippi and captured some five hundred Confederates at Rich Mountain, while the Confederates had killed, wounded, or captured nearly three thousand Union troops at Bull Run—but they were enough to prompt his urgent and hopeful summons to the capital. A special train was even dispatched to carry him. At Wheeling, Pittsburgh, and Philadelphia, as well as all the stops in between, the train was met by the shrill cheers of fevered throngs. Like a starving multitude at the sight of sustenance, a crowd hungry for the comforting news of victory mobbed him at the Washington station on July 26. Troops and Washington cops extricated him, then bundled him off to the White House. There President Abraham Lincoln took his hand and, without the delay of even the briefest ceremony, informed him that he was now commander of the Military Division of the Potomac. At the moment, this gave him responsibility chiefly for the defense of Washington, but McClellan understood that he was to use the division as the nucleus around which to build the major force of the Union army.

To his wife, Ellen Marcy McClellan, the new commander wrote, "I almost think that were I to win some small success now I could become Dictator or anything else that might please me." He was probably right. But what he wrote also revealed the sum of all that, in the end, made him unfit to command what would become the Army of the Potomac, the largest military formation ever raised on the continent to that time. For if "some small success" was all that was needed to elevate him to dictator, it was far short of what was needed to bring a quick and triumphant end to the Civil War. Reveling in the waves of adulation sweeping over him, McClellan nevertheless tragically underestimated the magnitude of his mission.

FROM WEST POINT TO WAR

But who could blame him? Born on December 3, 1826, into one of the leading families of Philadelphia, the son of a prominent physician, a pampered George McClellan was given a superb education at the preparatory school of the University of Pennsylvania and then, when he was only thirteen, possessed of an intellect just short of outright genius, was enrolled in the university itself. After two years of classes there, in which he was a standout, the fifteen-year-old McClellan was nominated to West Point, the realization of a dream to which he had first given voice at age ten. So impressed was the academy's board that it waived the minimum age requirement and admitted the lad.

The most promising West Point cadets were tapped for commissions in the Corps of Engineers, and McClellan, who graduated in 1846, second out of a class of fifty-eight, which included future Confederates Thomas "Stonewall" Jackson (seventeenth) and George Pickett (dead last), was so assigned. As is not always true in the case of overachievers, McClellan's classmates adored the young man. As one of them, William Gardner, later remarked, "We predicted real military fame for him."

Certainly the gods of martial destiny smiled on Second Lieutenant McClellan and the other graduates of 1846, who found that they had emerged into the biggest war the U.S. Army had fought since 1812, the war with Mexico, which prompted a two-fold increase in the size of the army and opportunities for glory to everyone smart and bold enough to seize them.

If McClellan assumed he would be marching from the West Point parade ground directly to Mexico, he was mistaken, however. His first assignment was local, as an aide to an engineer officer, tasked with helping him to train troops. Four long months would pass before he shipped out for Brazos de Santiago, where he served in the Southern Army under Winfield Scott. As an engineer, he was put to work drawing maps, a critically important function in Scott's fast- and far-moving army but one that kept him out of much of the hottest action, the kind of combat that made a young officer's military reputation and put him on the high road to rapid promotion. He did at last find himself in the midst of combat at the Battle of Contreras (August 19–20, 1847) on the outskirts of Mexico City. McClellan had two horses shot from under him by Mexican pickets, then was blown off his feet by Mexican artillery fire after he had taken over command of a howitzer when the battery officer fell mortally wounded. Brigadier General Persifer F. Smith, his commanding officer, singled him out in his after-action report, remarking that "nothing seemed . . . too bold to be undertaken, or too difficult to be executed." He was brevetted to first lieutenant for "gallant and meritorious conduct," and distinguished himself again, at the Battles of Molino del Rey (September 8, 1847) and Chapultepec (September 12–13, 1847), for which he was brevetted to captain.

After the burst of strenuous glory that was the U.S.-Mexican War, many of the newly minted West Point officers were cast down by the dreary dearth of opportunity that followed in the peacetime army. Unable to advance in their military careers, the likes of William Tecumseh Sherman and Ulysses S. Grant resigned their commissions early in the 1850s. Captain McClellan, however, managed to find opportunity. He taught engineering at West Point from 1848 to 1851, then supervised the construction of Fort Delaware near Delaware City before transferring from the Corps of Engineers to the cavalry and joining

Major Randolph Marcy in his Red River Expedition of 1852, an effort to discover the source of that strategic western waterway. Two years later, twenty-seven-year-old McClellan met Marcy's daughter, Ellen Mary Marcy, an eighteen-year-old beauty with whom he fell instantly in love. "I have not seen a very great deal of the little lady," he wrote to her mother, "still that little has been sufficient to make me determined to win her if I can." Greatly impressed with McClellan, Major and Mrs. Marcy did their best to prevail on Ellen, but neither they nor the captain himself could move the girl. She was in love with Lieutenant Ambrose Powell Hill—a dashing young officer who would go on to be a general in Robert E. Lee's Army of Northern Virginia.

INTO THE CRIMEA AND OUT OF THE ARMY

It must have seemed hopeless, but McClellan was undeterred. He believed that, in time, Ellen's heart would open to him. This attitude was typical of a man who, increasingly, was coming to believe that God had chosen him for great things and that he had only to wait for his destiny to unfold. As if to confirm this, in April 1855, the United States secretary of war, Jefferson Davis, himself a hero of the war with Mexico—and destined to become the first and last president of the Confederate States of America—quietly summoned Captain McClellan to his office in Washington. There McClellan was joined by Richard Delafield, an engineer and former superintendent of West Point, and Alfred Mordecai, an ordnance specialist. Davis told the three men that they were to consider themselves an official commission to visit the remote Crimean peninsula, where Britain, France, and the Ottoman Empire were at war against Russia. The commission's assignment was to discover just how modern Europeans fought their wars. Davis wanted to know about logistics (including camel transport), about medical provisions, and about artillery, especially a "secret weapon" the British were said to have, a rifled cannon with a radical elliptical bore dubbed the "Lancaster gun."

Delafield and Mordecai were recognized experts in their fields, but Davis had chosen McClellan, a promising officer who had yet to make his mark, over Robert E. Lee, the most distinguished engineer in the U.S. Army. In fact, Lee was both surprised and disappointed at being passed over. Clearly, there was something about McClellan that impressed people well beyond any actual achievements.

In the end, the trio of commissioners produced very little of value as a result of their tour of observation—though McClellan, inspired by a European military saddle he saw, modified its design slightly and produced a prototype that the U.S. Army quickly adopted. Soon, the "McClellan Saddle" became the cavalry standard. Later, he also introduced the shelter tent—popularly known as the "pup tent"—to the army, and he translated and edited the French bayonet and drill manuals for American use. But concerning modern warfare, which should have been the central object of the commission's study, neither McClellan nor his colleagues took away any significant insights. Nevertheless, feeling himself propelled by his own rising star, McClellan did not think twice before haughtily lecturing the secretary of war on precisely how the U.S. cavalry should be reorganized. Davis, who had been impressed with McClellan, now chafed at what he took to be his insolence. The two exchanged curt letters, and before the end of 1856, Captain George Brinton McClellan tendered his resignation from the United States Army.

CIVILIAN TRIUMPHS

In January 1857, McClellan, out of uniform now, was hired as chief engineer for the Illinois Central Railroad at the splendid yearly salary of $3,000. Within two years, he was vice president of the company and, in the course of his work,

became acquainted with Abraham Lincoln, who had been engaged by the railroad off and on since 1853 as a high-level attorney. McClellan also came to know Chicago private detective Allan J. Pinkerton, whom he hired to investigate a series of train robberies that had plagued the railroad. He would call on Pinkerton during the war to furnish intelligence during his major campaigns.

In 1860, McClellan left the Illinois Central to become president of the eastern division of the Ohio and Mississippi Railroad. Armed with a spectacular $10,000 salary, he resumed his pursuit of Ellen Marcy. In actuality, she had already accepted the proposal of A. P. Hill. This, however, provoked a campaign from both her parents. Her father warned her that Hill was a poor man as well as a Southerner, who supported slavery. Her mother took a more dramatic approach, disseminating rumors, which she knew would come back to her daughter, to the effect that Hill suffered from a sexually transmitted disease. To his credit, when McClellan became aware of the rumor, he wrote Mrs. Marcy to defend Hill, whom he called an honorable man and even a dear friend. Nevertheless, between the prospect of poverty, slavery, and VD, Ellen Marcy at last changed her mind. She accepted McClellan's proposal, and, in a transport of joy, he ratified in his own mind what he had long believed: God had a very special plan for him. He even became a devoted member of the Presbyterian Church.

Then, in April 1861, after the fall of Fort Sumter, he also became a member, once again, of the United States Army. He reentered the force initially as major general of Ohio volunteers, but the next month was commissioned a major general of regulars and assigned to command the Department of the Ohio. The only army officer senior to him was Winfield Scott himself.

GREAT EXPECTATIONS

Scott, Lincoln, and McClellan himself had every reason to believe that he would perform admirably. Gallant in battle, a brilliant West Point graduate who had seen European war-fighting close up, and, as a railroad executive, versed in the military potential of rail transportation, the commander his soon-to-be adoring soldiers would nickname "Little Mac"—he stood five-foot-eight, but his disproportionately short legs made him seem much shorter over-all—seemed nevertheless to tower head and shoulders over the great majority of officers, Union or Confederate.

As commander of Ohio forces, McClellan was assigned to a theater of war removed from the eastern seaboard, where the most intense action was about to take place. His mission was to clear out Confederate resistance in western Virginia, an area with strong Union sympathies (which, sometime after Virginia seceded, would break away and declare loyalty to the United States as the state of *West* Virginia). He scored easy victories against small forces at Philippi on June 3 and Rich Mountain on July 11, which moved *The New York Times* to predict (in a most peculiar turn of phrase) that McClellan, "wise and brave," had "a future behind him."

Appointed in the wake of Bull Run to command what would become the Army of the Potomac, he basked in public clamor for a hero and savior but hardly rushed to become either. Instead of leading his army straight into battle, he devoted the rest of the summer and early autumn of 1861 to building it, organizing it, and training it. At the same time, he went about the work of transforming Washington into a fortress city, ringing it with forty-eight strong points and a number of full-scale forts. Collectively, the capital's defenses bristled with nearly five hundred cannon, many of which, doubtless, would have been of more use in the field. But President Lincoln did not complain. He knew that to lose Washington to a Confederate attack would be to lose the war. Besides, the press had taken to calling "Little Mac" the "Young Napoleon," and who was the president, installed in the White House by a mere electoral plurality, not a majority, to argue with popular acclaim?

If McClellan was popular with the public, he made himself adored by his troops. He secured for the Army of the Potomac the best equipment, accommodations, and food he could requisition. He mingled with his men, demanding much of them in training and drill but also developing an extraordinary rapport. In an age that regarded soldiers as so much cannon fodder, McClellan made it clear that he cared about his troops—and it was no act; he really did care about them.

Even as he drilled and trained the soldiers he had, McClellan sent appeal after appeal to General Scott to lay aside the "Anaconda," his strategy of slow strangulation through naval blockade while gradually building up an army of invasion, and instead hurl everything into one force, namely the Army of the Potomac. As it approached one hundred thousand men, it was already the largest single military formation on the continent, but what McClellan insisted on having was a force of 273,000 and an artillery park of some six hundred guns. General Scott had come of age during the Napoleonic Wars, and he was a great admirer of Napoleon, having spent much of his early career in an effort to bring Napoleonic tactics and doctrine to the United States Army. Yet he knew enough about Napoleon to understand that the strategy and tactics of Austerlitz and Marengo would not work in the context of a civil war. Victory, he believed, had to be conceived in more than military terms. He did not want to pound the South into submission—such pounding would only make the people more determined in their resistance—but instead strangle and starve it, sapping both their will and their ability to fight before everything had been destroyed. Hence the blockade. McClellan, in contrast, believed that God had anointed him the Young Napoleon, and he needed all those men to stage one grand Napoleonic battle, an American Austerlitz that would crush the army of secession in a single blow.

To McClellan's credit, the notion of fighting an apocalyptic battle that would end the rebellion by wiping out its army did have the same objective as Scott's Anaconda: to end the war quickly and in a way that would do as little harm to the people of the South as possible. But it was based on the assumption that, once the Confederate army had been defeated, the people would end their rebellion. He took Lincoln at his word that the war was not a crusade against slavery, but a fight to restore the lawful Union. Neutralize the rebellion's army, therefore, and the Union would be restored. Unlike McClellan, Scott believed that the source of this civil war ran much deeper, which meant that the war could be won only by making it difficult or impossible for anyone, soldier or citizen, to continue fighting. In any case, both Scott and Lincoln understood that McClellan's request for a single force of nearly three hundred thousand men was impractical (if not impossible) for at least two reasons. First, it would take an inordinately long time to assemble and train such a force without committing it to battle. The Confederates would doubtless use this time to win victories intended to sap the will of the North to continue the war. It was unthinkable not to take aggressive action against the rebels as soon as possible. The army of the South could not be permitted to invade the North at will while generals bided their time building an idle army. Second, no single American general had ever tried to command a force so large. Even Napoleon himself discovered that the massive army he led into Russia in 1812 was beyond effective command. There was no reason to believe that this "Young Napoleon" would have fared better.

SAVED BY A SCAPEGOAT

So the message to McClellan was to fight with the army he had, yet to this message McClellan wordlessly replied by continuing to train it rather than commit it to battle. As the tension over McClellan's reluctance to fight increased, this officer who had such rapport with subordinates and soldiers turned bitterly against the one commander who was above him. He spoke openly of Winfield Scott as "a traitor, or an incompetent," complaining that he was being forced to "fight [his] way against him." Scott heard the complaints. Old and tired, he had no desire to challenge McClellan and therefore tendered his resignation to the president. Lincoln refused to accept it, but then he began to hear—albeit never directly from the Young Napoleon himself—that McClellan meant to resign if Scott did not step down. The rumors increased in volume and intensity. If Old Fuss and Feathers remained general-in-chief, McClellan, for the good of the nation, would lead a military coup!

Lincoln convened an emergency Cabinet meeting on October 18. Scott's resignation had been tendered; the Cabinet decided the president had better accept it. And so he did. The change of command would become official on November 1, but McClellan had immediate authority to act as chief.

What, then, would George McClellan, now general-in-chief of the U.S. Army, do with his unchallenged authority?

Far less than anyone expected.

On October 19, he sent a single division under Brigadier General George A. McCall to Dranesville, Virginia, not to fight a battle, but to gingerly probe Confederate movements there and around Leesburg. This accomplished, he immediately ordered McCall back to the division's main camp at Langley, Virginia, a few miles from the capital. No shots had been fired. In the meantime, he dispatched Brigadier General Charles Stone on another timid mission, to stage what he called "a slight demonstration" that was intended to provoke a Confederate response. In obedience to the tentative tone of the order, Stone sent a small force across the Potomac at Edwards Ferry. When the Confederates failed to react to this, he pulled the unit back but simultaneously ordered the commander of the 15th Massachusetts Infantry to send a twenty-man night patrol to reconnoiter the enemy position. In the darkness, Captain Chase Philbrick, the inexperienced leader of the patrol, mistook a stand of trees for Confederate tents and withdrew to regimental headquarters to report them. With a force of three hundred, Colonel Charles Devens attacked the trees at dawn on October 21. Realizing Philbrick's error, but having crossed the river with his raiding party, Devens decided to wait for instructions from General Stone before he turned back. Stone responded by sending the rest of 15th Massachusetts—350 more men—to join the raiding party and march with it toward Leesburg for a reconnaissance there. In the meantime, Edward Dickinson Baker, a U.S. senator *and* a Union colonel, arrived in Stone's camp. The general bade him welcome and promptly dispatched him to find out just what Devens was doing. Stone entrusted him with the authority either to withdraw the troops from Virginia altogether or to send in more.

While he was riding to Devens's position, Baker learned that a skirmish was under way. Itching for a fight, he ordered as many troops as could be quickly rounded up to cross the Potomac. Possessing more experience as a senator than as a colonel, he had not stopped to consider that very few boats were available to transport troops across the river. This resulted in a trickle of forces from one bank to another, even as the fighting heated up on the Confederate side of the river, at a place called Ball's Bluff, a thickly wooded, steep-sided hill thirty miles upriver from Washington. As the fire intensified, Baker was hit and fell dead, the only serving U.S. senator killed in action before or since.

Product of McClellan's timid, tentative orders from on high, the battle suddenly exploded, catching the mass of Devens's men, about 650 of them, huddled atop the steep bluff, without room to maneuver. The shortage of boats that

had impeded the arrival of reinforcements now bottled up the retreat back across the Potomac. Frantic troops were trapped on top of Ball's Bluff as well as between the bluff and the river.

That is when the 17th Mississippi Regiment arrived, charged up the bluff, and drove all the Union boys headlong down its steep slope. At bayonet point, the men ran, many leaping from the bluff, landing atop one another. Men impaled themselves grotesquely on the bayonets of those who had jumped before them. In an ecstasy of fear, soldiers piled into their pitiful few boats, overloading and swamping most of them. Soon, the lazy current of the Potomac carried the drowned and bloodied bodies to Washington.

Ball's Bluff was not a big battle, not compared to Bull Run or the titanic struggles that were yet to come; 223 Union troops were killed, 226 wounded, and 553 captured. But its effect on the psyche of the Lincoln government was devastating. The death of Senator Baker, a close friend of the president's, hit hard. The same Congress that fretted over a McClellan coup now speculated that Baker had not been killed in battle so much as assassinated in a conspiracy to undermine the Union. Although the Constitution exclusively assigns the president as commander in chief of the armed forces, Congress immediately created a Joint Committee on the Conduct of the War to look over the president's shoulder. Without consulting Lincoln, the committee haled General Stone to the Capitol, demanding that he explain the Ball's Bluff disaster. Unsatisfied with what it heard, the committee ordered Stone's arrest and imprisonment on "suspicion" (he was never actually charged) of treason.

Had the committee worked back from Stone, the failure of Ball's Bluff would have landed at the feet of the Young Napoleon himself. But the injustice meted out to Stone was an undeserved vindication for his commanding officer. With Stone neatly scapegoated, McClellan emerged from his biggest battle yet defeated but unscathed.

"GENERAL WAR ORDER NO. 1"

As the Civil War entered its second year, the Army of the Potomac, gigantic and magnificent, had almost nothing to show for itself. When Lincoln had made him general-in-chief of the U.S. Army, McClellan assured him, "I can do it all," then, that evening as almost every evening, he sat down to write to his wife. "Who would have thought," he mused, "when we were married, that I should so soon be called upon to save my country?" Despite the inaction, the Union public, most of it, still looked to the Young Napoleon for salvation. To the west, in Tennessee, in a theater of the war most people thought of as secondary to the battlefields of Virginia, the Battle of Shiloh (April 6–7, 1862) had just produced some thirteen thousand Union casualties, killed, wounded, and captured, earning Ulysses S. Grant widespread opprobrium and giving the public someone other than McClellan to blame for the tragic state of the war's conduct.

But on January 31, 1862, President Lincoln had issued his "General War Order No. 1," directing McClellan to begin an offensive against the enemy no later than February 22. When McClellan missed this deadline, Lincoln, despite continued support for McClellan among the public as well as from his own soldiers, relieved him on March 11 as general-in-chief of the armies, returning him to command of the Army of the Potomac only. The president hoped this sharp slap would prompt him to advance from Washington to Richmond. As Lincoln saw it, the logic of attacking Richmond directly was this: Menacing the capital of the South would force the Confederate armies to come to its defense, which meant that they would have to pull back and yield territory to Union control. Moreover, in the process of withdrawing, the armies would be vulnerable; turning one's back on an enemy was always dangerous.

But McClellan had a different idea. Instead of advancing overland against Richmond, he proposed transporting the entire Army of the Potomac by steamers down the Chesapeake Bay to the James River for an amphibious landing south of Confederate general Joseph E. Johnston's lines at Manassas, site of the Bull Run battle. By this movement, he intended to outflank Johnston's army, forcing it to pull back from Washington, which would free up reinforcements from the defense of the capital to join the Army of the Potomac in the field. With his force thus augmented, McClellan promised to carry out his attack against Richmond. Lincoln believed this approach was overly cautious. He understood that the longer McClellan waited to menace Richmond, the more time the Confederate armies would have to strengthen the city's defenses and the harder a target the Confederate capital would become. Nevertheless, pressured by subordinate officers who idolized McClellan, Lincoln endorsed the plan.

Neither Lincoln nor McClellan—who should have known better—figured on how much time would be consumed in embarking on a vast amphibious operation. McClellan was just getting under way when he learned that Johnston had left Manassas and marched south, to the Rappahannock River, closer to Richmond. When McClellan and his army finally reached Manassas and inspected the abandoned Confederate trenches there, they found them bristling with what they dubbed "Quaker guns," logs painted dull black to mimic cannon. "Our enemies," a reporter wrote, "like the Chinese, have frightened us by the sound of gongs and the wearing of devils' masks."

Of course, McClellan could point out that the enemy had withdrawn, yielding territory without firing a shot. The fact, however, was that Johnston was deliberately luring McClellan farther from his sources of supply and reinforcement to fight the consolidated bulk of the Confederate army in its home territory. Had McClellan followed Lincoln's original orders and attacked Richmond directly, he would have faced a much smaller enemy force.

McClellan had delayed in large part because he believed that the Confederate army vastly outnumbered him. Although he had been trained as an *engineer* to deal with hard facts, as a *combat commander* those very facts were consistently magnified in his imagination into wild overestimates of enemy numbers. In an effort to obtain accurate estimates, he extensively employed Allan J. Pinkerton, whose network of spies fed him an endless stream of numbers, all, unfortunately, as far off the mark as his own imagination. The figures Pinkerton delivered were inflated by factors of two or three, sometimes even more.

THE PENINSULA CAMPAIGN

Unable to accept the fact that *he* actually outnumbered Johnston all along, McClellan decided to continue avoiding a frontal attack on Richmond. Instead, he proposed to ferry his troops south to Fort Monroe, near Newport News and Hampton Roads, in the southeastern corner of Virginia. This would take him *south* of Richmond, so that he would advance *north* toward this objective, moving across the Yorktown Peninsula, which separated the York River from the James. His rationale was that by attacking Richmond from the south, he would force the Confederate capital's defenders to maneuver toward the north, which would present an opportunity to envelop both Richmond and the Confederate army in Virginia. The Young Napoleon dubbed the operation the Peninsula Campaign, echoing, intentionally or not, Napoleon Bonaparte's celebrated though ultimately failed "Peninsular War." But planning the biggest amphibious operation in American military history to that time consumed precious days and weeks, during which Johnston further

In the Battle of Fair Oaks during the Peninsula Campaign, McClellan hired balloonist Professor Thaddeus S. Lowe to do battlefield reconnaissance and observation from his tethered balloon Intrepid. The hydrogen-filled captive balloon seemed to McClellan a promising alternative to the rickety observation towers commanders often constructed, especially for artillery spotting.
LIBRARY OF CONGRESS

consolidated his position, making it a much tougher nut to crack.

On April 9, 1862, a supremely frustrated Lincoln wrote a letter: "It is called the Army of the Potomac but it is only McClellan's body-guard. . . . If McClellan is not using the army, I should like to borrow it for a while." He never sent it, but instead folded it and put it in his desk drawer.

In the meantime, at Yorktown, McClellan, as usual concluding that he was badly outnum-bered, decided to lay siege to the Confederate line rather than storm it. By the time McClellan set up his siege, Johnston had withdrawn all but fifteen thousand men from Yorktown. The wily Confederate general John Bankhead "Prince John" Magruder marched these men back and forth and back and forth to give the illusion of far greater numbers. Although he commanded some ninety thousand men, McClellan was thoroughly intimidated. He could have swal-lowed Magruder's entire command. Instead, he wasted a month, during which Robert E. Lee greatly strengthened the fortifications of Rich-mond, continuing to make it an ever more for-midable objective.

"THE SLOWS"

In one of the Peninsula Campaign battles, Seven Pines (May 31–June 1, 1862), General John-ston was so badly wounded that Robert E. Lee replaced him. A jubilant McClellan wrote to Lincoln that Lee was "cautious . . . weak . . . and . . . irresolute." But after going up against him in the so-called Seven Days Battles (June 25–July 1, 1862), he found out otherwise. At great cost to both sides—greater to the Confederacy than to the Union—Lee pushed McClellan northward, away from Richmond. The Peninsula Campaign cost the Army of the Potomac a total of sixteen thousand killed and wounded, lives spent in *los-ing* ground. McClellan sought to defend his per-formance by arguing that Lee's casualties were

much higher, totaling nearly twenty thousand. Yet the fact was that morale remained high in the South, while it eroded in the North. When McClellan protested that Lincoln and his secre-tary of war, Edwin Stanton, had withheld from him the reinforcements that he needed, Lincoln responded by putting McClellan under Major General John Pope, who was assigned com-mand of a catchall force called the Army of Vir-ginia, which effectively subsumed the Army of the Potomac and all other forces in and around Virginia. It was a much-deserved vote of no confidence against McClellan, but it resulted in protest and grumbling from the multitude of officers and men intensely loyal to him, and when Pope suffered a catastrophic defeat at the Second Battle of Bull Run (August 28–30, 1862), Lincoln formally restored McClellan to full command of the Army of the Potomac on September 1, 1862.

Some in Lincoln's Cabinet protested. The president admitted that while McClellan was competent in the defense, he had "the 'slows,'" which made him "good for nothing for an onward movement [offensive campaign]." Yet, Lincoln continued, he possessed "beyond any officer the confidence of the army." For this rea-son, despite the deficiencies Lincoln knew only too well, he believed that McClellan's "organiz-ing powers" had to be "made temporarily avail-able until the troops were rallied." More bluntly, he concluded: "There is no man in the army who can lick these troops of ours into shape half as well as he."

Of his reinstatement, the Young Napoleon wrote to his wife: "Again I have been called upon to save the country."

And now that country needed saving more than ever before.

On September 5, Robert E. Lee went on the offensive, marching across the Potomac and invading Maryland. The invasion plan was laid out in Lee's Special Order No. 191, which he distributed to his chief lieutenants, including

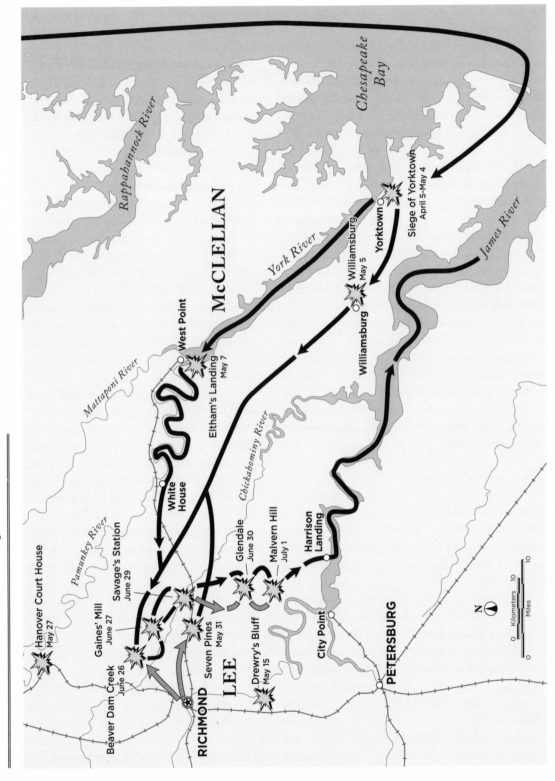

PENINSULA CAMPAIGN – APRIL 5–JUNE 1, 1862

Rappahannock River

Chesapeake Bay

Mattaponi River

James River

York River

McCLELLAN

West Point

Eltham's Landing
May 7

Williamsburg
May 5

Williamsburg

Yorktown

Siege of Yorktown
April 5–May 4

Chickahominy River

Pamunkey River

White House

Hanover Court House
May 27

Gaines' Mill
June 27

Savage's Station
June 29

Glendale
June 30

Malvern Hill
July 1

Harrison
Landing

Beaver Dam Creek
June 26

Seven Pines
May 31

RICHMOND

LEE

Drewry's Bluff
May 15

City Point

PETERSBURG

N

Kilometers   10

Miles   10

Stonewall Jackson, who had the order copied for General Daniel Harvey Hill. This copy was somehow discarded by Hill or lost before he received it, and on September 13, 1862, Union private W. B. Mitchell, 27th Indiana Infantry, while scrounging on what had been Hill's campsite, ran across a bunch of cigars wrapped in a piece of paper. Mitchell was most interested in the cigars, but he took time to examine the document, recognized that it might be important, and passed it up the chain of command. When McClellan received it, he exclaimed, "Here is a paper with which, if I cannot whip Bobby Lee, I will be willing to go home."

According to the plan, Lee intended to divide his forces—always a risky move in enemy territory. It was now up to McClellan to devise a counterattack that would defeat Lee in detail, before his divided forces could reunite.

Wonderful!

And then the familiar habits of doubt once again assailed George McClellan, who, as usual, fully believed he was massively outnumbered. He also took to heart a warning from the new army general-in-chief, Major General Henry Wager "Old Brains" Halleck, that this "lost order" might be a trick. Instead of making a decisive counterattack, therefore, McClellan timidly sent forces to probe three gaps in South Mountain on September 14. Stiff resistance from Hill bought Lee enough time to establish the main part of his army west of Antietam Creek, near the town of Sharpsburg. Still, McClellan almost managed to pull out of the situation a decisive victory with a planned three-pronged assault designed to hit both of Lee's flanks in preparation for a coup de grace attack on Lee's center. The plan was sound, but a combination of McClellan's continued timidity and the inability of his subordinates to execute the plan in a coordinated manner caused it to falter when the attack stepped off on September 17.

Of the nearly 75,500 men McClellan committed to battle, 2,108 were killed, 9,540 were wounded, and 753 were captured or went missing. Lee, who commanded no more than 38,000, saw 1,546 killed, 7,752 wounded, and 1,018 captured or missing. From a tactical point of view, McClellan secured a draw. Viewed strategically, however, Antietam was a Union victory because McClellan succeeded in ending the invasion by driving Lee off the field and out of Maryland. But McClellan had missed a much larger strategic opportunity, nothing less than the destruction of Lee's Army of Northern Virginia, which surely would have hastened the end of the Civil War. Although sick with yet another disappointment, Lincoln seized on what limited success McClellan had given him. With his general, Lincoln proclaimed Antietam a victory and used it as the occasion, to proclaim on September 23, 1862, the emancipation of the slaves throughout the Confederacy.

"You Will Immediately Turn Over Your Command"

Looking from the Emancipation Proclamation and back to George McClellan, Lincoln urged him to return to Virginia. McClellan responded that he needed time for the Army of the Potomac to recover from Antietam, then let more than a week pass without taking action. On October 1, the president wrote a formal order, commanding McClellan to "cross the Potomac and give battle to the enemy." Still, the general did nothing. A week later, Lincoln demanded to know why he had not obeyed the order. McClellan testily responded that his cavalry horses were exhausted. "Will you pardon me for asking," the president shot back, "what the horses of your army have done since the battle of Antietam that fatigues anything?"

McClellan at last got under way but moved so slowly that Lee easily interposed his Army of Northern Virginia between the approaching Army of the Potomac and Richmond. On November 5, the Union's new general-in-chief, Henry Halleck, sent McClellan a telegram: "On

Civil War field photographer Alexander Gardner turned his camera on this Union burial crew at work after the Battle of Antietam.

U.S. NATIONAL PARK SERVICE

receipt of the order of the President, sent herewith, you will immediately turn over your command to Major General Burnside. . . ." It was all over for the Young Napoleon.

HEARTBREAK

George Brinton McClellan never admitted failure. For the rest of his life, he portrayed Antietam as a great victory and any defeats he had suffered earlier as the result of Washington's refusal to furnish him with the men he demanded.

Viewed more objectively, on the positive side, McClellan had indeed taken a heavy toll on Confederate manpower, and while the North, with its greater wealth and much larger population, could make up the losses it incurred, the South could not. If the Civil War were evaluated solely as a war of attrition, McClellan did produce significant gains. Additionally, he transformed a dispirited rabble into a genuine army—only to expose that army to one brutal heartbreak after another.

On the negative side, McClellan failed to win the war, which, more than once, he might have done. Despite the waste of lives and missed opportunities, he remained popular with his men—decreasingly so with the public—and his relief and replacement created an abundance of bad blood in the army that may well have contributed to the difficulties that beset Ambrose Burnside and culminated in the catastrophic defeat he suffered at Fredericksburg (December 11–15, 1862). In November 1864, McClellan, a Democrat, tried to defeat Lincoln's reelection bid, but lost by a wide margin. After resigning his commission, he traveled in Europe for a time, worked as chief engineer for the New York City Department of Docks (1870–1873), was a trustee and subsequently president of the Atlantic & Great Western Railroad (1871–1872), then served as governor of New Jersey (1877–1881). He was only fifty-eight when he suffered a fatal heart attack on October 29, 1885.

Chapter 15

John Pope

RATING: ★ ★

Mathew Brady portrait of Brigadier General John Pope, probably taken in 1861. Library of Congress

Evaluation

Bright, politically well connected, educated in the military art, brave, enterprising, and inventive, John Pope was also arrogant, abrasive, and, as a young officer, hyper-ambitious, with a remarkable facility for offending subordinates, colleagues, and superiors alike. His success against fixed fortifications on the Mississippi River was of great strategic significance, but his subsequent failure to weld the Army of Virginia into an effective fighting force and to work collaboratively with other generals contributed to his ignominious defeat at the Second Battle of Bull Run (a Union disaster that dwarfed the comeuppance of the First Battle of Bull Run) and cost him his command in the Eastern Theater.

Principal Battles

PRE-CIVIL WAR

U.S.-Mexican War, 1846–1848

- Monterrey, September 21–24, 1846: Distinguished himself in what was often hand-to-hand combat
- Buena Vista, February 22–23, 1847: Served on Zachary Taylor's staff in this battle

CIVIL WAR

- Island No. 10, February 28–April 8, 1862: In Missouri; brilliant victory that seized a key Mississippi River fortification
- Second Bull Run, August 28–30, 1862: In Virginia; the catastrophic defeat that led to Pope's "exile" to a command effectively outside of the war zone
- Chantilly, September 1, 1862: In Virginia; Pope's game but unsuccessful counterattack after Second Bull Run

INDIAN WARS, 1862–1867

- Pope proved to be one of the more capable of the army's Indian-fighting commanders

RECONSTRUCTION

- Military governor, Third Military District (comprising Georgia, Florida, and Alabama), 1867: His adherence to Radical Republican Reconstruction policy prompted President Andrew Johnson to replace him with George Gordon Meade in December

INDIAN WARS

- From 1867 until his retirement in 1886, Pope variously directed the prosecution of the Indian Wars and police operations against Boomers (white squatters) in Indian Territory (Oklahoma).

Sometimes accused of executing a genocidal policy toward Plains Indians, especially the Sioux, Pope vigorously administered operations designed to evict squatters from reservation lands

A story buzzed throughout the Union army in 1862 that Major General John Pope made it a practice to preface all his written orders with the phrase "Headquarters in the Saddle." In response to this extraordinary piece of pomposity, some wag—no one knows who for sure—remarked that this precisely described the general's chief weakness: He had his headquarters where his hindquarters should be.

Repeat any story often enough, and a lot of people will simply assume it's true. That this particular article of apocrypha was so readily taken for gospel in the case of Pope speaks volumes about his personality: haughty, bombastic, abrasive, and contemptuous. John Pope of the Union army vies with Jubal Early of the Confedeerate army for the dubious honor of being deemed the least loved general of the Civil War, and his unpopularity greatly magnified his flaws as a commander.

Not that there weren't plenty of flaws to magnify. Nevertheless, like George B. McClellan, whom he unofficially displaced if not replaced, Pope showed so much early promise that there was every reason to believe—albeit briefly—that he was the man to bring the Civil War to a quick and victorious end.

A Career Begins

John Pope was born on March 16, 1822, in Louisville, Kentucky, but the family soon moved to Kaskaskia, Illinois, and John was raised there. Nathaniel Pope, his father, was a federal judge, a good friend of Abraham Lincoln, and an early and prominent member of the Republican Party. He was also an inveterate land speculator, and although he and his cultured wife, Lucretia, gave their son a far better education than what other children in the neighborhood received, they

could not afford to send John to college when the time came because the family's land investments all collapsed. Not to be thwarted, Nathaniel drew on his political connections, calling on Mary Todd Lincoln's brother-in-law, Ninian Wirt Edwards, son of the late Senator Ninian Edwards of Illinois, to help secure young John an appointment to the U.S. Military Academy at West Point. The sixteen-year-old enrolled in the Class of 1842 on March 20, 1838.

John Pope entered the academy with an especially complex chip on his shoulder. He had imbibed from his parents a sense of cultural superiority and social entitlement as well as the righteousness of committed abolitionism. Yet he was too poor to attend a civilian college. Moreover, while he had been educated well beyond the level of the typical Kaskaskia boy, he found himself at West Point suddenly surrounded by seaboard-raised cadets who were much more sophisticated and better prepared than he. At the same time, his father made no secret of his own expectations, which were for John to graduate first in his class. This combination of forces both stressed and drove Cadet Pope, who struggled, but struggled effectively, and while he won no close friends among his classmates, he did manage to claw his way to seventeenth place in a class of fifty-six, even earning the number-one slot among his peers in horsemanship. Although fellow 1842 graduate James Longstreet, future I Corps commander of the Confederate Army of Northern Virginia, pronounced him (despite a tendency to stoutness) a "handsome, dashing fellow" and a "splendid cavalryman," Pope shunned the cavalry and embraced what his respectable class standing qualified him for, a commission in the Corps of Engineers.

Although the engineers were the intellectual elite of the U.S. Army, Pope would regret his choice of service branch almost immediately. Assigned as an engineer to a post at Palatka in northeastern Florida, Second Lieutenant Pope grew bored and restless with life on a backwater outpost. He found himself picking fights with everyone, including his commanding officer, Captain Joseph E. Johnston, destined to become the highest-ranking U.S. Army officer to defect to the Confederacy. After a year in Florida, Pope could stand it no longer, secured leave, and traveled on his own dime to Washington to lobby directly for a new assignment. Habitually bickering with your commanding officer was bad enough, but breaking the chain of command by seeking a transfer not through ordinary channels but in the corridors of capital power was unforgivable. He did get his transfer, but at the price of the enmity of his Florida superiors and peers. To make matters worse, his new assignment, at Savannah, Georgia, pleased him no more than Florida did. Pope understood that leaping over others to get what he wanted had hurt him, but he simply didn't care. What he had done had gotten him transferred, and so, finding Savannah disagreeable, he repeated his earlier tactic, once again willfully breaching protocol. On October 23, 1844, the army sent Pope to Maine.

U.S.-MEXICAN WAR, 1846–1848

Pope, who had flaunted his Northern abolitionism under the proslavery noses of Captain Johnston and the other Southerners in Florida and Georgia, was pleased with his transfer to the northern fringes of free New England, but he would undoubtedly have soon enough found the backwoods of Maine as tedious as the environment of his first two assignments had he not been rescued, like so many others of his military generation, by the U.S.-Mexican War. He was transferred into Zachary Taylor's Northern Army as a lieutenant of engineers and fought in the Battle of Monterrey on September 21–24, 1846, distinguishing himself in Taylor's conquest of the city, which culminated in vicious hand-to-hand street combat. Major General Joseph Mansfield, Pope's commanding officer, reported that the lieutenant had "executed his duties with great coolness and

self-possession and deserves my highest praise," while another officer, Lieutenant Colonel John Garland, observed that he had "deported himself as a gallant soldier under the heaviest fire of the enemy." Brevetted to the rank of captain, Pope was elevated to the staff of General Taylor and served in this capacity at the Battle of Buena Vista on February 22 and 23, 1847.

Pope had every expectation of rapid promotion after the war. Not only had he performed gallantly under fire, he was, through his father, connected with any number of influential politicians. To his dismay, however, he was assigned after the war to dreary engineering duty in the West, his brevet promotion having, as a matter of routine, reverted to his prewar rank of second lieutenant. It was 1853 when he finally made first lieutenant and another three years passed before he attained the regular army rank of captain. Nevertheless, strenuous duty on the western frontier agreed with him better than eastern backwater assignments. Unlike other rising-star alumni of the U.S.-Mexican War, such as George B. McClellan, Ulysses S. Grant, and William T. Sherman, who, amid the dearth of military opportunity, resigned their commissions during the 1850s, Pope stuck it out. In the fall of 1859, he was reassigned to the exciting western gateway city of Cincinnati, Ohio. Here he picked up the thread of his earlier social pretensions, which he had dropped during seventeen years spent far from cities and towns. He met, wooed, and wed Congressman Valentine Horton's pretty daughter, Clara, on September 15, 1859, then watched, with his fellow countrymen, as the Union careened ever faster toward dissolution.

POPE AND LINCOLN

He did not watch quietly. On January 27, 1861, Pope wrote a seven-page letter to President-elect Lincoln not so much advising as instructing him on how to treat secession. He really didn't need seven pages, just the space for two words: *Be merciless.* Pope was uncompromising in his judgment that the secessionists were traitors and should be treated as such. Rather more deviously, he suggested to Lincoln that the army had more than its share of these traitors. It was true enough that many officers would soon resign to join the Confederate forces, but Pope was less interested in them than in undermining and casting doubt on those who remained in the U.S. Army with high rank. He was determined to leap over as many of them as he could and rise in their place. Lincoln's response to the letter does not survive—unless we consider his response to have been his invitation to Pope to accompany him on his inaugural train journey from Springfield, Illinois, to Washington.

En route with Lincoln, Pope talked, he talked a lot, and not just in confidence to the president-elect. His rant against outgoing president James Buchanan, whose inaction during the secession crisis had certainly accelerated the drift toward war, was picked up by a reporter for the *Cincinnati Gazette* and was both so sensational and so long that it was also rushed to publication independently in pamphlet form. By the time Lincoln's train rolled into Washington, Pope's remarks had circulated through army high command. As he descended to the platform, Pope was served with papers summoning him to a general court-martial. The charge was flagrant violation of the Fifth Article of War, which barred officers from criticizing a sitting president, who was, after all, their commander in chief. Fortunately for Pope, Buchanan had even less desire to have his actions put on trial than Pope had to be tried. The outgoing president put a stop to the process by countermanding the court-martial order. With this, the matter was instantly dropped. But there were still any number of officers gunning for the arrogant, impudent, and advancement-hungry Pope. He had won this round by default, but they were determined to hand him a noose, and they were confident that Pope would, sooner or later, give them ample rope.

BATTLE OF ISLAND NO. 10, FEBRUARY 28–APRIL 8, 1862

The talking stopped when Fort Sumter fell on April 13, 1861. Pope immediately called on Governor Richard Yates of Illinois, who commissioned him brigadier general of Illinois volunteers, in which capacity he was sent to Missouri at the head of a brigade for service under Major General John Frémont. If anything, Frémont was an even more ardent abolitionist than Pope and, without presidential authorization or authority of any kind, really, proclaimed martial law in Missouri, confiscated the property of prominent secessionists, and, most egregiously of all, issued a blanket emancipation of the state's slaves. Lincoln, who feared these actions would propel Missouri and the other still-loyal border states (at the time, Delaware, Kentucky, and Maryland) into the Confederate camp, demanded that Frémont rescind the order. When the general refused, Lincoln removed him from command in Missouri on November 2, 1861, and his troops were organized in the Department of Missouri under Henry Wager Halleck, who thus became Pope's new commanding officer. On February 23, 1862, Halleck assigned Pope command of the Army of the Mississippi and tasked him to lead it in an expedition against the key Confederate Mississippi River defenses at New Madrid, Missouri, and at Island No. 10. The Anaconda Plan of Winfield Scott, much derided in the North, was taken very seriously in the South. Aware of the grave danger posed by a Union invasion along the Mississippi, the Confederates rapidly erected and manned a series of fortifications along the river, including Fort Pillow, forty miles north of Memphis, and formidable fortifications at Columbus, Kentucky. These positions were coordinated with batteries on nearby Island No. 10, which commanded the approach to the New Madrid Bend in the Mississippi. Union forces under Ulysses S. Grant took two important defensive positions on the bend, Forts Henry and Donelson, early in February, thereby cutting off the fortifications at Columbus from the main body of the Confederate army. Confederate general P. G. T. Beauregard accordingly ordered Columbus to be evacuated, and the garrison withdrew to Island No. 10. In the meantime, Confederate positions on and around the island were greatly strengthened, so that by the middle of March, there were five rebel batteries on shore above the island, five batteries on Island No. 10 itself, and a floating battery moored in the river at the island's western tip. At New Madrid, Forts Thompson and Bankhead were erected, and the tiny Confederate navy was also pressed into service. Six gunboats were stationed between Fort Pillow and Island No. 10.

Pope swung into action as soon as he was named to command the Army of the Mississippi. Conventional practice at this time was for an army to go into winter quarters—in this case, the hamlet of Commerce, Missouri—and commence no major operation until spring. Pope, however, quickly got his twenty-five thousand men on the march. Too fast, really, for when he and his army arrived at New Madrid on March 3, Pope discovered that he had outrun the arrival of heavy artillery and the availability of Union gunboats under U.S. Navy Flag Officer Andrew H. Foote. The artillery would reach his position on March 12, but the gunboats would take longer, though, when they came, they would be supplemented by fourteen mortar rafts.

Aware that his winter march had stunned the Confederates, Pope decided not to await the arrival of the siege guns and gunboats before beginning the operation. He prudently held off on a full-out frontal assault against the New Madrid forts, but he did dispatch a brigade under Colonel Joseph B. Plummer to occupy Point Pleasant, on the right bank of the Mississippi, just opposite Island No. 10. Confederate gunboats opened fire on Plummer, but without much effect, and Point Pleasant was occupied by March 6. Six

days later, with the arrival of Pope's siege guns, the river was rendered impassable to Confederate gunboats, thereby preventing Confederate reinforcement of New Madrid. On March 13, Pope directed his guns against the New Madrid fortifications, forcing their abandonment on the night of March 13–14. Some Confederate troops withdrew south to Fort Pillow.

At this point, the restless and irascible Pope fell to arguing with the equally stubborn Foote over how to take Island No. 10. Pope wanted to build on his winning momentum with a major attack, while Foote proposed beating Island No. 10 into submission through unrelenting bombardment. Pope asked Foote to order two or three gunboats to run the gantlet of the Confederate batteries, so as to get below the island, which would cover Pope as he crossed the river from above in a bid to capture the entire garrison. Foote, who was still painfully convalescing from wounds he had received supporting Grant's operations against Forts Donelson and Henry, protested that this was far too risky. The two commanders argued for two solid weeks, during which the island was assaulted exclusively and ineffectively by long-range bombardment. At last, Foote declared his final refusal to send his gunboats in a run past Island No. 10.

Although exasperated, Pope was not out of ideas. Acting on a somewhat desperate suggestion from a subordinate officer, he ordered a canal to be excavated as a shortcut across the New Madrid Bend that would allow Union vessels to bypass the Confederate batteries entirely. Finished in just two weeks, the canal proved too shallow for the heavy gunboats, but it could be navigated by troop transports and supply boats, which drew less water. Still, Pope knew he needed at least one gunboat to cover his landing on the Tennessee side of the river. Foote finally surrendered—not to Pope, but to the personal request of Halleck. With profound misgivings, he sent the USS *Carondelet* to venture the run on the moonless night of April 4. Her success persuaded Foote to allow the USS *Pittsburgh* to make the same run on April 6.

Covered by two gunboats, Pope crossed the Mississippi and led a superb attack against New Madrid and Island No. 10, capturing the garrisons of both. It was by any measure a magnificent achievement, but Pope being Pope, he exaggerated the triumph nevertheless, claiming the capture of 273 officers and 6,700 enlisted men. Historians believe that fewer than 4,500 were actually taken.

ARMY OF VIRGINIA COMMANDER

Pope received official recognition for his Mississippi River victories in the form of a promotion to major general, but news flowing from the epic Battle of Shiloh, which was in progress at the time, overshadowed press coverage of the conquests of the Mississippi forts, despite Pope's unseemly courting of reporters. Still, one man did take note.

Abraham Lincoln had suffered through the heartbreak and disappointment of Irvin McDowell and George McClellan, not to mention the horrific bloodbath Grant was delivering at Shiloh. One general after another had failed to give him a victory. Now John Pope, tall, magnificently bearded, supremely military in bearing, had just won control of the upper Mississippi River. True, it had not been a picture-book triumph on a vast field of battle, banners waving, bugles calling. Nor was it a great tactical feat of maneuver. Instead, it was a victory of brute strength against fixed fortifications. But, strategically, it was the most important Union victory to date. The president accordingly directed his secretary of war, Edwin Stanton, to summon John Pope to Washington.

It was a measure of Pope's rapidly rising stock that his commanding officer, Halleck, tried to block Stanton's request. He did not want to let go of a winning commander. Stanton stood firm, however, Pope traveled, and the secretary of war informed him that he and the president were creating a new army, the Army of Virginia, which would bring together the disparate Union forces under Irvin McDowell, Nathaniel Banks, and John C. Frémont that were now fighting in that state. The new catchall army would operate in coordination with what was still George B. McClellan's Army of the Potomac, its initial mission to draw Confederate forces away from Richmond, so that McClellan could finally assault the rebel capital.

Prone to vainglory, Pope was highly susceptible to flattery, and doubtless Lincoln and Stanton expected him to jump at the chance to command a new army not in the West, but in the East, in what the public considered the most important theater of the war. Instead, Pope responded by complaining that he was being commissioned to serve as bait, a "forlorn hope," he called it, using the military term for a unit sent ahead as a sacrificial gambit. His mission, he correctly enough believed, was to make things easier for McClellan to win a great victory. As if that weren't bad enough, Pope pointed out that the generals who would be put under his command were all senior to him. It was hardly an enviable position for even the most genial of generals, and Pope was very far from being genial.

Pope bluntly told the president that the Army of Virginia was not a good idea, and he asked to be returned to the West. Lincoln, however, stood firm. Pope bowed to the inevitable and thus "entered that command with great reluctance and serious foreboding." No sooner did Pope take up his new post than Frémont, accusing his new commanding officer of having plotted against him to gain the command, resigned. He was replaced by Franz Sigel, a scrappy German immigrant who spoke broken English with a thick accent and, although he enjoyed the devotion of his mostly German-American troops, would prove to be a marginally competent commander at best.

For his part, Pope hightailed it back to Washington as soon as possible, devoting himself to a combination of public relations and political lobbying while he left his army to fend for itself in the field. Convinced that the Army of Virginia was doomed, he wanted nothing more than to use it as a stepping-stone to a more promising command. In Washington, he filled President Lincoln's ears with poison against McClellan, suggesting that the "Young Napoleon's" chronic tendency to an excess of caution was not so much a matter of military philosophy as it was a function of politics. As a Democrat, Pope told Lincoln, McClellan was in no hurry to win a war that would bring an end to slavery.

We don't know how Lincoln responded to such talk, though his record as a patient, tolerant moderate was consistent. The Radical Republicans in the Senate and Congress were not hesitant about making their views known, however. They relished every word Pope spoke, and they encouraged and supported his announced plan to feed and supply his army by taking whatever was necessary from the rebellious citizens of Virginia. Moreover, they applauded his promise of meting out the harshest of reprisals for any guerrilla or partisan attacks on Federal troops or property in the occupied territories. And they even approved of his proclamation that all Virginians were subject to the administration of a loyalty oath and that anyone who refused to submit would be sent beyond the lines with a stern warning that they would be shot on sight if they returned to the occupied territory. When McClellan voiced objection to Pope's policy, Pope amplified it even more outrageously. Anyone, he warned, man or woman, who corresponded with anyone in the Confederate army—son, brother, father, friend, no matter—would be subject to execution.

Pope's orders were never enforced and were largely unenforceable in any case; however, they earned the scorn of most of his military colleagues and the outright hatred of his enemies. Robert E. Lee, commanding the Army of Northern Virginia, called Pope a "miscreant"

and informed Stonewall Jackson that he wanted "Pope to be suppressed."

If the Radical Republicans in Washington embraced the new commander of the new army, the officers and men of the Army of Virginia itself were more than anything astonished by their commanding officer's apparently infinite capacity to offer insult. On July 14, 1862, he addressed a message to the soldiers of his new command:

Let us understand each other. I have come to you from the West, where we have always seen the backs of our enemies; from an army whose business it has been to seek the adversary and to beat him when he was found; whose policy has been attack and not defense. In but one instance has the enemy been able to place our Western armies in defensive attitude. I presume that I have been called here to pursue the same system and to lead you against the enemy. It is my purpose to do so, and that speedily. I am sure you long for an opportunity to win the distinction you are capable of achieving. That opportunity I shall endeavor to give you. Meantime I desire you to dismiss from your minds certain phrases, which I am sorry to find so much in vogue amongst you. I hear constantly of "taking strong positions and holding them," of "lines of retreat," and of "bases of supplies." Let us discard such ideas. The strongest position a soldier should desire to occupy is one from which he can most easily advance against the enemy. Let us study the probable lines of retreat of our opponents, and leave our own to take care of themselves. Let us look before us, and not behind. Success and glory are in the advance, disaster and shame lurk in the rear. Let us act on this understanding, and it is safe to predict that your banners shall be inscribed with many a glorious deed and that your names will be dear to your countrymen forever.

Almost instantly, the rumor that Pope addressed all orders as coming from

"Headquarters in the Saddle" swept through the army. His officers and men answered his patronizing sneers with their utter contempt.

Perhaps no general has ever assumed a new command more ineptly and obnoxiously than John Pope. Yet the authority of this most unpopular of officers was about to expand. Finally fed up with McClellan, Lincoln asked Pope to advance southward to attack Lee front-on while McClellan joined in with an attack on Lee's flank. Pope objected, whereupon Lincoln ordered McClellan and the Army of the Potomac to withdraw from the Yorktown Peninsula and join his great army to the Army of Virginia. Neither the president nor his secretary of war made clear whether McClellan or Pope would assume overall command. For his part, Lincoln was riveted on the problem of protecting Washington, and he didn't much care who did it. Pope, however, wrote an angry letter to the army general-in-chief Henry Halleck. "What," he demanded, "is to be my command? Am I to act independently against the enemy?" Worse, the Army of the Potomac did not march to its ordered merger with the Army of Virginia en masse, but in fragments, a unit here, a unit there. The soldiers, severed from contact with McClellan, for whom most felt a profound loyalty, could not bring themselves to accept Pope. Thus, isolated units drifted northward through a kind of limbo of command. Halleck's solution to the crisis was to urge McClellan to expedite the movement of his troops, so that Pope could move ahead to create a rational structure of command. But McClellan, plodding by inclination, now acted slowly by design. He was ambivalent, believing that Pope, an incompetent blowhard in his estimation, would lead "his" army to destruction (and since he cared deeply for his men, he did not want that), yet also half hoping that Pope would fail and fail catastrophically, if only to demonstrate to Lincoln and the rest that he, the Young Napoleon, offered the best prospect for the Union's salvation.

RAID, COUNTERRAID, AND THE BATTLE OF GROVETON, AUGUST 1862

Robert E. Lee could no more stop himself from swooping down upon the delay of ambivalence than a hawk could resist targeting its prey. With the Army of the Potomac migrating slowly and in piecemeal to the Army of Virginia, Lee ordered Stonewall Jackson on August 9, 1862, to strike part of Pope's force at Cedar Mountain, near Culpeper. The result was by no means a major battle, but it did force Pope to withdraw to the northern bank of the Rappahannock River. And that is precisely where Lee wanted him. The Army of Virginia, as yet lacking three corps from the Army of the Potomac, was vulnerable—provided Lee struck now.

To carry out the attack, the Confederate general deliberately broke one of the sacred commandments of offensive doctrine: Thou shalt not divide your army in the presence of the enemy. He placed half his forces under James Longstreet and tasked them with occupying Pope's front. The other half he assigned to Jackson, who marched his men rapidly around to the northwest, pointing them in a direction from which he would launch a surprise attack on the rear of the Army of Virginia.

While Longstreet and Jackson maneuvered, elements of the Army of Virginia made a lightning raid on the camp of Lee's dashing cavalry commander Jeb Stuart. They hoped to bag Stuart himself, and though he got away, the raiders did capture his adjutant—along with one more item of perhaps even greater value. In his haste, Stuart left behind his flamboyant and much-prized ostrich-plumed hat, together with a cape lined in shining crimson. These Pope's raiders gleefully made away with. On August 22, the unabashed Stuart would exact his vengeance. Galloping with a small raiding party into the heart of Pope's headquarters camp at Catlett's Station, Stuart took three hundred prisoners, seized $35,000 in Union army payroll money,

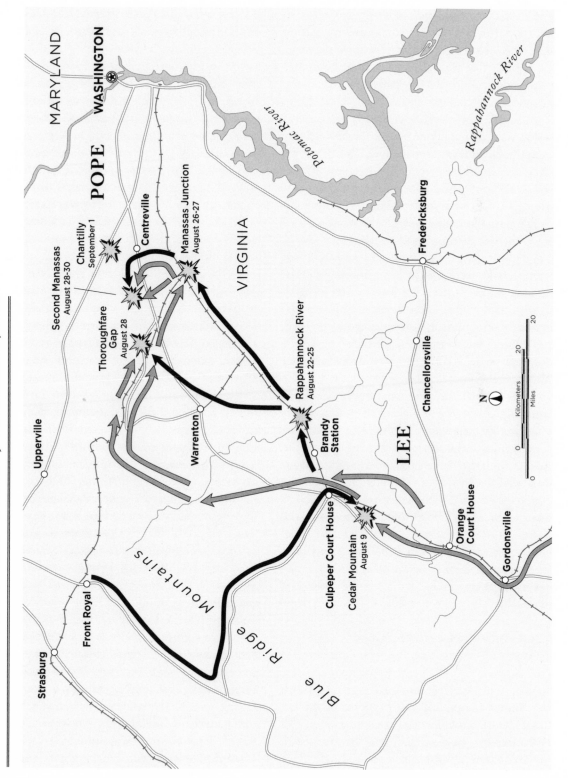
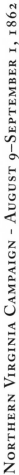

and ransacked Pope's personal baggage in search of the purloined hat and cloak. Failing to find these, he took Pope's dress uniform coat instead. And, since this was, after all, a military operation, Stuart also rode off with a bundle of the general's battle plans.

The raid, aimed as it was directly at the bombastic ego of John Pope, stung far beyond any quantifiable military damage it did, putting Pope dangerously off balance. When Stonewall Jackson lashed out four days after the raid, overrunning, looting, and destroying Pope's supply depot at Manassas Junction, Virginia, a stone's throw from the site of the disastrous Bull Run battle, Pope sputtered. He had suffered a serious loss of supplies, but, far worse, Jackson smashed his rail and telegraph connections, leaving him partially deaf, partially blind, and seriously hobbled. Pope commenced a pursuit, but Jackson was too fast, too nimble, and too stealthy for him.

Jackson did have a way of being found—but only at the moment of his strike.

On August 28, Jackson struck. Suddenly wheeling about, he attacked an isolated brigade led by Brigadier General Rufus King at Groveton. To the Union commander's credit, King responded to the surprise with a vigor and effectiveness that stunned Jackson. The commanders of both Confederate divisions engaged were badly wounded in the Groveton fight, but King's celebrated "Black Hat Brigade" (later called the "Iron Brigade," to acknowledge its consistent heroism), while inflicting many casualties, lost a third of its number, killed or wounded.

Second Battle of Bull Run, August 28–30, 1862

John Pope made a great show of shrugging off both the Manassas raid and the Battle of Groveton, Confederate victories though they were. All that mattered, he now said, was that Stonewall Jackson had revealed himself. Accordingly, Pope concentrated his forces around Groveton. He would, he announced, crush Stonewall Jackson and, in so doing, "bag the whole crowd."

Pope attacked on August 29 and did so with a ferocity beyond anything McClellan was capable of delivering. Yet, vigorous as his jabs were, they were never quite hard enough. Jackson managed to repulse each attack, albeit at heavy cost. This done, the Confederate withdrew at the end of the day. Given to believing whatever he wanted to believe, Pope concluded that he had utterly defeated Stonewall. He was tired, and so were his men. Assuming the Confederate had been whipped, the Union general called a recess. He would finish him off the next day.

While Pope knew exactly where Jackson was, he hadn't a clue to the whereabouts of Longstreet with the other half of Robert E. Lee's audaciously divided army. When Longstreet's command suddenly materialized around eleven o'clock on the morning of August 30, Pope was stupefied. History would remember it as the third day of the *Second* Battle of Bull Run.

A slow, methodical, lugubrious man—they called him "Old Pete" or sometimes "Gloomy Pete"—Longstreet was capable of decisive action when necessary. It was, he judged, necessary right now. All at once, he launched five of his divisions into the naked flank of the Army of Virginia along a vastly broad two-mile front. The resulting defeat he dealt Pope dwarfed that of Irvin McDowell at the *First* Bull Run. Commanding 62,000 men against Lee's divided army of 50,000, Pope suffered 10,000 killed and wounded, against some 8,300 casualties in the Army of Northern Virginia.

Pope, numbed, fell back on Centreville. Lee sent Jackson on a quick march to attempt to interpose his force between Pope's and Washington, D.C., but, pulling himself together, the Union commander counterattacked at the Battle of Chantilly on September 1. Tactically, the fight was an inconclusive draw, but it must be judged a strategic victory for the Confederates, since

Harper's Weekly *published this engraving of Major General Franz Sigel's corps at the Second Battle of Bull Run.*

Pope's army, even augmented at long last by elements of the Army of the Potomac, was brushed aside, putting Lee in position either to pursue Pope or to advance into Maryland, thereby invading the Union. Judging that the Army of Northern Virginia had pretty thoroughly spent itself at Groveton and Second Bull Run, however, Lee did not give chase and allowed Pope to limp away intact. With Pope marching away from him, Lee formed up the vanguard of his army on September 3 and sent it across the Potomac, into Maryland, where it would encounter the Army of the Potomac at a place called Antietam.

THE EXILE

At Antietam, Lee would be met not by John Pope, but George McClellan. Brigadier General Alpheus S. Williams, who had commanded

II Corps under Pope, spoke for many when he wrote of a "splendid army almost demoralized, millions of [dollars in] public property given up or destroyed, thousands of lives of our best men sacrificed for no purpose." He continued: "I dare not trust myself to speak of this commander [John Pope] as I feel and believe. Suffice to say . . . that more insolence, superciliousness, ignorance, and pretentiousness were never combined in one man. It can in truth be said of him that he had not a friend in his command from the smallest drummer boy to the highest general officer."

Practically friendless in the army, Pope had lost all his friends in Washington as well. On September 12, 1862, he was relieved of command, and his Army of Virginia, absorbed into the Army of the Potomac, was turned over to McClellan. Pope was not merely relieved of command of the Army of Virginia, he was virtually

Another Brady portrait of Pope, with the style of beard he adopted later in the war. NATIONAL ARCHIVES AND RECORDS ADMINISTRATION

exiled from the Civil War. He was sent to command what was being called the "Department of the Northwest," assigned not to fight rebels but to contain the obstreperous Santee Sioux of Minnesota.

Some egos are inflated but fragile, collapsing when pricked by defeat. No ego was more inflated than that of John Pope, yet few were tougher. He accepted his new assignment, held it through the rest of the war, then remained through the postwar years as one of the chief commanders in what the U.S. Army called the "Indian Wars." Pope served in a senior frontier command until his retirement in 1886, when he embarked on a career as a Washington-based historical journalist, writing Civil War articles for the *National Tribune.* Later still, he produced a personal memoir of surprising quality. The officer whose career had too often been defined by his outspoken contempt for colleagues, subordinates, and superiors alike now wrote of them with generosity and an evenhanded fairness that have made his book a valuable historical document rather than a mere autobiographical curiosity. He died in his sleep on September 23, 1892.

Chapter 16

AMBROSE E. BURNSIDE

RATING: ★ ★

Mathew Brady portrait of Ambrose Burnside.
LIBRARY OF CONGRESS

EVALUATION

Traditionally rated lowest of the principal Union commanders, more recently Ambrose E. Burnside's reputation has been the subject of controversial rehabilitation.

After delivering minor but welcome victories along the Carolina coast in 1862, Burnside was tapped by Lincoln to replace McClellan as commander of the Army of the Potomac. His disastrous leadership at the Battle of Fredericksburg, combined with his own self-critical modesty and sheer bad luck, undeservedly branded him as the

worst general of the Civil War, despite an overall battle record that, though hardly stellar, is superior to that of many other generals.

Principal Battles

CIVIL WAR

- First Bull Run, July 21, 1861: In Virginia; Union defeat in which Burnside performed better than most other commanders

- Burnside Expedition, February–April 1862: An early, albeit minor, victory for the Union

- Second Bull Run, August 28–30, 1862: In Virginia; Union defeat in which Burnside's units nevertheless performed magnificently

- Antietam, September 17, 1862: In Maryland; McClellan scapegoated Burnside for his own failure to win a decisive victory

- Fredericksburg, December 11–15, 1862: In Virginia; costliest Union defeat of the war

- Tennessee Campaign, fall of 1863: Succeeded in capturing Knoxville and establishing Union control of eastern Tennessee

- Overland Campaign, May–June 1864: In Virginia; performance praised by Grant

- Battle of the Crater, July 30, 1864: In Virginia; unjustly blamed for what Grant called "the saddest affair I have witnessed in this war"

In his *Personal Memoirs*, Ulysses S. Grant, general-in-chief of the Union armies, put it this way: Ambrose Burnside "was not . . . fitted to command an army. No one knew this better than himself."

There is plenty to back up the first as well as the second judgment. At Fredericksburg, Burnside led 106,000 men to the costliest Union defeat in the Civil War. Nearly thirteen thousand were killed or wounded in fourteen brave, foolish, and fruitless charges against fewer than seventy-three thousand Confederates. Burnside's longtime friend George B. McClellan, whom he replaced as commanding officer of the Army of the Potomac on November 7, 1862, believed him unfit "to command more than a regiment"; General William F. "Baldy" Smith rated "his merits . . . below zero"; and Henry Wager Halleck, general-in-chief of the U.S. Army at the end of 1862, blamed him for most of the many things that had gone wrong with the Union's war effort. As for Burnside's own belief that he was unfit to command an entire army, he had tried very hard to avoid promotion to that level. "The responsibility is so great," he wrote to a friend, "that at times I tremble at the thought of assuming so large a command."

Modern commentators are almost universal in their condemnation. Ezra J. Warner, author of the classic and rigorously objective *Generals in Blue: Lives of the Union Commanders*, could not resist beginning his entry on Burnside by calling him "the most unwilling and, perhaps, most unsuitable commander of the Army of the Potomac," and a recent edition of *Guinness World Records* lists him unambiguously as the worst general *in history*.

So why give Burnside two stars or any stars at all? Why even write about a general it may be simply better to forget?

When thoughtfully considered, Burnside's record reveals much to admire and is surely better than that of many, perhaps even most, Civil War generals. In 1862, he won a series of victories along the Carolina coast—at a time when the record of the Union army was uniformly a losing one. In 1863, he captured Knoxville, Tennessee, to the great satisfaction of Abraham Lincoln. In the desperate battles of Grant's Overland Campaign of 1864, his corps acquitted itself admirably at the Wilderness, Spotsylvania, and Cold Harbor before it suffered tragic humiliation in the Battle of the Crater (July 30, 1864) during the Petersburg siege. Even the many who have rained down criticism on Burnside concede

that he was (in Grant's words) "well liked"; more than anything, *this* may have been his downfall. Incurably genial, optimistic, and naïve, he was loath to criticize anyone and even less willing to believe that anyone would, out of malice, say anything bad about him. Moreover, he was so frank in expressing his self-doubts that he practically invited casual sniping from jealous rivals and defamation and scapegoating by subordinates and seniors alike.

Ambrose Burnside was born on May 23, 1824, in Liberty, Indiana, the fourth of nine children of Edghill and Pamelia Brown Burnside. Edghill Burnside was an associate circuit court justice and a state legislator, but, far from wealthy, he could not afford to send Ambrose to college. After elementary school, the young man apprenticed to a tailor and briefly ran his own shop until his father secured him an appointment to West Point in 1843. Ambrose managed to graduate in 1847, standing eighteenth in a class of thirty-eight, just in time to miss a combat assignment in the U.S.-Mexican War.

Like many young second lieutenants, Burnside found himself stagnating in the peacetime army, the tedium of his New Mexico posting punctuated only by the occasional encounter with Apaches. One such engagement left Burnside with an arrow through the neck and an idea in his head. Troops, while mounted, had only their sabers to use against hostile Indians. Revolvers were rarely issued (and then only to officers), and muzzle-loading rifle-muskets were impossible to load from the saddle and nearly impossible to fire. Burnside realized that the army needed a light, short, breech-loading rifle—a carbine. Promoted to first lieutenant in 1851, Burnside married and was transferred to Fort Adams, Rhode Island, in 1852. In October 1853, he resigned his commission to devote himself to perfecting his carbine design. This done, he borrowed money to open the Bristol Rifle Works to manufacture the weapon.

The army was predictably slow to warm to his invention, but at last he secured a big cavalry contract and, on the strength of it, took another risky loan to finance full-scale production. That was when John B. Floyd, secretary of war in President James Buchanan's Cabinet, took a bribe from a rival gun maker to break the contract. Wiped out, Burnside filed for bankruptcy, assigning everything he owned, including his carbine patent, to his investors.

Fortunately, Burnside had a friend, George B. McClellan, who, like himself, had recently resigned from the army; he was now vice president of the Illinois Central Railroad. McClellan got Burnside a job as the railroad's treasurer, and by 1860 he had paid his debts.

FIRST BULL RUN, JULY 21, 1861

The next year, Fort Sumter was fired on, and Rhode Island's governor invited Burnside to command a regiment of the state militia. He led his unit into battle at Manassas Junction, Virginia— Bull Run—where he was bumped up to command of a three-regiment brigade. At the time, whipping the rebels was seen as a cakewalk, and the defeat of the poorly trained boys in Union blue came as a terrific shock. Yet while most of the Union units fought in an uncoordinated, piecemeal fashion, Burnside's brigade made a cohesive attack and might even have saved the day had not the Union commander, Irvin McDowell, simply stopped fighting between noon and two on the afternoon of July 21. The pause gave the outnumbered Confederates time to bring up reinforcements—and that turned the tide irreversibly against the Union. By four o'clock, the Yankees were in full

and disorderly retreat. Even so, Burnside managed to keep his brigade intact until a Confederate shell overturned a wagon on a bridge he was crossing. When this happened, his men suddenly joined the rout.

BURNSIDE EXPEDITION, FEBRUARY–APRIL 1862

At First Bull Run, Burnside performed better than most other Union commanders, which is by any measure faint praise indeed. After the battle, his brigade disbanded, and he was released from the militia but was almost immediately commissioned as a brigadier general in the regular army. He was assigned to train recruits in the newly created Army of the Potomac, of which his friend McClellan was commander. From him, Burnside secured permission to form a coastal division of fifteen thousand men, whom he loaded onto a motley collection of ships and boats and, on January 9, 1862, commenced the "Burnside Expedition," which landed at Confederate-held Roanoke Island on February 7. The occupation was complete by the middle

Currier & Ives published this lithograph, "Capture of Roanoke Island, Feby. 8th 1862: By the federal forces, under Command of Genl. Ambrose E. Burnside . . .," in 1862. LIBRARY OF CONGRESS

of April, and although the "Battle of Roanoke" was, in the context of the greater war, a small-scale affair, it was a rare and welcome success in the Union's early war effort. Promoted to major general, Burnside was recalled to reinforce the Army of the Potomac, which, under "Tardy George" McClellan, had stalled on the Virginia peninsula.

SECOND BATTLE OF BULL RUN, AUGUST 28–30, 1862

Summoned to meet with President Lincoln and Secretary of War Edwin Stanton, Burnside was appalled to find himself invited to replace his friend as the army's commander. He demurred, protesting that McClellan was the better general and just needed more time to prove it. McClellan himself believed that what he needed was more and more troops. To his incessant appeals for men, Lincoln finally responded by ordering the Army of the Potomac back to Washington, where it would be enfolded into a newly formed Army of Virginia under Major General John Pope. But as McClellan withdrew from the peninsula, Confederate commander Robert E. Lee moved against Pope's army, and Burnside, commanding IX Corps, was therefore ordered to return to northern Virginia to protect Pope's left flank and the road to the nation's capital. In response to Pope's urgent call for reinforcements, Burnside sent him two of his divisions on August 12 while he remained behind to hold the Union line at the Rappahannock River. Pope now found himself engulfed in the Second Battle of Bull Run (April 28–30, 1862) and suffered a defeat far larger than that of the earlier Bull Run battle. The two divisions Burnside had given him, however, performed magnificently, and Burnside was rewarded with command of *two* corps, the IX as well as the XII.

ANTIETAM, SEPTEMBER 17, 1862

At the beginning of September 1862, Lee boldly invaded Maryland, prompting a beleaguered Lincoln once again to offer Burnside command of the Army of the Potomac. Yet again, Burnside declined and advised the president to restore full control of the army to McClellan. Pope had failed, and Lincoln, remarking that "we must use the tools we have," ordered McClellan to absorb the short-lived Army of Virginia into the Army of the Potomac. In this process, McClellan assigned Burnside to command only IX Corps and, with it, Burnside joined the march into Maryland on September 5.

Lee's entire Army of Northern Virginia was in Maryland by September 7, with McClellan cautiously tracking along a parallel route. One of McClellan's soldiers stumbled across a bundle of cigars wrapped in a piece of paper. More interested in the cigars than the paper, he nevertheless took time to read it and, discovering that it was a description of the disposition of Lee's army, he turned it over to his commanding officer, who sent it to McClellan. "Here is a paper with which if I cannot whip Bobby Lee," McClellan reportedly exclaimed, "I will be willing to go home."

As usual, however, McClellan hesitated just long enough to give Lee time to outguess him. The Confederate commander concentrated at Antietam Creek, where the armies clashed on September 17, 1862. McClellan wanted Burnside's IX Corps to hit Lee's right while "Fighting Joe" Hooker attacked in greater strength on his left. To get into position, IX Corps had to cross the Antietam near Sharpsburg. Burnside moved his four divisions to a hill above a stone bridge known locally as Rohrbach's Bridge and awaited McClellan's order to move. But Hooker had suffered a repulse, and McClellan, always cautious, withheld the order until the arrival of Major General William Franklin's VI Corps as reinforcement. When the order was finally released, it made no mention of Hooker's reversal, so Burnside proceeded in the belief that his IX Corps was still supposed to create nothing more than a diversion for Hooker's main attack. There was, therefore, no great urgency driving Burnside, who patiently and persistently fought to gain possession of Rohrbach's Bridge instead of simply fording the shallow Antietam. The resulting delay needlessly cost Burnside many men and gave Confederate major general A. P. Hill time to bring up his light division. The appearance of this relatively small force persuaded McClellan that a much larger wave of Confederate reinforcements was about to materialize and, instead of proceeding with his attack, he ordered Burnside and Franklin to hold their ground. For all practical purposes, that ended the battle.

More than twenty thousand Confederate and Union soldiers were killed or wounded on this, the costliest single day in American military history. Antietam, which should have been a decisive Union victory, must be judged instead as a very narrow win or perhaps even a draw. Although he had allowed the Army of Northern Virginia to retreat back into Virginia battered but intact, McClellan chose to misrepresent the battle as an out-and-out triumph, and when both Lincoln and much of the Union public objected, he put the blame on Burnside, claiming that his delay in crossing the Antietam had wrecked his grand plan. True to form, Burnside declined to defend himself against his commander and friend.

FREDERICKSBURG, DECEMBER 11–15, 1862

Despite the black mark against Burnside, Lincoln was so heartily disgusted with McClellan's refusal to pursue Lee that he sent an envoy to offer Burnside the Army of the Potomac command for the *third* time, arming his messenger with an additional incentive. The reluctant general was told that, if he declined the position, it would be given to Joseph Hooker. Burnside was affable to a fault, and one would have to look far and wide to find a single brother officer for whom he had no affection. Hooker was that officer, however, and everyone knew it. Burnside was convinced that Hooker, crude, full of empty boasts, and almost congenitally disloyal to his superiors, was unfit for major command. Presented with this ultimatum, he reluctantly accepted command of the Union army's flagship force.

Burnside's reign of error began even before he took the Army of the Potomac into combat. He decided to simplify the organization of the army, reducing its structure to three huge "Grand Divisions," each consisting of two corps. This made for a magnificent paper chart, but, in the field, it created problems of communication and logistics that impeded rather than streamlined the progress from order to execution and compounded the already formidable difficulties of efficiently maneuvering a vast body of men. Nevertheless, having completed his reorganization, Burnside (to Lincoln's infinite relief and satisfaction) got the army on the move, completing in early November what McClellan had only begun, an advance to Warrenton, Virginia, where he deployed his forces on the north bank of the Rappahannock River.

Lee's Army of Northern Virginia was within his reach and consisted of just two corps, which were widely separated from one another. Burnside's logical move would have been to attack between these corps, entering between them like a thick wedge, then striking out at the flanks of both. Given his superiority in numbers, he might thus have defeated Lee's army not one corps at a time, but the two simultaneously.

If Burnside lacked talent as a tactician, he possessed in overabundance a desire to please, and what would please the political leaders in Washington was his delivering *their* idea of absolute victory. This meant nothing more or less than capturing Richmond, the Confederate

Printed from a damaged glass-plate negative, this group portrait was made on November 10, 1862, at the Warrenton, Virginia, headquarters of the Army of the Potomac and shows Ambrose Burnside, standing center, with some of his officers. LIBRARY OF CONGRESS

west. By December 11, when the Union's pontoon bridges were finally in place, more than seventy thousand Confederates were entrenched just south of Fredericksburg, the town lying between them and the south bank of the Rappahannock.

Burnside ordered a massive artillery barrage not against the Confederate defensive positions, but against the town itself. Presumably, this was intended to suppress sniper fire that emanated from the streets of Fredericksburg, but employing cannon against snipers is like using the proverbial elephant gun to kill the proverbial fly. The cannonade did little to suppress enemy fire, but it did gratuitously destroy much of Fredericksburg, and when Burnside's troops began to enter what was left of the place, they broke ranks to swarm over the ruins in search of anything sufficiently intact to loot.

To the Confederates who watched from the hills, the Yankees looked like so many blue insects picking over the corpse of what had been a fine old Virginia town. There was only one thing to do to these bugs. "Kill 'em," Stonewall Jackson ordered. "Kill 'em all."

That killing began just south of town at 8:30 in the morning of December 13 when Major General William Franklin, another of Burnside's Grand Division commanders, pushed through a gap in the Confederate defenses. It was a promising start, but Burnside, overeager to carry the battle to its climax, ordered the first in a series of headlong charges against what were essentially unassailable enemy positions dug into the hills. In this operation there was an utter absence of strategy and no discernable tactic, except to charge directly into the guns of the enemy.

capital. Burnside therefore passed up Lee's divided and vulnerable main force and instead advanced well to the south of Warrenton to attack Fredericksburg.

The two-corps Grand Division of Major General Edwin V. Sumner was the first portion of the Army of the Potomac to get into position before Fredericksburg, on November 17. Sumner's men were separated from the town by the broad Rappahannock. Because Sumner had managed to reach the river before General James Longstreet's Confederate corps arrived—it would not get there until November 18—Burnside should have seized the moment to order him to cross the river immediately. Instead, he directed Sumner to await the arrival of five pontoon bridges, which (predictably) were delayed. It was a fatal blunder. Sumner obediently bivouacked his men on the north bank of the Rappahannock, thereby giving Longstreet ample time not only to reach Fredericksburg, but to dig into the hills overlooking the town from the south and

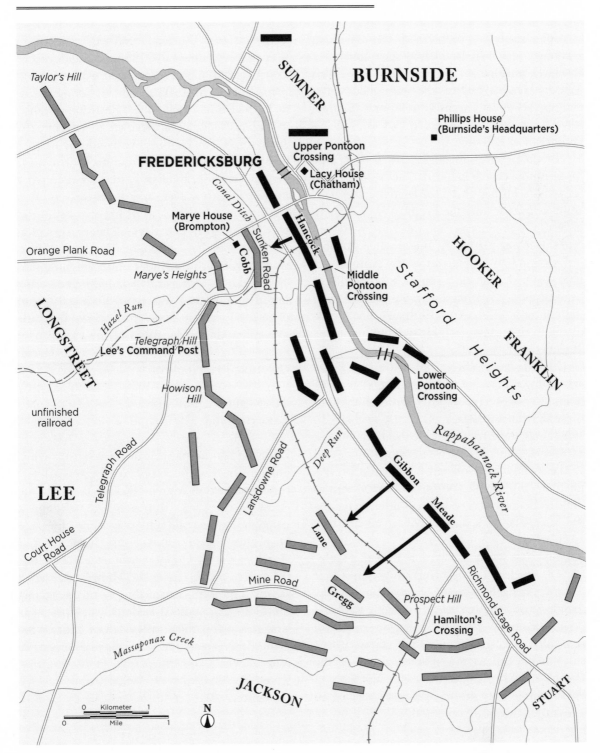

Taylor's Hill

SUMNER

BURNSIDE

Phillips House
(Burnside's Headquarters)

Upper Pontoon
Crossing

FREDERICKSBURG

Lacy House
(Chatham)

Canal Ditch

Hancock

Marye House
(Brompton)

Cobb

Sunken Road

Middle
Pontoon
Crossing

Stafford

HOOKER

Orange Plank Road

Marye's Heights

Hazel Run

Telegraph Hill
Lee's Command Post

LONGSTREET

unfinished
railroad

Howison
Hill

Lower
Pontoon
Crossing

Heights

FRANKLIN

Rappahannock River

Telegraph Road

Lansdowne Road

Deep Run

Gibbon

Meade

LEE

Court House
Road

Lane

Mine Road

Gregg

Prospect Hill

Richmond Stage Road

Hamilton's
Crossing

Massaponax Creek

JACKSON

STUART

0 Kilometer 1

0 Mile 1

N

Burnside was nothing if not determined. He saw his blue-clad soldiers, dead men now, falling on top of one another, a berm of corpses accumulating before a stone wall that ran along a sunken road just beneath the Confederates' strongest position at a place the locals called Marye's Heights. Even as the berm piled higher and spread wider, Burnside sent one doomed wave after another. "Murder, not warfare," a Union officer said of it.

By dusk, Burnside judged that he had time for one more charge before darkness made battle impossible. He had already ordered fourteen separate assaults against the heights. With tears in his eyes, he announced that, this time, he would lead the charge personally. That is when the officers around him counseled that the Army of the Potomac had done all it could. Another charge would produce nothing but more casualties. In the failing light, Ambrose Burnside finally saw reason in this assessment. He ordered his army's buglers to call Retreat.

"To the brave officers and soldiers . . . I owe everything," he wrote to Henry Wager Halleck in his after-action report on Fredericksburg. "For the failure in the attack I am responsible." To "the families and friends of the dead," he offered all that he could: his "heartfelt sympathies"; and to the wounded, he offered his "earnest prayers for their comfortable and final recovery"; but to Halleck he made a very different offer: to recross the Rappahannock and launch a fresh attack against Lee.

Burnside was quite unaware that, in a violation of the chain of command as egregious as it is understandable, a group of subordinate commanders had already conveyed directly to President Lincoln the gist of the new plan. Appalled, the chief executive immediately stayed Burnside's hand, and so the battered Army of the Potomac, surely the most misused major force in American military history, was idled once again and settled into winter quarters.

"MUD MARCH" AND RELIEF FROM COMMAND

To his credit, Burnside refused to yield to despair. On January 20, 1863, he began execution of what might have been a pretty good plan. Instead of striking out at Lee head-on, as he had done with such catastrophic results at Fredericksburg, he decided to envelop the Army of Northern Virginia by advancing into position across the Rappahannock at a more distant crossing, Banks's Ford. This required a long march, however, and Burnside, as often the victim of bad luck as of his own bad ideas, was pounded by two days of heavy sleet that churned the hard ground into a quagmire, transforming the advance into the infamous "Mud March." The symbolism of his great army mired in the mud was more than enough to persuade President Lincoln to relieve Burnside as commander of the Army of the Potomac on January 26, 1863, and replace him with Joseph "Fighting Joe" Hooker.

TENNESSEE CAMPAIGN, FALL OF 1863

Burnside had ample reason to resign his commission. Instead, he asked to be given a lesser command, and in March 1863 was assigned the Army of the Ohio. Burnside had to suppress Confederate guerrilla activity in Kentucky while he planned an invasion of east Tennessee and also coped with Copperheads and other Confederate sympathizers in the Midwest. He acted swiftly but with reasonable restraint against the Ohio Copperhead leader Clement L. Vallandigham, and then, in the fall of 1863, commenced his Tennessee Campaign, entering the state via the Cumberland Gap and occupying Knoxville, which he succeeded in holding for the Union.

On May 3, 1863, Captain Andrew J. Russell photographed the effects of a thirty-two-pound shell from the gun of the 2nd Massachusetts Heavy Artillery at Fredericksburg. A Confederate caisson and eight horses were destroyed.

DEFENSE VISUAL INFORMATION CENTER

OVERLAND CAMPAIGN AND THE BATTLE OF THE CRATER, MAY–JUNE AND JULY 30, 1864

In the spring of 1864, Burnside was transferred from the Army of the Ohio and returned to command of IX Corps, which, at the time independent of any army, was sent to Virginia to support the Army of the Potomac in Grant's Overland Campaign. Burnside's role in helping to repel Lee's final attack at the Battle of the Wilderness (May 5–7, 1864) earned Grant's praise, and the general-in-chief formally attached IX Corps to the Army of the Potomac, which was commanded by George Meade.

At the Battle of Cold Harbor (May 31–June 12, 1864), IX Corps had the rare good fortune to be positioned on the extreme right flank of the Army of the Potomac, and so avoided the worst of the horrific bloodletting in that tragic battle. Throughout the rest of the Overland Campaign, Burnside and his men acquitted themselves

admirably, and IX Corps was assigned a central position in the Siege of Petersburg, which commenced on June 9, 1864.

One of Burnside's regimental commanders, Colonel Henry Pleasants, a mining engineer in civilian life who now commanded the Forty-eighth Pennsylvania Infantry, a regiment made up almost entirely of coal miners, proposed a daring plan to tunnel out to the Confederate line, pack several tons of black powder beneath it, and blow a hole in the Confederate defenses, through which elements of the Union army could break through, thereby ending the siege and opening a way to Richmond. Innovative and open-minded, Burnside promoted the plan to Generals Grant and Meade, who grudgingly agreed to it. Pleasants and his men then dug a shaft more than five hundred feet long—the longest military tunnel in history—which they completed after a month's work on July 27, 1864.

While Pleasants's men dug, Burnside saw to the special training of a division of the United

States Colored Troops to exploit the gap that would be blasted into the Confederate lines. He understood the critical importance of charging through the enemy entrenchments without getting trapped in the blast crater and without slowing or stopping, lest the attackers pile up on one another, bog down, and make easy targets for the defenders. Ensuring the rapidity of the advance required the division assigned to the initial attack to master a series of complex movements, which were choreographed with the precision of a ballet and rehearsed to perfection.

The day before the blast was set to be detonated and the attack launched, Meade summoned Burnside to his headquarters. He and Grant had had second thoughts about using black troops for what was clearly an extraordinarily hazardous mission. They felt that, if the attackers suffered heavy losses—which was likely—the two of them would be pilloried by the public, press, and politicians for having deliberately sacrificed black lives instead of risking white ones. Meade therefore summarily ordered Burnside to find a white division to lead the assault. Burnside protested, arguing that sending an unprepared division into the breach would almost certainly mean the failure of the mission. Meade insisted.

Frustrated, exhausted, and following his orders, Burnside summoned the generals of his white divisions, explained the situation, then simply abdicated command by ordering them to draw straws to determine which division would lead the assault. The short one fell to Brigadier General James H. Ledlie, the very worst of the bad bunch of Union commanders known as the "political generals."

That the Battle of the Crater, July 30, 1864, would end in failure was now inevitable. The Pleasants "mine" worked perfectly, blasting to oblivion 175 feet of Confederate entrenchments, but, when it came time for Ledlie's division to charge through the gap, the general pleaded illness, turned over command to a subordinate, and took refuge with a bottle of "medicinal" whiskey

in a bombproof (blast shelter). Untrained, unrehearsed, and thoroughly confused, the doomed division blindly charged *into* the crater instead of around it. Men soon piled up within it. Those who managed to climb out were soon lost in the wreckage of what had been a complex warren of Confederate entrenchments. The Confederate defenders, appalled by the horrific and treacherous nature of the attack they had suffered, closed in from all sides on the attackers. They killed the men wallowing in the trenches, and they poured into the crater itself musket fire supplemented by rocks and other debris. Before the struggle ended under a sweltering sun, Union casualties, killed, wounded, and captured, topped five thousand, with nearly four thousand in IX Corps alone.

This time, Burnside was not willing to absorb the blame. He criticized Meade to his face, and Meade responded by charging Burnside with insubordination and demanding a court of inquiry. Not surprisingly, the court, stacked with Meade's officers, found Burnside, along with his corps, substantially culpable for the failure of the Crater. Despite this, Burnside, on furlough after the inquiry, offered his continued services to the Union in a telegram of March 23, 1865. But when Secretary of War Edwin Stanton failed so much as to acknowledge the message, Burnside sent him a letter of resignation, along with a personal note congratulating him for his role in the victory. The letter was dated April 14, 1865. That evening, John Wilkes Booth murdered Abraham Lincoln.

POSTWAR

Although Burnside ended the war with his military reputation ruined, his postwar life was a success. He not only prospered in railroad and industrial directorships, but he was elected governor of Rhode Island in 1866, 1867, and 1868, and, in 1874, was sent to the U.S. Senate, where he served until he succumbed to a heart attack on September 13, 1881.

Chapter 17

HENRY WAGER HALLECK

RATING: ★ ★

Henry Wager Halleck: "Old Brains" photographed by Mathew Brady. LIBRARY OF CONGRESS

EVALUATION

Henry Wager Halleck was a military scholar who did much to create and promote the quasi-Napoleonic war-fighting doctrine that dominated the officer corps on both sides of the Civil War. He also did much to promote an ethos of military professionalism. Despite his academic and professional achievements, however, Halleck was an unimaginative, overly cautious tactician, whose views on the nature of warfare lagged

behind the realities of modern combat fought on massive scales. As general-in-chief of the Union armies, he defined his role too narrowly, functioning as an administrator rather than a genuine military leader. Too often, he impeded rather than aided the field commanders (including Ulysses S. Grant) who reported to him. Although he proved to be an able administrator, logistician, and liaison between civilian and military leaders, Halleck was personally arrogant, defensive, aloof, uninspiring, and unsupportive. Nevertheless, after (at his urging) Grant was appointed general-in-chief of the Union armies, Halleck invented the role of chief of staff, singlehandedly creating the modern concept of the staff officer and thereby profoundly influencing the ways America would fight future wars, especially in the twentieth and twenty-first centuries.

Principal Battles

PRE-CIVIL WAR
U.S.-Mexican War
- Capture of Mazatlán, November 11, 1847: His duty with the Third U.S. Artillery included a limited combat role

CIVIL WAR
- "Siege" of Corinth, April 29–May 30, 1862: In Mississippi; after relieving Grant, Halleck assumed field command; his excessive caution allowed P. G. T. Beauregard to withdraw his Confederate forces intact
- General-in-chief of the Union armies, 1862–1864, and chief of staff, 1864–1865: Played a combination of non-field command, advisory, administrative, and liaison roles in the conduct of the war from 1862 to 1865

Among casual students of the Civil War, Henry Wager Halleck is best known for nearly nipping in the bud the Civil War career of the most aggressive, effective, and promising general under his command in the Western Theater: Ulysses S. Grant. When Grant, having acquitted himself well in command at the Battle of Belmont (Missouri) in November 1861, proposed ambitious amphibious operations on the Cumberland and Tennessee Rivers, Halleck initially turned him down until President Lincoln, yearning for his commanders to seize the initiative, pressured him to authorize the operations. The result was Grant's triumphs against Forts Henry and Donelson in February 1862, as the Union wrested control of these strategically vital rivers from the Confederacy. Despite this achievement, Halleck believed that Grant's reputed penchant for strong drink (most modern scholars believe tales of his drinking were greatly exaggerated) made him unreliable. He relieved Grant of command in response to rumors of alcoholism, but soon reversed himself and restored Grant, claiming that, in doing so, he was setting right a grave injustice—though most historians believe he was once again yielding to pressure from the president and the War Department. Less than a month later, however, after the Battle of Shiloh, he effectively demoted Grant a second time.

If Grant held any grudge against Halleck, it was hardly apparent from the praise he lavished upon him. "A man of gigantic intellect," he called him. Not only was he "well studied in the profession of arms," Grant wrote, but he was, in fact, "one of the greatest men of the age."

Grant's assessment of Halleck, when he delivered it after the war, was distinctly a minority opinion. But it was founded, in large part, on Halleck's formidable credentials. He had graduated from West Point in 1839, number three of a class of thirty-one, and, like all top-performing graduates of the academy, was commissioned as a second lieutenant of engineers. A report the new second lieutenant drew up for the Senate on seacoast defenses, grandiosely titled *Report on the Means of National Defence*, thrilled the army's

senior-most officer, General Winfield Scott, who immediately packed Halleck off to Europe in 1844 to study classic and modern fortifications and the French military, considered at the time the state of the art. When he returned to the United States, Halleck delivered a dozen lectures at Boston's Lowell Institute, which were collected and published in 1846 as *Elements of Military Art and Science*. It became a key text at West Point and was studied by virtually every officer who fought in the Civil War, North and South. For it, he earned the sobriquet "Old Brains," and when the Civil War erupted, Scott, now the superannuated general-in-chief of the Union armies, pushed through an urgent recommendation that Halleck be commissioned a major general. The following year, on July 23, 1862, Abraham Lincoln confidently tapped Halleck to replace the profoundly disappointing George B. McClellan as the Union's top commander.

Lincoln expected great things of Halleck, the man who literally wrote the book on war. He would, in fact, serve for nearly two years as general-in-chief, but by March 1864, when he was relegated to chief of staff as Grant was elevated to replace him, "Old Brains" had become an epithet of sheer contempt. While Grant and William T. Sherman remained loyal to Halleck, practically everyone else reviled him, and history mostly remembers him as yet another in the heartbreaking line of Lincoln's failed generals.

"OLD BRAINS" AS A YOUNG MAN

Born on January 16, 1815, in Westernville in New York's Mohawk Valley, Henry Wager Halleck was the first of thirteen children and was fully expected to take over the family farm on which he worked until he was sixteen. But having had his fill of an overcrowded household and a life of agricultural drudgery, the teenage Halleck did what the adult Halleck would never think of doing: He took a chance, went against the grain, even rebelled, leaving his father's house to find a new life. He took up residence with an uncle, David Wager, who sent him to Fairfield Academy in Hudson, New York, then encouraged him to continue his studies by financing his enrollment at Union College in Schenectady. At the advanced age of twenty, Halleck left the civilian college to accept an appointment as a West Point cadet. The combination of Halleck's maturity relative to the other cadets, the high level of his educational preparation, and his own scholarly bent prompted Dennis Hart Mahan (1802–1871), the academy's first notable military theorist, to take this cadet under his wing. Mahan soon assigned him to teach other cadets, instructing them not in the rudiments of martial drill but in the elements of military theory.

Mahan introduced Halleck to the work of the Swiss-born Napoleonic general and military theorist Antoine-Henri Jomini (1779–1869). Jomini's approach to strategy and tactics was highly prescriptive: Identify the decisive point in any battle, and concentrate your main forces there. He defined the "decisive point" as the place at which you could do the "greatest damage to your opponent by the least exposure of your troops to those of the enemy," and his discussions of tactics coolly stressed the geometry of maneuver and position. All of this contributed to a view of warfare as a highly intellectualized combination of art and science. This appealed to Halleck's scholarly inclinations, while the idea of limiting exposure to the enemy fed his natural tendency to approach battle conservatively and with caution. It is often said that the generation of officers, both North and South, who fought the Civil War were thoroughly steeped in often outmoded Napoleonic strategy and tactics. This is true, as far as it goes. But the further point that must be made is that the graduates of West Point and other officers of the regular army got their Napoleon via Jomini as taught by Halleck and those of like mind.

After his graduation in 1839, Second Lieutenant Halleck taught French at West Point for a year before he was assigned to the Board of Engineers in Washington, D.C. His next assignment was to improve the defenses of New York Harbor. This mission occasioned his Senate study, *Report on the Means of National Defence,* and earned him a military tour of Europe in 1844. Two years later, when the United States was rushing headlong into war with Mexico, Halleck published his *Elements of Military Art and Science,* which firmly established him as an acolyte of Mahan and Jomini and an advocate of American military professionalism. The book was destined to be adopted as one of the definitive tactical treatises used by officers, both experienced and inexperienced, in the Civil War. Yet to read its opening pages today is to enter a genteel world far removed from the violent realities of that war or any of the others that followed it. Halleck observed in his 1846 volume "that, in the sixty-two years that have elapsed since the acknowledgment of our national independence, we have enjoyed more than fifty-eight of general peace," dismissing "our Indian border wars" as "too limited and local in their character to . . . disturb the general conditions of peace" and apparently forgetting the nearly ruinous War of 1812 altogether. The attitude displayed in *Elements of Military Art and Science* may seem to a modern sensibility aberrant in a professional military man, but it was, if anything, typical of the United States even as it fought Mexico and began its slide toward civil war. Americans at mid-century, H. W. Halleck among them, thought of themselves as a distinctly unmilitary people.

THE U.S.-MEXICAN WAR AND AFTERWARD, 1846–1860

Having recently returned from studying European fortifications, Halleck was assigned to California at the outbreak of the U.S.-Mexican War to inspect and build forts. Sailing on the sloop-of-war USS *Lexington,* an old ship that had been launched in 1825 and converted into a troop transport, Halleck spent seven months at sea, rounding Cape Horn at the tip of South America, then journeying up the coasts of South and Central America to California. During this time, Lieutenant Halleck served as aide-de-camp to U.S. Navy Commodore William Shubrick and produced a translation of Jomini's seminal *Political and Military Life of Napoleon,* which would become another mainstay of the U.S. Army's small professional library.

Thus Halleck passed much of the war with Mexico quietly writing aboard ship, then working on California fortifications. His combat experience was limited to service with Shubrick in his capture of the port of Mazatlán on November 11, 1847, which included duty with the 3rd Artillery under Colonel H. S. Barton. Although Halleck's combat performance earned him a brevet promotion to captain "for gallantry," he was in short order assigned the administrative post of military lieutenant governor of occupied Mazatlán, then was sent north to serve under General Bennet Riley, at the time governor general of the short-lived California Territory. Halleck was named military secretary of state, a post in which he represented Riley at the 1849 state constitutional convention. Indeed, the convention bowed to his scholarly reputation, and Halleck found himself assigned to undertake primary authorship of the new constitution.

At this point, his career might have changed profoundly. Halleck accepted nomination as one of two U.S. senators for the brand-new state; however, he garnered only enough votes to come in third after the two front-runners. His failure to win popular support foreshadowed what would be one of his great weaknesses as general-in-chief of the Union armies. While his credentials and intellectual achievements were impressive and his performance as military secretary of state—reconciling the chaotic and conflicting interests of occupied California's American and Mexican residents and

almost singlehandedly writing a state constitution—was even extraordinary, he was a prickly individual, cold, aloof, often contemptuous of subordinates, colleagues, and superiors alike. He was, in short, uninspiring and unlikable.

Still, while he proved to everyone, including himself, that he was no politician, he was a talented organizer and administrator, and, in the course of helping to create the state of California, he learned the law. By the end of 1849, he joined two San Francisco lawyers in founding the law firm of Halleck, Peachy, and Billings, which quickly proved so remunerative that Halleck, like many other career U.S. Army officers of the period (Sherman and Grant among them), resigned his commission in 1854.

Halleck traveled briefly back east, to New York, where he met, courted, and wed no less a society figure than the granddaughter of Alexander Hamilton, Elizabeth Hamilton, whom he brought back with him to the Golden State. Already prosperous on account of his law firm, Halleck became even wealthier through shrewd speculation in California land; real estate development in San Francisco, Monterey, and Marin County; and as a director of the Almaden Quicksilver Company of San Jose and president of the Atlantic and Pacific Railroad. Although he had resigned from the regular army, Halleck remained active in local military affairs, and in 1860, with the nation hurtling toward war, he was appointed major general of the California Militia.

WESTERN COMMAND, NOVEMBER 1861–JULY 1862

Although Halleck was a Northerner born and bred, he was also a Democrat who felt strong sympathy for the Southern cause. This was not, however, sufficient to trump his allegiance to the Union, so that when, on August 19, 1861, Congress acted on Winfield Scott's urgent recommendation that he be commissioned a major

Halleck as photographed by J. A. Scholten early in the war.

general in the regular army, Halleck enthusiastically accepted this leap from his last official rank, captain, to suddenly become the army's fourth most senior commander, behind Scott himself, George B. McClellan, and John C. Frémont.

On November 2, 1861, the unruly, impulsive, and ultimately incompetent Frémont was relieved as commander of the Western Department, which was then divided into the Department of Kansas (under Major General David Hunter) and the Department of Missouri, which became Halleck's first assignment, on November 9. While Hunter was content with his portion of command, Brigadier General Don Carlos Buell, who replaced William Tecumseh Sherman as commander of the Department of the Ohio after

Sherman suffered something akin to a nervous breakdown, coveted the commands of Hunter as well as Halleck. Indeed, both Buell and Halleck wanted the Western Department reconstituted under their leadership, and Halleck, seeking to thwart Buell's aspirations, focused his attention on expanding the Department of Missouri at the expense of Hunter. While this process was sometimes unseemly and added names to the list of fellow officers who had no fondness for him, Halleck also worked diligently to clean up the corrupt and chaotic mess he had inherited from Frémont. For this, his California experience of reconciling conflicting interests came in handy. His command, headquartered in St. Louis, was subjected to demonstrations of contempt by the city's large pro-Southern faction. Women, in particular, took to prominently displaying on their dresses red rosettes as symbols of their disdain for what they deemed a Union force of occupation. Instead of cracking down with a decree banning the emblems, Halleck bought up as many rosettes as he could obtain, then assigned troops to distribute them to St. Louis's not inconsiderable army of ladies of the evening. No respectable woman would allow herself to be seen wearing what had now become the badge of a streetwalker, and so the rosettes of protest disappeared virtually overnight.

It would prove for Halleck a rare public triumph.

While he had managed the disgruntled women of St. Louis brilliantly, his attitude toward Buell became increasingly contentious and petty precisely when collaboration and coordination were most urgently needed. Buell wanted to seize the initiative in the Western Theater by advancing against Nashville, an operation that required Halleck's cooperation so that Buell could safely move up the Tennessee and Cumberland Rivers. Buell called for the very operation Ulysses S. Grant had advocated: the neutralization of the Confederate river forts. Halleck told Buell and Grant that he did not have sufficient manpower,

The Western Theater of the Civil War

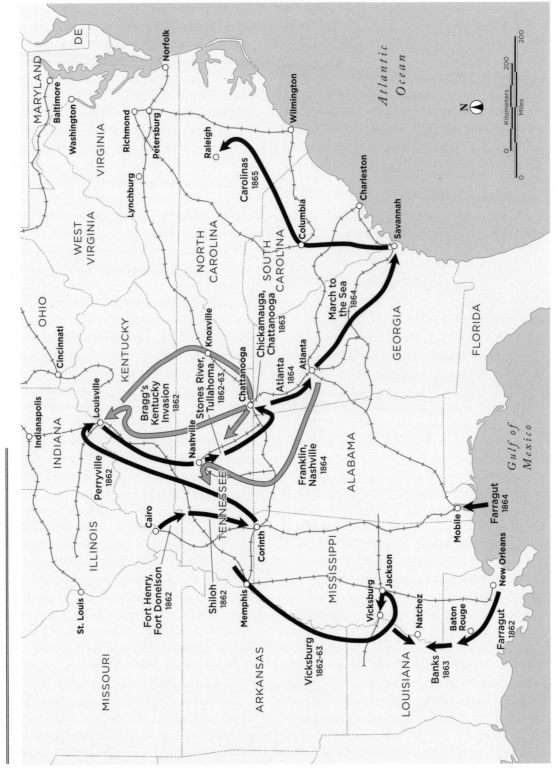

and so *both* armies—Buell's Department of the Ohio and Halleck's Department of Missouri—idled unproductively through the rest of November and clear through the end of December. A message from a frustrated Lincoln ordering Buell and Halleck to communicate and launch a joint offensive operation seems to have prompted Halleck to move on his own. At the end of January 1862, he ordered Grant to do what Grant had earlier proposed, attack Fort Henry on the Tennessee River. In issuing the order to Grant, Halleck pointedly avoided informing Buell. Only with the operation under way and having discovered that Confederate general P. G. T. Beauregard was advancing into Tennessee with fifteen thousand men did Halleck make a last-minute call for Buell's support.

Grant followed the capture of Fort Henry (February 6, 1862) with the capture of Fort Donelson on the Cumberland River (February 11–16, 1862), which together represented a crucial Union breakthrough. Halleck moved with unaccustomed speed not only to usurp personal credit (he had never left his desk in St. Louis) but also to parlay the victories into a claim on the coveted command of a reconstituted Western Department. "I ask this," he wrote to General-in-Chief McClellan, "in return for Forts Henry and Donelson." Understandably, McClellan declined, but, incredibly, Halleck vaulted over the chain of command and made the same request of Secretary of War Edwin Stanton, who likewise refused.

BATTLE OF SHILOH AND THE "SIEGE" OF CORINTH, APRIL 6–7 AND APRIL 29–MAY 30, 1862

Halleck salved the wounds of thwarted ambition by basking in the success of his subordinates, Grant and John Pope. The fall of Fort Donelson was followed by Pope's capture of the fortified Island No. 10 (February 7–April 8, 1862) in the New Madrid Bend of the Mississippi. Together, these victories drove Confederate forces out of Nashville and all of Kentucky. What is more, Pope's victory was won without incurring a single casualty, which seemed to Halleck a splendid example of his idol Jomini in action: victory with minimal cost.

Such a cut-rate victory would not be repeated.

Having left his encampment at Pittsburg Landing, Tennessee, inadequately guarded, Grant was surprised on April 6 by a massive three-corps attack under Albert S. Johnston. Overwhelmed that first day, Grant managed to collect himself, received reinforcements from Buell, rallied his army, and defeated the Confederates, who were now under the command of P. G. T. Beauregard after Johnston fell in battle. While the Battle of Shiloh (as it came to be called after the name of a nearby church) was moved into the Union victory column, Grant's losses were nevertheless staggering: 13,047 killed, wounded, or captured. Calls came from Congress and the public to remove Grant, but Halleck, who had been so willing to deprive him of credit for his victories at Forts Henry and Donelson, showed himself equally eager to rise to Grant's defense at Shiloh. He blamed the high casualty count on poorly trained subordinate officers, well-meaning volunteers who had not had the benefit of a West Point education. Nevertheless, having verbally exonerated Grant, Halleck took personal charge of his troops on April 11 and effectively demoted him to a subordinate position.

While Grant pondered resigning his commission, Halleck prepared to attack Corinth, Mississippi. Acting out of his usual abundance of caution, he waited until he received reinforcements before advancing, then advanced, only to linger at the outskirts of the town—just long enough, as it turned out, to enable Beauregard to determine that Halleck greatly outnumbered him. Deciding that discretion was the better part of valor, Beauregard pulled back, cleverly covering his withdrawal with a display that duped Halleck

Although the Battle of Shiloh was later hailed as an important Union victory, at the time of the bloody engagement Halleck was among Union commanders who saw it as evidence that Grant really was what some newspapers would later call him, a Butcher. FROM PAUL WILHELMI, *DEEDS OF VALOR: HOW AMERICA'S HEROES WON THE MEDAL OF HONOR* (1901)

May 30, "Old Brains" took Corinth—without firing a shot, and without losing a man, but also without winning a victory.

GENERAL-IN-CHIEF, JULY 1862–MARCH 1864

What saved Halleck from humiliation and Grant from following through on thoughts of resignation was a development in another theater of the war. On March 11, 1862, President Lincoln ordered General McClellan's relief as general-in-chief, justifying this not so much as the demotion that it really was but as a means of allowing McClellan to focus exclusively on the campaign to take Richmond. While McClellan fought the Peninsula Campaign, Lincoln, throughout part of April and well into June, functioned as de facto general-in-chief. At last, in July, he summoned Halleck to Washington and gave him the job.

Halleck had achieved nothing actually commanding troops in the field, but he had presided from his desk over the successes of Grant, Pope, and others. In comparison with the Eastern Theater, which was marked by one Union heartbreak after another, the war in the Western Theater, Halleck's theater, was going well. What better choice for overall command was there?

For his part, ambitious though he was, Halleck did not want the job. He believed he could and should continue to build on "his" success in the West. But he acceded to the president's wishes, assumed top command on July 23, 1862, and immediately visited McClellan, who was by this time bogged down on the peninsula.

Halleck got the same earful McClellan had been delivering ad nauseam to Lincoln: He was hopelessly outnumbered; he needed many, many more troops to continue the campaign. Like Lincoln, Halleck readily concluded that no matter how many men McClellan commanded he would always believe himself outnumbered and would therefore never attack. Unlike Lincoln,

into believing that the Confederate general was actually receiving massive reinforcements. As his command stole quietly out of Corinth, Beauregard ordered locomotives to steam in and out of town, over and over again, blowing their whistles, every "arrival" greeted by loud rebel cheers. Each round of movement and noise appeared to Halleck as if it were the delivery of a fresh regiment. Only when he heard another sound, the detonation of the supplies the enemy could not carry with them, did Halleck realize that Beauregard had withdrawn and thereby saved his army. On

Halleck was a military man, so his assessment of what Lincoln had labeled McClellan's case of "the slows" carried bona fide professional weight.

And that was good. But it could have been much better. Having accurately evaluated McClellan, Halleck acted on his judgment by committing both a strategic and a psychological blunder. He ordered McClellan to begin withdrawing the Army of the Potomac back to northern Virginia to coordinate if not consolidate it with the newly formed Army of Virginia under John Pope. Halleck's intention was to use Pope to bolster McClellan by creating one huge force to throw against Robert E. Lee. This was Halleck's strategic blunder. Had he kept the Army of the Potomac in its advanced position, he could have used it to attack Lee on one front while Pope's Army of Virginia attacked on another. Instead, by pulling back the Army of the Potomac, Halleck relieved the pressure on Lee, who was now free to advance against the Army of Virginia, which consisted of only about fifty-six thousand men and was therefore quite vulnerable.

Only after the withdrawal was under way did Halleck realize the danger to which he had exposed Pope. He therefore issued orders to McClellan to proceed back to northern Virginia with all deliberate speed so as to build up a force around Pope. That, of course, was Halleck's psychological blunder. Asking McClellan for speed was by definition a futile request. Perhaps resenting his effective subordination to Pope, perhaps resisting what he believed was the wrong strategic move, or perhaps acting out of his habitual "slows," McClellan predictably dragged his feet, leaving Pope to face Lee alone. On August 25, 1862, the worried commander of the Army of Virginia pleaded with Halleck to know the whereabouts of McClellan. In a curiously misdirected tantrum of ill temper, the general-in-chief invited Pope to "just think of the immense amount of telegraphing" he would have to do if he were "expected to give you any details as to the movements of others, even when I know them."

If there was one man in the Union army whose reputation for a porcupine's disposition exceeded that of Halleck, it was Pope, who responded to the general-in-chief's telegram by requesting that *he*, Halleck, come down to Manassas to take over command of the Army of Virginia himself. Halleck should have replied with conciliation and a morale-building expression of confidence in Pope. Such gestures, however, were beyond him. Instead, he responded as if he took Pope's invitation seriously, saying only that it was "impossible" for him to leave Washington just now. Next, on the eve of what would be the Second Battle of Bull Run, when Pope asked Halleck to rush him additional artillery, the general-in-chief admonished Pope to "make your requisitions on the proper office" because he, as general-in-chief, had "no time for these details." The battle of August 28–30 was a defeat far more crushing than the First Battle of Bull Run had been. Of sixty-two thousand men engaged (Pope had been reinforced by elements of the Army of the Potomac and Burnside's IX Corps), some ten thousand were killed or wounded.

Both history and Halleck have blamed Pope for the catastrophe of Second Bull Run. Halleck accordingly relieved him on September 12, 1862, and Abraham Lincoln, at a loss, wearily recalled McClellan to assume once again the largest field command in the Eastern Theater, to include the Army of the Potomac, the Army of Virginia (which was effectively absorbed into the Army of the Potomac), and the defenses around Washington.

BATTLE OF ANTIETAM, SEPTEMBER 17, 1862

Yet again, Halleck and Lincoln put their reliance on McClellan, a commander in whom neither—and with good reason—had confidence.

In September, when Lee crossed into Maryland, Halleck ordered McClellan to offer battle. On September 13, Union private W. B. Mitchell, 27th Indiana Regiment, was traipsing about an abandoned Confederate campground, foraging for valuables, when he made a most welcome find: a bundle of fine cigars. They were wrapped together in a piece of paper, which, despite his eagerness to get at the cigars, the private fortunately took time to examine. Deciding that the document looked important, he passed it up the chain of command. When McClellan received it, he realized that "Special Order No. 191" was nothing less than Lee's detailed plan for the invasion of the Union.

"Here is a paper," McClellan jubilantly exclaimed, "with which, if I cannot whip Bobby Lee, I will be willing to go home."

But like the proverbially misfortunate man who, seeing that it has suddenly begun to rain soup, rushes outdoors with a fork, McClellan groundlessly fretted that Lee outnumbered him two to one. Worse, Halleck reinforced his doubts by suggesting that the "lost order" could be bait in a trap. The result was, as it always was with McClellan, hesitation and dilution of effort. The Battle of Antietam was fought to an incredibly bloody draw on September 17, 1862, which, because Lee was driven out of Maryland in the end, McClellan claimed as an overwhelming victory.

It is difficult to believe that Halleck wholeheartedly shared McClellan's optimistic opinion as to the outcome, but he acted as if he did, sending the Army of the Potomac reinforcements in the hope that McClellan would pursue the retreating Lee and destroy his Army of Northern Virginia. But nether Halleck nor Lincoln could induce him to give chase.

POLITICAL HELL, MILITARY LIMBO

Powerless to motivate McClellan, Halleck turned his attention temporarily to another source of trouble, his old rival Major General Don Carlos Buell, whose Army of the Ohio had done precious little from June to October 1862. When Buell managed to halt Braxton Bragg's incursion into Kentucky at the Battle of Perryville on October 8, 1862, only to fail to pursue the Confederate's withdrawing army, Halleck relieved him of command, replacing him with William S. Rosecrans.

"Neither the country nor the government," Halleck proclaimed after relieving Buell, "will much longer put up with the inactivity of some of our armies and generals." Never mind that the cautious policies of Halleck himself had encouraged much of this "inactivity." But it was Abraham Lincoln, not Henry Wager Halleck, who next instigated the final relief of McClellan, ordering Halleck on November 7, 1862, to replace him with Ambrose Burnside.

For his part, Halleck increasingly saw himself as having fallen into what he described to Grant as a "political hell." In fact, it more nearly resembled a military limbo. In one respect, he understood his job to be the president's chief advisor, translating military matters into civilian terms for him and, in turn, putting Lincoln's strategic wishes into a militarily executable context. As he later wrote to General Sherman, "I am simply a military advisor of the Secretary of War and the President, and must obey and carry out what they decide upon, whether I concur in their decisions or not. As a good soldier I obey the orders of my superiors. If I disagree with them I say so, but when they decide, it is my duty faithfully to carry out their decision."

If this advisory and executive aspect of his job was inherently thankless, even worse was its other aspect. Lincoln habitually used Halleck as a buffer between himself and the army. Whenever he had a potentially unpopular military decision to make, he set up Halleck as his mouthpiece. "I wish not to control," the president responded to those who questioned what they considered *his* military decisions. "That I now leave to General Halleck. . . . [He] commands."

Did anyone see through Lincoln's smoke-screen? If McClellan's perception is typical, surprisingly not. "Of all the men whom I encountered in high positions," the "Young Napoleon" wrote in his postwar memoirs, "Halleck was the most hopelessly stupid." Clearly, McClellan blamed him, not Lincoln, for his relief. "I do not think he ever had a correct military idea from the beginning to end." Whatever his other failings, Halleck proved eminently successful as a scapegoat.

Disasters

Halleck, Lincoln said, *commands*. This was a fiction. Lincoln knew it. Halleck knew it. Yet it was not simply that Halleck functioned as Lincoln's dummy, mouthing whatever words the president gave him to say. He did earnestly advise the president, as he was supposed to. But he also *advised*, rather than *ordered* or even *directed*, the generals in the field.

Sometimes, this style of leadership was a good thing. Halleck refused to micromanage his subordinates, leaving virtually all decisions about how to execute strategy and tactics to them. Yet he refused to micromanage both his best and his worst subordinates, apparently making no judgment as to a commander's strengths, weaknesses, aptitude, genius, or lack thereof. Regardless of what he may have thought of a given commander, Halleck always withheld prescriptive, detailed direction.

At times, this approach had the direst of consequences. When Burnside presented Halleck with his plan for advancing on Richmond via Fredericksburg, the general-in-chief criticized it. He believed that crossing the Rappahannock at Fredericksburg invited disaster. Yet instead of pushing back when Burnside insisted on the plan, Halleck called in President Lincoln, who bowed to Burnside's judgment, only warning him that success depended on speed. As for Halleck, having expressed his opinion, he

argued no further, but instead left Burnside and the Army of the Potomac to their fate—which proved to be the Union's costliest defeat thus far: 12,653 Union soldiers killed, wounded, captured, or missing.

Halleck pinned the blame for the Fredericksburg disaster on Burnside and Burnside alone. The public and press were not so sure, however, and there was a clamor for the removal of Halleck as well as Stanton. In the end, it was Lincoln, not Halleck, who relieved Burnside and replaced him as commanding general of the Army of the Potomac with Joseph Hooker. In doing this, the president did not even consult his military advisor. Had he done so, Halleck would undoubtedly have counseled against the choice. He was not alone in distrusting Hooker, who had a reputation for selectively opportunistic loyalty and disloyalty. Halleck's low opinion of Hooker, however, was based on something arguably irrelevant to his capacity for command. Back in California, Hooker had borrowed money from Halleck—and had never repaid him. For his part, incredibly, Hooker laid down as a condition for accepting appointment as commanding general of the Army of the Potomac that he must be allowed to deal directly with the president and labor under no obligation to go through the general-in-chief.

If anything is more incredible than Hooker's demand that he be allowed to bypass the chain of command, it is the fact that Lincoln agreed to it. Not that Halleck was blameless in creating this dangerous situation. He acceded to the unorthodox arrangement, and made no objection to the circumvention of his authority.

Halleck reaped the bitter fruit of his abrogation of command. Burnside had clumsily reorganized the Army of the Potomac into unwieldy "Grand Divisions." Hooker undid this and made other sweeping changes. Not only did he fail to consult the general-in-chief, he ignored the unsolicited suggestions Halleck made, choosing not even to give his superior officer the courtesy of an acknowledgment or any reply at all. Halleck did nothing, and Hooker went on to fight and lose at Chancellorsville (April 30–May 6, 1863) without any intervention from the general-in-chief.

After Chancellorsville—in which 17,197 Union soldiers were killed, wounded, or went missing—President Lincoln solicited Halleck's opinion on Hooker's latest proposal, which was to attack and capture Richmond while Lee was still up north. Lincoln rejected the proposal, and Halleck concurred.

The alternative to Hooker's plan, which Lincoln and Halleck agreed on, called for the destruction of the Army of Northern Virginia rather than the occupation of Richmond. In this, it foreshadowed the strategic approach Grant had long advocated and practiced in the West. The idea was this: *Occupying cities did not win wars; killing the enemy won wars.* Yet Hooker's rationale for grabbing Richmond was to force Lee to withdraw from the North to defend the capital. This would force him to wearily march to battle on his enemy's terms. And *that* could well be the means of killing his army. Did Lincoln and Halleck lack the vision to see this? Or had they both—understandably—lost confidence in Hooker? And was Halleck's agreement with Lincoln based on military judgment or his personal dislike of Hooker?

Whatever the answers to these questions, Hooker demanded reinforcements before he would begin to execute the alternative plan Halleck and Lincoln ordered. His stubborn delay allowed Lee to invade Pennsylvania and prompted an outraged president to replace Hooker as commander of the Army of the Potomac with George Gordon Meade on June 28, 1863. Yet again, neither Halleck nor Secretary of War Stanton was consulted in this choice.

FROM GENERAL-IN-CHIEF TO CHIEF OF STAFF

Without input from Henry Wager Halleck, the Army of the Potomac and its new commanding officer fought and won the Battle of Gettysburg (July 1–3, 1863), but when it came to the immediate aftermath of the battle, Halleck issued what was for him a relatively rare direct order. Hoping to avoid a repetition of the squandered aftermath of Antietam, he commanded Meade to pursue the defeated Lee and his Army of Northern Virginia.

It was, of course, the right order, and Halleck did give it, but Meade did not obey it, and Halleck, who in the past had not scrupled at victimizing scapegoats, now found himself blamed for Meade's failure to follow through on the hard-won victory at Gettysburg. The general-in-chief may have been disappointed, but he was not surprised. He had become accustomed to a thankless job, and he was about ready to give it up.

For most of the nation, the Gettysburg victory overshadowed the fall of Vicksburg, which came the very next day, on July 4, 1863. For Lincoln, however, the Vicksburg triumph, which gave the Union control of the Mississippi River and severed the Confederate West from the Confederate East, shone brightly. "Grant," the president declared, "is my man, and I am his the rest of the war."

Halleck not only wholeheartedly concurred with Lincoln's choice to give Grant command of everything in the West, but, after Grant triumphed in the Chattanooga campaign and drove Braxton Bragg into Georgia, it was Halleck himself who requested that Lincoln appoint Grant general-in-chief while he made room by willingly accepting "demotion" to the newly created post of chief of staff. The change in top command became effective as of March 12, 1864, and while Grant approached his new office very differently from Halleck—Grant commanded at the front, in the field, not from behind a Washington desk—Halleck used *his* new office to continue to do pretty much the same job he had been doing all along: administering rather than leading the Union armies. As chief of staff, he juggled reinforcements and supplies among the armies, and, when asked, he gave advice to subordinate commanders. His relationship to Lincoln had changed. Instead of advising the president, he now served as a liaison between the new general-in-chief and the president on the one hand and between Grant and his subordinate commanders on the other.

For the first time in almost two years, Henry Wager Halleck enjoyed his work. Lincoln once derided him as "little more than a first-rate clerk," and Secretary of the Navy Gideon Welles complained that he "originates nothing, suggests nothing, is good for nothing." Cruel and ultimately unjust as these judgments were, there is a grain of truth in them. For Halleck was the first of a new breed of officer: the staff officer—the military manager, whose job really and truly was to "originate" nothing but, rather, to enable the successful *execution* of what the top commanders—the president and the general-in-chief—originated. One great deficiency of Civil War leadership, on both sides, was the paucity of the middle level of command, the staff officers who ensured that field commanders executed what high command ordered. Halleck ended the war by becoming the prototype of this new military professional, a role as unglamorous as it was to prove essential in modern, complex, highly political, and highly technological warfare.

Halleck served after the war briefly as commander of the Military Division of the James, headquartered in Richmond, then was transferred far from the former theaters of the Civil War, assuming command of the Division of the Pacific in California from August 1865 to March 1869. He was returned to the heart of Reconstruction administration as commander of the Division of the South, headquartered in Louisville, Kentucky, and served there until his death on January 9, 1872.

Chapter 18

ULYSSES S. GRANT

RATING: ★ ★ ★ ★

Lieutenant General Ulysses S. Grant, photographed by the Brady studio. LIBRARY OF CONGRESS

EVALUATION

During his tenure as commander of the Army of the Tennessee and as general-in-chief of the Union armies as well as in historical retrospect, the criticism most often leveled against Ulysses S. Grant was his willingness to outspend the Confederacy in human sacrifice. Aware that the Union could replace men and equipment, while the Confederacy could not, Grant often traded man for man in combat, knowing that the losses would hurt the enemy more than they hurt

him. For this, Grant was—and, by some, still is—condemned as a "butcher." That Grant, by the time of the Overland Campaign, conducted a war of attrition is true. That he spent many lives is also true. But so did the Union generals who had preceded him. The difference was that Grant purchased victory with the blood he spilled, while his predecessors had gained nothing for it. Grant was not a butcher. He was a skillful leader who had a natural grasp of tactics and strategy. He redirected Union military doctrine from expending blood and treasure to conquer territory and towns to killing the army of the enemy—a means by which the final objective, a victorious end to the war and restoration of the Union, could most efficiently be achieved. To achieve this objective, he willingly exploited the economic, industrial, and demographic advantages of the North to overwhelm and overcome the South. In this, he exhibited a profound understanding of the nature of modern warfare as well as the moral courage to pay the price of winning a modern war.

Principal Battles

PRE-CIVIL WAR

U.S.-Mexican War, 1846–1848

- Palo Alto, May 8, 1846 and Resaca de Palma, May 9, 1846: Performed impressively in his first two combat experiences

- Monterrey, September 21–24, 1846: Made a spectacular ride through sniper-infested streets

- Veracruz, March 9–29, 1847: Saw sporadic combat throughout the operation

- Molino del Rey, September 8, 1847: Brevetted to first lieutenant for gallantry

- Chapultepec, September 12–13, 1847: Positioned a howitzer in a belfry against Mexicans defending San Cosme gate; brevetted to captain

CIVIL WAR

- Belmont, November 7, 1861: In Missouri; achieved an inconclusive result here
- Forts Henry and Donelson, February 6 and February 11–16, 1862: In Kentucky and Tennessee; capture of these two key Confederate forts put the spotlight on Grant
- Shiloh, April 6–7, 1862: In Tennessee; surviving a first-day disaster, Grant achieved a costly victory on day two
- Vicksburg Campaign, December 1862–July 4, 1863: In Mississippi; Grant's conquest of this fortress city split the Confederacy in two and gave the Union control of the Mississippi River
- Chattanooga Campaign, October–November 1863: In Tennessee; Grant effectively secured the war's Western Theater for the Union
- Overland Campaign, May–June 1864: In Virginia, comprised the Battles of the Wilderness, Spotsylvania Court House, and Cold Harbor; the first two were inconclusive, Cold Harbor was a Union defeat, and all were horrifically costly to both sides, but Grant continued his southward offensive as he bled the Army of Northern Virginia white
- Siege of Petersburg, June 9, 1864–March 25, 1865: In Virginia; after failing to make a quick—and probably war-winning—breakthrough at Petersburg, Grant settled in for a long siege, ultimately forcing the evacuation of the Army of Northern Virginia
- Appomattox Campaign, March 29–April 9, 1865: In Virginia; the final pursuit and defeat of Robert E. Lee and the Army of Northern Virginia, ensuring the end of the Civil War

It wasn't the name his parents gave him, after he was born on April 27, 1822, in the Ohio hamlet of Point Pleasant. Baptized Hiram Ulysses Grant, he proved such an inept young man as he puttered in his father's tannery that townsfolk—the family moved to Georgetown, Ohio, during the boy's first year—took to calling him "Useless."

For his part, Jesse Root Grant didn't rise to his son's defense, probably because, like his neighbors, he saw little in his son to suggest much of a future. As soon as possible, the senior Grant packed him off to boarding school in Maysville, Kentucky, and shortly after the boy returned to Georgetown, Jesse Grant goaded him into accepting the West Point nomination he had obtained from Congressman Thomas L. Hamer. Young Hiram was hardly enthusiastic about an army career, but his father told him that the military academy was an opportunity to get an engineer's education at no charge. After brief service in the army, he could resign his commission and take a civilian job that at least promised a decent paycheck. Hiram—"Useless"—surrendered to the older man's logic and enrolled in 1839 as part of the Class of 1843.

That is when he got his next name. For some reason, Congressman Hamer had nominated him as "Ulysses S. Grant," and when Hiram, arrived at the academy, pointed out that this was not his name, the adjutant replied that it was now—at least as long as he stayed in the U.S. Army. So yet again Grant surrendered. Since Hamer hadn't specified what the *S* stood for, Grant wrote in his mother's maiden name, *Simpson*, and he soon learned to enjoy having the initials "U. S.," which quickly invited his classmates to call him Uncle Sam—though by the end of his plebe year, he was generally known as Sam Grant. The plain name was fine with him.

But this was hardly the end of Grant's naming and renaming. Of all the Civil War generals, North or South, none evolved more surprisingly, more dramatically, or more profoundly than the man who started life as Hiram and Useless, became Uncle Sam and plain old Sam, and subsequently earned the sobriquet of "Unconditional Surrender" followed later in the war by the epithet of "Butcher," before finally collecting the titles of *savior of the Union* and *Mr. President*.

THE RELUCTANT CADET

Ulysses Simpson Grant was destined to become one of America's few genuine warrior leaders. Like George S. Patton Jr. in the century after him, Grant understood and accepted the nature of modern war. Like Patton, Grant was willing to spend—never to squander—lives to achieve victory. But while Grant, like Patton, took to the grisly business of war as if it were his second nature, Grant never intended to be a soldier, whereas Patton, from earliest childhood, never thought about being anything else.

"I never went into battle willingly or with enthusiasm," Grant wrote late in life. His father had regarded West Point not as a portal by which his son might realize a great military destiny, but as a backdoor to some civilian profession by which hapless "Useless" might support himself in adult life. And young Grant agreed. "If a man graduates here," he said of the academy, "he is safe for life, let him go where he will."

Patton would struggle through West Point. Entering in 1904, he had to repeat his plebe year and did not graduate until 1909. But never once did he doubt his martial destiny. In stark contrast, Grant enrolled in fear and trembling, terrified that he would yet again disappoint, even disgrace, his family by failure that seemed to him inevitable. "A military life had no charms for me," he recalled in his 1885 *Personal Memoirs*, "and I had not the faintest idea of staying in the army even if I should be graduated, which I did not expect." In fact, when Congress debated in December 1839 a bill to abolish the United States Military Academy once and for all, Cadet Grant "saw in this an honorable way to obtain a discharge," and he "read the debates with much interest" and much impatience; "for I was selfish enough to favor the bill."

Except for mathematics, for which he had a flair, Grant plodded joylessly through his classes. When Winfield Scott visited the academy to review the cadets, Grant was awed by "his quite colossal size"—he himself was a puny five-foot-eight and 135 pounds—and "showy uniform." He thought Scott "the finest specimen of manhood my eyes had ever beheld" and believed he "could never resemble him in appearance" but nevertheless confessed to "a presentiment for

a moment that some day I should occupy his place on review. . . ." Prospects for the realization of this "presentiment" hardly looked good, however. Cadet Grant racked up demerit after demerit for slovenly appearance, tardiness, and all-around "unsoldierliness." While other cadets vied for promotion, Grant failed to be named corporal in his second year but was sixteenth among eighteen sergeants in his third. That promotion, he wrote in his *Personal Memoirs*, "was too much for me. . . . I was dropped, and served the fourth year as a private."

Because he graduated twenty-first in the thirty-nine-member Class of 1843, a commission in the engineers was out of the question (that was reserved for the best and the brightest, young men like George B. McClellan and Robert E. Lee), as was one in the artillery (the place for the academy's second best). Grant had always loved horses and was very good with them, having earned a reputation as a superb and daring rider and setting a West Point record in the equestrian high jump that endured for nearly a quarter century. He seemed a natural for a cavalry commission, but the U.S. Army has never been known for making the natural choice, and Grant was assigned to the 4th U.S. Infantry Regiment.

U.S.-Mexican War, 1846–1848

Quartered at Jefferson Barracks in St. Louis, Grant met seventeen-year-old Julia Boggs Dent, the plantation-bred daughter of a slaveholding family, squinty and plain, yet in the young second lieutenant's eyes beautiful. He courted her doggedly from 1843 until she finally accepted his proposals, and they were married on August 22, 1848, after he had returned from the U.S.-Mexican War.

The war with Mexico broke out in May 1846. Grant wrote in his *Personal Memoirs* that he "was bitterly opposed" to the war "as one of the most unjust ever waged by a stronger against a weaker nation." He believed that its purpose was to acquire more territory into which slavery might be spread. "I know the struggle I had with my conscience during the Mexican War. I have never altogether forgiven myself for going into that," but, he declared with his invariable candor, "I had not moral courage enough to resign. . . . I considered my supreme duty was to my flag."

There is no evidence that he ever shared his objections or reservations with fellow officers. Grant hated argument. He swallowed his doubts and embraced his duty, which was a dull assignment as a quartermaster—essentially a supply clerk. Yet in the war with Mexico, in which U.S. forces were almost always outnumbered, every soldier, regardless of his official assignment, was first and foremost a rifleman, and Grant saw action at Palo Alto (May 8, 1846), Resaca de Palma (May 9, 1846), Monterrey (September 21–24, 1846), Veracruz (March 9–29, 1847), Molino del Rey (September 8, 1847), and Chapultepec (September 12–13, 1847). At Monterrey, he put his brilliant horsemanship to use by volunteering to run a snipers' gantlet to deliver an urgent request for ammunition. "I adjusted myself on the side of my horse furthest from the enemy," he wrote, "and with only one foot holding to the cantle of the saddle, and an arm over the neck of the horse exposed, I started at full run. It was only at street crossings that my horse was under fire, but these I crossed at such a flying rate that generally I was past and under cover of the next block of houses before the enemy fired." At Chapultepec, he led a small party of men in hauling a howitzer up into the belfry of a church to bear down Mexicans defending the capital's San Cosme gate. For earlier gallantry at Molino del Rey, Grant had been brevetted to first lieutenant; for his performance at Chapultepec, he received a second brevet, to captain. Both battles he later dismissed as having been "wholly unnecessary."

RETURN TO FAILURE, 1848–1861

Heroic action gave way after the war to the tedium and penury of the peacetime United States Army. Reverting to the rank of first lieutenant at the end of the war, Grant married Julia in 1848 and, like others of his age and rank, served in various out-of-the-way posts. His bride dutifully followed him until he was sent to Fort Vancouver, Washington Territory, in 1853. Pregnant with the couple's second child, she was unable to accompany him since there was no hope of a lieutenant's pay supporting her and two children on the frontier. The following year, Grant achieved promotion to the regular army rank of captain and was assigned to an infantry company command at Fort Humboldt in northern California. The jump in pay grade should have made it possible for him to reunite with his family, but in his *Personal Memoirs*, he cites his continued inability to support a wife and two children on an army officer's salary as his reason for suddenly resigning his commission in July 1854, weeks after he was promoted.

This may well have been his true reason for leaving. Nevertheless, at the time, rumor had it that his commanding officer, Brevet Lieutenant Colonel Robert C. Buchanan, had caught him drunk on duty as a pay officer. It was said that Buchanan offered him the choice of court-martial or voluntary resignation. There is no official record of the incident or the ultimatum, but the story would dog Grant for the rest of his career—would, in fact, outlive him—and he never made any effort to deny it.

At thirty-two, Grant was a civilian. His father's calculations notwithstanding, neither West Point nor the army had prepared him for anything lucrative, and for the next four years, he worked a farm outside of St. Louis. Although he was personally opposed to slavery, he used slaves his father-in-law lent him and even purchased one of them outright. Nevertheless, he could not make a go of it and gave up the farm in 1858 to become, of all things, a bill collector. That employment lasted barely a year. After abortive stabs at a few more occupations, he sought the help of his disapproving father, who, in 1860, took him on as a clerk in his Galena, Illinois, tannery and leather shop. Buying raw hides and selling tack and other leather goods was not so different from being an army quartermaster, but it was just as dull, and the future could not have appeared very bright to Grant as he slid into middle age.

BATTLE OF BELMONT, NOVEMBER 7, 1861

The Civil War, when it came, didn't so much make Grant as save him. On April 15, two days after Confederate batteries commenced fire on Fort Sumter, President Lincoln issued a call for seventy-five thousand volunteers. Grant immediately responded by helping to recruit a company of volunteers, which he led to the state capital, Springfield. There, Governor Richard Yates asked him to recruit and train the state's volunteers. He was happy to get the assignment, but he wanted a field command, not a training job, and in June, the governor appointed him a colonel in the Illinois militia. He was assigned to command the 21st Illinois Infantry. At the end of the following month, President Lincoln appointed him brigadier general of federal volunteers. Major General John C. Frémont, who held command of the army's Western Department, named Grant to command the District of Southeast Missouri, a critical region violently torn between pro-Union and pro-Confederacy factions.

Setting up headquarters at Cairo, Illinois, where the Mississippi and Ohio Rivers meet, Grant was quick to take strategically decisive action. Kentucky, a "border state" (slaveholding but loyal to the Union), had declared itself neutral in the war. When Confederate forces violated its neutrality by taking the town of Columbus,

BRIGADIER-GENERAL U. S. GRANT

Brigadier General Grant, photographed at Cairo, Illinois, on September 4, 1861. FROM THE PHOTOGRAPHIC HISTORY OF THE CIVIL WAR (1911)

Grant responded by occupying Paducah on September 6, 1861, at the confluence of the Ohio and Tennessee Rivers. This action was followed on November 7 by the Battle of Belmont, Missouri, which was inconclusive; Grant initially took Fort Belmont but was forced to withdraw to Cairo after Confederate general Gideon Pillow was reinforced so that he outnumbered Grant by a margin of five to three. Nevertheless, the Illinois brigadier's aggressive spirit, so unlike the tentative passivity and caution that prevailed among other Union generals, drew President Lincoln's attention.

Brigadier General U. S. Grant is pictured with the staff of his Cairo, Illinois, headquarters in October 1861.

BATTLES OF FORT HENRY AND FORT DONELSON, FEBRUARY 6 AND FEBRUARY 11–16, 1862

Three months after the Battle of Belmont, Grant coordinated operations with the U.S. Navy's Flag Officer Andrew H. Foote to capture Fort Henry on the Tennessee River and Fort Donelson on the Cumberland. These were the Union's first strategically important victories, loosening the Confederate chokehold on two vital arteries and beginning to pry the West from enemy hands.

Fort Henry had fallen quickly, but Fort Donelson was a tougher nut to crack. Foote had unsuccessfully attacked it on February 14, prompting Pillow, the Confederate general, to seize the initiative the next day by attacking one of Grant's divisions (under Brigadier General John A. McClernand) and sending it into a rout. Grant, four miles from the front in conversation with Foote, hearing the distant thunder of cannon and the rattle of musketry, rode to the sound of the guns. Rounding up his subordinate commanders, he took control of the situation, rallied his troops, and counterattacked so fiercely that

the Confederate line broke. At the same time, he blocked the Nashville road, thereby forcing the enemy to withdraw back into Fort Donelson. Generals Pillow and John B. Floyd summarily decamped, leaving Simon Bolivar Buckner behind to ask Grant for surrender terms. Grant replied to him in writing: "Sir: Yours of this date proposing an Armistice, and appointment of commissioners, to settle terms of capitulation just received. No terms except unconditional and immediate surrender can be accepted. I propose to move immediately against your works." And so, for a time, a jubilant Union public came to know him as "Unconditional Surrender" Grant. President Lincoln promoted him to major general of volunteers.

BATTLE OF SHILOH, APRIL 6–7, 1862

Praise poured in on "Unconditional Surrender" Grant, and because a newspaper story reported his affection for cigars, cigars were showered upon him as well. In point of fact, Grant was a pipe man, but he dared not waste the gifts that were being sent him, so, just as he had acceded to the name changes thrust upon him, he conceived an affection for cigars, which became his trademark. Soon he was puffing through as many as twenty in a day.

For the public, it became his trademark—that is, along with whiskey.

There is no doubt that Grant drank. On occasion, he may well have drunk too much—though not, perhaps, by the standards of the day. In any event, no one has ever presented more than a rumor of his being drunk on duty. Yet, after his victories at Forts Henry and Donelson, his commanding officer, Henry "Old Brains" Halleck, heeded tales of his rising general's bibulousness and seems to have gone gunning for Grant. What prompted him to pull the trigger was news that Grant had met in Nashville with Don Carlos Buell, Halleck's chief rival for power.

On March 4, 1862, Halleck relieved Grant of field command of a new expedition up the Tennessee River. Hearing of this, Abraham Lincoln pressed him to restore his "fighting general." Old Brains quickly capitulated, rescinded his order, and, on March 17, gave Major General Grant command of what would be known as the Army of the Tennessee.

Halleck did not, however, heed Grant's plea to allow him to coordinate his forces with Buell's and pursue those Confederates who had been dislodged from the river forts and from Columbus, Kentucky. Instead, Halleck dragged his feet, and the two principal Confederate commanders, P. G. T. Beauregard and Albert Sidney Johnston, were able to link up and regroup at Corinth, Mississippi.

Had Halleck moved swiftly and had Buell cooperated with Halleck, some seventy thousand Union troops would have been ready to attack perhaps fifty thousand Confederates. As it was, however, Grant encamped at Pittsburg Landing, Tennessee, on the west bank of the Tennessee River, northeast of the Confederate position at Corinth, Mississippi, with just forty-two thousand men. He was frustrated, tired, and plagued by a badly sprained ankle. He erected his headquarters tent beside a log-built Methodist meeting house called Shiloh Chapel. Shiloh was the Canaanite town where the Tabernacle and the Ark of the Covenant had been lodged. In Hebrew, the name means "peaceful place," and Grant assumed that he would enjoy an interval of peace as the Confederates holed up at Corinth. Acting on this assumption, he chose not to dig entrenchments to defend his camp, nor did he mount cavalry patrols or pickets.

On Sunday morning, April 6, the peace was shattered as Johnston and Beauregard descended upon Grant and his men.

For twelve mortal hours, the Confederates had their way. Panic-stricken Union troops hid instead of fought, and by the end of that Sunday, Shiloh Chapel was in Confederate hands and the Federal lines had been shoved nearly into the river. Thanks in part to the actions of William Tecumseh Sherman, who, Grant later remarked, inspired "confidence in officers and men that enabled them to render services on that bloody battlefield worthy of the best of veterans," Grant was able to begin turning back the tide.

"Well, general," Sherman remarked to him as night fell on Sunday, "we've had the devil's own day."

"Yes," Grant agreed, then added: "Lick 'em tomorrow, though."

Where others would have joined the panic, Grant mastered it. Sherman bought time for the arrival of reinforcements on Monday morning, and Grant used them to counterattack, forcing Beauregard—who had assumed overall command of Confederate forces upon the death of Johnston—to fall back on Corinth following a ten-hour fight.

THE BUTCHER

Grant ended up winning the Battle of Shiloh, but he had lost 1,754 killed, 8,408 wounded, and 2,885 missing in the victory. Among politicians, the press, and the public alike, many turned about-face on their hero. "Unconditional Surrender" Grant was on his way to earning the epithet that would be attached to him during the bloody battles of his 1864 Overland Campaign: "Butcher Grant."

There were many calls for his relief, but Halleck—he who had so recently relieved Grant on the basis of mere rumor—now leaped to his defense. The heavy casualties, he said, were the fault of poorly trained subordinates, not the leadership of U. S. Grant. Then, having supported him publicly, Halleck quietly relegated Grant to a subordinate position as he himself, on April 11, took personal charge of his troops. In effect demoted, Grant considered resigning then and there but was talked out of it by Sherman and backed to the hilt by Lincoln. "I can't spare this man," the president answered those who called for his dismissal. "He fights."

VICKSBURG CAMPAIGN, DECEMBER 1862–JULY 4, 1863

Halleck, as we saw in Chapter 17, scored a hollow victory at Corinth, then was kicked upstairs by Lincoln, becoming the Union's new general-in-chief in July 1862. With Halleck safely out of the way in Washington, Grant had nominal command of Union forces at the Battle of Iuka (September 19, 1862) and the Second Battle of Corinth (October 3–4, 1862), but left actual field command to William S. Rosecrans while he turned his attention to taking Vicksburg, Mississippi.

Even the often obtuse Halleck understood the great strategic importance of capturing the rebel city of Vicksburg, which commanded high bluffs above a hairpin turn of the Mississippi River and thus controlled the river. "In my opinion," he said, "the opening of the Mississippi River will be to us more advantage than the capture of forty Richmonds." But the Confederates had transformed Vicksburg into what they called the "Gibraltar of the West," a formidable fortress standing virtually impregnable on its bluff. With artillery positioned to sweep the river bend, a direct naval assault would be suicide. Grant proposed instead to develop a combined land and water operation, but even he had no idea how long it would take.

In December 1862, Grant established an advance base at Holly Springs, Mississippi, preparatory to a planned movement of some forty thousand troops down the Mississippi Central Railroad to link up with thirty-two thousand river-borne troops led by William Tecumseh Sherman. Raids by Confederate generals Earl Van Dorn and Nathan Bedford Forrest checked Grant's advance, and Sherman, thus deprived of Grant's support at Chickasaw Bayou (also known as Chickasaw Bluffs) (a few miles north

of Vicksburg), failed as well. Undaunted, Grant took a new tack. He decided to dig a canal to bypass the river bend below Vicksburg and thereby avoid the fortress artillery. This time, heavy rains and high water during February 1863, not Confederate resistance, defeated him. Grant attempted another canal, at Duckport, but couldn't dig one deep enough to accommodate combat vessels and troop transports.

Ever tenacious, Grant next sent Major General James B. McPherson on a mission to open up a spectacular four-hundred-mile route through Louisiana swamps, lakes, and bayous to a position on the river below Vicksburg. Grant later abandoned this in favor of a more roundabout water route through the so-called Yazoo Pass but was blocked by a new Confederate fort erected ninety miles north of Vicksburg. On March 11, Grant abandoned the Yazoo Pass Expedition and tried yet another water route, through Steele's Bayou. Admiral David Porter led an eleven-boat flotilla with Sherman's infantry following but was stopped and nearly annihilated on March 19 at Rolling Fork, Mississippi, north of Vicksburg.

Military historians have speculated that Grant never actually harbored much hope that all the labor-intensive preliminaries would succeed, but he undertook them just the same in the interest of keeping his offensive campaign alive, keeping the enemy guessing, and keeping his army busy and therefore disciplined. When his superiors ordered him to break off the campaign and move south to link up with forces under Nathaniel Banks, who was engaged in his Red River Campaign, which Grant saw as clearly futile, he instead moved immediately against Jackson, Mississippi, which produced the Battle of Champion's Hill on May 16. Grant scored a costly victory here, which at last positioned him for an assault on Vicksburg.

It failed on May 19 and again on May 22. Grant then laid siege, pounding the city from late May through early July with no fewer than two hundred heavy artillery pieces and siege mortars, turning it into a hell. "We are utterly cut off from the world, surrounded by a circle of fire," a resident recorded in her diary as, like others, she huddled in the improvised shelter of a cave. Vicksburg's surrender came on July 4, 1863, a day after George Meade's victory at Gettysburg. If Gettysburg rescued and reasserted the Union's will to continue the fight, Vicksburg broke the very back of the Confederacy.

OVERLAND CAMPAIGN, MAY–JUNE 1864

Lincoln congratulated Grant on a victory he called "one of the most brilliant in the world," a triumph that was of "almost inestimable service" to the country. After Grant next presided over the battles for Chattanooga during October and November, the president was persuaded that he had at last found *the* general to lead the Union armies to final victory. Success at Chattanooga bashed open the door to Atlanta—logistical hub of the Confederacy—and to the very heart of the South. On March 12, 1864, the president named Grant general-in-chief, replacing Henry Halleck, who was only too willing to step down and accept what was at the time the novel role of chief of staff.

Unlike Halleck, who had commanded the Union armies from behind a desk in Washington, Grant took to the field, accompanying George Meade, who retained operational command of the Army of the Potomac. While Halleck had promoted the traditional strategy of capturing enemy cities and territory, Grant focused on killing the enemy army. Destroy it, he argued, and you end the war. The conquest of cities and territory was secondary. These were to be attacked only to draw the enemy army into battle under conditions favorable to the Union.

Chosen as Lincoln's warrior-in-chief, Grant in turn tapped William T. Sherman as his deputy. He divided his war plan between himself and Sherman. The Confederates were now fighting with two principal armies. While Grant and the Army of the Potomac would destroy the Army of Northern Virginia under Robert E. Lee, Sherman, assigned command of the armies of the West, was tasked with destroying the Army of Tennessee under Joseph E. Johnston.

Grant commenced his Overland Campaign in pursuit of Lee on May 4, 1864, by crossing the Rapidan River into the so-called Wilderness. If Grant saw himself as a predator, Lee refused to oblige by playing the role of prey. Enlisting the rugged and tangled Wilderness as an ally, the outnumbered Confederate commander attacked Grant's columns as they struggled through. The terrain made it impossible for Grant to mass his superior numbers in order to overwhelm and blunt Lee's attacks. Intense exchange of fire on May 5 and 6 set the brushy woods on fire, suffocating or burning to death as many as two hundred men during the night of May 7–8. By this time, the Army of the Potomac, defeated, had already disengaged.

But, even in defeat, Grant never forgot what he knew to be the controlling equation of this Civil War. The North had more men, more money, more industry, and more of everything than the South. Every man, every cannon Grant lost could be replaced, while Lee could replace nothing. Instead of retreating back north in defeat, Grant sidestepped Lee and advanced southward, to Spotsylvania Court House, at a crossroads en route to Richmond. Lee, his Army of Northern Virginia victorious but depleted, had no choice but to fight Grant again.

For eleven days, from May 8 to 21, the Battle of Spotsylvania Court House spawned some of the most violent combat ever seen on the North American continent. Grant did not merely pound and absorb pounding in return, he maneuvered brilliantly, continually shifting his army to the left, probing, always probing, for his enemy's vulnerable flank, which Lee, seemingly inexhaustible, always managed to cover. Tactically, the long battle ended inconclusively—except that,

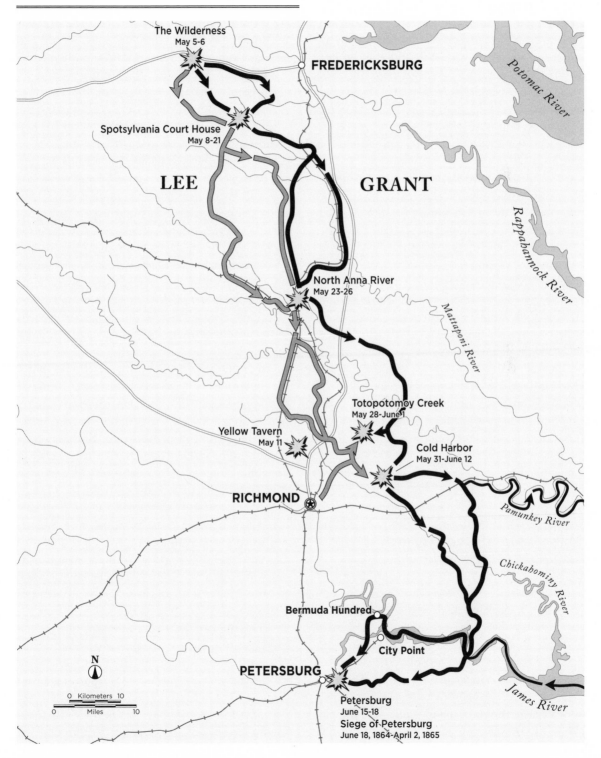

The Wilderness
May 5-6

FREDERICKSBURG

Spotsylvania Court House
May 8-21

LEE

GRANT

North Anna River
May 23-26

Mattaponi River

Rappahannock River

Potomac River

Totopotomoy Creek
May 28-June 1

Yellow Tavern
May 11

Cold Harbor
May 31-June 12

Pamunkey River

RICHMOND

Chickahominy River

Bermuda Hundred

City Point

PETERSBURG

Petersburg
June 15-18
Siege of Petersburg
June 18, 1864-April 2, 1865

James River

N

0   Kilometers   10

0   Miles   10

for a certain fact, the Army of the Potomac had suffered more than eighteen thousand casualties, killed, wounded, captured, or missing, and had inflicted on the Army of Northern Virginia somewhat more than thirteen thousand. Grant had fielded a hundred thousand men, Lee about half that number. Strategically, in what was now a war of attrition, Lee, even when tactically victorious, was losing, and, what is more, the Overland Campaign continued and pushed ever southward.

"I think," Grant wrote in a telegram to the War Department in Washington on May 11, "the loss of the enemy must be greater [than ours]," and, he continued: "I propose to fight it out on this line, if it takes all summer."

He moved next, on May 31, to a crossroads called Cold Harbor, no more than six miles northeast of Richmond. On June 3, at 4:30 in the morning, he hurled sixty thousand Army of the Potomac troops against Lee's entrenched forces, which were all but invisible to the attackers. Out of a total of 108,000 Union soldiers engaged through June 12, Grant would lose 12,737 killed, wounded, captured, or missing. Of these, perhaps seven thousand fell in the first hour of the June 3 attack—and most of them were hit within the engagement's first eight minutes. Years later, the general wrote: "I have always regretted that the last assault at Cold Harbor was ever made."

SIEGE OF PETERSBURG, JUNE 9, 1864–MARCH 25, 1865

Grant was decried as "the Butcher," but Lincoln asserted his absolute faith in him. Since the Overland Campaign had begun, the Army of the Potomac had suffered some fifty thousand casualties—41 percent of its original strength. Lincoln knew this was terrible. He also knew, however, that Grant had inflicted on the Army of Northern Virginia a casualty rate of 46 percent. After the horror of Cold Harbor, the Army of the Potomac was quickly reinforced to

full strength, while Lee could find no one with whom to rebuild his army.

Never one to lick his wounds, Grant quietly slipped the Army of the Potomac out of Cold Harbor and crossed the Chickahominy River. Lee could only assume that he was bound for Richmond and so sent most of his Army of Northern Virginia to cover the capital. But Grant had for once deceived the masterful Lee. Feinting toward Richmond, he marched instead against Petersburg, a rail junction vital to the supply of Richmond and much of inland Virginia.

When the first sixteen thousand Union soldiers arrived outside of Petersburg on June 15, a mere three thousand Confederates defended the city. Tragically, the general commanding this lead Union contingent, William Farrar "Baldy" Smith, bungled what should have been an overwhelming assault. The Confederates quickly reinforced their positions. Grant relieved Smith and personally led two more assaults, on June 16 and 18, but it was too late for a breakthrough, and Grant settled in for yet another siege.

It would last for nine months of misery, the opposing armies hunkered down in a grim and filthy network of entrenchments surrounding Petersburg. In the meantime, Sherman took Atlanta and collaborated with Grant on a change of tactics. Instead of pursuing and killing what was now John Bell Hood's Army of Tennessee, Sherman proposed turning *away* from that army and marching out of conquered Atlanta not west, toward Hood, but east, all the way "to the sea," burning a great swath of countryside and making, as he said, "Georgia howl." From Savannah on the Georgia coast, he would turn toward South Carolina to devastate and punish the state that had brought down this terrible war on the nation. Sherman's objective was fourfold. His operations would deprive the Confederacy of the means of war—the means, indeed, of existence itself. They would break the will of the Confederate people to continue the fight, since the march of destruction would demonstrate the

Artist George P. Healy painted The Peacemakers *about 1868. Shown here is the White House copy of the lost original. Pictured from left to right are Generals Sherman and Grant, President Lincoln, and Admiral David Porter in conference aboard the sidewheel steamer* The River Queen *during March 27–28, 1865. Grant used the vessel as his private dispatch boat plying the Potomac. In February,* The River Queen *hosted the Hampton Roads Conference, at which Lincoln and his secretary of state, William H. Seward, met with Confederate vice president Alexander H. Stephens, Confederate senator Robert M. T. Hunter, and Confederate assistant secretary of war John A. Campbell in an unsuccessful attempt to bring the war to an end.* The White House Historical Association

Confederate government's utter inability to protect and defend the population. They would draw Hood back east, giving Sherman an opportunity to turn against him and destroy his army. Finally, Sherman's long route of march would take his forces up through the Carolinas, to attack the Army of Northern Virginia from the south even as Grant continued to bear down on it from the north. Lee would be crushed in the jaws of a great Union vise.

As Grant continued to hold and batter the Army of Northern Virginia at the Petersburg front and as Sherman harrowed the Confederate heartland, Philip Sheridan, in command of the Army of the Potomac's cavalry, laid waste to the "breadbasket of the Confederacy," the lush Shenandoah Valley. Sheridan promised Grant that, by the time he was through, "if a crow wants to fly down the Shenandoah, he must carry his provisions with him."

APPOMATTOX CAMPAIGN, MARCH 29–APRIL 9, 1865

Out of food, out of ammunition, out of manpower, Robert E. Lee was out of options on April 2, 1865, when what was left of the Army of Northern Virginia evacuated both Petersburg and Richmond. He hoped to continue the fight by moving south to join forces with the Army of Tennessee (now once again under the command of Joseph E. Johnston), but the Federals blocked his way, and so Lee and his diminished and dwindling army moved west, toward Appomattox Court House, in search of railroad transport and rations.

Elements of the Army of the Potomac dogged his march. On April 7, Grant, having reached the town of Farmville, wrote to Lee not so much to demand his surrender as to persuade him of its necessity: "The results of the last week must convince you of the hopelessness of further resistance on the part of the Army of Northern Virginia in this struggle. I feel that it is so, and regard it as my duty to shift from myself the responsibility of any further effusion of blood, by asking of you the surrender of that portion of the Confederate States army known as the Army of Northern Virginia." This led to an exchange of notes between the two commanders, culminating in an offer of terms very different from what might have been expected from "Unconditional Surrender" Grant: ". . . peace being my great desire," he wrote to Lee, "there is but one condition I would insist upon, namely: that the men and officers surrendered shall be disqualified for taking up arms again against the Government of the United States until properly exchanged."

Grant's own account, in his *Personal Memoirs*, speaks volumes of his character as a human being, a warrior, and a leader of warriors. The two generals met in the farmhouse of one Wilmer McLean:

When I had left camp that morning I had not expected so soon the result that was then taking place, and consequently was in rough garb. I was without a sword, as I usually was when on horseback on the field, and wore a soldier's blouse for a coat, with the shoulder straps of my rank to indicate to the army who I was. When I went into the house I found General Lee. We greeted each other, and after shaking hands took our seats. I had my staff with me, a good portion of whom were in the room during the whole of the interview.

What General Lee's feelings were I do not know. As he was a man of much dignity, with an impassable face, it was impossible to say whether he felt inwardly glad that the end had finally come, or felt sad over the result, and was too manly to show it. Whatever his feelings, they were entirely concealed from my observation; but my own feelings, which had been quite jubilant on the receipt of his letter [offering surrender], were sad and depressed. I felt like anything rather than rejoicing at the downfall of a foe who had fought so long and valiantly, and had suffered so much for a cause, though that cause was, I believe, one of the worst for which a people ever fought. . . .

We soon fell into a conversation about old army times. . . . Our conversation grew so pleasant that I almost forgot the object of our meeting. After the conversation had run on in this style for some time, General Lee called my attention to the object of our meeting, and said that he had asked for this interview for the purpose of getting from me the terms I proposed to give his army. I said that I meant merely that his army should lay down their arms, not to take them up again during the continuance of the war unless duly and properly exchanged. He said that he had so understood my letter.

Grant declined to accept Lee's proffered sword, and he permitted Confederate officers to retain their sidearms and soldiers to keep their horses; he knew that most were farmers and would need the animals desperately. When Lee pointed out that his men "had been living for some days on parched corn," Grant opened his commissary to him and his army.

Technically, Lee had done no more and no less than surrender the one army under his command. The war would continue until the other Confederate forces had surrendered as well, but both men knew that the loss of the Army of Northern Virginia signaled the end of it all. Both men also knew that there were some in Washington who wanted the top Confederate leaders to be arrested and tried for treason. They wanted men to hang. Grant gave Lee his word that there would be none of that. The general peace, when it came, would be on the same terms he had given Lee. Grant had no legal authority to make such a guarantee, but he knew that the people of the Union would hail him as a hero, and he intended to use this popular acclaim to make it difficult, if not impossible, for politicians to bring down vengeance on the vanquished. In a way perhaps impossible to measure, Grant's conduct at the McLean house made it possible for this civil war to end instead of, like so many others, continuing endlessly, fought on by embittered bands of irregulars and guerrillas.

The exchange at Mr. McLean's table was perhaps the finest of Grant's many fine hours. A natural soldier who hated battle and bloodshed but was willing to fight with matchless ferocity and shed blood in unprecedented quantity, Grant ended the war as a peacemaker who compelled his countrymen to forswear revenge.

PRESIDENT, FINANCIAL FAILURE, AND AUTHOR OF A MASTERPIECE

Ulysses S. Grant's hard-won stature as the Union's savior made him an almost inevitable candidate for high office. No politician, he was nevertheless elected president of the United States by a landslide in 1868 and reelected four years later.

Mathew Brady's portrait of President U. S. Grant.
LIBRARY OF CONGRESS

Both terms of his administration were blighted by cynical, systematic corruption and casual criminality unequaled even by the notorious Harding administration of the 1920s. Grant's personal reputation remained remarkably unsullied, except that he was marked as something of a dupe, naïve and feckless. When he left office in 1877, he and Julia Grant embarked on a two-year world tour and were feted by the leaders and the people of every country they visited. On his return to the United States, grateful financiers—who were grateful for both the salvation of the Union and for the limitless license to profit the eight years of the Grant administration had given them—bought the Grants a New York mansion, and William H. Vanderbilt personally loaned him $150,000 to found a brokerage.

Not surprisingly, Grant rapidly failed as a financier. Penniless, he gave Vanderbilt everything he owned. In an effort to help him out, Congress restored Grant's rank—he had been named "general of the army," the first of that lofty grade since George Washington—together with full pay. It hardly made a dent. Mark Twain, who saw in Grant's story a monumental publishing opportunity and who saw in Grant's financial plight a national disgrace, offered him the biggest advance ever paid by a publisher to that date, $150,000, for his memoirs. By this time, the savior of the Union had met an enemy he knew he could not defeat. Diagnosed with cancer of the throat, he could not tolerate the thought of leaving behind an impoverished widow. He not only completed the two-volume, 250,000-word *Personal Memoirs of U. S. Grant* in well under a year, but he also created a best-selling masterpiece of first-person historical writing. On July 16, 1885, he penned the concluding paragraphs: "I feel that we are on the eve of a new era, when there is to be great harmony between the Federal and the Confederate. I cannot stay to be a living witness to the correctness of this prophecy. . . ." He died seven days later.

Chapter 19

WILLIAM TECUMSEH SHERMAN

RATING: ★ ★ ★

William Tecumseh Sherman in the uniform of a major general. LIBRARY OF CONGRESS

EVALUATION

A doctrinal and strategic visionary, William Tecumseh Sherman was also a charismatic leader of troops, but he did suffer tactical lapses that on occasion proved costly, as at the Battle of Kennesaw Mountain (June 27, 1864). His profound understanding of the essential brutality of war may have contributed to mental collapse early in the Civil War, but it also drove his strategic and tactical thinking, which were unhampered by illusions of martial glory. Although there is no evidence that Sherman was influenced by the

work of the European military theorist Carl von Clausewitz (1780–1831), he may be regarded as the first important American practitioner of what Clausewitz called "total war," combat practices directed against the enemy civilian population as well as enemy military formations. With Winfield Scott and Ulysses S. Grant on the Union side and Confederate Robert E. Lee, Sherman was one of the key shapers of Civil War combat.

Principal Battles

PRE–CIVIL WAR

Second Seminole War, 1835–1842
- Light combat experience

U.S.-Mexican War, 1846–1848
- Logistical and support duties only

CIVIL WAR
- First Bull Run, July 21, 1861: In Virginia; one of few Union commanders who performed with distinction
- Shiloh, April 6–7, 1862: In Tennessee; in the opinion of H. W. Halleck, "saved the fortunes of the day on [April 6] and contributed largely to the glorious victory of [April 7]"
- Vicksburg Campaign, December 1862–July 4, 1863: In Mississippi; despite a costly defeat at Chickasaw Bayou (December 26–29, 1862), was instrumental in supporting Grant throughout the campaign
- Chattanooga Campaign, October–November 1863: In Tennessee; his attack against Braxton Bragg at Missionary Ridge (November 25, 1863) faltered, but Sherman was subsequently more successful
- Meridian, February 14–20, 1864: In Mississippi; a dress rehearsal for the "total war" tactics practiced on a large scale during the "March to the Sea"
- Atlanta Campaign, May 7–September 2, 1864: In Georgia; despite a costly defeat at the Battle of Kennesaw Mountain (June 27, 1864), the centerpiece of Sherman's strategic genius and controversial execution of a "total war" doctrine

- March to the Sea, November 15–December 21, 1864: In Georgia; brutal, controversial exercise of a scorched-earth "total war" strategy designed to destroy the Confederacy's ability and will to continue to fight
- Carolinas Campaign, February–March 1865: Strategically, a continuation of the March to the Sea: combat directed at civilian production and infrastructure as much as against the enemy army

POST-CIVIL WAR
- The Plains Indian Wars, 1866–1891: First as commander of the Military Division of the Missouri (1865–1869) and then as commanding general of the U.S. Army (1869–1884), Sherman established a "total war" policy, at times verging on genocide, with regard to "hostile" tribes refusing confinement to reservations

Like Ulysses Simpson Grant, William Tecumseh Sherman never set out to be a soldier, but, also like Grant, he proved to be a natural warrior although he remained forever ambivalent about the morality of the profession of arms. As he told the graduating class at the Michigan Military Academy on June 19, 1879, "War is at best barbarism. . . . Its glory is all moonshine. It is only those who have neither fired a shot nor heard the shrieks and groans of the wounded who cry aloud for blood, more vengeance, more desolation. War is hell." Grant would have agreed.

Yet, unlike Grant, who believed wars were won by killing the enemy army, Sherman embraced the doctrine of waging war not only against the enemy army but against the enemy people. *On War*, in which the early nineteenth-century European military theorist Carl von Clausewitz expounded on this "total war" concept, was published in 1832 but was not generally available in the United States until the 1870s. Sherman did not read it when he was a West Point cadet from 1836 to 1840, and there is no evidence that he read it in later life. But that he believed in waging war against soldiers and civilians alike cannot be doubted. During the Civil War, he persuaded Grant, his commanding

officer, to let him "march to the sea" and, in so doing, "make Georgia howl" by burning towns, villages, and farms, and pillaging and destroying all civilian means of productive undertaking. After the Civil War, when he was in charge of creating and executing military policy against the Indians of the western Plains, Sherman expressed "pity" for the Native Americans as victims of the onslaught of white civilization, but he advised Grant in 1866 that "we must act with vindictive earnestness against the Sioux, even to their extermination, men, women, and children."

To the mayor of Atlanta and two city councilmen, who had protested his order that all citizens evacuate the city he had conquered, Sherman replied in a letter of September 11, 1864, "You cannot qualify war in harsher terms than I will. War is cruelty, and you cannot refine it." Was this the heartless creed of a sadistic militarist? Or was it the frank assessment of a military realist? In either case, of all the generals of the Civil War usually judged "great," Sherman is the most difficult to call "heroic" as well. He understood and accepted war as it was fought on a truly terrible scale, which embraced a continent and its civilization. He did not shrink from this understanding, and he commanded others on the basis of it. For this, he became both a highly successful general and a profoundly disturbing figure in American history.

EARLY LIFE AND WEST POINT

For all his similarities to Grant, there was one great difference between them. Grant's roots were humble, while Sherman was born very well connected on February 8, 1820, in Lancaster, Ohio. Charles R. Sherman, his father, was a cultivated man—he had attended Dartmouth College—who practiced law in his father's prosperous office until he was elevated to the Supreme Court of Ohio. According to persistent legend, he named his sixth child (there would be five more) Tecumseh, after the fiercely brilliant Shawnee warrior chief who had led a tribal confederacy in the Ohio country during the American Revolution and the War of 1812. In his *Memoirs* (first edition, 1875), however, Sherman himself claimed that his father named him William, inserting Tecumseh only as a middle name because he had "caught a fancy for the great chief." What is indisputable is that family members and close friends soon took to affectionately calling him "Cump."

In rural Ohio, being a lawyer or even a State Supreme Court justice was a strenuous life of circuit riding in all weather, and during his father's frequent and prolonged absences, Cump was raised by his older siblings, his mother, and his formidably overbearing grandmother. It was a life of comfort and security that was shattered by the sudden death of Charles R. Sherman, who, while on the road, succumbed to a high fever on June 24, 1829. He was forty-one years old.

The man's death was shock enough. Added to it was the realization that most of the judge's earnings had long been siphoned off to pay the massive debt created by a failed business venture. All that was left to his widow and eleven children was the house and everything in it, along with a portfolio of bank stock that produced a very modest annual return. Friends and relatives rushed in to help. But this meant breaking up the large family, which was parceled out to live with others. Cump didn't have to go far. Neighbors Thomas and Maria Ewing took the boy in.

It was a stroke of good fortune amid the tragedy of loss. Like Sherman's father, Thomas Ewing was educated, cultivated, and well connected. A successful country lawyer, he would be elected to the U.S. Senate within a year, in 1830 (and would serve one term, later becoming secretary of the treasury under Presidents Harrison and Tyler, then secretary of the interior under Zachary Taylor). A devout Catholic, his wife, Maria Ewing, insisted that her new foster child, who had been raised a Presbyterian, be baptized in the Catholic Church. This fact reinforced the persistent legend that the name *William* was added to the original *Tecumseh,* the Dominican priest who baptized Cump having chosen it because it was St. William's Day.

The Ewings saw to Sherman's education and, when Cump was sixteen, Senator Ewing exercised the prerogative of his office by appointing him to the U.S. Military Academy at West Point. An earnest and able student as well as a fine athlete—classmate and future Civil War general William Rosecrans called him "one of the brightest and most popular fellows"—Sherman graduated an impressive sixth in the Class of 1840, yet he never had much taste for the military life and, as he wrote in his *Memoirs,* "was not considered a good soldier [at the academy], for at no time was I selected for any office, but remained a private throughout the whole four years." Rosecrans remembered him as "bright-eyed" and "red-headed . . . always prepared for a lark of any kind," which apparently led to a fair number of demerits. "Then, as now," Sherman later wrote, "neatness in dress and form, with a strict conformity to the rules, were the qualifications required for office, and I suppose I was found not to excel in any of these."

Yet his West Point experience did leave at least one indelible impression on him. In a required course on "moral philosophy," Cadet Sherman read *Commentaries on American Law* (1826–1830) by the eminent jurist James Kent (1763–1847). In this work, Kent held that war trumped all ordinary morality and that, in the event of *civil* war, the government was obligated "to defend the laws of the union by force of arms." History buffs and historians alike have often jumped to the conclusion that Sherman, both in the Civil War and the Indian Wars that followed, showed himself to be a disciple of "total war" as advocated by Clausewitz. But Clausewitz did not figure in the West Point curriculum, while Kent did. Sherman had grown up in the law and the practice of law and would himself briefly practice as a lawyer. If he derived his conception of war and morality from any outside authority, it was not the Prussian general, but the American legal scholar.

SECOND SEMINOLE WAR AND U.S.-MEXICAN WAR

It would be more than twenty years, however, before he put that conception into action. Commissioned a second lieutenant in the 3rd U.S. Artillery upon graduation in 1840, Sherman was sent to Florida, where he saw desultory action in the Second Seminole War (1835–1842), which was more of a police action than anything resembling a full-scale war. The army had the thankless—and ultimately hopeless—task of rounding up recalcitrant Seminoles and Creeks and setting them on the march to Indian Territory (present-day Oklahoma and parts of adjacent states), which had been reserved for them pursuant to the Indian Removal Act of 1830.

Outside of a few skirmishes, Sherman experienced nothing of combat in Florida. Subsequently transferred to posts in Georgia and South Carolina, he was especially well received in Charleston, where upper-crust Southerners enjoyed entertaining the foster son of a politician whose Whig sympathies were very much in tune with the interests of the South, including the institution of slavery.

The outbreak of the war with Mexico in 1846 seemed to offer some opportunity for action, glory, and advancement, but Sherman, having failed to make an impression as a soldier, was not assigned to front-line combat, but to supply and commissary duties first in Pennsylvania and then in California. He saw no substantial action, even in California, although he was brevetted to captain, mainly on the strength of his proximity to a combat zone.

Like many other military officers his age, Sherman grew bored and frustrated by prospects for advancement that were slim to none. In his case, he was also haunted by the penury that

had been his father's legacy. He did not want to remain poor. In 1850, Sherman married Ellen Ewing, his foster father's daughter, and shortly afterward wrote to foster brother Hugh Ewing that he "often regretted that your father did not actually, instead of sending me to West Point, set me at some useful trade or business." Thomas Ewing did help Sherman support his bride in the manner to which she was accustomed, but Sherman found the financial aid humiliating. In 1853, three years after his marriage, he ended thirteen years of profound dissatisfaction with his military career by resigning his commission to accept a position a former army friend offered him. Sherman opened and managed the San Francisco branch of a St. Louis-based bank. A financial panic that swept the nation in 1857 hit California especially hard, and the branch failed. Sherman was sent to the firm's New York branch, but that soon collapsed as well.

Deeply in debt, he sold his property, paid off most of his creditors, and thought of returning to the army, but resolved to do so only if he could reenter at a higher rank. Thomas Ewing Jr., his foster father's eldest son, intervened, however, with an invitation to join his law firm in Leavenworth, Kansas Territory. Admission to the frontier bar without a law degree or legal experience proved an easy hurdle. Sherman's "general intelligence and reputation" were sufficient credentials. Hopeful though he was, clients did not come his way. The single case he tried he lost. He wrote to his wife, Ellen, that he looked upon himself "as a dead cock in the pit."

As often as he fell on his face, Sherman seemed always to have family or friends willing to help set him on his feet again. Major Don Carlos Buell, an army buddy who had stayed in the service, told Sherman that the brand-new Louisiana State Seminary of Learning & Military Academy in Pineville, Louisiana—it was scheduled to open on January 2, 1860—was looking for a superintendent. Two more army friends, future Confederate generals Braxton

Bragg and P. G. T. Beauregard, wrote glowing letters of recommendation, and the job was his.

OUTBREAK OF THE CIVIL WAR

Sherman quickly settled in. He liked the South—the climate, his job, and the people. The first academic year of the new institution went very well for him. He was forty now, a time when most men of substance had long settled into comfortable lives. At last, he, too, had found a position that offered at least a whiff of financial stability. On Christmas Eve 1860, while dining with the institution's professor of classics, the meal was interrupted by breaking news. Hours earlier this very day, South Carolina had proclaimed its secession from the United States of America.

"This country will be drenched in blood," Superintendent Sherman warned his dinner companion, "and God only knows how it will end. It is all folly, madness, a crime against civilization! You people"— he meant the *Southern* people—"speak so lightly of war; you don't know what you're talking about. War is a terrible thing!"

Having seen almost nothing of combat himself, this last statement was something of an assumption on his part—an assumption, in fact, few others shared. Nevertheless, Sherman tried to talk sense into his dinner companion, as if this one man represented the whole of the Southern population:

You mistake . . . the people of the North. They are a peaceable people but an earnest people, and they will fight, too. They are not going to let this country be destroyed without a mighty effort to save it. . . . Besides, where are your men and appliances of war to contend against them? The North can make a steam engine, locomotive, or railway car; hardly a yard of cloth or pair of shoes can you make. You are rushing into war with one of the most powerful, ingeniously mechanical, and determined people on

Earth—right at your doors. You are bound to fail. Only in your spirit and determination are you prepared for war. In all else you are totally unprepared, with a bad cause to start with. At first you will make headway, but as your limited resources begin to fail, shut out from the markets of Europe as you will be, your cause will begin to wane. If your people will but stop and think, they must see in the end that you will surely fail.

Of course, neither his dinner companion nor anyone else heeded him. North and South hurtled toward war. Early the following month, when the U.S. Arsenal at Baton Rouge surrendered its stock of arms and ammunition to the Louisiana State Militia, it fell to Sherman, as a quasi-official employee of the state, to sign a receipt for the weapons. He refused. "On no earthly account will I do any act or think any thought hostile . . . to the . . . United States," he declared to the governor and, with this, resigned as superintendent of the academy on January 18, 1861.

John Sherman, now a U.S. senator, advised his jobless brother to call on Abraham Lincoln—who, on March 4, had been sworn in as the sixteenth president of the disintegrating nation—and offer his military services. When he arrived at the capital, William T. Sherman was shocked at how unmilitary the city looked. Even with the enemy at its doorstep, Washington was still playing the part of the sleepy little Southern town it had always been. Military defenses consisted of no more than a hundred regular army troops, many of them more comfortable behind a desk than a musket, and three, perhaps four hundred marines, who were quartered in the old barracks at the corner of Eighth and I Streets. The handful of private volunteer militia companies in town were far more social clubs than genuine military formations.

In his postwar *Memoirs*, Sherman vividly recalled his first meeting with Lincoln. His brother presented him to the president, explaining that he had just resigned from a post in the South.

"Ah," Lincoln exclaimed affably, "how are they getting along down there?"

The commander-in-chief's lightly bantering tone stunned Sherman.

"They think they are getting along swimmingly," he replied grimly. Then, hoping to shake Lincoln up, he sternly observed, "They are preparing for war."

The president nodded. "Oh, well, I guess we'll manage to keep house."

Sherman said nothing more to the president and departed with his brother as fast as rudimentary courtesy permitted. Once the White House door was safely behind him, he exploded to his brother: "You have got things in a hell of a fix and you may get them out as best you can." With this, he turned his back on both Washington and military service, traveling instead to St. Louis, where he accepted an appointment as president of the local streetcar company.

Having sought to get away from the war, Sherman, now a resident of Missouri, a strife-torn border state, found himself in the very midst of it. Still, he persisted in his effort to avoid being sucked in. When, early in April, President Lincoln offered him a position in the War Department with the understanding that it would lead to his appointment as assistant secretary of war, Sherman declined. And after Fort Sumter was bombarded a few days later, he responded to the president's call for seventy-five thousand three-month volunteers with outright ridicule: "Why, you might as well attempt to put out the flames of a burning house with a squirt-gun."

No one, he feared, North or South, appreciated just how big and just how terrible this war would be. But he couldn't keep himself out for long. In May, he called on his brother and others to get him an officer's slot in the regular army. He was commissioned as colonel of the 13th U.S. Infantry.

BATTLE OF BULL RUN, JULY 21, 1861

The reality was that the 13th did not yet exist—at least not beyond a few of Lincoln's three-month volunteers. The rawest of raw recruits, they were precisely the kind of soldiers who would dissolve into confusion in the first major battle of the war, Bull Run, on July 21, 1861. Sherman, who took the war far more seriously than most, crammed as much training into them as he could, then led them into battle with great skill. Untested in combat himself, Sherman performed with conspicuous gallantry, receiving glancing but painful bullet wounds in the knee and shoulder.

The Union's humiliating defeat at Bull Run caused Sherman to doubt his fitness to command, in much the same way as the financial panic of 1857 had shattered his self-confidence as a businessman. But Sherman's performance drew enough notice to come to the attention of President Lincoln, who immediately promoted him to brigadier general of volunteers. Assigned to the Department of the Cumberland, headquartered in Louisville, Kentucky, he served under Brigadier General Robert Anderson but, in October, was suddenly vaulted into command of the department after Anderson stepped down due to illness.

PROMOTION AND BREAKDOWN

In a frenetic time in which inexperienced "political generals" vied for just such prominence, Sherman's first reaction was to shrink from it. He had welcomed service under a senior commander, writing to his wife, Ellen, "Not till I see daylight ahead, do I want to lead." Just now, what he saw was pitch black. Thrust into command responsibility over the bitterly contested border state of Kentucky, in which the Confederates occupied the strategic towns of Columbus and Bowling Green, the officer who had acquitted himself with such gallantry in combat at Bull Run began to lose his nerve. He poured telegrams into the

War Department about the shortages of man-power and equipment that he faced. These were all too real, but he also wildly inflated his estimates of the strength of Confederate forces nearby.

While his local estimates were way off, his predictions that the war as a whole would soon involve hundreds of thousands of troops would prove to be all too prescient. For the present, however, they seemed to observers part and parcel of his hysteria. When War Department superiors responded to his entreaties for reinforcements by suggesting that he use what he had to move against east Tennessee and "liberate" it, Sherman suddenly believed he saw the situation clearly: Washington intended to sacrifice him and his command. To his wife, he wrote that the "idea of going down in History" as such a sacrifice "nearly makes me crazy, indeed I may be so now."

Members of the press and fellow officers certainly thought he was. In an age of overfed military "types" of ample girth, Sherman in 1861 stood out as a gaunt scarecrow of a figure, unshaven yet without a full beard, his unruly hair a flaming red, his eyes wild, his manner alternating restless energy with periods of moody, staring contemplation. When Secretary of War Simon Cameron visited him early in November, a badly shaken Sherman requested relief from command.

Cameron obliged, explaining to a reporter that Sherman was "unbalanced" to such a degree "that it would not be wise to leave him in command." His old friend Don Carlos Buell replaced him, and, it seemed, his career was at an end. Major General Henry Wager Halleck, at the time commanding the Department of Missouri, was a friend. Ignoring reports of Sherman's instability, he reassigned him to central Missouri. Assessing the situation there, however, Sherman promptly reported to Halleck that local Confederate forces were far too strong to be defeated. This contrasted sharply with prevailing reports

Detail of George P. A. Healy's idealized portrait painting of Sherman, about 1866. NATIONAL PORTRAIT GALLERY

by others that the Confederates were notably weak in the region. Halleck believed he had no alternative but to deem Sherman unfit for duty and, in December, he put him on leave. Sherman limped off to Lancaster, Ohio, seeking rest and recuperation. "I am so sensible now of my disgrace," he wrote to his foster brother John Ewing, "that I do think I would have committed suicide were it not for my children. I do not think I can be entrusted with a command."

Yet, even now, Halleck refused to blithely write Sherman off. Just before Christmas, he assigned him to a noncombat role recruiting, training, and administering logistics at Benton Barracks, St. Louis. In this duty, Sherman rapidly recovered his bearings and was soon reassigned as commander of the District of Cairo, headquartered in Paducah, Kentucky, his primary mission to provide logistical support to

Ulysses S. Grant in his campaign to capture Fort Donelson. In Grant, Sherman recognized a bold, supremely competent commander—just the superior under whom he wished to serve. On March 1, 1862, Halleck obliged him by assigning him command of the Fifth Division in Grant's Army of the Tennessee.

BATTLE OF SHILOH, APRIL 6–7, 1862

Like Grant, Sherman was totally surprised by the April 6 Confederate attack on the Union army's encampment at Pittsburg Landing, Tennessee, near Shiloh Chapel. Like Grant, he had turned a blind eye to reconnaissance reports suggesting that the Confederates under Albert Sidney Johnston were moving out of their encampment at Corinth, Mississippi. Like Grant, Sherman had taken almost no defensive measures to protect his own camp, perhaps fearing (as he wrote to his wife) that "they'd call me crazy again" if he did so.

Taken by surprise, however, Sherman continued to pattern himself after Grant. In the midst of bloody chaos, he refused to panic. Far from appearing crazy, he remained supremely calm and collected, as he rallied his division and held his position protecting the Union's right flank. When the first day of battle was over, Sherman was well aware of just how narrowly he had averted a total rout. Approaching Grant, the subject of retreat crossed his mind, but, as he later wrote, "some wise and sudden instinct" prevented his even uttering the word. Instead, he nonchalantly observed that "we've had the devil's own day, haven't we?" To which Grant replied in identical tone, "Yes. Lick 'em tomorrow, though."

With this, the two commanders meshed in thought and spirit. On the second day of battle, Sherman led Grant's counterattack with such ferocity that its success was assured. Three horses were shot from under him, and though bullets penetrated his hand and his shoulder, the battle cured his mental wounds, which had been

far graver. Grant singled Sherman out in his post-battle dispatches, and Halleck reported to Washington the "unanimous opinion here that Brig. Gen. W. T. Sherman saved the fortunes of the day on the Sixth and contributed largely to the glorious victory of the Seventh." Promoted to major general, Sherman wrote to his wife that this gave him "far less emotion" than had his "old commission as First Lieutenant of Artillery," a promotion he had been confident was "merited" while "this [one] I doubt." Yet despite his persistent self-questioning, Sherman would never again falter in command. From Shiloh on, he was Grant's strong right hand and, after Atlanta, would be his strategic counterpoint.

VICKSBURG CAMPAIGN, DECEMBER 1862–JULY 4, 1863

Sherman fully agreed with Grant on the strategic importance of capturing Vicksburg, the Confederate fortress city perched on an impregnable bluff above a hairpin turn in the Mississippi River. Take this objective, and control of the river would fall to the Union while the Confederacy would be effectively broken in two.

Sherman led the initial attack of the campaign, the Battle of Chickasaw Bayou, December 26–29, 1862, in an effort to position the Union army for a frontal assault against Vicksburg itself. Outnumbering the Confederates under Lieutenant General John C. Pemberton better than two to one, Sherman intended to use his thirty thousand men to overwhelm Pemberton's fourteen thousand with a crushing frontal attack but was repulsed in the Mississippi swamp by the well-dug-in Confederates. In the end, Sherman suffered 1,176 killed, wounded, captured, or missing versus Pemberton's modest losses of 187 killed, wounded, or missing.

Undiscouraged by this failure, though not always completely confident of Grant's Vicksburg plan, Sherman continued to serve his commanding officer faithfully and efficiently through the long campaign and siege, which culminated in victory on July 4, 1863. He and his wife suffered a personal tragedy, however, when their son Willie, age nine, succumbed to typhoid contracted during a visit to the Union's camp outside of Vicksburg.

CHATTANOOGA CAMPAIGN AND MERIDIAN EXPEDITION, OCTOBER 1863–FEBRUARY 20, 1864

After the fall of Vicksburg, Sherman was sent to Chattanooga. En route, his train stopped at Collierville, Tennessee, on October 11, just as the 550-man Union garrison there fell under attack by some 3,500 Confederate cavalrymen. Sherman immediately assumed command of the vastly outnumbered force and managed to repulse the attack before continuing to Chattanooga. Shortly after this, when Grant was assigned command of the newly created Military Division of the Mississippi, Sherman took over his former command, the Army of the Tennessee. In November, during the Chattanooga Campaign, Sherman found himself initially struggling at Billy Goat Hill on the north end of Missionary Ridge above the city while the rest of Grant's forces made rapid progress.

After Chattanooga fell to the Union, Sherman was dispatched with a portion of his army to reinforce Ambrose Burnside at Knoxville. From here, in February 1864, he led more than twenty-six thousand men in an expedition against Meridian, Mississippi (February 14–20, 1864), a major Confederate arsenal and logistical center. Ordering his troops to "wipe [Meridian] off the map," Sherman conducted the kind of massively destructive "total war" operation he would soon bring to Georgia and the Carolinas. Railroads were utterly destroyed, and the town itself razed. "Meridian," he subsequently reported, "with its depot, store-houses, arsenal, hospitals, offices, hotels, and cantonments no longer exists."

ATLANTA CAMPAIGN, MAY 7–SEPTEMBER 2, 1864

On March 12, 1864, Abraham Lincoln named Ulysses S. Grant general-in-chief of the Union armies, whereupon Sherman took his place at the head of the Military Division of the Mississippi, thereby becoming commander of the war's Western Theater.

In his new position, Grant's primary mission was to defeat Robert E. Lee and his Army of Northern Virginia. He in turn assigned Sherman to pursue and defeat the Army of Tennessee (first commanded by Joseph E. Johnston, then John Bell Hood, and, later, once again by Johnston). These were the two principal military formations of the Confederate States of America. In targeting them for coordinated destruction, Grant turned his back on the strategy that had dominated the Eastern Theater of the war since the beginning. Formerly, Union commanders had focused on the capture of cities and territory; instead, Grant would direct all efforts to the destruction of the enemy *armies*. Destroy them, he reasoned, and the war would end.

Sherman initially accepted this strategy and commenced the invasion of Georgia with the three armies of what was now his Military Division of the Mississippi: the Army of the Cumberland, sixty thousand men commanded by George Henry Thomas; the Army of the Tennessee, twenty-five thousand under James B. McPherson; and the Army of the Ohio, thirteen thousand troops commanded by John M. Schofield. He led them in frustrating pursuit of the Army of Tennessee over mountainous terrain that made a coordinated showdown battle all but impossible. Nevertheless, Sherman forced Johnston to continually fall back toward Atlanta.

While Grant battled Lee in Virginia, Sherman bore down on the Georgia city that was a manufacturing center and the major rail hub of the Confederacy. The Meridian Expedition had shown Sherman the strategic potential of targeting and destroying infrastructure, both civilian and military, but he was also intent on destroying the Army of Tennessee. Johnston, however, continually eluded destruction, and when he and his artillery took up a position behind formidable defenses erected on Kennesaw Mountain near Marietta, Sherman decided he had had enough of maneuvering.

On June 19, Sherman deployed his forces into positions from which he hoped he could flank Johnston. To achieve this, he had to get troops south of the Confederate left to take and hold the road leading to Marietta. An able tactician, Johnston instantly grasped Sherman's intentions and sent John Bell Hood to defend the

road. On June 22, Hood handily checked Union forces under Joseph Hooker, but, an impulsive and aggressive commander, instead of holding his strong defensive position, Hood counterattacked, suffering heavy casualties as a result. Hooker, however, was intimidated, and Sherman became discouraged at having lost momentum. In the extremity of frustration, Sherman decided to do precisely what had failed earlier during the opening of the Vicksburg Campaign: He made a frontal assault on Kennesaw Mountain.

Sherman launched the attack at eight o'clock on the morning of June 27. Rain and dense undergrowth doomed the uphill assault from the beginning. Johnston's well-placed artillery killed,

Sherman and his staff. Standing left to right: O. O. Howard, William B. Hazen, Jefferson Columbus Davis, and Joseph Anthony Mower. Seated left to right: John A. Logan, Sherman, and Henry Warner Slocum. LIBRARY OF CONGRESS

wounded, or captured some three thousand of the 16,225 troops Sherman committed to the battle. Having bloodied his enemy, Johnston pulled back to the Chattahoochee River on the outskirts of Atlanta, picking up reinforcements in the process. Sherman was able to advance closer to the city, but he understood that Johnston was playing for time, trying to wear him down and force a costly siege. Everyone knew that Abraham Lincoln, who swore to continue the war until the "rebellion" had been defeated, was standing for reelection in November. The platform of the Democratic Party opposing him was to end the Civil War immediately with a negotiated peace. If Johnston could delay the capture of Atlanta long enough to cost Lincoln reelection, he might buy the Confederacy a favorable settlement.

Fortunately for Lincoln, the Union, and Sherman, Confederate president Jefferson Davis did not appreciate Johnston's strategy. Davis saw only that this general had allowed Sherman's army to reach the threshold of a key city. Accordingly, on July 17, 1864, Davis relieved Johnston and replaced him with John Bell Hood, ordering his new commander to prevent Sherman from taking Atlanta at all costs. In attacking Kennesaw Mountain, Sherman had lapsed into rash impetuosity. Now Davis had put one of the Confederacy's two principal armies in the hands of a commander capable of nothing but such impetuous action.

Sherman was determined not to make the mistake of attacking Atlanta head-on, as he had attacked Kennesaw Mountain. Instead, his plan was to cut the four rail lines that led into the city. This would force Hood to come out for a fight or to retreat. It was an excellent plan, but in executing it Sherman betrayed a certain weakness of execution by leaving a gap between McPherson's Army of the Tennessee and Schofield's Army of the Ohio on the one hand and Thomas's Army of the Cumberland on the other. While Schofield and McPherson moved in on the city from the

east, Thomas crossed Peachtree Creek, north of the city. At the gap between these forces, Hood attacked, beginning the Battle of Peachtree Creek on July 20. Had Thomas faltered in his defense during this engagement, his army might have been rolled up and defeated before he could join it with the armies of McPherson and Schofield. But he stood firm.

Two days later, on July 22, having failed to roll up Thomas, Hood turned to McPherson's Army of the Tennessee and very nearly succeeded in flanking it. This action marked the transition from the Battle of Peachtree Creek to the Battle of Atlanta proper. In the initial attack, McPherson was killed as his army struggled to fight off simultaneous assaults on its front and rear. In the end, however, the Union's superior numbers prevailed, and Hood withdrew into the defensive works of the city.

By this time, Sherman had severed the northern and eastern rail lines. He now marched down to the southwest to cut the Macon and Western Railroad. This brought Hood out into the open on July 28 to attack the Army of the Tennessee, which was now under the command of O. O. Howard. In a sharp fight at Ezra Church, west of the city, Howard drove Hood back, inflicting heavy losses on him.

With Atlanta clearly within his grasp, Sherman made a surprising move. Despite occasional tactical lapses, he always retained a keen strategic grasp. He saw and he understood the big picture. He saw and understood that Hood could keep him occupied at Atlanta's doorstep long enough for Nathan Bedford Forrest to march east from Mississippi to attack his army's rear. Rather than take a chance on facing enemies both ahead and behind, he suddenly ceased the artillery bombardment of Hood's entrenchments on August 25. The next day, he slipped away from Hood's front, leading the Confederate commander to assume that he had retreated.

What Sherman had actually done was complete his movement to the south, so that he

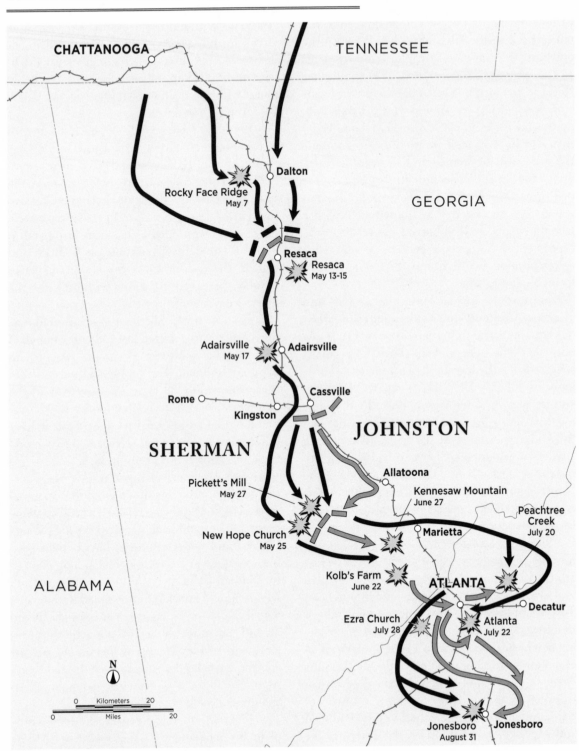

CHATTANOOGA

TENNESSEE

GEORGIA

Dalton

Rocky Face Ridge
May 7

Resaca

Resaca
May 13-15

Adairsville
May 17

Adairsville

Rome

Cassville

Kingston

JOHNSTON

SHERMAN

Allatoona

Pickett's Mill
May 27

Kennesaw Mountain
June 27

Peachtree
Creek
July 20

New Hope Church
May 25

Marietta

Kolb's Farm
June 22

ALABAMA

ATLANTA

Decatur

Ezra Church
July 28

Atlanta
July 22

N

Jonesboro
August 31

Jonesboro

0   Kilometers   20

0   Miles   20

could cut the final rail line into the city. It was September 1 before Hood realized what Sherman had carried off. Now, to avoid being trapped in Atlanta, which was completely cut off from rapid rail reinforcement, supply, and communication, Hood evacuated his army and gave up the city.

On the very next day, Sherman marched in and ordered the people of Atlanta to evacuate. When the mayor and a pair of city councilmen protested, Sherman wrote them a letter in which he declared that: "War is cruelty. . . . You might as well appeal against the thunderstorm as against the terrible hardships of war. They are inevitable, and the only way the people of Atlanta can hope once more to live in peace and quiet at home is to stop the war. . . ."

MARCH TO THE SEA, NOVEMBER 15–DECEMBER 21, 1864

Sherman rapidly transformed the Southern city into a Northern fortress. His victory had deprived the Confederacy of its principal rail nexus and major industrial city and, in the process, had virtually assured President Lincoln of reelection. It also prompted Sherman to collaborate with Grant on a modification of the exclusive focus on the destruction of enemy armies. Instead of pursuing Hood, who was moving west to link up with Forrest, Sherman proposed to leave a large garrison to hold Atlanta and to take most of the rest of his army and turn *away* from Hood, advancing instead to Savannah in a "March to the Sea." This movement would cut through the heart of the Confederacy and would bring Sherman into position to attack Lee's Army of Northern Virginia from the south as Grant continued to bear down on it from the north. At the same time, Sherman and his men would live off the land, pillaging and burning whatever they didn't need. The purpose of this wanton devastation was the demoralization of the South by the destruction of its physical capacity and spiritual

will to continue the war. As for Hood and Forrest in the West, Sherman argued that they were nearly irrelevant to the overall strategy, and if they chose to march east to attack, then they could be dealt with and disposed of.

With Grant's approval, Sherman turned away from Hood in November. For his part, Hood believed that if he could link up with Forrest, he would be able to menace the Union army under Major General George Thomas in Tennessee, thereby forcing Sherman's garrison out of Atlanta to save Thomas. Hood believed he might be able to recover Tennessee for the Confederacy and even launch an invasion of Kentucky and perhaps raid Ohio. Sherman, however, was confident that the redoubtable Thomas could fend for himself. He therefore marched southeast from Atlanta, cutting a flaming swath of destruction all the way to Savannah, which surrendered without a fight on December 21, 1864. Sherman telegraphed Abraham Lincoln: "I beg to present you as a Christmas gift the city of Savannah, with one hundred and fifty heavy guns and plenty of ammunition; also about twenty-five thousand bales of cotton."

Sherman's men had left much of Atlanta in smoldering ruins when they marched out in November, and shortly before his army left Savannah to invade South Carolina, fire broke out in that city as well. Leaving those flames behind, his juggernaut rolled into Columbia, capital of South Carolina. Sherman had promised Grant that he would "make Georgia howl." Now he swore to "punish South Carolina as she deserves." Although Columbia quickly surrendered, fires razed half that town on February 17, 1865. The next day, the Confederates abandoned Fort Sumter as elements of Sherman's forces drew near Charleston. The proud port city quickly surrendered, and the Stars and Stripes were raised once again above Fort Sumter. Sherman did not linger to savor the moment but instead pressed north, targeting the rear of Lee's Army of Northern Virginia.

Carolina Ending, April 26, 1865

In the public eye, Sherman's dramatic March to the Sea overshadowed Grant's dogged siege of the Army of Northern Virginia at Petersburg, and there was much speculation that Sherman was about to replace Grant as general-in-chief of the Union armies. Sherman protested to his senator brother, John Sherman, against any such action. It was reported that he declared his loyalty to Grant by pointing out that "he stood by me when I was crazy, and I stood by him when he was drunk; and now, sir, we stand by each other always."

As it turned out, Grant prevailed at Petersburg without the necessity of Sherman's pincer attack. After Lee surrendered the Army of Northern Virginia to Grant at Appomattox Court House on April 9, 1865, Sherman continued his campaign in North Carolina, occupying Raleigh on April 13. Four days later, he met with Joseph E. Johnston and drew up an armistice far more elaborate than the simple agreement Grant had made with Lee at the McLean house in Appomattox. In fact, the two generals composed what amounted to a full and formal peace treaty, the main provision of which exchanged a blanket amnesty for absolute military surrender.

Sherman (seated third from left center) and treaty commissioners in council with Indian chiefs at Fort Laramie, Wyoming, 1868. Department of the Army, Office of the Chief Signal Officer

Andrew Johnson, who ascended to the presidency on the death of Lincoln on April 15, angrily repudiated the "treaty" on April 21. Five days later, Johnston accepted a simple armistice modeled on the one between Grant and Lee. While President Johnson was willing to let the matter end with this, Secretary of War Edwin Stanton continued to vent his outrage publicly, accusing Sherman of insubordination, stupidity, and even treason. These egregious accusations brought Sherman's soldiers, who idolized their "Uncle Billy," to the verge of insurrection. Officials in Washington wisely sought to defuse the situation by staging a grand victory review through the city's streets, with Grant leading the Army of the Potomac on May 23 and Sherman leading the Army of the Tennessee the next day. To the surprise of the Johnson administration, Sherman's parade outdrew Grant's, and the hard feelings vanished.

Postwar Career

After the war, Sherman was given command of the newly created Military Division of the Missouri, which put him in charge of all army activity west of the Mississippi River. In this post, he took over the direction of warfare against those Indian tribes that refused to submit to reservation life and that interfered with, attacked, or otherwise menaced the western railroads and other manifestations of white settlement in the West. Sherman carried into the Indian Wars the same policy he had carried out in his March to the Sea. He refused to confine military operations to combating warriors and instead endeavored to destroy all "enemy" resources, including game (his troops killed large numbers of buffalo, a staple of the Plains Indians), villages, encampments, and food stores. As Sherman saw it, extermination was the only alternative an Indian had to the reservation. In combat against hostile tribes, Sherman admonished his commanders and soldiers not "to distinguish between male and female, or even discriminate as to age," but to attack all equally.

With Grant's elevation on July 25, 1866, to the rank of general of the army, Sherman was promoted to lieutenant general, and when Grant became president in 1869, he was named commanding general of the United States Army. Although Sherman served in this role until November 1, 1883, shortly before his voluntary retirement from the army on February 8, 1884, his tenure was often stormy, and in 1874, seeking to escape Washington, he moved his headquarters to St. Louis, remaining there until 1876. His two-volume *Memoirs*, published in 1875, are, like Grant's of a decade later, a distinguished historical and literary achievement. On his retirement, there was much talk of his being offered the Republican presidential nomination. Sherman sternly rejected this in a ringing phrase as celebrated as it was emphatic—"I will not accept if nominated and will not serve if elected"—and he spent his last years quietly in New York City, where he died on February 14, 1891.

Chapter 20

JOSEPH HOOKER

RATING: ★ ★

Mathew Brady portrait of Joseph Hooker.
LIBRARY OF CONGRESS

EVALUATION

Bright, aggressive, personally courageous, tactically skilled, an effective leader of men, and a competent administrator, Joseph Hooker had the makings of a fine general officer, but he was also afflicted with an abrasive personality, an egocentric orientation, overweening ambition, opportunistic lapses in loyalty, and a lack of personal discipline, all of which tended to turn subordinate officers, colleagues, seniors, and civilian politicians against him. Hooker's great strength was his individual aggressive initiative, a quality sorely lacking in Union commanders early in the war. This, however, was also the source of his greatest weakness, what U. S. Grant described as a personal ambition that cared "nothing for the rights of others" and a tendency "when engaged in battle, to get detached from the main body of the army and exercise a separate command." In more modern terms, Hooker was not a team player. When his brash, self-centered self-confidence was put to the ultimate test against Robert E. Lee at Chancellorsville, Hooker failed catastrophically and for this reason is remembered—unjustly— far more for his personal peccadilloes (a legendary, probably exaggerated, overfondness for strong drink and women of easy virtue, and an addiction to gambling) than he is for his very real, if flawed, achievements as a military officer.

Principal Battles

PRE-CIVIL WAR

Second Seminole War, 1835–1842
- Light combat experience

U.S.-Mexican War, 1846–1848
- Monterrey, September 21–24, 1846: Brevetted to captain for his gallantry
- National Bridge, March 29, 1847: Brevetted to major for his actions in the culmination of the Siege of Veracruz

- Chapultepec, September 12-13, 1847: Singled out for praise by Winfield Scott and brevetted to lieutenant colonel

CIVIL WAR
- Williamsburg, May 5, 1862: In Virginia, during the Peninsula Campaign; Hooker first exhibited his trademark aggressive approach to combat in his clash with James Longstreet's rear guard
- South Mountain, September 14, 1862: In Maryland; vigorously checked Confederate major general D. H. Hill at Turner's Gap in this prelude to Antietam
- Antietam, September 17, 1862: In Maryland; made the initial assault in this single bloodiest day in U.S. history; claimed that he could have achieved a decisive victory, had he not been sidelined by a severe wound to the foot
- Fredericksburg, December 11-15, 1862: In Virginia; sharply disagreed with and protested Ambrose Burnside's disastrous frontal attacks and was vocal in his condemnation of Burnside for this disastrous Union defeat
- Chancellorsville, April 30-May 6, 1863: In Virginia; in command of the Army of the Potomac, Hooker created a careful plan to destroy Lee and his Army of Northern Virginia but faltered catastrophically in the execution and suffered a costly defeat by Lee's far smaller force
- Battle of Lookout Mountain, November 24, 1863: In Tennessee, Chattanooga Campaign; led a brilliant uphill assault on the mountain's north slope, driving the Confederates from their defenses
- Atlanta Campaign, May 7–September 2, 1864: Commanding XX Corps in George Henry Thomas's Army of the Cumberland, was instrumental in repulsing a dangerous attack by John Bell Hood on July 20

Desperate for anything hopeful to say about George B. McClellan's perpetually stalled Peninsula Campaign, Northern newspapers ran a story wired from the field about III Corps, Second Division and its commander, Joseph Hooker. The reporter who wrote the piece headlined it, "Fighting—Joe Hooker Attacks Rebels," but the papers all picked it up as "Fighting Joe Hooker Attacks Rebels," and with this omission of a lowly em dash was born a Civil War sobriquet and reputation to live up to.

There was good reason to believe Hooker could in fact live up to his accidental name, and there was perhaps even more compelling reason to believe that he could do no such thing.

EARLY LIFE AND WEST POINT

Born on November 13, 1814, Joseph Hooker was the fifth in a line of Joseph Hookers reaching back a century and a quarter through the history of Hadley, Massachusetts. Though locally prominent, the Hookers were no longer wealthy since Joseph's father was, at the time of his son's birth, in the process of losing his fortune in business speculations during the ongoing War of 1812. He soon had to take a menial job as a cattle purchaser while the children, three daughters and Joseph, worked whatever odd jobs they could find as soon as they came of age. Keeping up appearances remained a high priority despite financial hardship, and the family managed to hold onto their large and comfortable house and to finance a fine education for all four children at the local Hopkins Academy.

There was much talk in the Hooker household of young Joseph's preparing for the ministry—his mother, Mary, certainly wanted this—but he himself found the law far more appealing. As the family continued to struggle financially, however, the question became increasingly moot, since college funds were unavailable. That is when one of Joseph's teachers used his influence to wrangle a West Point appointment as an alternative to a civilian college. Thus, like Grant, Sherman, and some others who would fight the Civil War, training for a military career was a matter of expedience rather than the answer to some distinct martial calling.

Joseph Hooker enrolled at the U.S. Military Academy in 1833 as a member of the Class of 1837. He was eighteen, melancholy at having to leave the only home and only life he had known, yet eager to excel academically and especially zealous to proselytize fellow cadets on the thorny subject of abolition. He read avidly and learned rapidly, earning high academic grades but also acquiring a reputation for arrogant argumentativeness in the classroom, as he freely challenged both his classmates and his instructors. This was often abrasive enough, but far more offensive to many—for a large proportion of West Point cadets were plantation Southerners—was Hooker's self-righteous insistence on the absolute rightness of abolition and the absolute evil of Southern slavery. Although his academic achievements should have put him near the top of his class, his overbearing and obnoxious conduct earned him a formidable bundle of demerits, so that he graduated in 1837 twenty-ninth out of a class of fifty.

SECOND SEMINOLE WAR AND U.S.-MEXICAN WAR

Second Lieutenant Hooker's middle-of-the-pack class ranking was insufficient to merit placement in the engineers—reserved for top-ranking graduates—but just barely good enough to get him into the First U.S. Artillery. He was dispatched to Florida to fight in the Second Seminole War. The insurgent nature of the conflict, combined with the dense tangle of the swampy terrain, meant that artillery was of little use, and Hooker found himself involved in sporadic infantry skirmishes rather than anything resembling the kind of Napoleonic battles for which West Point cadets of the era were trained.

In the spring of 1838, with the capture of the Seminole war leader Osceola, the main phase of the war wound down, though not before Hooker achieved promotion to first lieutenant. In 1841, he returned to West Point, this time as adjutant, a position awarded to those marked by their superiors as likely candidates for eventual higher command.

The fact was that Lieutenant Hooker cut an impressive military figure. A fellow officer

recalled him as "handsome" and "polished in manner, the perfection of grace in every movement." If anything, growing up in the distinguished but financially strained Hooker household had taught the young man the art of making an impressive appearance. Beneath the elegant surface, however, some who served with him already noted a certain brash recklessness, boastfulness, and an overfondness for hard liquor, soft women, and the high life.

Still, he had reason to look forward to a successful career, especially when war broke out with Mexico in 1846. Most New Englanders, especially old Massachusetts folk like the Hooker family, opposed the war as an instance of cynical expansionist aggression aimed at extending slavery into the Southwest. Lieutenant Hooker may well have felt this to be the case; however, he did not allow his moral qualms—if he had any—to trump an opportunity for martial glory and rapid professional advancement. Like others of his West Point vintage, he plunged into the war with a passion.

Hooker was assigned as a staff officer successively under three generals, P. F. Smith and two who would play important roles in the Civil War, Benjamin Butler and Gideon J. Pillow. His staff assignments were not quiet desk jobs; Hooker spent much of his time on the front lines, acting as liaison between headquarters and field commanders and ensuring that orders were properly executed. His performance was so outstanding that he was brevetted three times for staff leadership and gallantry. As a result of the Battle of Monterrey (September 21–24, 1846), he was brevetted to captain (and earned among local *senoritas* the appellation of "the Handsome Captain"); after the Battle of National Bridge (March 29, 1847), he was jumped to brevet major; and after Chapultepec (September 12–13, 1847), lieutenant colonel. It was a record of brevet promotion that no other first lieutenant broke during the war with Mexico. General Pillow officially acknowledged that Hooker had "distinguished himself by his extraordinary activity, energy, and gallantry," and no less a figure than Winfield Scott singled him out for his performance at Chapultepec and the capture of Mexico City.

RISE AND DECLINE

Brevet Lieutenant Colonel Hooker had achieved what all of his West Point brethren had hoped to achieve in Mexico: a shower of glory. Yet he soon managed to cloud this achievement. Tennessee-born Gideon Johnson Pillow used his friendship with President James K. Polk to obtain promotion to major general on April 13, 1847, and in September of that year, he was given credit for the American victories at Contreras and Churubusco in a letter signed "Leonidas" and published in the *Orleans Delta*. The letter outraged Winfield Scott, the actual commander in both of these battles, who then exploded in vengeful fury when he discovered that "Leonidas" was in fact none other than Pillow himself. Accusing him of gross insubordination, Scott arrested and held Pillow for court-martial. Both Scott and Pillow had praised Hooker. Scott was general-in-chief of the army, but Pillow had the continued support of the president of the United States. Weighing his options, Hooker decided to testify on Pillow's behalf, thereby making an enemy of the most senior officer in the U.S. Army.

After reverting to his regular army rank at the conclusion of the war, Hooker was promoted to regular army captain in the 1st Artillery Regiment on October 29, 1848. The appointment was vacated the very day it was made. No one knows why, and although he retained his promotion to captain, the record of his military activities is strangely silent until June 9, 1849, when he was named assistant adjutant general for the Pacific Division.

By 1851, the boredom that characterized life in the peacetime army had taken a particularly heavy toll on Hooker. Reportedly, he beguiled his tedious days and nights with liquor, ladies, and gambling, all financed with loans from the likes of William T. Sherman and Henry Halleck. (Though no one denies his penchant for gambling, several historians believe that his reputation as an imbiber was greatly exaggerated in that he was never reported as drunk on duty. As for his womanizing, a persistently popular folk etymology claims that *hooker*—as a synonym for prostitute—originated in Joseph Hooker's notorious appetite for ladies of the evening. Some authorities have suggested that the word was born at this time, the product of Hooker's locally notorious habits. Others assert that the word arose from the disreputable atmosphere of Hooker's headquarters encampments during the Civil War, which were said to be so rife with prostitutes that people took to calling the women "hookers." In fact, the word was in widespread use in Britain and America long before the Civil War as a synonym for *streetwalker*, a woman who entices, snares, or *hooks* her clients.)

Burdened by debt, Hooker took a leave from the army before the end of the year, and when his leave was over in 1853, he resigned his commission on February 21—without bothering to make arrangements to repay either Sherman or Halleck. Like Scott, they would not forget the wrong that Hooker had done them.

"The dashing army officer," Civil War historian Bruce Catton wrote of the next five years of Hooker's life, "descended almost to the level of beachcomber." Settling in Sonoma County, California, he farmed, tried his hand at real estate, and took a stab at state politics, all without success. At last, in 1858, he appealed to Secretary of War John B. Floyd to present his name to President James Buchanan as a candidate for a commission in the regular army as a lieutenant colonel. Presumably due in some measure to the intervention of Winfield Scott, nothing came of this entreaty, and from 1859 to 1861 Hooker served only as a colonel in the California Militia.

RETURN TO THE U.S. ARMY

With the outbreak of the Civil War, Hooker drew upon the militia ranks to organize a California regiment that he intended to offer for service in the Union army back east. When no orders to federalize the regiment materialized, however, Hooker wrote another letter to the president. This time, the president was his personal friend, Abraham Lincoln. Friend or not, however, Lincoln passed the appeal on to General-in-Chief Scott, who promptly buried it in a recess of his War Department desk. Still intent on getting a hearing, Hooker borrowed enough money for the long trip to Washington. Like many another civilian in the Washington area, Hooker followed Brigadier General Irvin McDowell as he led the newly created Army of Northeastern Virginia out of the capital and down to Manassas. Here Hooker closely observed the First Battle of Bull Run on July 21, 1861. Afterward, he called on President Lincoln at the White House. "I was at the Battle of Bull Run the other day," he told him, "and it was neither vanity nor boasting in me to declare that I am a damned sight better general than you, sir, had on the field."

Far from being insulted by Hooker's brash words and insolent tone, Lincoln was receptive. McDowell had proven inept, the army and its officers were demoralized, and most of Lincoln's other generals were full of *ifs, ands,* or *buts.* Here, in welcome contrast, was a forthright man brimming with confidence.

"Colonel—not Lieutenant Colonel—Hooker," Lincoln cooed to him, laying a large hand on his shoulder, "Stay. I have use for you and a regiment for you to command."

Drunk, reprobate, deadbeat, "beachcomber," spurned by no less than Winfield Scott, Joseph Hooker had nevertheless gotten himself back into the army and into a field command. Remarkably, he regarded the colonelcy as a toehold only, and he immediately put the moves on other influential men of his acquaintance to exchange his regimental eagle for the single star of a brigadier general in command of an entire brigade. His efforts quickly paid off, and on August 3, 1861 (retroactive to May 17), he was commissioned a brigadier general of volunteers, occupying a slot two positions *above* Brigadier General Ulysses Simpson Grant.

Despite his own notable absence of personal discipline, Hooker was very much in tune with the efforts of his commanding officer, George B. McClellan, to create in the newly constituted Army of the Potomac a disciplined military formation of the highest morale. His own brigade of that army, which was camped just outside of Washington, became a model of thoroughly drilled spit and polish, tempered by Hooker's insistence that the men under *his* command be given the best food and uniforms available. They adored him for this, and they responded enthusiastically to his demands. Within two months, Hooker's command was expanded from a single brigade to a full division.

He was also given a mission at this time, assigned to sweep southern Maryland clean of Confederate spies and sources of Confederate supply. The timidity and narrow scope of the assignment were all too typical of McClellan, and Hooker, eager to achieve much more, repeatedly appealed to his commander to allow him to lead raids across the Potomac and into rebel territory. McClellan would have none of this, however, and, descending once again into the familiar boredom of army routine, Hooker reputedly retreated into the bottle.

After McClellan, in March 1862, finally commenced his Peninsula Campaign, Hooker's division was called into action in April. Its mission was not to engage in glorious battle but to dig trenches for McClellan's laborious siege of Yorktown. Hooker resented the work, and he empathized with his men, who had signed on to be soldiers, not common laborers. Accordingly, he rewarded them in a way he himself apparently appreciated: with a special ration of whiskey. By and by, a lowly private made bold to present the general with a sample of the ration. Hooker smiled, accepted the soldier's canteen, quaffed a shot, then spat it out. It had been watered shamelessly by officers who, as the portion passed down the chain of command, each siphoned off their share. Promising his men that they would never again be subjected to diluted "rations," Hooker announced that, from then on, the whiskey would be issued directly and exclusively from his own headquarters. He gave his soldiers reason to believe he could do no wrong.

YORKTOWN SIEGE AND SEVEN PINES, APRIL 5–MAY 4 AND MAY 31–JUNE 1, 1862

As Confederate general Joseph E. Johnston made a mockery of McClellan's Yorktown siege by withdrawing his troops and falling back on Richmond early in May 1862, Hooker, supremely frustrated by his superior's inaction, led Second Division, III Corps in a reckless assault on Johnston's rear guard. Confederate major general James Longstreet, commanding the rear guard, counterattacked furiously, taking a heavy toll on Hooker's division. Throughout, the tenacious and gallant Hooker rode through the ranks of his troops, issuing a string of clear personal commands that held his division together. After Hooker directed the placement of artillery, the opening cannon volley spooked his horse. The animal first threw him and then fell on top of him. As his dazed men watched, Hooker crawled out from under the mount and continued to rally his troops.

While ferocious, Hooker's aggression achieved little in proportion to its heavy cost. Nevertheless, the press ate it up. It was in reporting this action that the "Fighting—Joe Hooker Attacks Rebels" headline was printed without the dash, and Hooker would complain about the nickname from then on, claiming that it made people think he was "a hot-head, furious young fellow" who sacrificed his men needlessly. Nevertheless, he made liberal use of the platform the press coverage provided to denounce McClellan for his persistent unwillingness to support his aggressive initiative.

At the Battle of Seven Pines (May 31–June 1, 1862), Hooker's aggressive swagger was well on its way to becoming the stuff of legend. He told a fellow commander, whose troops were moving too slowly ahead of him, to "get out of the way" and make room for his own "two regiments . . . that can go anywhere." To McClellan he boasted that he could hold his position against a hundred thousand of the enemy. Soon the *New York Times* assigned a reporter to cover Hooker and his division exclusively. Yet if he was capturing the attention of the press and public, Hooker noted bitterly that McClellan was ignoring him altogether. There was not one mention of Hooker and the Second Division in the commanding general's report on Seven Pines. "If I had commanded," Hooker testily declared, "Richmond would have been ours." McClellan, he sputtered, "is not only not a soldier, but he does not know what soldiership is."

When, instead of relieving the braggart for insubordination, McClellan notified him that he intended to recommend him for corps command, Hooker executed an abrupt about-face, suddenly shifting all blame from McClellan to McClellan's present roster of corps commanders. "If these officers are still to be imposed upon him [McClellan]," he wrote to Senator James Nesmith of Oregon, "God help him." Then he went on to issue a threat of resignation: "If I cannot be placed upon the same footing of other officers of the Army, the sooner I quit it the better. I will not fight their battles for them with the doors of promotion closed to me." This missive was but one of a veritable barrage he delivered to a number of influential senators. The result? In July 1862, Hooker was duly promoted to major general of volunteers.

SECOND BATTLE OF BULL RUN, SOUTH MOUNTAIN, AND ANTIETAM, AUGUST 28–30 AND SEPTEMBER 14 AND 17, 1862

Beaten down by the Seven Days Battles (June 25–July 1, 1862), McClellan began a slow and ignominious withdrawal from the peninsula under orders to link up with the newly constituted Army of Virginia commanded by Major General John Pope. Hooker and his 2nd Division, still part of III Corps under Major General Samuel P. Heintzelman, were transferred from the Army of the Potomac to the Army of Virginia.

Hooker fought with his customary aggression and confidence in the Second Battle of Bull Run (August 28–30, 1862) and was one of the very few Union commanders to come out of this catastrophe looking good. There was talk not merely of elevating him to corps command but of relieving Pope and making Hooker commanding officer of the entire Army of Virginia. Lincoln nipped this conversation in the bud with a vague comment that the others seemed to understand perfectly. Hooker, Lincoln said, "gets excited."

Postmaster General Montgomery Blair put his own objection in more concrete terms, calling Hooker "too great a friend of John Barleycorn."

At a loss for Pope's successor, Lincoln turned back to none other than George B. McClellan, reaffirming him as commander of the Army of the Potomac, which would be enlarged by its absorption of the Army of Virginia. On September 6, 1862, Joseph Hooker was given V Corps in the combined army.

He and his new corps soon found themselves at the tip of the spear in confronting Robert E. Lee's Army of Northern Virginia as it invaded Maryland. At the Battle of South Mountain (September 14, 1862), he was relentlessly aggressive in checking Confederate major general D. H. Hill at Turner's Gap, then moved on to Sharpsburg on the Antietam Creek, where,

on September 17, he made the opening attack in what would prove to be the bloodiest single day in U.S. history. Hooker slammed into Stonewall Jackson's corps, at first pushing it back, then fighting it to a standstill.

Hooker was at his best in this assault. He inspired his men to carry out a sustained main-strength effort, but his presence on the battlefield ended prematurely when he received a severe wound in the foot. He claimed—and seems sincerely to have believed—that Antietam would have been a decisive rather than a razor-thin Union victory if only he had been able to remain in the field to keep his men pushing. Remarkably, McClellan, perpetual butt of Hooker's criticism, expressed this very same opinion: "Had you not been wounded when you were," he wrote in a letter immediately after the battle, "I believe the result of the battle would have been the entire destruction of the Rebel's army."

As it was, Hooker moved once again into the running for Army of the Potomac command, this time to replace McClellan. To Lincoln and others who came to visit him as he recovered from his wound, Hooker unabashedly touted his prowess in contrast to McClellan's feebleness. If he had had just three more hours on the field, he said to Lincoln, he would have made "the rout of the enemy sure."

The president listened, but he could not bring himself to choose Hooker. Twice, he had tried to recruit Ambrose Burnside to command the Army of the Potomac, and each time, Burnside protested that he was not up to the task. At last, Lincoln stopped asking. Instead, he issued General Order No. 182, which relieved McClellan and replaced him with Burnside. When Major General Catharinus Putnam Buckingham delivered the order to him, Burnside once again protested his inadequacy. This time, Buckingham knew precisely how to respond. *Very well, if you don't accept the order, Joe Hooker will.* Affable to a fault, there was, it seemed, no one Burnside *didn't* like and admire. No one, that is, except Joseph Hooker, whom Burnside (like so many others) condemned as hyper-ambitious, disloyal, and unreliable. Faced with Buckingham's ultimatum, Burnside took the job.

BATTLE OF FREDERICKSBURG, DECEMBER 11–15, 1862

On assuming command of the Army of the Potomac, Burnside carried out an operational reorganization as sweeping as it was ill-advised. He replaced the time-honored conventional corps structure with three huge and inherently unwieldy "grand divisions," assigning Hooker to command the largest, composed of forty thousand men. Eager to show himself as boldly decisive as McClellan had been overcautious, Burnside proposed a frontal assault on the elaborately defended Confederate positions in the hills behind Fredericksburg, Virginia.

Hooker dismissed the plan as "preposterous." Had he appended the adverb "tragically" to this word, his assessment would have been entirely accurate. Hooker protested each of the fourteen futile assaults Burnside ordered, but he always attempted everything the commander required. In the end, the Army of the Potomac suffered 12,653 killed, wounded, captured, or missing—for which Hooker tore into Burnside immediately after the battle, describing him as a "wretch . . . of blundering sacrifice." Later, he elaborated on this in testimony before the congressional Joint Committee on the Conduct of the War. For his part, Burnside sought Lincoln's approval to remove Hooker from command as insubordinate and "unfit to hold an important commission during a crisis like the present." When Lincoln refused to dismiss Hooker, Burnside challenged the president to choose between them. If his choice was Hooker, Burnside would tender his resignation.

In fact, as Lincoln saw it, the choice was no longer between Burnside and Hooker, but between Hooker and George Gordon Meade.

Burnside was out as commander of the Army of the Potomac.

Meade was a solid, if uninspired performer. Although notoriously prickly and ill-tempered, there was never a question of his loyalty. Hooker, however, had incurred widespread resentment and distrust over the years. His reputation as a schemer was well deserved, yet most of the army had begun to see his elevation to command of the Union's biggest, most important force as well-nigh inevitable. Whatever else he had shown himself to be, he was consistently and undeniably aggressive. And that was the kind of general the president and the public demanded.

TAKING COMMAND

Fighting Joe Hooker was appointed to command the Army of the Potomac on January 26, 1863. On that day, Abraham Lincoln sent him a letter remarkable for the absolute frankness of its appraisal of the addressee:

I have placed you at the head of the Army of the Potomac. Of course I have done this upon what appear to me to be sufficient reasons. And yet I think it best for you to know that there are some things in regard to which, I am not quite satisfied with you. I believe you to be a brave and a skillful soldier, which, of course, I like. I also believe you do not mix politics with your profession, in which you are right. You have confidence in yourself, which is a valuable, if not an indispensable quality. You are ambitious, which, within reasonable bounds, does good rather than harm. But I think that during Gen. Burnside's command of the Army, you have taken counsel of your ambition, and thwarted him as much as you could, in which you did a great wrong to the country, and to a most meritorious and honorable brother officer. I have heard, in such way as to believe it, of your recently saying that both the Army and the Government needed a Dictator. Of course it was not for this, but in spite of it, that I have given you the command. Only those generals who gain successes, can set up dictators. What I now ask of you is military success, and I will risk the dictatorship. The government will support you to the utmost of its ability, which is neither more nor less than it has done and will do for all commanders. I much fear that the spirit which you have aided to infuse into the Army, of criticising their Commander, and withholding confidence from him, will now turn upon you. I shall assist you as far as I can, to put it down. Neither you, nor Napoleon, if he were alive again, could get any good out of an army, while such a spirit prevails in it.

And now, beware of rashness. Beware of rashness, but with energy, and sleepless vigilance, go forward, and give us victories.

Yours very truly
A. Lincoln

What nobody expected of Hooker was the skill with which he administered his new command. He saw his most important task as rebuilding the morale of the Army of the Potomac. Toward this end, he substantially improved rations, he saw to it that camps observed basic principles of sanitation and hygiene, he did much to end inefficiency and corruption in the quartermaster system, he modernized hospital services, and he created a generous and equitable furlough system to give personnel more opportunities to visit their loved ones. Hooker also cracked down on deserters (they were to be shot, summarily) and generally improved training and drill. He scrapped Burnside's unwieldy grand divisions and returned to the more traditional corps structure, but, at the same time, made a radical reform of the cavalry—always a weak link in the Union forces—by consolidating it into its own corps. He introduced one further innovation, assigning to the men of each of the seven Army of the Potomac corps distinctive hat badges to identify their corps membership. The emblems worked wonders for morale, as

the soldiers came to regard them not merely as badges of identification, but badges of honor. In the end, Hooker boasted—not, this time, about himself, but about what he called "the finest army on the planet . . . the finest army the sun ever shone on."

And he continued: "May God have mercy on General Lee, for I will have none."

CHANCELLORSVILLE, APRIL 30–MAY 6, 1863

Much as Burnside had sought to distinguish himself from the chronically dilatory McClellan by quickly planning an offensive, so Hooker laid out a fresh campaign plan for an advance against Richmond. In contrast to Burnside, Hooker planned carefully and subtly. He did not intend to repeat Burnside's catastrophically simplistic frontal assault. Instead, he would send his newly created cavalry corps deep behind enemy lines to disrupt supply and communications from the rear. This would serve to draw Lee's attention from the main attack. Then, exploiting his far superior numbers, Hooker planned to use a portion of the Army of the Potomac to hold down Lee at Fredericksburg from the front while most of the rest of his army made a wide flanking sweep to hit the Army of Northern Virginia from the rear. With Lee battered into submission, the next step was on to Richmond at long last.

It was a good plan, and Hooker had done a fine job of conditioning his army. Yet it all nevertheless went wrong, very wrong in the execution.

Under an overly cautious Brigadier General George Stoneman, the cavalry corps failed totally in its mission of penetration, and the large-scale raid was ineffective. In the meantime, although the infantry and artillery accomplished their flanking march and were positioned for a surprise attack on Lee's rear, Hooker suddenly and uncharacteristically suffered a failure of nerve. The first reports of contact with the Army of Northern Virginia on May 1, 1863, should

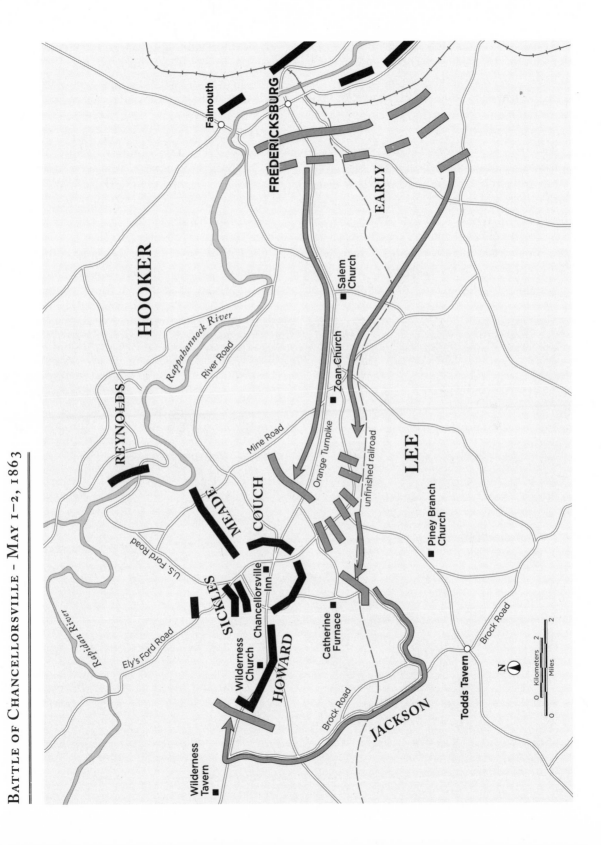

have been his signal for all-out effort at Fredericksburg. Instead, Hooker relinquished the initiative by withdrawing to nearby Chancellorsville, where he deployed his troops into positions not for an offensive, but to respond to Lee's anticipated attack.

Robert E. Lee, however, did not oblige by attacking in the manner Hooker expected. It is an inviolable tactical maxim that a general never divides his army in the face of the enemy. But this is precisely what Lee did, splitting his forces, outnumbered though they were, so as to confront both elements of Hooker's own divided army. Even more remarkably, he split his forces a second time, dispatching Stonewall Jackson's corps on a flanking march to hit Hooker's vulnerable right. This attack routed XI Corps, prompting Hooker to assume a fully defensive posture. At Chancellorsville, the Army of the Potomac numbered nearly 134,000 men against just under 71,000 in the Army of Northern Virginia. His nerve failing him at the last minute, Hooker squandered this huge advantage, absorbed a staggering 17,197 casualties, killed, wounded, or missing, and went into retreat. About half his men had never even been committed to the battle.

History has tended to oversimplify what happened by portraying Chancellorsville as nothing more or less than "Lee's masterpiece."

Captain Andrew J. Russell photographed these Confederate dead, killed during the Battle of Chancellorsville, behind the stone wall of Marye's Heights, Fredericksburg. NATIONAL ARCHIVES AND RECORDS ADMINISTRATION

There is no denying that it was an extraordinary achievement. Using daring high-risk tactics, the Confederate commander defeated a much larger adversary.

But it wasn't that simple. Even in victory, the cost to Lee was terrible. Of 60,892 Army of Northern Virginia men actually engaged in the battle, 13,303 became casualties, killed, wounded, or missing—nearly a 22 percent casualty rate versus about 13 percent for the Union. Perhaps worst of all, Thomas "Stonewall" Jackson was mortally wounded by friendly fire during the battle. Upon Jackson's death, Lee moaned: "I have lost my right arm." His "masterpiece" was, in fact, a Pyrrhic victory.

As for Hooker's reported "failure of nerve," it is important to note that, in the thick of combat on May 3, a Confederate cannonball struck his headquarters, splintering a wooden pillar against which he was leaning. Half of it (Hooker later wrote) struck him "in an erect position from my head to my feet." Knocked unconscious, Hooker was out cold for more than an hour. Groggy, he nevertheless refused to yield command, even temporarily. It is possible that the immediate and lingering effects of this trauma to the brain adversely affected his performance throughout the rest of the battle.

Abraham Lincoln's verdict on Chancellorsville was stark. "My God!" he groaned. "My God! What will the country say?"

For his part, Hooker first tried desperately to shift blame for the defeat on subordinates, especially (with some justification) cavalry commander Stoneman, whom he summarily relieved. The ultimate, inescapable fact of the battle, however, even Hooker could not bring himself to evade. In a jumble of botched execution, he had failed to commit fully half of his forces to the battle, and he had employed the rest (as one officer remarked) like a "disjointed army." Reportedly, Hooker himself admitted, "Well, to tell the truth, I just lost confidence in Joe Hooker." Some historians doubt he actually said this, but,

if he did, it was surely the most candid and least political statement he ever made.

RELIEVED

President Lincoln was not quick to remove Hooker; however, while Lincoln had earlier agreed to allow him to bypass General-in-Chief Henry Halleck (whom Hooker despised and who, in turn, despised him) and to communicate instead directly with the White House, the president now ordered Hooker to communicate only with Halleck before taking any major action.

In the wake of Chancellorsville, Hooker seemed to those close to him (in the words of a friend from California days) "broken . . . dispirited, and . . . ghostlike." Nevertheless, he had a new plan. After Chancellorsville, Lee had pulled out, clearly intending to launch a new invasion of the North. Instead of pursuing Lee or otherwise defending against the invasion, however, Hooker proposed making an immediate assault against Richmond, arguing that this would bring Lee out for a showdown battle that would destroy him.

Whether from his kneejerk conservative conventionality or a desire to thwart Hooker and thereby prompt his resignation, Halleck vetoed the plan, and, what is more, Lincoln concurred. Hooker was admonished to keep the Army of the Potomac north of the Rappahannock, its mission first and foremost to protect Washington, D.C., and Baltimore and, only secondarily, to locate the Army of Northern Virginia as it slipped down the Shenandoah Valley into Pennsylvania, intercept it, and defeat it.

The undeniable truth was that Abraham Lincoln had lost confidence in Hooker. When Hooker subsequently fell into a dispute with Halleck over the status of defensive forces at Harpers Ferry, he impulsively offered his resignation. This time, the president didn't blink. On June 28, three days before the Battle of Gettysburg, he replaced Hooker as commander of the Army of the Potomac with Major General George Gordon Meade.

CHATTANOOGA AND ATLANTA CAMPAIGNS, OCTOBER-NOVEMBER, 1863, AND MAY 7-SEPTEMBER 2, 1864

Relieved as Army of the Potomac commander, Hooker was assigned command of XI and XII Corps and sent to reinforce the Army of the Cumberland around Chattanooga, Tennessee. On November 24, he sent three of his divisions against Confederate positions on the northern slope of Lookout Mountain. In a remarkable action, the Union troops completely dislodged the Confederates, forcing Braxton Bragg to abandon his mountain defenses. For this, Hooker was rewarded with a brevet to major general in the regular army, only to be mortified by General Grant's pointed omission of the triumph in his official report.

Hooker's next major command was in Sherman's Atlanta Campaign (May 7–September 2, 1864) at the head of a unit now designated the XX Corps. On July 20, 1864, Hooker's corps was instrumental in repulsing an attack by the Confederate Army of Tennessee under John Bell Hood against the Union's Army of the Cumberland. Visiting Hooker's headquarters the next day, Sherman brutally dismissed both the accomplishment and the great sacrifice it had cost. To Hooker's report of his heavy losses, Sherman responded, "Oh, most of 'em will be back in a day or two," implying that his brave men had neither been killed nor wounded but had (in the word of the day) "skedaddled."

Sherman's ill will toward Hooker was confirmed after Major General James McPherson, the Union Army of the Tennessee commander, was killed on July 22, 1864, during the Battle of Atlanta. In terms of seniority, Hooker was an obvious choice to replace McPherson. Sherman chose O. O. Howard, a former Hooker subordinate, instead. To his immediate superior, Army

of the Cumberland commander Major General George H. Thomas, Hooker submitted his resignation. "I have learned that Major General Howard, my junior, has been assigned to the command of the Army of the Tennessee," he wrote to Thomas. "If this is the case, I request that I may be relieved from duty with this army. Justice and self-respect alike require my removal from an army in which rank and service are ignored."

Thomas thought sufficiently of Hooker's claim to refer the matter to Sherman and President Lincoln. Siding with Hooker, Lincoln sent Sherman a telegram requesting that he name Hooker to replace the slain McPherson. Sherman, however, stood firm on his choice of Howard, and when Lincoln pressed him, he offered his *own* resignation. With this, Lincoln bowed to the inevitable, and Hooker was allowed to resign from the Army of the Cumberland.

For his part, Sherman was glad to be rid of a man he deemed an "envious, imperious . . . braggart," for whom "[s]elf" always "prevailed." In his 1885 *Personal Memoirs*, Grant finally gave Hooker the credit he had earlier withheld for his achievements at "Lookout Mountain and into Chattanooga Valley," calling them "brilliant." But, he added, "I nevertheless regarded him as a dangerous man. He was not subordinate to his superiors. He was ambitious to the extent of caring nothing for the rights of others." Grant condemned him as a lone wolf: "His disposition was, when engaged in battle, to get detached from the main body of the army and exercise a separate command, gathering to his standard all he could of his juniors."

Having resigned from the Army of the Cumberland, Fighting Joe Hooker was effectively exiled from further significant participation in the war. In September 1864, he was assigned command of the Northern Department, which encompassed Michigan, Ohio, Indiana, and Illinois. His mission was to supervise the draft, to guard the Confederate prisoners of war confined in the region's large and squalid camps, and to stand guard over the northern frontier. He found time to court and (shortly after the war) to marry the sister of Ohio congressman William S. Groesbeck, Miss Olivia Augusta Groesbeck, and on June 27, 1865, he assumed command of the Department of the East, which took in New England plus New York and New Jersey. Later in the year, Hooker was gratified by a report of the Joint Committee on the Conduct of the War that exonerated him for the defeat at Chancellorsville. In November, however, he was felled by a stroke that left him temporarily paralyzed on his right side. Recovering by the summer of 1866, he resumed active command of the Department of the East, only to be felled by another stroke in 1867, which forced him to obtain a leave of absence. Seeking a cure in travel, he and his wife set sail for Europe, returning in July 1868. A short time after this, Mrs. Hooker died, and on October 15, 1868, Joseph Hooker retired from the army with the regular army rank of major general. Although he took up the writing of a memoir, he did very little else before he, too, died—on October 31, 1879.

Another Brady image of Hooker. LIBRARY OF CONGRESS

Chapter 21

GEORGE H. THOMAS

RATING: ★ ★ ★

George H. Thomas is shown in an engraving published in Harper's Pictorial History of the Civil War, *1866.*

AUTHOR'S COLLECTION

EVALUATION

In an era of glory seekers, George H. Thomas put steadfast devotion to duty, perseverance, methodical professionalism, courage, and loyalty above all else. His Virginia birth cost him the rapid promotion to independent command he deserved even as his absolute devotion to the Union cost him his relationship with his Southern family. Deliberate in manner, partly by his nature and partly because of a back injury sustained before the war, his West Point cavalry students nicknamed him "Slow Trot Thomas," which underscored his methodical approach

to combat. This was sometimes confused with uncertainty and delay, even by superiors, such as U. S. Grant, who should have known better. Possessed of a solid tactical and strategic grasp, he was sure and determined in both attack and defense. Unflappable and fearless, his refusal to yield at Chickamauga saved the Union army from disaster there and earned him a far more laudatory sobriquet: the "Rock of Chickamauga." Ezra J. Warner, long deemed an authority on Civil War biography, judged his combat performance unsurpassed "by any subordinate commander in this nation's history."

Principal Battles

PRE–CIVIL WAR

Second Seminole War, 1835–1842

- Although assigned to the artillery, Thomas led infantry patrols in numerous skirmishes

U.S.-Mexican War, 1846–1848

- Fort Brown (Fort Texas), May 3–9, 1846: Served with Zachary Taylor in the opening battle of the war
- Resaca de la Palma, May 9, 1846: Commanded a gun crew
- Monterrey, September 21-24, 1846: Showed extraordinary heroism in positioning and commanding a gun in a narrow alley during this urban operation, for which he was brevetted
- Buena Vista, February 22-23, 1847: Praised by his commanding general for his coolness and accuracy in command of his gun crew

CIVIL WAR

- Mill Springs, January 19, 1862: In Kentucky; won the first significant Union victory of the war at Perryville, October 8, 1862: In Kentucky; arrived on the field too late to make a significant impact
- Stones River, December 31, 1862–January 2, 1863: In Tennessee; dramatic demonstration of Thomas's "do or die" approach to combat

- Chickamauga, September 19–20, 1863: In Georgia; his heroic stand amid a crumbling Union situation saved the Army of the Cumberland from annihilation and established Thomas as the "Rock of Chickamauga"
- Chattanooga Campaign, October–November 1863: In Tennessee; chosen to replace William Rosecrans as commanding general of the Army of the Cumberland, Thomas vowed to hold Chattanooga "till we starve"; he was overall commander of the Battle of Missionary Ridge (November 25, 1863), which drove the Confederates from their positions on Lookout Mountain
- Atlanta Campaign, May 7–September 2, 1864: Thomas's Army of the Cumberland supplied more than half the force Sherman employed in the campaign
- Nashville, December 15–16, 1864: Methodical in planning, this battle neutralized John Bell Hood's Army of Tennessee, effectively taking it out of the war

Just before dawn on August 22, 1831, Nat Turner, fiery lay preacher and slave, led what slaveholding Southerners termed a "servile insurrection," a fierce rampage that resulted in sixty murders and sent waves of terror throughout the South. It started at the home of Turner's master, Joseph Travis, in Southampton County, Virginia, as Turner and his cohorts killed every white member of the Travis household. Fanning out into the county, they killed every white person who happened to cross their path. As they swept through the region, more slaves joined in a campaign of mayhem that lasted until the next morning. Among those who fled before Turner and his fellow slaves were fifteen-year-old George Henry Thomas, his sisters, and their widowed mother, all of whom cowered in the woods until the danger had passed.

When the Civil War began in April 1861, the majority of U.S. Army officers were Southerners, most of whom summarily resigned their commissions to join the Confederate forces. If any son of the South would have been assumed to count himself among this number, it was George Thomas, raised on a plantation and nearly the victim of a slave rebellion. For his family, the matter of allegiance was never in question. As with Robert E. Lee and so many others, Virginia, not the United States, was their "country," and they were shocked when Major George Thomas, U.S. Army, turned down Virginia governor John Letcher's offer on March 12, 1861, of a post as chief of ordnance in the Virginia Provisional Army. When Southern states had begun to secede in 1860, Thomas was at first ambivalent about his loyalty, but when war actually came, however, Thomas's Northern-born wife explained that "whichever way he turned the matter over in his mind, his oath of allegiance to his government always came uppermost."

Once Thomas fully realized his commitment to his oath, he was a rock—that word would come to characterize him—and one of the most tenacious and effective combat leaders in the war. The price he paid was terrible. His family disowned him during the war and refused to reconcile with him after it.

EARLY LIFE AND WEST POINT

He was born the fifth of nine children at Newsom's Depot, Southampton County, Virginia, just five miles from the North Carolina line. His father, John, was a prosperous and ambitious planter, who worked alongside his three male children and twenty-four slaves to farm his 685 acres. When George was just thirteen, John Thomas died in a farm accident, leaving his large family in straitened circumstances. Despite this and the terror of Nat Turner's Rebellion, it was said that young George knowingly broke Virginia law by teaching his family's slaves to read (some historians dismiss this as a legend unfounded in fact).

George Thomas had never intended to follow in his father's footsteps as a planter. Educated at a local academy, he went to work in the law office of his Uncle James Rochelle. In the end, however, like Ulysses S. Grant, William Tecumseh

Sherman, and Joseph Hooker, young men of good families with limited funds, George Thomas found both a means of present sustenance and future career in the United States Military Academy at West Point. In 1836 Congressman John Y. Mason secured his appointment to the Class of 1840. When a grateful Thomas made a special trip to Washington to thank the congressman, he was met by a stern warning: "If you should fail to graduate, I never want to see your face again." It seems that every other young man from Southampton County Mason had appointed to the academy had failed miserably.

The congressman's ultimatum would prove to be but the first of many do-or-die military assignments George Thomas would accept.

At twenty when he enrolled, Thomas was sufficiently mature in age and manner to merit the nickname "Old Tom," and he cultivated friendships with classmates William T. Sherman, Philip Sheridan, William Rosecrans, Don Carlos Buell, Joseph Hooker, and U. S. Grant as well as future Confederate officers Daniel Harvey Hill, Braxton Bragg, and William Hardee. Far from letting Congressman Mason down, he earned a promotion to cadet officer in his second year and performed well enough to come in twelfth in a class of forty-two when he graduated in 1840. This respectable showing was not sufficiently stellar to get him into the engineers—reserved for the very highest achievers—but it did secure him a second lieutenant's commission in Company D, 3rd U.S. Artillery.

SECOND SEMINOLE WAR AND U.S.-MEXICAN WAR

His first posting was to Fort Lauderdale, Florida, late in 1840 during the Second Seminole War. The mission of the 3rd U.S. Artillery was the same as that of the other army units assigned to Florida: hunt down and round up recalcitrant Seminoles and Creeks and set them marching west to Indian Territory pursuant to the Indian

Removal Act of 1830. Since cannon were of no use in this mission carried out in tangled, swampy terrain, Second Lieutenant Thomas led infantry patrols, doing so with sufficient success to merit a brevet promotion to first lieutenant on November 6, 1841.

In 1842, he was transferred to New Orleans, and by 1845 served at Fort Moultrie in Charleston Harbor and Fort McHenry in Baltimore. As war with Mexico began to look inevitable, the 3rd U.S. Artillery was ordered to Texas in June 1845. Thomas was in command of gun crews at the Battles of Fort Brown (May 3–9, 1846), Resaca de la Palma (May 9, 1846), Monterrey (September 21–24, 1846), and Buena Vista (February 22–23, 1847). General Zachary Taylor himself praised "the services of the light artillery" at Buena Vista, and Brigadier General John E. Wool singled out Thomas, without whom "we would not have maintained our position a single hour." The commander of Thomas's battery described his "coolness and firmness," calling "Lieutenant Thomas . . . an accurate and scientific artillerist." Coolness, firmness, "scientific" accuracy, all these were qualities Thomas would display in one Civil War battle after another. But his heroism at Monterrey was even more predictive of his later combat style. In this urban battlefield, he positioned a cannon in a narrow alley to blast a Mexican barricade. Before long, snipers began picking off his gun crew, whereupon Thomas was ordered to withdraw. He lingered long enough, however, to get off another shot, which repulsed a Mexican infantry charge. Then, instead of abandoning the gun, he and his surviving crew members pulled it out of the alley. Captain Braxton Bragg, with whom Thomas served in Mexico and against whom he would fight in the Civil War, wrote that "no officer of the army has been so long in the field without relief" and characterized his service as "arduous, faithful, and brilliant." Courage and sheer endurance under fire: These were the fighting hallmarks of George Henry Thomas.

BETWEEN THE WARS

Breveted in Mexico from first lieutenant to captain and from captain to major, he was reassigned in 1849 to duty in Florida. Bragg recommended Thomas for a post as an artillery instructor at West Point, but it was filled by another officer senior to him. When that officer died in 1851, the position became his, and Thomas was additionally assigned as an instructor in cavalry. At the time, Lieutenant Colonel Robert E. Lee, a fellow Virginian, was the academy superintendent, and the two developed a close professional relationship and personal friendship. Among Thomas's star pupils in cavalry were J. E. B. Stuart and the superintendent's nephew Fitzhugh Lee, both of whom would become celebrated Confederate cavalry commanders.

While teaching at West Point, Thomas married Frances Lucretia Kellogg, of Troy, New York (November 17, 1852), and was gratified by promotion to regular army captain on December 24, 1853, which carried with it a sorely needed bump in pay.

In the spring of 1854, Thomas left West Point to rejoin his artillery regiment, which was transferred to California. Captain Thomas was put in charge of transporting two companies to San Francisco via ship to the Isthmus of Panama, overland across the stifling and disease-ridden isthmus, then, via another ship, to San Francisco, from which the units embarked on an overland march to Fort Yuma, California, across the Colorado River from Yuma, Arizona.

In 1855, Franklin Pierce's secretary of war, the future Confederate president Jefferson Davis, formed the 2nd U.S. Cavalry. Historians have long speculated that Davis, believing that civil war was imminent, purposely staffed the new regiment with top-notch officers who were also strongly identified with the South, hoping to create, in effect, a ready-made elite unit for a projected Southern army. Braxton Bragg personally recommended the promotion of Thomas

to major and his assignment to the new unit. Presumably, he based his recommendation both on Thomas's impressive military record and on his identity as an old-line Virginian. Thomas was the third-ranking officer in the regiment, which was commanded by Colonel Albert Sidney Johnston, with Lieutenant Colonel Robert E. Lee as his second in command. Two years later, in October 1857, with Johnston and Lee performing other duties, Major Thomas became acting commander of the regiment and continued as such for two and a half years.

The 2nd was stationed in Texas, where clashes with local Indians were frequent. At Clear Fork, on the Brazos River, Major Thomas was wounded by a Comanche arrow in a skirmish on August 26, 1860. The arrow passed through the fleshy part of his chin and lodged in his chest. He responded by pulling it out himself and then summoning the surgeon, who made a hasty field dressing, after which the major resumed his place at the head of the patrol.

Although he had been in the thick of battle in Mexico and would again be so during the Civil War, the arrow shot was the only combat wound Thomas ever received. However, in November 1860, during a leave of absence in which he journeyed back to Virginia to see his family, he suffered a freak accident at Lynchburg, when he fell from a train-station platform. He injured his back so severely that he thought he would have to close his military career; he recovered but was doomed to suffer from nearly debilitating back pain for the rest of his life.

His injury was not his only concern on this trip. As the nation hurtled toward dissolution, he agonized over reconciling his loyalty to the U.S. Army and the government it served with his Virginia birth and the sentiments of his Virginia family. He must have known that this could be the last time he would visit his siblings. After staying with them, he boarded a northbound train, intending to visit his wife's family in Troy. He made it a point, however, to stop over in Washington, so that he could inform General-in-Chief Winfield Scott that Major General David E. Twiggs, in command of the Department of Texas, was a secessionist whose allegiance to the U.S. Army could not be relied upon. Clearly, Thomas was preparing to choose the Union over the Confederacy.

OUTBREAK

Despite the information he gave Scott, many in the U.S. government and the army doubted Thomas's loyalty. It is true that as late as January 18, 1861, three months before Fort Sumter, Thomas applied for the post of superintendent of the Virginia Military Institute (VMI), yet he also turned down Governor Letcher's offer in March to become ordnance chief of the Virginia Provisional Army. When Virginia seceded on April 17, 1861, days after the fall of Fort Sumter, Thomas made his absolute decision to fight for the Union. With ritual solemnity, his sisters turned his portrait to the wall and burned every letter he had ever written to them. His West Point cavalry pupil J. E. B. Stuart was equally unsparing in his condemnation, writing to his wife on June 18 that he "would like to hang, *hang* him as a traitor to his native state."

Of the thirty-six officers of the 2nd U.S. Cavalry, nineteen, including Johnston, Lee, and Hardee—resigned their commissions to join the Confederate army, a circumstance that catapulted Thomas through a rapid series of promotions, to regular army lieutenant colonel on April 25 (replacing Lee) and colonel on May 3 (replacing Johnston) and to brigadier general of volunteers on August 17.

WAR AND POLITICS

Even before he was officially promoted to brigadier general, Thomas led a brigade under Major General Robert Patterson in the Shenandoah Valley during the First Bull Run Campaign but was immediately thereafter transferred to the Western Theater. In Kentucky, he reported to Major General Robert Anderson, who assigned him to train the raw recruits who had answered President Lincoln's call for short-term volunteers. Soon after this, on December 2, 1861, he was assigned independent command of a group of five understrength brigades consolidated as the First Division of Don Carlos Buell's Army of the Ohio.

On January 19, 1862, Thomas led four brigades—4,400 men—of the First Division in its first battle, against 5,900 Confederates led by George B. Crittenden at Mill Springs, Kentucky. Thomas achieved a quick victory with few casualties (39 killed, 207 wounded), which blunted the Confederate threat from east Tennessee and sent a thrill of elation through a Union public whose morale had been sorely tested by Bull Run and the other defeats that followed. It was the first significant Union victory of the war.

In what would become something of a pattern in the war, Thomas received remarkably little credit for his achievement while four colonels under him were elevated to brigadier general. It is likely that, despite his superb performance, higher command, Lincoln included, still distrusted the Virginian. Nevertheless, he was sent with his division to Shiloh, to reinforce Grant at that nearly disastrous battle, but arrived on April 7, just as the second day's combat had come to an end.

Although he had missed the battle, he benefited from the reorganization of the Department of the Mississippi that Henry Wager Halleck engineered to squeeze Grant (whose losses at Shiloh unnerved Halleck) out of field command. The department's three armies were juggled and transformed into three "wings." Seeing to it that Thomas was promoted to major general of volunteers, Halleck assigned him to command right wing, which consisted of four divisions of what had been Grant's Army of the Tennessee plus one division from the Army of the Ohio.

William T. Sherman became Thomas's subordinate, and neither he nor Grant ever fully forgave Thomas for what they regarded as his usurpation of their rightful authority.

With Grant out of the way, Halleck assumed field command of some 120,000 men. The center was under Buell's command, the left under that of Major General John Pope, and the right led by Thomas. Major General John McClernand commanded the reserve. Under Halleck's sluggish leadership and hampered by the mediocrity of Buell, Pope, and McClernand, Thomas could do very little. Halleck's massive forces arrived at Corinth only after the Confederates had withdrawn, making the occupation of this town a hollow victory. Lincoln kicked Halleck upstairs by naming him general-in-chief of the Union armies, replacing George B. McClellan, and, with his departure, Thomas was made acting commander of the Army of the Tennessee at Corinth until June 10, when Grant was restored to field command. Turning Corinth and the army over to Grant, Thomas led his First Division to link up with the Army of the Ohio under Buell, who had direct orders from Lincoln to advance against Chattanooga and Knoxville.

Buell proved to be in the Western Theater what McClellan was in the East: supremely reluctant to go on the offensive. General-in-Chief Halleck offered command of the Army of the Ohio to Thomas, who, unwilling to behave in any manner that seemed disloyal to Buell, a longtime friend and comrade-in-arms, refused the promotion. He served as Buell's second in command at the Battle of Perryville, Kentucky, on October 8, 1862, a bloody contest in which Buell was poised to annihilate Braxton Bragg's army but was unable to coordinate the disparate units of his sixteen-thousand-man force. Thomas did not engage until mid-afternoon, by which time the critical moment had passed and Bragg was preparing to slip away. In the end, Buell garnered some credit in the popular press for *driving* Bragg out of Kentucky (though he had taken

substantially heavier casualties than Bragg), credit he generously shared with Thomas. Halleck and Lincoln didn't see Buell as victorious, however, and he was relieved. This time, when Thomas's name again came up as his replacement, Lincoln countered with that of William Rosecrans. The president acknowledged that Thomas had shown himself to be aggressive—which was precisely the kind of commander he always clamored for—but he was a Virginian, and Lincoln was reluctant to replace the Virginian Buell with the Virginian Thomas. Besides, Rosecrans was Catholic, which, Lincoln believed, would be helpful in generating support for the war among Catholics, especially such immigrant groups as the Irish. Thus the president sacrificed the very military quality he had missed in McClellan and Buell—a willingness to fight—in order to achieve certain political ends.

BATTLE OF STONES RIVER, DECEMBER 31, 1862–JANUARY 2, 1863

Having declined command of the Army of the Ohio when it had been offered him the first time, Thomas was angry at being passed over the second time. This fact said much about his character and sense of justice. Buell was his senior, and so he considered it wrong—disloyal and unseemly—to take a command away from him. By the same token, Rosecrans was *his* junior and therefore should not have been offered the command. A forthright man, Thomas brought this up with Rosecrans and requested a transfer. Rosecrans responded by asking for Thomas's help. Put this way, Thomas found that he could not refuse. Rosecrans offered him a range of commands. Thomas chose to lead the center corps.

When Lincoln and Halleck pressed Rosecrans to attack Bragg at Murfreesboro, Tennessee, Thomas advised Rosecrans not to hurry. While Thomas was aggressive, he was also highly methodical and believed that careful preparation was an indispensable key to victory. As long as

Rosecrans did not feel fully prepared to launch the offensive, Thomas advised resisting the pressure from Washington.

But if Rosecrans wasn't ready for a fight, Bragg was. On December 31, 1862, he attacked Rosecrans's right flank at Stones River, achieving total surprise as the Union soldiers were busy preparing breakfast. Union retreat was orderly, but relentless. At the end of the first day, Rosecrans met with his generals to decide whether to continue the fight tomorrow or withdraw now. When he asked Thomas, "General, what have you to say?" the reply was stark and calm: "Gentlemen, I know of no better place to die than right here." The words put spine into Rosecrans, who dismissed his commanders with, "We must fight or die."

And fight and die many did. On both sides, casualties were stunning. Of 43,400 Union troops engaged, 13,249 became casualties, killed, wounded, captured, or missing; on the Confederate side, the number was 10,266 out of 37,712: casualty rates of 30 and 27 percent respectively— the highest of any major engagement in the war. In the end, it was Bragg who retired from the field, thereby putting the victory in the Union column, though nothing, really, was decided by the horrific battle.

BATTLE OF CHICKAMAUGA, SEPTEMBER 19–20, 1863

Because Rosecrans had achieved so little at the bloody Battle of Stones River, by the early spring of 1863, President Lincoln was making noises about relieving him. "Old Rosy" heard him and reluctantly bestirred himself to bottle up Bragg in Tennessee so as to prevent his troops from reinforcing Vicksburg, to which Grant was laying siege.

Rosecrans relied heavily on Thomas to lead a series of brilliant feints and deceptions, executed during seventeen miserable days of driving rain, which positioned his troops behind Bragg's right flank near Tullahoma, Tennessee. On July 4, Bragg, outnumbered, withdrew from Tullahoma and fell back on Chattanooga, which is precisely where Rosecrans wanted him. However, without reinforcements, Rosecrans decided not to risk a frontal assault but instead recommended maneuvering, with Thomas leading a stunning surprise crossing of the Tennessee River thirty miles west of Chattanooga and then marching through a series of gaps in Lookout Mountain, the long ridge south-southwest of Chattanooga, to sever the Western and Atlantic Railroad, Bragg's supply and communications artery to Atlanta. By cutting this, Rosecrans and Thomas gave Bragg no choice other than to evacuate Chattanooga— which he did, without firing a shot.

Buoyed by his remarkable victory at Chattanooga, Rosecrans, so reluctant to start his campaign, now didn't want to stop. Thomas counseled him to rest and consolidate his forces at Chattanooga before marching on. Instead, he kept going after Bragg, his three worn-out corps becoming separated from one another in the heavily forested mountain passes. In the meantime, Bragg halted at LaFayette, Georgia, twenty-five miles south of Chattanooga, where he took on substantial reinforcements. Thus fortified, Bragg positioned his men for a counterattack at Chickamauga Creek, Georgia, a dozen miles south of Chattanooga.

On September 18, the night before the battle, both commanders shifted and moved troops. In the dense woods, neither side knew the other's position. Even worse, none of the commanders on either side was fully aware of the disposition of his own troops. With daybreak on September 19, Thomas ordered a reconnaissance near Lee and Gordon's Mill, a local landmark on Chickamauga Creek. These troops, led by Brigadier General John Brannan, encountered and drove back the dismounted cavalry of Nathan Bedford Forrest. He, in turn, called on nearby Confederate infantry units for help, and with this an all-out battle exploded, with every division of

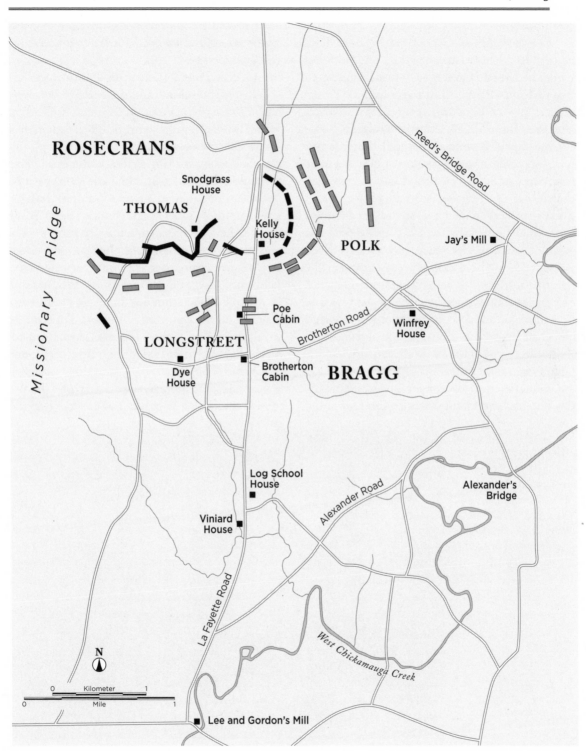

ROSECRANS

Snodgrass
House

THOMAS

Kelly
House

POLK

Jay's Mill

Missionary Ridge

Reed's Bridge Road

Poe
Cabin

Brotherton Road

Winfrey
House

LONGSTREET

Dye
House

Brotherton
Cabin

BRAGG

Log School
House

Alexander Road

Alexander's
Bridge

Viniard
House

La Fayette Road

West Chickamauga Creek

N

Kilometer

Mile

Lee and Gordon's Mill

the three Union corps engaged. At the end of a terribly bloody day, neither army had gained an advantage.

On the night of September 19, both sides worked feverishly to improve their positions, but while the Union men dug in, James Longstreet's two divisions arrived to further reinforce Bragg, who, at 9:00 on Sunday morning, September 20, attacked. The Federals held their own for some two hours, but Rosecrans, befuddled by the terrain, lacked an accurate picture of how his units were deployed. By mid-morning, he decided that it was urgently necessary to plug a gap in his right flank and therefore ordered troops from what he believed was his left to plug the gap in the right. But there was no gap. Even worse, thinking he was moving troops from the left to the right, he actually moved them out of the right flank, thereby *creating* the very gap he had meant to close. Longstreet saw this and launched an attack at the newly opened gap, shattering two Union divisions and driving the Union right onto its left.

Rosecrans and two of his corps commanders, Thomas Leonidas Crittenden (brother of the

Confederate general George B. Crittenden) and Alexander McDowell McCook, unable to rally their routed forces, believed a total collapse was inevitable and therefore joined a chaotic retreat to Chattanooga.

George Henry Thomas did not run.

Instead, he rallied units under Brigadier General Thomas John Wood and Brigadier General John Brannan, using them to block Longstreet on the south. Because Bragg had made an all-out attack, holding nothing in reserve, he was unable to exploit Longstreet's initial breakthrough. In the meantime, Union general Gordon Granger, grasping the significance of Thomas's bold action, violated his own orders to remain in place to protect the Union army's flank. Instead, he rushed two brigades to reinforce Thomas, who held the field until nightfall, thereby saving the Army of the Cumberland from annihilation, even in the absence of its commanding officer. For this, he would be hailed as the "Rock of Chickamauga," a sobriquet bestowed on him by Brigadier General James Garfield.

Thanks to Thomas, the Battle of Chickamauga became a Pyrrhic victory for Braxton

Combat artist Alfred Waud painted this evocative watercolor of the Confederate line advancing uphill through the woods toward the Union line at the Battle of Chickamauga, September 20, 1863.
LIBRARY OF CONGRESS

Bragg. Although he had driven Rosecrans from the field, his losses exceeded those of the Union: 18,454 killed, wounded, captured, or missing versus 16,170 for the Union. Having achieved a tactical victory, Bragg could not exploit his gains to claim a strategically decisive triumph.

BATTLES FOR CHATTANOOGA, NOVEMBER 23–25, 1863

After Chickamauga, the Army of the Cumberland fell back on Chattanooga, whereupon Bragg deployed his forces in the surrounding mountains and laid siege, seeking to starve the Union out. The desperate situation suddenly riveted Washington's focus on this theater of the war, and two corps were detached from George G. Meade's Army of the Potomac and sent west by rail under Joe Hooker. They were transferred from the banks of eastern Virginia's Rappahannock River to Bridgeport, Alabama, arriving on October 2. In the meantime, William T. Sherman led part of the Union's Army of the Tennessee east from Memphis, and Ulysses S. Grant was given command of almost all military operations west of the Alleghenies.

During this time, Lincoln and his Cabinet discussed the removal of Rosecrans as commander of the Army of the Cumberland. Secretary of War Edwin Stanton and Secretary of the Navy Gideon Welles both agreed that George H. Thomas should replace him, but Lincoln at first hesitated to promote a Virginian. He delayed his decision for nearly a month, until October 19, 1863. Grant's first telegram to the new army commander was to "hold Chattanooga at all hazards." The Rock of Chickamauga replied: "We will hold the town till we starve."

While Union forces prepared to break the siege of Chattanooga, Grant set up the celebrated "Cracker Line" to funnel food and other supplies to the bottled-up Army of the Cumberland. On November 23, Hooker and Sherman commenced the battle for Chattanooga, and on the afternoon

of November 25, Grant ordered Thomas to lead the Army of the Cumberland forward from the city to take the Confederate rifle pits at the base of Missionary Ridge south of Chattanooga and east of Lookout Mountain. Grant's intention was to apply sufficient pressure on Bragg to force him to pull back troops from Sherman's front on Missionary Ridge; this, he hoped, would allow Sherman to break through. Grant knew the Army of the Cumberland had endured a long, debilitating siege, and he assigned to them a relatively modest mission. But precisely because they had been immobilized for so long, they performed like men who had something to prove. The Army of the Cumberland not only captured the rifle pits as assigned, they kept going, without orders from Grant or from Thomas, charging up the slope of Missionary Ridge and sweeping everything before them. Astoundingly, the soldiers of the Army of the Cumberland broke Bragg's line exactly where it was the strongest, sending the Confederates into retreat. Gordon Granger, commanding officer of the unit that had so exceeded its orders, exclaimed to an assembly of his men, "You ought to be court-martialed, every man of you. I ordered you to take the rifle pits, and you scaled the mountain!" According to a correspondent who witnessed this exchange, Granger's "cheeks were wet with tears as honest as the blood that reddened all the route."

ATLANTA CAMPAIGN, MAY 7–SEPTEMBER 2, 1864

In February 1864, Sherman took charge of three armies: the Ohio, the Tennessee, and the Army of the Cumberland, under Thomas. If he rankled at being subordinated to Sherman, his junior, Thomas did not let on, but he did frequently disagree with Sherman over basic tactics. While Thomas favored making a simultaneous flanking and frontal attack against the Confederate Army of Tennessee (now under Joseph E. Johnston, who had replaced Bragg), in an effort to finish it off once and for all, Sherman wanted to pursue that army toward Atlanta, and so the march to the outskirts of Atlanta consumed 113 days. In this advance, Thomas's sixty thousand men of the Army of the Cumberland constituted more than half of Sherman's Atlanta Campaign force.

En route to Atlanta, Thomas fought numerous engagements. Sherman relied on Thomas's own staff officers to carry out logistics for the entire advance. Thomas played an especially central role in the Battle of Peachtree Creek (July 20, 1864), offering another rocklike stand, against which Lieutenant General John Bell Hood, who had replaced Johnston as commanding officer of the Army of Tennessee, battered fruitlessly, absorbing heavy casualties. Thanks to Thomas's steadfast work at Peachtree Creek, Hood was unable to break Sherman's siege of Atlanta.

BATTLES OF FRANKLIN AND NASHVILLE, NOVEMBER 30 AND DECEMBER 15-16, 1864

In the fall of 1864, Grant agreed to allow Sherman to embark on his March to the Sea. Leaving a portion of his armies to garrison Atlanta, Sherman therefore turned away from Hood and advanced on Savannah, sending Thomas with thirty-five thousand men of the Army of the Cumberland west to deal with Hood.

Thomas raced the Confederate general to Nashville, Tennessee, where he would link up with other Union forces in the region. Reaching the city early in November, Thomas made preparations to stand against and defeat the combined forces of Hood and Nathan Bedford Forrest. In the meantime, the XXIII Corps of Major General John Schofield's Army of the Ohio found itself backed into a vulnerable position at Spring Hill, Tennessee, on November 29. Hood, however, failed to envelop Schofield, who was able to continue his withdrawal toward Thomas. Schofield took up a position at Franklin, and on November 30, Hood, frustrated and impulsive as ever, ordered an ill-advised frontal assault on

Schofield. Of some 27,000 men under his command, Hood lost 6,252 killed, wounded, missing or captured, against 2,326 casualties he inflicted on Schofield. The Battle of Franklin won, Schofield continued his withdrawal to Nashville, where he linked up with Thomas. With XXIII Corps attached to it, the Army of the Cumberland now outnumbered Hood nearly two to one.

Grant and others in Union high command understood this. What they could not understand was why, with such a clear numerical advantage, Thomas delayed counterattacking Hood. What Grant perceived as delay, however, was actually a key aspect of Thomas's tactical style. In sharp contrast with the likes of Hood, he was methodical—perhaps to a fault. As Thomas saw the situation, he was in complete control in and around Nashville. So he took the time he felt necessary to set up a decisive battle.

Back in Virginia, Grant became alarmed and feared that Thomas would allow Hood to slip away. He therefore cut an order relieving Thomas of command but had not yet transmitted it when, on December 15 and 16, Thomas finally attacked. Deploying about fifty-five thousand men against Hood's thirty thousand, he inflicted some six thousand casualties, killed, wounded, captured, or missing, neutralizing the Confederate Army of Tennessee as a fighting force for the rest of the war and thus accomplishing Sherman's original mission. The "Rock of Chickamauga" now became known as the "Sledge of Nashville."

FINAL PURSUIT AND POSTWAR CAREER

Both Secretary of War Stanton and William Tecumseh Sherman sent congratulatory telegrams to Thomas; however, Grant was still oddly dissatisfied with his performance, complaining to Sherman of "a sluggishness" in his pursuit of the defeated Hood after Nashville, which, Grant told Sherman, "satisfied me [that Thomas] would never do to conduct one of your campaigns."

Nevertheless, Stanton wired the news to Thomas that he had been promoted from major general of volunteers to major general in the regular army. Despite this, Thomas felt considerable bitterness toward Grant, whose conduct toward him he considered unwarranted and mean-spirited.

Thomas's pursuit of Hood ended on December 29, 1864, when Hood was replaced by the very man he had earlier replaced, Joseph E. Johnston. By this point, the Army of Tennessee had been so reduced that it was no longer worth harrying, and Thomas and the Army of the Cumberland engaged in no more major battles before the force was dispersed on May 9, 1865.

In the aftermath of the war and through 1869, Thomas was assigned command of the

Major General George Henry Thomas, the "Rock of Chickamauga," by Mathew Brady. LIBRARY OF CONGRESS

Department of the Cumberland in Kentucky and Tennessee, with occasional additional command responsibilities in West Virginia and portions of Georgia, Mississippi, and Alabama. This general whose loyalty had been frequently called into question because of his Virginia roots, proved to be an enthusiastic exponent of Reconstruction, acting vigorously to provide protection to freedmen who were menaced by the abuses of white Southern officials and others, including the recently founded Ku Klux Klan.

In 1868, President Andrew Johnson, facing impeachment, sent Thomas's name to the Senate for promotion to brevet lieutenant general. His intention, clearly, was to position Thomas to replace Grant as general-in-chief, doubtless in a bid to impede Grant's looming presidential candidacy. Whatever personal resentment Thomas may still have harbored toward Grant, he requested that his name be withdrawn from Senate consideration. It was, he said, a matter of military loyalty, which he was unwilling to sacrifice to politics.

Having taken himself out of consideration to succeed Grant as America's top soldier, Thomas requested and received command of the Division of the Pacific in 1869. He succumbed to a stroke early the following year, on March 28, 1870, in his headquarters at the Presidio of San Francisco. It was said that, at the time of his collapse, he had been composing a response to a critical article published by John Schofield, who had served under him in Tennessee but had always seen himself as a rival. Burial was at Oakwood Cemetery, in his wife's hometown of Troy, New York; his body was not welcome in Virginia. None of his Virginia family came north to attend the funeral, his sisters reportedly explaining to their neighbors that "our brother George died to us in 1861."

Chapter 22

WINFIELD SCOTT HANCOCK

RATING: ★ ★ ★

Winfield Scott Hancock: "The Superb." LIBRARY OF CONGRESS

EVALUATION

In his *Personal Memoirs* of 1885, Ulysses S. Grant gave what may be the most comprehensive concise evaluation of Winfield Scott Hancock. He stands, Grant wrote, as "the most conspicuous figure of all the general officers who did not exercise a separate [that is, army-level] command. He commanded a corps longer than any other one, and his name was never mentioned as having committed in battle a blunder for which he was responsible. He was a man of very conspicuous personal appearance. . . . His genial disposition made him friends, and his personal courage and his presence with his command in the thickest of the fight won for him the confidence of troops serving under him. No matter how hard the fight, the 2d corps always felt that their commander was looking after them."

Hancock always fought under the command of others, and no field officer was more universally admired than he, who emerged from the Civil War as perhaps the model soldier-general. He is deservedly most celebrated for the leading role he took at Gettysburg, where his command decisions and personal presence on days one and two made Union victory possible, and his sacrifices on day three ensured the defeat of Lee.

Principal Battles

PRE–CIVIL WAR

U.S.-Mexican War, 1846–1848

- Contreras, August 19–20, 1847: His maiden battle
- Churubusco, August 20, 1847: Although wounded himself, assumed command of his company after its commander was disabled by a more serious wound; brevetted to first lieutenant
- Molino del Rey, September 8, 1847: Fought despite the fever that had developed from his wound; was too sick to fight at Chapultepec, the culminating engagement of the war

Third Seminole War, 1855–1858

- Served in the noncombat role of quartermaster

"Bleeding Kansas" Guerrilla Border War, 1854–1860

- Saw little action here

Mormon Rebellion, March 1857–July 1858

- Arrived after the violence had ended and the "rebellion" had been resolved

CIVIL WAR

- Peninsula Campaign, March–July 1862: In Virginia; fought throughout the campaign but was outstanding for his leadership at the Battle of Williamsburg,

May 5, 1862, in which he led his brigade in a spectacular encircling movement against the Confederate left flank; had McClellan followed up on this, the Peninsula Campaign might well have been a Union triumph

- Antietam, September 17, 1862: In Maryland; assuming First Division command after the mortal wounding of Major General Israel B. Richardson, he rallied the troops at "Bloody Lane," but followed McClellan's instructions to hold his position instead of counterattacking; promoted to major general of volunteers

- Fredericksburg, December 11–15, 1862: In Virginia; although he protested Burnside's suicidal plan for making a frontal attack against Marye's Heights, he managed to lead his division closer to this objective than anyone else; was wounded in the abdomen

- Chancellorsville, April 30–May 6, 1863: In Virginia; provided magnificent and effective cover for the retreat of the Army of the Potomac from this catastrophe

- Gettysburg, July 1–3, 1863: In Pennsylvania; assumed field command after the death of John Reynolds; held the high ground on day one and effectively poised the Union for victory on day two; on day three, led II Corps in repulsing Pickett's Charge; suffered a severe wound; received the thanks of Congress

- Overland Campaign, May–June 1864: In Virginia; although not fully recovered from his Gettysburg wound, joined the campaign at the Battle of the Wilderness, May 5–7, 1864, where he led II Corps in a breakthrough at the Bloody Angle in the assault on the Mule Shoe; at the Battle of Spotsylvania Court House, May 8–21, 1864, defeated the famed Stonewall Division; at the Battle of Cold Harbor, May 31–June 12, 1864, his II Corps fought fiercely but suffered catastrophic losses from which it would never fully recover

- Siege of Petersburg, June 9, 1864–March 25, 1865: Participated throughout, but missed opportunity for an early breakthrough in June and, on August 25, 1864, at Reams's Station, suffered a humiliating and tremendously costly defeat

- Discouraged by the Battle of Reams's Station and suffering as a result of his still troublesome Gettysburg wound, Hancock served out the rest of the war in mainly administrative roles

POST–CIVIL WAR

Hancock's Campaign, April–July 1867

- A fruitless pursuit of Cheyenne and Sioux in Kansas, conducted in the field by George Armstrong Custer

Reconstruction, 1865–1877

- As Fifth Military District commander supervised Reconstruction in Texas and Louisiana from late 1867 to early 1869, controversially endeavoring to minimize military government

Department of Dakota Commander, 1869–1872

- Relatively peaceful military command in an area encompassing Minnesota, Montana, and the Dakotas

Great Railroad Strike of 1877

- As commander of the Department of the Atlantic, took charge of suppressing widespread labor violence

---

On February 14, 1824, Elizabeth Hoxworth Hancock of Montgomery Square, Pennsylvania, gave birth to identical twin boys. One was given the name Hilary Baker and the other Winfield Scott. That a boy should be named for family relations, in the case of Hilary Baker, was hardly unusual, but to name his twin brother not after relatives but a soldier—a hero of the War of 1812 who was just entering mid-career by 1824—was rare in early nineteenth-century America. Most Americans had an innate dislike of standing armies and professional military men (the quartering of troops had played a big part in triggering the American Revolution). What is more, the Hancocks were hardly a military family. Father Benjamin was a schoolteacher who studied law and would soon become a lawyer, while Mother Elizabeth worked as a milliner. It was, therefore, almost as if, in naming their son, the Hancocks had inadvertently predicted his destiny. From childhood, he would exhibit an early fascination with things military, and, as an adult, he would prove to be a kind of natural and instinctive soldier and leader of soldiers. In the U.S.-Mexican War, his first experience of battle, he would even serve directly under his namesake.

And in the Civil War, he would earn the romantic warrior sobriquet of "Hancock the Superb."

EARLY LIFE AND WEST POINT

A few years after the Hancock twins were born, the family moved from Montgomery Square, outside of Lansdale, to Norristown, where Benjamin Hancock began practicing law. He also became increasingly prominent in local Democratic politics and served with great devotion as a deacon in the Baptist church. The twins were educated at Norristown Academy until a public school opened up in town late in the 1830s. As boys, they were inseparable, yet identical only in physical appearance. While Hilary was quiet and well-behaved, the boisterous Winfield often got into trouble of the boys-will-be-boys variety. His conduct, however, was not so naughty as to disqualify him from the dose of higher education his school grades merited, and his rapidly developing interest in the military—he organized a military company among his classmates— prompted his father to call in a political favor from the local congressman, Joseph Fornance. In 1840, Fornance obliged Benjamin by nominating Winfield to the U.S. Military Academy at West Point.

Already tall—he was six-foot-two in an era when five-foot-seven was average for a man— handsome, and soldierly in appearance, Winfield Scott Hancock was also a genial and popular cadet. His academic performance was, however, on the lower end of average. Graduating eighteenth in the twenty-five-cadet Class of 1844, he was automatically sent to the infantry and commissioned in the 6th Regiment, assigned to serve in Indian Territory.

INDIAN TERRITORY, RECRUITING DUTY, AND THE U.S.-MEXICAN WAR

For the next two years, little happened in the Red River Valley, Hancock's corner of Indian Territory, and he saw nothing of combat before he was sent back east to recruiting duty in Cincinnati, Ohio, and across the river in Kentucky. While he was there, the U.S.-Mexican War began in Texas and California, prompting Hancock to request his immediate return to the 6th Regiment, which was stationed in the thick of the developing action. The problem was that the good-looking and genial Hancock had proved to be a talented recruiter, not only signing up more than his quota of men, but also knowing which men to reject. He was just too good at his job, and the army wanted him to continue in it as long as possible. Orders to rejoin his regiment did not come until May 31, 1847.

To Second Lieutenant Hancock's vast relief, there was still plenty of war to be fought when he rejoined the 6th at Puebla, Mexico, as it served in the invading army led by his namesake, Major General Winfield Scott.

From Puebla, the army advanced to Contreras, which became Winfield Scott Hancock's maiden battle on August 19 and 20, 1847. By the afternoon of August 20, the battle had moved to Churubusco. Here Hancock suffered his first wound—a shallow musket ball penetration below the knee—yet he not only kept fighting, but took over command of his company after its commander was felled by a more grievous wound. Hancock's gallantry and initiative at Churubusco earned him a brevet to first lieutenant, and in both Contreras and Churubusco, he served alongside three officers who would become notable Confederate generals, James Longstreet, George Pickett, and Lewis Armistead—a man with whom Hancock also developed a close personal friendship.

The wound Hancock sustained at Churubusco became infected and resulted in a fever. Despite this, he fought at Molino del Rey (September 8, 1847) but was laid up during the culminating battle of the war, Chapultepec (September 12–13), and the subsequent occupation of Mexico City. That these momentous events should have passed him by was a source of lifelong regret.

PRELUDE TO THE CIVIL WAR

Hancock and his regiment remained in Mexico until after the Treaty of Guadalupe Hidalgo was signed in February 1848. Having earned a reputation as an able administrator while he served as a recruiter, Hancock was next assigned to a number of quartermaster and adjutant postings, including at Fort Snelling, Minnesota, and St. Louis, Missouri. In this city, he met Almira Russell, whom he married on January 24, 1850. "Allie" was universally admired by Hancock's fellow officers for her beauty, charm, and kindness, and when he was promoted to captain in 1855 and transferred to Fort Myers, Florida, she and their five-year-old son accompanied him—she the only woman on this primitive post. Although the sporadic fighting of the Third Seminole War

Hancock's wife, Almira ("Allie") Russell Hancock, was celebrated among U.S. Army officers for her charm, beauty, and kindness. WIKIMEDIA

was under way, quartermaster Hancock saw no combat.

He was transferred again, this time to Fort Leavenworth, Kansas, in 1856, during the height of the "Bleeding Kansas" guerrilla violence between proslavery and antislavery factions. Hancock saw relatively little of the bloodshed, however, before he was tasked with helping to prepare an expedition to Utah Territory to put down the so-called Mormon Rebellion, an antigovernment uprising, which included the Mountain Meadows massacre of September 11, 1857, in which the Mormon Militia and their Paiute Indian allies killed more than 120 non-Mormon California-bound settlers. By the time Hancock and the 6th Infantry arrived, however, the conflict was over, and Hancock was told that he was being sent to a new posting with the 6th in Benicia, California.

Obtaining a leave of absence, he traveled back east to fetch his wife, who had given birth to a second child, a daughter, before he left for Utah. For the first time in their lives together, Allie was reluctant to follow her husband, but she was gently counseled by none other than Colonel Robert E. Lee, who persuaded her that an army officer needed his wife and family to be with him, if at all possible. Thus the family made the arduous journey to California together. At Benicia, in the San Francisco Bay area, they were presented with orders to travel even farther, down to Los Angeles, some four hundred miles to the south. Here they remained, Captain Hancock serving as assistant quartermaster under future Confederate general Albert Sidney Johnston, and here Hancock formed his close friendship with Armistead.

When news of the outbreak of the Civil War reached Los Angeles in the spring of 1861, Johnston, Armistead, and the other Southern officers who had decided to resign their commissions and join the Confederate cause gathered at the Hancock home for a farewell party. Almira Hancock later recalled that Major Armistead was "crushed . . . tears . . . streaming down his face." He laid his hands upon her husband's shoulders, she wrote, and looked him "steadily in the eyes." "Hancock," he said, "good-bye. You can never know what this has cost me."

Armistead then turned to Allie and placed in her hands a small satchel filled with keepsakes to be sent to his family if he should be killed. There was also a little prayer book, which he said was for her and her husband. On its flyleaf he had inscribed: "Trust in God and fear nothing." Before he left that evening, Armistead also offered Hancock his major's uniform, but the captain could not bring himself to accept it.

INTO WAR

Like his Southern comrades, Winfield Scott Hancock was also determined to leave California—in his case, however, to serve with the Union. Since the end of the war with Mexico, he had been studying the campaigns of history's "great captains," from Julius Caesar to Napoleon Bonaparte, and he hoped that he would not only receive a speedy transfer back east, but would also exchange his administrative duties for a combat assignment.

He was sent to Washington but was instantly loaded down with quartermaster work for the Union army, which, by the late summer of 1861, was rapidly expanding. George B. McClellan, however, soon picked out Hancock's name from a list of officers. He remembered him from West Point as well as from the Mexican war, and he recognized him as a courageous, intelligent, and skilled officer. Thanks to McClellan, Hancock was, on September 23, 1861, jumped from captain to brigadier general (and thus would not have had use for the major's uniform he had declined to accept from Armistead) and assigned to command an infantry brigade in a division under Brigadier General William F. "Baldy" Smith in McClellan's Army of the Potomac.

McClellan soon realized that he had every reason to be pleased with his choice of Hancock. The man was a thoroughgoing military officer, who prized military discipline but also understood men and how to motivate them on a human level. In contrast to most of his regular army colleagues, he enjoyed working with volunteers, whom he did not regard as necessarily inferior to regular army troops. Treated with respect and confidence, these citizen soldiers gave Hancock their very best in return.

BATTLE OF WILLIAMSBURG, MAY 5, 1862

Thanks to General McClellan's dilatory approach to campaigning, the Confederates were able to withdraw from their positions at Yorktown, Virginia, before the Army of the Potomac closed in on them during the Peninsula Campaign. A division under Joseph Hooker opened the Battle of Williamsburg on May 5 by attacking an earthen fortification known as Fort Magruder. He was repulsed, however, and Confederate general James Longstreet followed up the repulse with a counterattack on the Union left. A Union division under Brigadier General Philip Kearny arrived in time to blunt the counterattack and stabilize the Union position as Hancock led his brigade in a spectacular encircling movement against the Confederate left flank, forcing the enemy to abandon two key redoubts, which Hancock's men occupied.

McClellan both recognized and appreciated what Hancock had done and even telegraphed Washington to report that "Hancock was superb today," thereby giving birth to the sobriquet he would carry with him through the rest of the war, "Hancock the Superb." Yet, being McClellan, he declined to exploit the counterattack. Instead of following up on what Hancock had gained, McClellan released the pressure, allowing the Confederates, now on the defensive, to withdraw intact.

BATTLE OF ANTIETAM, SEPTEMBER 17, 1862

A subordinate commander, Winfield Hancock was perpetually at the mercy of those above him, and his tactical achievement at Williamsburg came to nothing strategically as McClellan's Peninsula Campaign shriveled on the vine. McClellan was ordered to withdraw north to link up his Army of the Potomac with John Pope's newly formed Army of Virginia, and because McClellan moved slowly, Pope and his army were left cut off and vulnerable to Robert E. Lee at the Second Battle of Bull Run (August 28–30, 1862).

With Pope's failure, President Lincoln reluctantly recalled McClellan to top field command, and when Lee invaded Maryland in September 1862, Hancock found himself deep in the blood of Antietam. After 1st Division, II Corps commander Major General Israel B. Richardson fell mortally wounded, Hancock assumed divisional command, making a magnificent entrance, galloping at top speed, staff in train, between the division's troops and the enemy, parallel to the Sunken Road that had been transformed by desperate battle into "Bloody Lane." Deliberate exposure to enemy fire was and would always be part and parcel of the Hancock style of command.

The men of the division were impressed and inspired. As Hancock's adjutant Francis Walker later wrote, "An hour after Hancock rode down the line at Antietam to take up the sword that had fallen from Richardson's dying hand, every officer in his place and every man in his ranks was aware, before the sun went down, that he belonged to Hancock's division."

It was a magnificent display of what modern officers call "command presence," and yet Hancock did not fully exploit it. He had his men in the palm of his hand and might have led them in highly effective counterattacks against the Confederates, who were by this time thoroughly exhausted. Instead, he clung to and carried out the orders McClellan had given him, which were to do no more than hold his position. He did what he had been told. Bold as Hancock was, an even bolder combat leader would have given his commander more than he had asked for and, in so doing, might have transformed a narrow Union victory into a decisive triumph.

FREDERICKSBURG AND CHANCELLORSVILLE, DECEMBER 11–15, 1862 AND APRIL 30–MAY 6, 1863

What Hancock did achieve at Bloody Lane was sufficient to get him a promotion to major general of volunteers on November 29, 1862. By this time, however, President Lincoln had once again relieved McClellan (if Hancock had exceeded his orders from McClellan, he might have saved his commanding officer's job), and Hancock was leading his newly acquired division in an Army of the Potomac commanded by Ambrose Burnside.

Like most of the officers and men of the Army of the Potomac, Hancock was not happy about McClellan's removal. Unlike many of them, however, he was determined to give the new commander his full loyalty. He believed, he said, that "we are serving no one man: we are serving our country."

But his determination to serve his country by demonstrating loyalty to the new commander was soon sorely tested. Learning of Burnside's plan to make a frontal assault against thoroughly entrenched Confederate positions, including artillery, on Marye's Heights at Fredericksburg, Hancock could not stop himself from protesting its suicidal foolishness. Hearing of this, Burnside summoned Hancock to remind him of his obligation to execute without complaint whatever orders his commanding general might give. Hancock agreed but pointed out that the proposed objective was extraordinarily difficult. Burnside nevertheless stood firm on his plan, and when Hancock received his orders to attack at eight o'clock on the morning of December 13, 1862, he followed his orders.

Between his division's starting position and the stone wall at the foot of Marye's Heights were some 1,700 feet of flat, open, exposed plain, all thoroughly raked by fire from Confederate artillery and muskets dug in on the high ground. To advance across this expanse was to walk into death itself. But Hancock led his men across. A Confederate bullet sliced through his coat and grazed his abdomen. Had he walked a split second faster, he would have been dead. As it was, the wound did not stop him. Hancock shuttled back and forth across the exposed plain, through the ceaseless storm of musket and cannon fire, always urging his men forward.

His exertions were sufficient to drive the soldiers of his division closer to the stone wall than any other Union troops that terrible day. But, like the rest, Hancock's men were forced to break off and retreat.

"Out of the fifty-seven hundred men I carried into action," he wrote the next day, "I have this morning in line but fourteen hundred and fifty."

As Second Bull Run had cost Pope his command and Antietam had spelled the end for McClellan, so Fredericksburg brought the relief of Ambrose Burnside and his replacement by Joseph Hooker. Hooker's plan was to return to Fredericksburg, attack far more intelligently and with greater numbers, and in this way break through to advance at long last against Richmond.

The plan, Hancock believed, was sound, yet he had overheard Hooker declare to another general the day before the fight that "God almighty could not prevent me from winning a victory tomorrow." And that made Hancock doubt. "Success," this son of a Baptist deacon wrote, "cannot come to us through such profanity."

Profane and blustering as he was, Hooker had a good plan and outnumbered Lee by two

to one. His problem was that he lost his nerve in the execution, and instead of pushing Lee out of Fredericksburg, he relinquished the initiative by waiting for him at Chancellorsville.

Hancock's chief contribution to the disastrous battle that resulted was to use his division with great skill and courage to cover the withdrawal of the Army of the Potomac. In the course of carrying out this operation, he was wounded by shell fragments, his injuries adding to the heavy sense of depression this latest defeat had loaded upon him. "I have had the blues ever since I returned from the campaign," he admitted in a letter to Allie.

BATTLE OF GETTYSBURG, JULY 1–3, 1863

Hancock endured his "blues." But for some commanders, it was beyond endurance. After Chancellorsville, Major General Darius Crouch, commanding officer of II Corps, requested to be relieved of command. On May 22, command of II Corps was awarded to Winfield Scott Hancock.

He established an immediate rapport with these veterans who, like the rest of the Army of the Potomac, had fought hard, deserved triumph, and yet suffered nothing but wounds, deaths, and heartbreak. As when he commanded a brigade and then a division, corps commander Hancock took steps to make himself personally known to his officers and men and to get to know them with the same degree of intimacy. Captains and lieutenants were amazed that the commanding general singled them out, saluted, and addressed them by name.

As Lee's victory at the Second Battle of Bull Run emboldened him to invade Maryland, so his victory at Chancellorsville propelled him to invade Pennsylvania. George Meade, newly appointed to replace Hooker as commanding general of the Army of the Potomac, led his troops to intercept Lee's Army of Northern Virginia. Contact between the two forces came at a crossroads town called Gettysburg, and the first day of battle, July 1, 1863, began badly for the Union. Major General John Reynolds, a good friend of Hancock's and universally respected—many believed *he*, not Meade, should have been placed at the head of the Army of the Potomac—had control in the field. On his arrival at the front, the army cheered, only to fall into stunned silence when Reynolds was killed a few moments after his arrival.

Hearing the news, Meade summoned Hancock. He told him that he needed a replacement for Reynolds, a man who would take control and restore the situation until the bulk of the army arrived at Gettysburg. Hancock responded by reminding Meade that Major General O. O. Howard was senior to him and next in line for the command. But Meade knew what he wanted. He replied to Hancock that he understood but had made his choice.

By a stroke of death and decision, Winfield Scott Hancock assumed effective command of the entire left wing of the Army of the Potomac, consisting of his own II Corps plus I, III, and XI Corps. When Howard disputed Hancock's authority, Hancock quickly asserted himself and set about organizing the critical Union defenses on Cemetery Hill. The Confederates, who at this point outnumbered the Union forces at Gettysburg, were relentlessly driving I and XI Corps back through the streets of Gettysburg. That, Hancock decided, was acceptable. But the high ground at Cemetery Hill had to be held at all costs. Lose the high ground, and the battle would be lost. Acting on the authority Meade had given him to withdraw the forces holding the town proper, Hancock ordered I and XI Corps to fall back on Cemetery Hill, to take a stand there, and to fight it out there.

Thus when Meade arrived after midnight to assume direct command, the contour of the Battle of Gettysburg had already been determined—by Hancock. The morning of July 2 found Hancock's II Corps occupying Cemetery Ridge, in the center of the Union line. Lee attacked both ends of the line. Union III Corps, on the left, absorbed a terrific blow dealt by Lieutenant General James Longstreet. To meet this assault, Hancock sent his own 1st Division, commanded by Brigadier General John C. Caldwell, to reinforce III Corps in a place called the Wheatfield. At the same time, Confederate Lieutenant General A. P. Hill led his corps against Hancock at the Union center. With extraordinary agility, Hancock shuttled and rushed units to each critical point as they developed. Looking to save the army, he sacrificed the 1st Minnesota Regiment by sending it to attack an entire brigade—representing about four times more men than were in the regiment—a suicide mission (the Minnesotans took 87 percent casualties, killed, wounded, or missing) that nevertheless bought Hancock the time he needed to re-form the Union line.

Throughout the second day, Hancock often personally led reinforcing units as needed. He seemed to be everywhere, and when III Corps commander Daniel Sickles was wounded, Meade added III Corps to Hancock's command. Now directly controlling all of the Union line from Cemetery Hill to Little Round Top, Hancock kept the defense both strong and flexible, so that, by the end of July 2, the Battle of Gettysburg had yet to be decided.

July 3 found Hancock still holding his center position on Cemetery Ridge. His II Corps absorbed the main impact of Pickett's Charge—the twelve-thousand-man frontal assault Lee desperately hoped would dislodge the Union from the high ground. It had been preceded by a horrific artillery bombardment, most of it concentrated against Union II Corps. During the pounding, Hancock rode back and forth along his lines to keep his troops in place. "General," one subordinate officer protested, "the corps commander ought not to risk his life that way." Hancock replied: "There are times when a corps commander's life does not count."

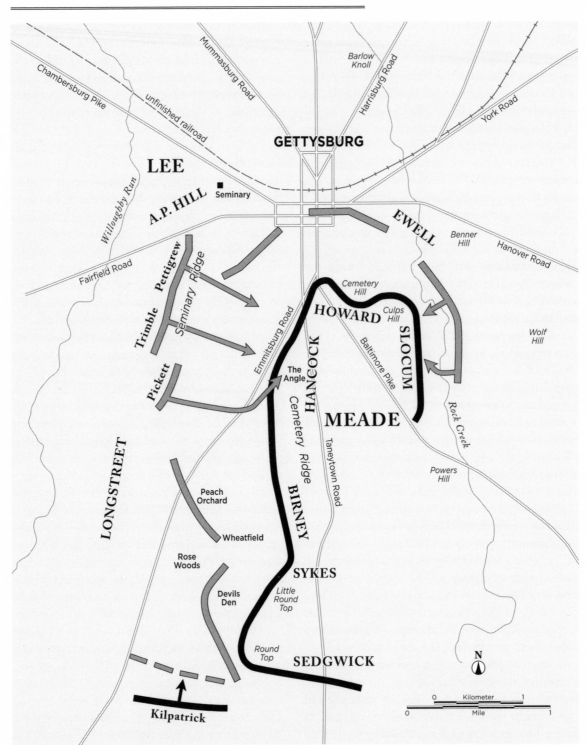

In the end, Pickett's Charge proved both futile and tragic. Among its casualties was Brigadier General Lewis A. Armistead, who led a brigade in Pickett's division. Severely wounded in the charge, he would die two days later.

Hancock learned of his friend's wounding as he himself lay painfully injured. On July 3, a Confederate bullet had ricocheted off the pommel of his saddle. The bullet tore into his inner right thigh, pushing through wood splinters and one bent nail from the shattered pommel.

"My eyes were upon Hancock's striking figure," a Lieutenant George Benedict recalled, "when he uttered an exclamation, and I saw that he was reeling in his saddle. General Stannard bent over him as we laid him on the ground, a ragged hole an inch or more in diameter, from which blood was pouring profusely, was disclosed in the upper part of his thigh." Aides applied a tourniquet, and Hancock, quite conscious, pulled out the nail himself. "They must be hard up for ammunition," he commented, "when they throw such shot as that." Hancock asked his aides to prop him where he lay on Cemetery Hill so that he could continue to direct the battle.

In the meantime, Captain Henry H. Bingham, one of his staff, brought the news of Armistead's wound and reported that it was mortal. He conveyed to Hancock a message from his friend. "Tell General Hancock for me," Armistead had said, "that I have done him and done all an injustice which I shall regret or repent the longest day I live." Bingham then handed to Hancock Armistead's spurs, pocketbook, watch and chain, and a personal seal, explaining that the Confederate general had wanted him to have these.

Hancock allowed himself to be evacuated only after he was certain the Battle of Gettysburg had been won. Armistead would die within two days. Hancock would recover slowly but never completely. Meade had entrusted most of the conduct of the battle to him. Only when Hancock urged a full counterattack after Pickett's Charge had been repulsed did Meade overrule him. It was a serious error on Meade's part, since it allowed Lee to begin his withdrawal, his Army of Northern Virginia badly beaten but still intact, back into Virginia. "My God," President Lincoln would moan after he'd heard that Meade had allowed Lee to slip away, "is that all?"

OVERLAND CAMPAIGN, MAY–JUNE 1864

Hancock convalesced at his father's house in Norristown, returning to limited duty as a recruiting officer during the winter of 1863–1864, then resuming field command of II Corps in the spring, in time to march in Grant's Overland Campaign.

Although those who knew Hancock reported that his wound and long convalescence had diminished his former passion and energy, his corps performed extraordinarily well at the Battle of Spotsylvania Court House (May 8–21, 1864), achieving a breakthrough at the so-called Bloody Angle in the assault on the Mule Shoe salient. The Confederates' vaunted Stonewall Brigade was splintered, most of those who weren't killed becoming prisoners. Indeed, II Corps captured some three thousand men in Richard Ewell's corps.

II Corps was next committed to Grant's ill-conceived assault at Cold Harbor (June 3, 1864), where it absorbed the brunt of the slaughter, losing more than 3,500 men, killed, wounded, or captured. Already battered in its long service with the Army of the Potomac, II Corps would never be restored to its full strength after Cold Harbor.

SIEGE OF PETERSBURG, JUNE 9, 1864– MARCH 25, 1865

Hancock had known the awful bitterness of being the victim of his commanders' blunders, from McClellan, to Pope, to Burnside, to

Hancock with his division commanders at Cold Harbor, Virginia, 1864. Standing from left to right: Francis C. Barlow, David B. Birney, and John Gibbon. Hancock is seated. NATIONAL ARCHIVES AND RECORDS ADMINISTRATION

Hooker, and now even Grant at Cold Harbor. After Cold Harbor, Grant did what he had done after the Battles of the Wilderness and Spotsylvania Court House. Though defeated, he sidestepped Lee and the Army of Virginia and, instead of retreating, advanced, forcing Lee to stretch his deteriorating lines yet thinner. As the Army of the Potomac trudged across the James River, Hancock's II Corps was positioned to make an assault against Petersburg, which was weakly defended because Lee, assuming Grant intended to attack Richmond, had shifted troops from the Petersburg front to the Confederate capital. Had Hancock struck and struck hard, the war would surely have ended much sooner than it did. Instead, he deferred to XVIII Corps commander "Baldy" Smith, who wanted to delay action until all of the men were consolidated in position and rested. Had Hancock been less depleted by the lingering effects of his Gettysburg wound and the carnage of Spotsylvania and Cold Harbor, he might have acted in spite of Smith's counsel. But he did not, and by the time Grant and the bulk of the Army of the Potomac arrived at the Petersburg front, Lee had reinforced it, and the opposing armies settled in for a siege that would last until early spring of the next year.

During the long siege, Hancock led his corps in the two battles of Deep Bottom (July 27–29 and August 14–20, 1864), both feints toward Richmond intended to draw Confederate forces away from Petersburg so that Grant might effect a breakthrough. The Confederate defenders prevailed in both encounters, however. Nevertheless, Hancock's accumulated record of achievement was recognized by his promotion to brigadier general in the regular army on August 12, 1864.

After the Second Battle of Deep Bottom, Hancock led II Corps south of Petersburg to destroy the tracks of the Wilmington and Weldon Railroad in an ongoing effort to ensure that the city was totally cut off. Hancock committed a rare blunder, leaving his position exposed at Reams's Station, where Confederate generals Henry Heth and A. P. Hill attacked on August 25, inflicting on the roughly nine thouand II Corps men engaged 2,747 casualties, including 2,046 captured or missing. Confederate casualties in this lopsided battle were light, 814 killed, wounded, or missing out of eight to ten thousand engaged. Hancock blamed himself for having deployed his men in a faulty manner, but he was far more appalled by their performance under fire. They crumbled, broke, and ran—despite his own efforts to rally them, which included, as usual, deliberately exposing himself in the teeth of enemy fire.

The truth he was forced to face was stunning. His beloved corps had at last been broken. In November, when his Gettysburg wound, never having fully healed, partially reopened, the debilitated and depressed Hancock resigned field command.

COMMANDER, FIRST VETERANS CORPS

Hancock was assigned to command the garrison at Washington, D.C., and to create and command a ceremonial First Veterans Corps. On March 13, 1865, he was promoted to brevet major general in the regular army in somewhat belated recognition of his heroism at Spotsylvania.

His new duties were comparatively light, but, following the assassination of President Abraham Lincoln and the subsequent trial and conviction of John Wilkes Booth's conspirators, Hancock was charged with carrying out the group execution—by hanging on July 7, 1865—of Lewis Powell, David Herold, George

Atzerodt, and Mary Surratt. Hancock believed that Surratt's sentence was a gross miscarriage of justice, and he was so hopeful that it would be commuted at the last minute that he stationed a relay of couriers between the gallows at Fort McNair and the White House. To the judge who presided over the trial and pronounced the death sentence on Mrs. Surratt, Hancock remarked that he had "been in many a battle and [had] seen death, and shell and grapeshot, and, by God, I'd sooner be there ten thousand times over than to give the order this day for the execution of that poor woman." He paused, then continued: "But I am a soldier, sworn to obey, and obey I must."

HANCOCK'S CAMPAIGN, APRIL–JULY 1867

Shortly after he carried out the executions of the assassination conspirators, Hancock was given command of the Middle Military Department, headquartered in Baltimore. Promoted to regular army major general in 1866—upon Grant's recommendation—Hancock was assigned to command the Military Department of the Missouri, headquartered at Fort Leavenworth, Kansas, and encompassing Kansas, Missouri, Colorado, and New Mexico.

General Sherman, who had command of all army forces west of the Mississippi, assigned Hancock to negotiate—forcefully—with the Southern Cheyenne, the Southern Arapaho, the Kiowa, and the Oglala and Southern Brulé Sioux. On April 8, 1867, Hancock marched a column of soldiers to a combined Cheyenne and Sioux village with the intention of awing the Indians with the might of the army. Fearful of the soldiers, the women and children of the village scattered into the hills. Hancock ordered his main field officer, Lieutenant Colonel George Armstrong Custer, acting commander of the 7th Cavalry, to surround the village to prevent the men from escaping as well. Despite this, the lodges were all deserted by morning, and

Hancock ordered Custer to hunt down the flee-ing Indians.

From April through July, Custer and the 7th Cavalry chased Cheyenne and Sioux, some of whom raided settlements in Kansas. Custer and his command withdrew in exhaustion, and "Hancock's Campaign" quickly petered out into a series of mostly futile attempts to defend civil-ian settlements.

RECONSTRUCTION GENERAL

Shortly after the end of Hancock's Campaign, the commander of the Department of the Mis-souri was called back east by President Andrew Johnson, who was eager to replace hard-line Republican generals with Democrats to admin-ister Reconstruction in the South. Accordingly, Republican Philip Sheridan (who was especially harsh in handling ex-Confederates) was ordered to trade assignments with Hancock. As Sheri-dan went to Fort Leavenworth, Hancock trav-eled to New Orleans as the new commander of the Fifth Military District.

Tasked with overseeing Reconstruction in Texas and Louisiana, Hancock made a highly favorable first impression on the white people of the region by issuing General Order No. 40 on November 29, 1867: "The great principles of American liberty are still the lawful inheritance of this people, and ever should be. The right of trial by jury, the habeas corpus, the liberty of the press, the freedom of speech, the natural rights of persons and the rights of property must be pre-served. Free institutions, while they are essential to the prosperity and happiness of the people, always furnish the strongest inducements to peace and order."

Essentially, the order retracted the martial law policies of Sheridan and other Republican generals and asserted in their place the prin-ciples of President Johnson. Not surprisingly, Republicans in Congress condemned the order, which was the start of friction between them

Winfield Scott Hancock after the Civil War, by Mathew Brady. LIBRARY OF CONGRESS

and Hancock, who refused to overturn the elec-tion results and court verdicts to which they objected. Hancock made it clear that he would use his military authority only to suppress actual open insurrection, should any occur. Instantly popular with the struggling Democratic Party, Hancock was briefly considered for nomination as its presidential candidate in the 1868 election.

DEPARTMENT OF DAKOTA

With the ascension of Republican Ulysses S. Grant to the presidency in 1869, Hancock was removed from his Reconstruction duties and returned to the West, this time to the more remote Department of Dakota, encompass-ing Minnesota, Montana, and the Dakotas. In contrast to his earlier assignment as command-ing general of the Department of the Mis-souri, Hancock enjoyed a degree of success in negotiating reasonably peaceful relations with the Indians, and he even found the resources to provide military support for the expeditions that explored the Yellowstone region in 1870 and 1871, thereby laying the foundation for what would become the nation's first national park.

FROM GOVERNORS ISLAND TO A RUN FOR THE WHITE HOUSE

With the death of George Gordon Meade in 1872, Hancock became the U.S. Army's senior major general. President Grant, still unwilling to put him in charge anywhere in the sensitive Southern region, named him to command the Division of the Atlantic, with headquarters at Governors Island, New York City. It was a large command, encompassing virtually the entire Northeast, but his tenure was uneventful except for military involvement in suppressing the Great Railroad Strike of 1877, a mission that was controversial and sometimes bloody.

Hancock used his office to keep himself in the public and political eye, but he was soundly outpolled at the 1876 Democratic National Convention by Governor Samuel J. Tilden of New York. Hancock asserted his political ambitions more forcefully in 1880 and won the presidential nomination on the second ballot. In the general election, he received 4,444,952 votes versus 4,454,416 for Republican James A. Garfield, a narrow popular defeat, after which he returned to command of the Division of the Atlantic. While serving in this post, he was elected president of the National Rifle Association in 1881, an organization, he believed, that contributed to "the military strength of the country by making skill in the use of arms as prevalent as it was in the days of the Revolution."

In 1885, Hancock presided over the funeral of Ulysses S. Grant. By this time, his own health was in precipitous decline. The death of his son, Russell, in December 1884 had greatly depressed him, and he began also to suffer from diabetes. Early in 1886, a carbuncle on the back of his neck became infected, he developed a fever, and he died in his quarters at Governors Island on the afternoon of February 9.

Chapter 23

George Gordon Meade

RATING: ★ ★ ⯪

George Gordon Meade. LIBRARY OF CONGRESS

and he was notoriously irritable and famous for fits of anger. Politically inept, he was abrasive, readily giving as well as taking offense. Yet he had a strong sense of duty, placed a high value on loyalty, was fearless in combat, and, at his best, took a methodical approach to war-fighting, from logistics to engagement. As a subordinate commander, leading a brigade, a division, or a corps, he was aggressive, taking more initiative than most other Union generals. When he ascended to independent command as leader of the Army of the Potomac, however, he fell back on his natural tendency to caution. Calm, steady, competent, a good judge of men, and a leader willing to empower his subordinates, Meade assumed command of the Army of the Potomac from a badly shaken Joseph Hooker, who made no attempt to create a seamless transition of leadership. Three days after he took over, Meade fought the Battle of Gettysburg and managed to wring a critical turning-point victory using entirely defensive tactics. His failure to pursue the defeated Robert E. Lee, however, almost certainly prolonged the war unnecessarily, and his performance after Gettysburg, still as Army of the Potomac commander but very much in the shadow of Ulysses S. Grant, was adequate at best, careless at worst, and generally lackluster.

EVALUATION

Like a number of other young men of his generation, George Gordon Meade had entered West Point as an alternative to paying for a college education he could not afford. He never intended to make the army his career, and he possessed neither a soldierly appearance nor a soldierly temperament. His command presence was nil,

---

Principal Battles

PRE-CIVIL WAR

U.S.-Mexican War, 1846–1848

- Palo Alto, May 8, 1846
- Resaca de la Palma, May 9, 1846
- Monterrey, September 21–24, 1846: Meade served in staff and engineering capacities and did not lead troops in combat, but was brevetted to first lieutenant for gallantry at Monterrey

CIVIL WAR

- Seven Days, June 25–July 1, 1862: In Virginia; led a brigade of Pennsylvania volunteers at Beaver Dam Creek (Mechanicsville), June 26, at Gaines's Mill, June 27, and at Glendale, June 30; Meade displayed extraordinary valor under heavy attack at Glendale and was severely wounded—twice

- Second Bull Run, August 28–30, 1862: In Virginia; rendered heroic service covering the retreat of the bulk of the Army of the Potomac

- South Mountain, September 14, 1862: In Maryland; led aggressive action against D. H. Hill, which McClellan failed to exploit to advantage

- Antietam, September 17, 1862: In Maryland; competently led Hooker's corps after Hooker was wounded, but without the fire he had shown at South Mountain

- Fredericksburg, December 11–15, 1862: Meade's division was the only one that broke through the Confederate line, but, lacking support, Meade was forced to withdraw, his heavy losses having been suffered in vain

- Chancellorsville, April 30–May 6, 1863: In Virginia; Hooker kept Meade's corps in reserve throughout most of the battle, despite Meade's pleas that he be allowed to fight

- Gettysburg, July 1–3, 1863: In Pennsylvania; named to command the Army of the Potomac just three days earlier, Meade achieved a turning-point victory using only defensive tactics; had he followed up by pursuing the defeated Lee, his victory might have been war-winning

- Overland Campaign, May–June 1864: In Virginia; commanding the Army of the Potomac very much in Grant's shadow, Meade sometimes chafed under Grant, but performed to his satisfaction, despite tragic blunders at Cold Harbor, May 31–June 12, 1864

- Siege of Petersburg, June 9, 1864–March 25, 1865: In Virginia; still subordinate to Grant, Meade failed to coordinate attacks by his corps at the start of the siege, sacrificing an opportunity for an early, probably war-winning breakthrough; his failure of command at the Battle of the Crater, July 30, also sacrificed an early opportunity to break through to Petersburg and resulted in many needless deaths

His features pinched and ascetic, he looked more like an old-time Puritan preacher than a Civil War general, but, as one of his staff officers observed, "I don't know any thin old gentleman with a hooked nose and cold blue eye, who, when he is wrathy, exercises less of Christian charity than my well-beloved Chief." Ulysses S. Grant, who worked closely with him during the culminating campaigns of the war, praised Meade as "brave and conscientious" but also considered him cautious, dull, and quarrelsome—"of a temper that would get beyond his control . . . and make him speak to officers of high rank in the most offensive manner." Like Robert E. Lee, Meade had a natural talent for mathematics and had taken readily to engineering at West Point, but, in razor-sharp contrast to Lee, he was void of charisma and, it sometimes seemed, deficient in spirit and heart with little understanding of what truly was at stake in the war.

Learning that he would face Meade at Gettysburg, Lee assessed him with great accuracy: "General Meade will commit no blunder on my front, and if I make one he will make haste to take advantage of it." That was George Gordon Meade in full and in sum: cautious, competent, vigilant, unimaginative, and ill-tempered, ready to pounce, whether the enemy wore a uniform of gray or of blue. But who would have thought that it would be his destiny, of all generals, to command the Union army in the biggest, most famous, most storied, and arguably most consequential battle of the Civil War?

RELUCTANT CADET

Richard Worsam Meade had made a fortune as a Philadelphia merchant and was on his way to making that fortune even bigger in Cádiz, Spain, where he worked as a naval agent for the U.S. government. But by the time the eighth of his eleven children, George Gordon Meade, was born on December 31, 1815, his fortune was rapidly melting away. He had extended massive sums in credit to the government of Spain and, by the conclusion of the Napoleonic Wars, there was no one left in power with the authority, means, or willingness to pay him. Leaving his family in Spain, Richard Meade returned to the United States in an effort to recoup some of his losses. He died trying, penniless, in Washington, D.C., in 1828. Six months later, Margaret Coats Butler Meade and those of her children who still lived with her returned to Philadelphia.

Although Mrs. Meade was Protestant, her husband had been a staunch Irish Catholic, and George was admitted to Mount Hope College, a Catholic preparatory school in Baltimore. After three years there, he hoped to attend college, but because his widowed mother could not afford to send him, he reluctantly accepted an appointment to the United States Military Academy at West Point, which was obtained for him through one of his late father's political contacts. For many young men of limited means during this era, including several who would become the most important commanders of the Civil War, West Point did not loom as a portal to a military career but was a source of higher education that required no payment other than a commitment of one year's service in the U.S. Army. Young Meade didn't even want to commit to that year—but he did, figuring that it was a modest price to pay for valuable training as a civil engineer.

He enrolled in 1831 and almost instantly regretted it. If he made a hawklike appearance as a middle-aged general, he looked in his youth like a small bird, thin and delicate. He did not like marching. He did not like training. He did not like the bullying ways of upperclassmen. But he persevered, managing to graduate nineteenth in the fifty-six-member Class of 1835.

SECOND SEMINOLE WAR AND U.S.-MEXICAN WAR, 1835–1842 AND 1846–1848

His class standing, in the upper half but not the upper quarter, was insufficiently lofty to gain him

a commission in the engineers, but he did make it into Company C of the 3rd U.S. Artillery, which was stationed in Florida, where it participated in the Second Seminole War. Because artillery was of little use in what amounted to an insurgency carried out in overgrown, swampy terrain, Meade served primarily as an infantry officer in Florida before he was assigned to the U.S. arsenal in Watertown, Massachusetts, a center for the manufacture of cannon.

From the beginning of his reluctant military career, Meade's intention had been to serve out his statutory year and then resign. In 1836, he did just that, using his West Point engineering background to get a job as a civil engineer for the Alabama, Georgia, and Florida Railroad. At first he prospered in this work, but in 1837, a severe recession swept the nation, and it became increasingly difficult to remain employed. When his railroad job dried up, he took a cut in pay to work as a civilian engineer for the War Department. He had begun to court Margaretta Sergeant, the oldest daughter of Pennsylvania Congressman John Sergeant, who had been the running mate of Henry Clay in the 1832 presidential election. The couple married on December 31, 1840, but as money became scarcer, Meade looked to the U.S. Army for his salvation. He joined the Corps of Topographical Engineers on May 19, 1842, at his former rank of second lieutenant.

If engineering work was hard to come by in the civilian sector, it was abundant in the military. Meade was busy in the construction of lighthouses and breakwaters and in coastal survey as well as geodetic survey for mapmaking purposes. When war with Mexico broke out in 1846, he was assigned as a staff officer under Generals Zachary Taylor, William J. Worth, and Robert Patterson. He also served as an engineering officer, and although he was never a combat leader in the war, he did see action at Palo Alto (May 8, 1846), Resaca de la Palma (May 9), and Monterrey (September 21–24), during which he

made a sufficient impression on his commanding officer to merit a brevet promotion to first
lieutenant.

RETURN TO ENGINEERING

With the end of the U.S.-Mexican War, Meade
returned to his work with the Corps of Topographical Engineers and filled the months and
years before the Civil War with a list of impressive engineering achievements. There were more
lighthouses and breakwaters to build, a number
of which still stand and are well-loved land-
marks, including, along the New Jersey shore,
Barnegat Light on Long Beach Island; Absecon
Light in Atlantic City; Cape May Light in Cape
May; and, in Florida, the Jupiter Inlet Light and
Sombrero Key Light. Meade even turned his
hand to invention, designing a hydraulic lamp
that was widely used in lighthouses throughout
the United States.

Promoted to captain in 1856, Meade was
sent the following year to Detroit to relieve
Lieutenant Colonel James Kearney as leader of
the Lakes Survey project on the Great Lakes.
Meade oversaw completion of the Lake Huron
survey and the extension of the surveys of Lake
Michigan down to Grand Bay and Little Traverse Bay. His work was the foundation of the
first detailed statistical report on the Great
Lakes, published in 1860, and his measurements
and recommendations for measurement procedures remain the basis for lake-level studies that
continue to this day.

OUTBREAK

While carrying out his peaceful work on the
Lakes Survey, Meade grew increasingly concerned about the nation's drift toward civil war,
especially since two of his married sisters lived
in Southern states. Despite this family connection with the South, however, Meade's total
allegiance to the Union was always a foregone

conclusion. When Fort Sumter fell in April, he
was still at work in Detroit. When he received
no response to his requests for reassignment to a
combat command in the East, he boarded a train
for Washington in June to call on Secretary of
War Simon Cameron. He made his request for
reassignment in person, then returned to Detroit,
expecting word daily. Failing to hear from the
secretary by July, he appealed to Senator David
Wilmot and Governor Andrew G. Curtin, both
of Pennsylvania. This produced, on July 31, 1861,
a promotion from captain to brigadier general of
volunteers and command of one of three Pennsylvania brigades Curtin had organized.

After waiting so long, the sudden leap in rank
and responsibility unnerved Meade. "Sometimes
I have a little sinking in the heart," he admitted
in a letter to his wife, "when I reflect that perhaps I may fail at the grand scratch." What he
wrote next speaks volumes about his personality: "But I try to console myself with the belief
that I shall probably do as well as most of my
neighbors." Having graduated near the middle
of his West Point class, Meade seemed content
to aspire to a middling status of performance as
a general.

THE SEVEN DAYS, JUNE 25–JULY 1, 1862

As an engineer, Meade led his Pennsylvania volunteers in their first war-related assignment, to
extend and strengthen the fortifications around
Washington. This project occupied the winter;
come spring, Meade and his Pennsylvanians
were assigned to the Army of the Potomac under
Major General George B. McClellan.

Meade commanded his brigade in McClellan's Peninsula Campaign, fighting in the Seven
Days Battles (June 25–July 1, 1862) at the Battle of Beaver Dam Creek (Mechanicsville) on
June 26, at Gaines's Mill the next day, and at
Glendale on June 30. In this bitterly contested
battle, three Confederate divisions pounced on
the retreating Army of the Potomac at Frayser's

Farm in Glendale, Virginia. As the fighting became increasingly desperate, Meade rose to the occasion, fearlessly encouraging his men and exhorting them to keep up the fight. Those who were accustomed to the methodical, even plodding and certainly noncharismatic Meade were astonished by the fire he summoned in himself. The cost he paid, however, was high. Almost simultaneously, he was hit twice, once through the fleshy part of the forearm, and once into his right side, the bullet exiting just above the spine. He refused to quit the field until blood loss made it impossible for him to stand. As he was carried away, he called out to his artillerists: "Fight your guns to the last, but save them if possible."

Second Battle of Bull Run, August 28–30, 1862

Meade was invalided back home to Philadelphia but rejoined his brigade on August 17, at Falmouth, Virginia. His men cheered him as he rode through camp. In less than two weeks, he and his brigade, assigned to Irvin McDowell's corps in John Pope's Army of Virginia, were facing Lee at the Second Battle of Bull Run. In this disastrous Union defeat, Meade and his men performed heroically by standing firm on Henry House Hill to provide a rear guard for the retreating Union forces.

Battles of South Mountain and Antietam, September 14 and 17, 1862

The debacle at Second Bull Run brought the removal of Pope and the return front and center of George B. McClellan, who now led the Army of the Potomac to intercept Robert E. Lee as he invaded Maryland. In the run-up to the Battle of Antietam, Meade, who had jumped from brigade command to command of a division in Joseph Hooker's corps, led his troops against a part of the Confederate army under D. H. Hill at the Battle of South Mountain on September

14. Hooker, observing the battle, was impressed. "Look at Meade!" he exclaimed. "Why, with troops like those, led in that way, I can win anything!" And one of Hill's own soldiers, captured in the battle, admiringly remarked to one of Meade's officers, "Your men fight like devils."

When a foot wound took Hooker from the field at the Battle of Antietam on September 17, McClellan tapped Meade to replace him as I Corps commander, even though he was junior to several other generals. He performed adequately, but without the fire he had shown at South Mountain. Later, Hooker and McClellan would agree that the bloody battle would have ended in a more decisive defeat of Lee had not Hooker's wound forced him off the field. Beyond question, however, was Meade's courage. A thigh wound was not enough to take him out of the battle.

Battles of Fredericksburg and Chancellorsville, December 11–15, 1862, and April 30–May 6, 1863

No one, including President Lincoln, criticized Hooker or Meade for the failure to bring the Battle of Antietam to a more decisive conclusion. Justly or not, McClellan took all the blame, and when he idled the Army of the Potomac for more than a month following the battle, an exasperated president relieved him, replacing him with an initially reluctant Ambrose Burnside on November 5.

Eager to act vigorously where McClellan had procrastinated, Burnside drew up a plan to capture Richmond by crossing the Rappahannock River rapidly at Fredericksburg. Speed was the critical element in the plan. Delay would be fatal, since it would give Lee the time he needed to reinforce the Fredericksburg crossing. Meade criticized Burnside's plan as impractical because "true logistics were being ignored." It was, he believed, compounded more of wishful thinking than of realistic tactical formulation.

And later, when the Rappahannock crossing was delayed by the failure of pontoon boats to show up in time, Meade knew the operation was doomed. Nevertheless, on December 13, he dutifully formed up a line of his five thousand men opposite the well-fortified high ground held by Major General D. H. Hill's division. The defenders' fire was withering, as it was everywhere along the line, but Meade's division was the only one on that terrible day that succeeded in breaking through the Confederate lines. Tragically for Meade and his men, Burnside did not see to it that the breakthrough was supported, exploited, and followed up. "The slightest straw," Meade later remarked, "almost would have kept the tide in our favor." But without backup, he was forced to withdraw, having suffered 1,800 casualties out of the five thousand men engaged—a horrific 36 percent casualty rate that was made all the more ghastly by the fact that it was all for nothing. Nevertheless, Meade received promotion to major general of volunteers and command of V Corps.

He led his corps in the Army of the Potomac under its new commander, Joseph Hooker, at the Battle of Chancellorsville (April 30–May 6). Meade was satisfied with Hooker's plan, which was far more sophisticated than Burnside's simple and suicidal frontal approach. Besides, although he had reservations about Hooker—as virtually all of Hooker's brother officers did—Meade was confident that he was a substantial improvement over Burnside, a man he believed had been unfit for independent, army-level command. What disturbed him, however, was Hooker's loudmouthed confidence in an easy victory. It not only seemed unrealistic, given the toll Robert E. Lee had already taken on the Army of the Potomac, it rang hollow.

And hollow it proved to be. While Hooker's plan was sound, his execution was timid, a sudden shift from offense to defense, which yielded the initiative to Lee while also allowing him to operate from "the Wilderness," as the environs of Chancellorsville were called. This dense and tangled landscape robbed Hooker of the maneuverability he needed to make productive use of his two-to-one superiority in numbers. In the thick of combat, Hooker kept Meade's corps in reserve throughout the most critical phase of the battle on May 2, when Stonewall Jackson smashed the Union army's right flank. Even with the situation desperate, most of Meade's men were never allowed to enter the fight.

The next day, May 3, Meade advised a strong counterattack, but the unnerved Hooker withdrew into a fully defensive position. "I opposed the withdrawal with all my influence," Meade later wrote, "and I tried all I could . . . to be permitted to take my corps into action, . . . but I was overruled." Still, when a number of Army of the Potomac subordinate commanders organized a movement to bring about the removal of Hooker, Meade, always loyal, refused to join, telling the officers that only if President Lincoln officially solicited his opinion would he speak out about Hooker's performance.

BATTLE OF GETTYSBURG, JULY 1–3, 1863

Lincoln did not consult Meade but did meet confidentially with Major General John F. Reynolds, one of the officers agitating for Hooker's removal. Most historians believe that, in this June 2 meeting, the president offered him the Army of the Potomac command. He was, after all, one of the most universally respected generals in the U.S. Army. What happened next has been subject to much speculation and debate. It is widely believed that Reynolds was willing to accept the offer on condition that he would be given an entirely free hand, without political interference. Lincoln, who had the Joint Committee on the Conduct of the War in Congress continually looking over his shoulder, could not agree to this, and so Reynolds declined. Others, however, believe that Lincoln decided to withhold the command from Reynolds because he feared that this would create a war hero who would challenge him in his bid for reelection. Some have suggested that Lincoln turned to Meade, a solid figure but one who was not high on anyone's list for independent command, because his foreign birth in Spain supposedly disqualified him from becoming a presidential contender. (As constitutional law goes, this contention was the thinnest of reeds; Meade's father was in Spain on official U.S. government duty.)

Whatever the reasons for Lincoln's decision, having made it, he dispatched a messenger who arrived at Meade's camp to tell him that he had been appointed as Hooker's replacement. Again, Meade's response to the arrival of the messenger at three o'clock in the morning of June 28, 1863, suggests much about the man's psychology. Roused from bed, his first thought was that military/political enemies had sent a War Department agent to arrest him. When the messenger delivered his message, Meade replied that others were more senior and more qualified than he, and he therefore respectfully declined. The messenger pointed out, however, that what he bore was not an invitation but an order. "Well," Meade told him, "I've been tried and condemned without a hearing, and I suppose I shall have to go to the execution."

He wasted little time in what he assumed would be the most unpleasant task of telling Hooker the news. Instead of responding with his customary bluster, Hooker calmly took it in like the beaten man he was. Meade wrote to his wife that Hooker said he was "ready to turn over to me the Army of the Potomac; that he had enough of it, and almost wished he had never been born." Thus washing his hands of his former command, Hooker left Meade neither plans nor counsel nor even any information on the current disposition of the troops. From his field headquarters at Prospect Hall in Frederick, Maryland, Meade had no choice but to make things up as he went along. Knowing only that Lee was invading Pennsylvania, he started the army marching toward the Susquehanna River, while at the same time ensuring that it screened Washington and Baltimore from possible attack.

On July 1, just three days after he had taken command, a cavalry division of the Army of the Potomac under Brigadier General John Buford made contact with infantry elements of the Army of Northern Virginia at the quiet Pennsylvania crossroads town of Gettysburg. Neither unit had intended to begin a battle here, but a battle there would be.

Greatly outnumbered, Buford set up necessarily thin defensive lines north and west of the town, desperately holding on until the closest Union infantry, I Corps under John Reynolds, could arrive. The gallant Reynolds galloped out ahead of his corps' 1st Division, consulted with Buford, agreed that Gettysburg should be held, and then began directing the fight. He was supervising the placement of the 2nd Wisconsin Regiment, when a Confederate bullet slammed into his neck, tumbling him off his horse, and killing him instantly.

The loss of this popular general, who most officers of the Army of the Potomac believed should rightfully be their commander, was stunning. Many modern historians believe that Reynolds, more than any other available Union commander, possessed the heart and brain to shape Gettysburg into a war-winning battle. As it was, in his brief time on the scene, he had created the conditions that made it the place at which the Army of the Potomac would meet the Army of Northern Virginia for a showdown. Reynolds had approved Buford's decision to defend the ground, and he had committed his I Corps to it. Having been cast adrift by Hooker, Meade welcomed the direction that had been thrust upon him.

His most urgent problem was that, at the moment, he was greatly outnumbered at Gettysburg. He had to hold on until he could bring to bear the rest of the widely scattered Army of the Potomac. To replace Reynolds and manage the holding action, he dispatched Major General Winfield Scott Hancock. Much as Meade had not been the obvious choice to replace Hooker, Hancock was junior to other candidates, most notably O. O. Howard. But Meade knew Hancock better than he knew Howard, and he believed he could rely on his fighting spirit.

Under Hancock on July 1, two Union infantry corps absorbed terrible casualties and withdrew through the streets of Gettysburg to take up positions on the high ground, which they managed to hold against fierce Confederate assaults as Meade efficiently consolidated his army and rushed it into position.

Because Buford, Hancock, and other subordinate commanders were the first on the ground, Meade is often given little credit for what was achieved at Gettysburg. In fact, over the course of the three-day battle, it was his willingness to trust and his ability to use his subordinates—especially Hancock—that brought victory. On the other hand, Meade's prickly temper and sometimes ham-handed political ineptitude caused potentially catastrophic difficulty with some subordinates, most notably with the III Corps commander, Major General Daniel Sickles. Sickles was politically ambitious and eager for advancement at Meade's expense. He also resented Meade because he erroneously believed that Meade had deliberately engineered the ouster of his friend Hooker. Apparently by way of revenge, Sickles acted against Meade's explicit orders by advancing his corps a half mile ahead of the Union defensive line, thereby exposing himself to attack in the area called the Peach Orchard northwest of the Big and Little Round Tops, the high ground positions that formed the left flank of the entire Army of the Potomac.

All the Confederates had to do was break through III Corps in the Peach Orchard, and they could punch through to roll up the entire Union position. For the Union, this would have meant the battle was lost and, with it, quite possibly, the Civil War. Fortunately, Meade's chief engineer, Brigadier General Gouverneur K. Warren, saw that Sickles's advance had left Little Round Top essentially undefended, and he immediately sent his staff officers to round up a brigade to hold the position. Other units were rushed into place as well, including the battered 20th Maine Regiment under the command of Colonel Joshua Lawrence Chamberlain, by trade a professor of rhetoric at Bowdoin College. With no more than five hundred men, Chamberlain managed to defeat an attack by a superior Alabama regiment and thus save the Union flank, the Union army, and the Union cause.

Widely considered the single most significant Union victory of the war, Gettysburg could easily have gone the other way—and not just thanks to the insubordination of Dan Sickles. At the end of the second day of battle, July 2, Meade seemed not to share the aggressive fire of his best field officers. Nor did he exhibit an understanding of all that was at stake in this battle, that the only approach to it was do or die. Instead of simply and unambiguously committing to a third day of combat, he convened a council of war with his subordinates and asked them, "Should we remain and fight or should we withdraw?" Only when he was certain of a consensus to remain, did he decide to fight on, but, even then, as he wrote to Union army general-in-chief Henry Wager Halleck, he was "not prepared to say . . . whether my operations will be of an offensive or defensive character."

For Meade, the shape of the final day of battle, July 3, would be dictated by caution, while Lee would throw caution to the wind and hurl at the Union a desperate infantry charge by twelve thousand of his finest soldiers. Meade's defense shattered Pickett's Charge, inflicting some 6,555 casualties—about half the men engaged—and sending a broken Army of Northern Virginia into retreat out of Pennsylvania. The next day, July 4, Meade did not even discuss mounting a counterattack. He had fought a totally defensive battle, and he had won. But in declining to shift

The great Civil War photographer Timothy O'Sullivan titled this "Incidents of the war. A harvest of death, Gettysburg, July, 1863." LIBRARY OF CONGRESS

to the offensive when Lee was at his most vulnerable, he threw away an opportunity to kill the enemy army and so failed to push the war to a faster end.

Initially relieved and overjoyed by the victory at Gettysburg, President Lincoln quickly became depressed by Meade's failure to exploit the costly triumph. When he read Meade's proclamation to the soldiers of the Army of the Potomac, in which the general spoke of driving "from our soil every vestige of the presence of the invader," he exploded in rage. "Drive the invaders from our soil," he gasped. "My God! Is that all? Will our generals never get that idea out of their heads? The whole country is our soil!" The president

sat down and wrote a stern letter to Meade: "I do not believe you appreciate the magnitude of the misfortune involved in Lee's escape. He was within your easy grasp, and to have closed upon him would . . . have ended the war."

But Lincoln folded the missive and put it in his desk, alongside many other letters he had composed in anger but had never sent.

IN GRANT'S SHADOW

When Henry W. Halleck informed Meade of what he called the president's "disappointment" over the aftermath of Gettysburg, Meade offered the general-in-chief his resignation. Halleck

The Gettysburg Campaign - June–July 1863

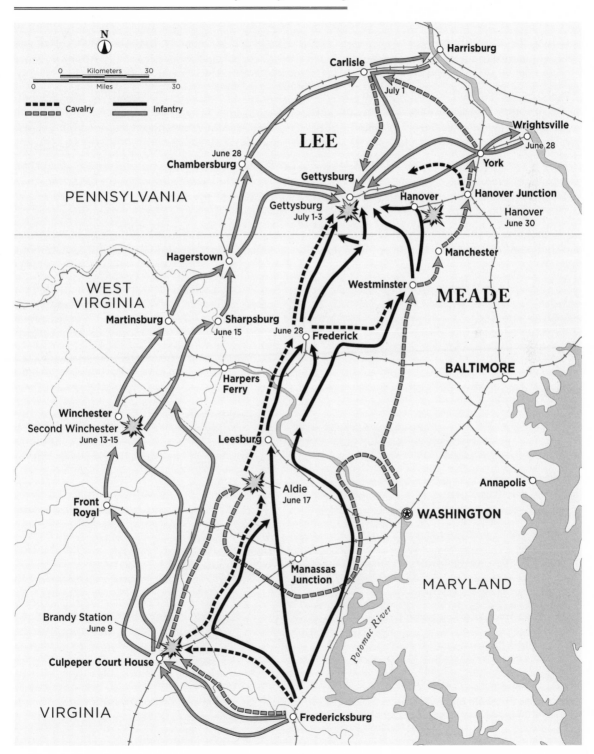

refused it and quickly changed the subject by praising Meade for having handled the "troops . . . as well, if not better, than any general has handled the army during the war." Expressed this way, it was, in fact, a just assessment.

As for Lincoln, initially disgusted with Meade, he subsequently resisted calls from some in his Cabinet to remove him. "What can I do with such generals as we have?" he asked. "Who among them is better than Meade?" That also was a just assessment—as far as it went. Of course, Lincoln did have a better general, Ulysses S. Grant, whom he appointed general-in-chief of the U.S. Army in March 1864. In contrast to the desk-bound, Washington-based Halleck, who willingly made room for Grant by moving down from general-in-chief to chief of staff, Grant was determined to command from the field, which meant that he would travel with the Army of the Potomac. Fearing that this would create an intolerably awkward command situation, since the Army of the Potomac was the principal constituent of the U.S. Army wielded against Lee, Meade, feeling superfluous, offered to step down as its general. Grant refused to accept his resignation, and thus Meade found himself "commanding" the army on orders from Grant. A further complication was introduced by the presence in the Army of the Potomac of Ambrose Burnside, who had been reduced to command of a single corps—IX Corps—but who was nevertheless senior to Meade. Grant solved the difficulty by giving his orders to Meade and then issuing them separately to Burnside.

Grant consistently professed great admiration for Meade, and yet Grant's willingness to fight a relentlessly aggressive war of attrition in the Overland Campaign, in which the Army of the Potomac absorbed fifty-five thousand to sixty-five thousand casualties, conflicted with Meade's cautious stewardship of the army. Aggressive as a subordinate commander, Meade had become far more conservative in independent command, and now he was asked to stand by while Grant spilled the blood of men Grant knew he could replace in order to kill men he knew Robert E. Lee could not.

Meade with his Army of the Potomac staff, March 1864. Major General John Sedgwick, second from right, would be killed at the Battle of Spotsylvania on May 9, 1864. FROM THE PHOTOGRAPHIC HISTORY OF THE CIVIL WAR (1911)

Perhaps because he keenly felt the limitation of his authority, Meade suffered some uncharacteristic lapses in judgment. At the Battle of Cold Harbor (May 31–June 12, 1864), his failure to ride herd on his corps commanders by insisting that they obtain adequate pre-assault reconnaissance substantially contributed to the catastrophic casualties of an ill-advised frontal assault—for which, however, Grant accepted full blame. During the Siege of Petersburg (June 9, 1864–March 25, 1865), Meade's failure or inability to effectively coordinate the otherwise piecemeal attacks of his corps gave Lee ample time to reinforce the elaborate fortifications that ringed Petersburg. What might have been a quick and decisive breakthrough here became a ten-month siege and stalemate. A short time later, when Ambrose Burnside conveyed to Meade a plan two of his officers had formulated to blast a gap in the Confederate defenses by digging a mine under the enemy lines and packing it with explosives, he passively permitted the project to proceed, only to make a last-minute decision that ensured its failure. Burnside had used the weeks required to dig the mine to train a division of the United States Colored Troops in the complex choreography required to exploit the breach. Suddenly fearing a public relations disaster if he and Grant were seen as "sacrificing" black troops in a suicide mission, Meade ordered Burnside to pull the black division and substitute an untrained, unprepared white division to make the initial assault. The result was the Battle of the Crater (July 30, 1864), which has been called the greatest Union fiasco of the war, as 3,798 men of IX Corps were killed, wounded, captured, or went missing in a grotesque slaughter that achieved absolutely nothing.

Still, Grant consistently praised Meade and saw to it that he was promoted to major general of the regular army—a gesture that the ill-tempered Meade managed to interpret as a slight because the promotion came after those of William T. Sherman and Philip Sheridan, favorite officers of Grant. Nor did Grant ask that Meade be present when Robert E. Lee surrendered at the McLean house in Appomattox Court House on April 9, 1865.

(Lee and Meade did visit one another after the surrender, however. It was the first time they had seen each other since they had served together in the war with Mexico.

"What are you doing with all that gray in your beard?" Lee good-naturedly chided his former comrade-in-arms.

"You have to answer for most of it," Meade responded.)

POSTWAR COMMANDS AND DEATH

After the war, Meade held a succession of major commands, including the Department of the East, the Department of the South, and the Military Division of the Atlantic, headquartered in Philadelphia, where he also served as a commissioner of the city's celebrated Fairmount Park and was the beneficiary of a gift presented by the people of Philadelphia, a magnificent house at 1836 Delancey Place. It was here that he succumbed to pneumonia on November 6, 1872.

Chapter 24

Philip H. Sheridan

RATING: ★ ★ ★

A Mathew Brady portrait of Philip Sheridan. NATIONAL ARCHIVES AND RECORDS ADMINISTRATION

EVALUATION

In an era and a war in which it was common for men, Union and Confederate, to be commissioned as general officers based on their political connections, Philip Henry Sheridan rose to top command strictly on his merits as a warrior and leader of warriors. Trained as an infantry officer, he ended up reinventing the Union cavalry, raising it to a level that challenged the vaunted Confederate cavalry while also radically revising its mission from reconnaissance, screening, and guarding trains and rear areas to more strategic attack roles, especially as shock troops directed against the enemy army and civilian population. In this redesign of the cavalry mission, he had mixed success, especially in Grant's Overland Campaign, in which his neglect of the traditional cavalry functions almost certainly deprived Grant and Army of the Potomac commander George G. Meade of vital battlefield intelligence when it was most needed. On the other hand, his use of mixed cavalry and infantry in the Shenandoah Campaign introduced scorched-earth "total warfare" tactics that presaged William T. Sherman's more famous "March to the Sea" and proved both cruel and effective. He would reprise these, most controversially, in his postwar assignment as chief architect of the Indian Wars in the West.

Despite the mixed results of his approach to cavalry and the moral ambiguity (in the Indian Wars verging on genocide) of his policy of waging war on civilians, it cannot be denied that Sheridan was a superb leader of troops, a fine tactician, and an aggressive fighter, who was especially effective in forcing Lee to surrender his Army of Northern Virginia in the closing weeks of the Civil War.

Principal Battles

PRE-CIVIL WAR

Rogue River War, 1855–1856

- North of the present California-Oregon border; while attached to a topographical survey mission, Sheridan was involved in skirmishes with so-called Rogue Indians while most of the army in the area was fighting the Yakima War

Yakima War, 1855–1858

- In Oregon Territory; attached to a topographical survey mission, Sheridan led small combat units

in sharp fights with followers of the Yakima chief Kamiakin, who resisted incursions led by territorial governor Isaac Stevens; was slightly wounded on March 28, 1857

CIVIL WAR

- Pea Ridge, March 6–8, 1862: In Arkansas; served under Brigadier General Samuel R. Curtis in the battle, mostly in a noncombat role as quartermaster general

- "Siege" of Corinth, April 29–May 30, 1862: In Mississippi; served on H. W. Halleck's staff and as an assistant to the Department of the Missouri's topographical engineer

- Booneville, July 1, 1862: In Mississippi; Sheridan's first real combat command in the Civil War and first time commanding cavalry; brilliantly blunted a Confederate cavalry attack by Brigadier General James R. Chalmers on the main Union force, greatly impressing his seniors

- Perryville, October 8, 1862: In Kentucky; drove the Confederates from the field, discouraging a major offensive

- Stones River, December 31, 1862–January 2, 1863: At Murfreesboro, Tennessee; delayed Confederate advance to buy time for William S. Rosecrans to regroup at a stronger defensive position, which led to a Union victory in this very bloody fight

- Tullahoma Campaign, June 24–July 3, 1863: In Tennessee; commanded the lead division into Tullahoma

- Chickamauga, September 19–20, 1863: In Georgia; made a remarkable stand at Lytle Hill with his division against Lieutenant General James Longstreet's corps; regrouped and joined George H. Thomas in his counterattack, arriving too late to participate in the main phase

- Missionary Ridge (during Battle of Chattanooga), November 25, 1863: At Lookout Mountain, Tennessee; Sheridan's division was among elements in Thomas's Army of the Cumberland that forced the Confederates out of their defensive positions on Missionary Ridge

- Wilderness, May 5–7, 1864: In Virginia; the densely forested terrain impeded cavalry operations, and Sheridan's troopers enjoyed little success

- Spotsylvania Court House, May 8–21, 1864: In Virginia; again, Sheridan's cavalry turned in a poor performance, allowing Robert E. Lee to beat Ulysses S. Grant to critical defensive positions

- Yellow Tavern, May 11, 1864: In Virginia; Sheridan scored a tactical victory against the Confederate cavalry of J. E. B. Stuart, who was mortally wounded, but produced strategic results of little value—except to shatter the myth of the invincibility of the Confederate cavalry

- Haw's Shop, May 28, 1864: In Virginia; a high-cost victory that drove the Confederates from the field, but, again, produced nothing of strategic significance

- Trevilian Station, June 11–12, 1864: In Virginia; the largest all-cavalry battle of the war, it produced mixed results: Sheridan created a diversion that prevented Lee from quickly seeing that Grant had shifted his target from Richmond to Petersburg, but Sheridan failed to destroy the Virginia Central Railroad, one of his key objectives

- Shenandoah Valley Campaign, August 7–October 19, 1864: In Virginia; commanding the newly created Army of the Shenandoah, Sheridan pursued Jubal Early, neutralizing him as a force in the war, and conducted a scorched-earth campaign designed to deprive the Confederacy of its Shenandoah Valley "breadbasket"

- Third Battle of Winchester, September 19, 1864: In the Shenandoah Valley; Sheridan pursued and battered Jubal Early

- Fisher's Hill, September 22, 1864: In the Shenandoah Valley; Sheridan continued to hammer at Early

- Cedar Creek, October 19, 1864: In the Shenandoah Valley; culmination of the Shenandoah Valley Campaign: Sheridan rallied his army, converting a rout into a spectacularly decisive Union victory

- Waynesboro, March 2, 1865: In Virginia; destroyed what remained of Jubal Early's army

- Five Forks, April 1, 1865: Severed Lee's last line of supply and communications, forcing him to evacuate Petersburg, thereby precipitating the Appomattox Campaign and the ultimate loss of the Army of Northern Virginia

- Sayler's Creek, April 6, 1865: About one-quarter of the depleted Army of Northern Virginia surrendered to Sheridan here, prompting him to advise Grant to "press" the war to its end

- Appomattox Court House, April 9, 1865: Sheridan blocked Lee's only remaining escape route, forcing surrender of the Army of Northern Virginia on this day

POST-CIVIL WAR

Occupation of Texas, 1865–1866

- Sheridan's prompt action along the border put an end to a threatened invasion by French troops propping up the puppet Mexican government of Austrian Archduke Maximilian

Military governor, Fifth Military District, 1867

- Military governor of Louisiana and Texas; his harsh Radical Republican policies clashed with President Andrew Johnson's lenient approach to Reconstruction, and Sheridan was relieved after six months

Indian Wars

- As commanding general of the Department (later, Division) of the Missouri, 1867–1878, and of the Military Divisions of the West and Southwest, 1878–1883, was the prime architect of U.S. Army campaigns against the Plains Indians
- Ended his career as commanding general of the Army, 1883–1888

He was hardly the image of the powerful soldier that he in fact was. Five-foot-five with an outsized bullet head that made him appear even smaller, he looked up to most men and way up to Abraham Lincoln, who described him as a "brown, chunky little chap, with a long body, short legs, not enough neck to hang him, and such long arms that if his ankles itch he can scratch them without stooping." But within that unprepossessing frame were the mind, the heart, and the sheer energy that make up the kind of senior combat commander rare in any war and in especially short supply, on both sides, during the Civil War.

The iconic moment, the occasion that showed it all, came on October 19, 1864, when, confident he had whipped the wily Confederate raider Jubal Early, Sheridan, long in the field, was taking a precious opportunity to touch base with Washington. He was resting en route at a house in Winchester, Virginia, when an aide woke him early with news of artillery fire back at Cedar Creek, where he had camped his men. Sheridan dressed, mounted up, and began to ride the twenty miles back to Cedar Creek. It was a comfortable trot until, as he later described, "the

appalling spectacle of a panic-stricken army—hundreds of slightly wounded men, throngs of others unhurt but utterly demoralized . . . burst upon our view." All were "pressing to the rear in hopeless confusion."

Sheridan broke into a gallop and was soon met by Major General William Emory riding in the opposite direction. A division of his corps, he panted, was all set to cover a mass retreat of the Army of the Shenandoah.

Sheridan locked eyes on Emory.

"Retreat, hell! We'll be back in camp tonight."

With that, Sheridan rallied and re-formed his army.

"We'll raise them out of their boots before the day is over!" he promised his soldiers. And by late afternoon, Jubal Early, scourge of the Valley, was finished as a force in the Civil War.

COMING OF AGE

No one has ever quite pinned down the facts of Philip Henry Sheridan's humble pedigree. It is generally accepted that he was born on March 6, 1831—a date he himself mentioned several times—but other dates have also been suggested. In his own memoirs, he claimed to have been born in Albany, New York, but other birthplaces have been suggested as well. It is known that he was the third child of six born to John and Mary Meenagh Sheridan, second cousins who had wed in their home parish of Killinkere, County Cavan, Ireland, then, like so many others, immigrated to the American promised land. And, like so many others, found that the promise made far exceeded the promise kept. Having struggled as tenant farmers in Ireland, they arrived in Albany only to discover that jobs were scarce. Hearing, however, that work gangs were needed for the National Road that was being cut from the Chesapeake Bay to the Mississippi River, they moved west to Somerset, Ohio. Here Philip Sheridan grew up, raised mostly by his mother while his father was away at work on the road and, later, on canal and railroad projects.

The boy started school when he was ten and left when he was fourteen, typical for the time and place. He worked hard as a helper and clerk in Somerset's general stores and, in his teen years, found a steady job as head clerk and bookkeeper in a dry goods establishment. As an Irish Catholic, Sheridan might have expected to run into trouble, but Somerset had a fairly large Catholic community into which the family fit. The scrapes he did get into as a youngster mostly had to do with his short yet gawky frame. According to his own recollections, the necessity of dealing with bully boys moved him to develop fighting skills. He decided to tolerate abuse from no one, to make no threats, but to respond to any attack swiftly and fiercely, preferably when his adversary least expected it. In this way, he built a local reputation that gained him a good deal of respect, even if some of it was grudging.

Like small-town lads everywhere, young Sheridan became restless and longed to see more of the wider world. He relished tales his father and other workers brought with them from the West, and he became especially excited by what he heard and read of the U.S.-Mexican War (1846–1848), which seemed to him a great adventure. He learned of West Point and imagined it as his portal to a bigger life. But poor, first-generation Irish Catholic immigrants lacked the political pull needed to cajole a senator or a congressman into a nomination. Sheridan's prospects looked dim until he heard that the nominee from his district had been disqualified for failing the math portion of the entrance exam and displaying an all-around "poor attitude." Pouncing on the opportunity, long shot though it was, Sheridan wrote to Congressman Thomas Ritchey, asking for the still-vacant slot. To his surprise, the reply came quickly. Sheridan was nominated, passed the entrance exam, and was duly enrolled in the Class of 1852. Although Sheridan's sketchy educational preparation was

typical of nineteenth-century small-town America, it was significantly below the level of most West Point cadets. At first, Sheridan struggled academically and was grateful for the tutoring and coaching offered by his roommate, a sophisticated cadet from New York named Henry Slocum. Yet Slocum's friendship proved to be the exception for Sheridan. He was by nature pugnacious and argumentative, he was physically odd, and he was Irish Catholic. None of these characteristics made him popular among his classmates. On September 9, 1851, in his third year, he responded to an insult—probably less real than perceived—from Cadet William R. Terrill by proposing to run him through with a bayonet. As the two squared off, a cadet officer intervened, thereby preventing what might otherwise have been a beating (Terrill was by far the bigger of the two) or murder (Sheridan had the bayonet). What he did not prevent was a sentence of suspension from classes, which compelled Sheridan to repeat his third year and meant that he would graduate in 1853 rather than with the rest of his class in 1852. Although the combination of Slocum's tutelage and his own hard work had earned him respectable grades, his collection of demerits—mostly related to exercises of ill temper—put him thirty-fourth in a class of fifty-two.

Northwest Indian Wars

Brevet Second Lieutenant Sheridan was assigned to the 1st U.S. Infantry regiment at Fort Duncan, Texas. It was, for the most part, an uneventful assignment, and he occupied his time in learning the countryside. He devoured maps, and where adequate maps didn't exist, he drew his own. He understood intuitively that prevailing in battle required intimate, firsthand knowledge of the topography. The idea was to enlist the land as an ally, and this is what he practiced.

Promoted to regular army second lieutenant in November 1854, he was transferred to the 4th

Fresh out of West Point, Brevet Second Lieutenant Philip Sheridan, 1st Infantry Regiment, was photographed about 1853 or 1854. LIBRARY OF CONGRESS

U.S. Infantry at Fort Reading, California. The gold rush of 1848–1849 having rapidly populated the country, the army was faced with the mission of policing it, which mostly meant dealing with clashes between white settlers and local Indians. Sheridan's interest in maps led to his being attached to a topographical survey mission in the Willamette Valley in 1855, but this soon segued into a combat mission when the survey team got into scrapes with Indian warriors during the Rogue River War (1855–1856) and Yakima War (1855–1858). The second lieutenant became adept at small-unit tactics, but he also learned—on the job—the delicate, dangerous, and often cynical art of negotiating with tribes. On March 28, 1857, at Middle Cascade, Oregon Territory, Sheridan suffered his

first combat wound when an Indian rifle bullet grazed his nose. Like many soldiers stationed in remote outposts of the tiny U.S. Army of the time, Sheridan took an Indian lover, living for a time with Sidnayoh—whites called her Frances—the daughter of a Klickitat chief.

CIVIL WAR OUTBREAK

The enormous manpower demands of the Civil War would lead, on both sides, to the creation of many "political generals," men elevated to high military office on the strength of who, not what, they knew. While some of these men would rise to their responsibilities, becoming competent, even excellent officers, most remained mediocrities at best. Sheridan, born poor and thoroughly unconnected, was the diametric opposite of the political general. He would rise on his military merit, which began to be recognized very early. Promoted to first lieutenant in March 1861, on the eve of the Civil War, he was jumped to captain in May, just after the fall of Fort Sumter.

Sheridan was no abolitionist—the issue of slavery moved him neither one way nor the other—but he was passionate about the preservation of the Union, and he was eager to get into the fight. In September 1861, he was ordered to the 13th U.S. Infantry at Jefferson Barracks, Missouri. This meant an arduous journey from Fort Yamhill, Oregon, overland to San Francisco, where he boarded a ship bound for the Isthmus of Panama. Crossing this disease-ridden jungle overland, he took another ship bound for New York City. After a brief home leave in Somerset, Ohio, he boarded a train for St. Louis. Before reporting to Jefferson Barracks and his ordered assignment, he paid what he apparently intended as nothing more than a courtesy call on Major General Henry W. Halleck, who had just relieved John C. Frémont as commanding officer of the Department of the Missouri. Halleck effectively hijacked his visitor, assigning the mathematically adept former clerk and bookkeeper to audit the byzantine financial records that Frémont, who had badly mismanaged the department, had left behind.

The task, which proved herculean, Sheridan tackled single-handedly. Amazed and delighted by the results, Halleck marked Sheridan out as prime staff officer material. It was hardly a job he sought, but he threw himself into it nonetheless, and in December, he was appointed chief commissary officer of the Army of Southwest Missouri. Apparently seeking to make the most of the desk job he didn't want, Sheridan also talked Halleck into making him quartermaster general as well.

MAIDEN BATTLE

In January 1862, while serving in his staff posts, Sheridan was assigned to duty under Major General Samuel Curtis. Although he saw action at the Battle of Pea Ridge (March 6–8, 1862), his true maiden battle was fought on another field and against a Union commander, not a Confederate one. In his roles as departmental commissary officer and quartermaster, he discovered that war profiteering was rampant among many officers, and Curtis was doing nothing to stop it. The scam was both brazen and simple. Officers stole horses from civilians, turned them over to Curtis's army, then demanded payment from quartermaster Sheridan. Clearly, he was expected to play along. When he refused, Curtis demanded that he pay. To this *general*, the *captain* responded, "No authority can compel me to jayhawk or steal."

Taken aback, Curtis ordered Sheridan's arrest for insubordination and prepared a court-martial. Halleck intervened before charges were actually brought, and he saw to Sheridan's expeditious transfer from Curtis's command back to his own headquarters. While once again a staff officer for Halleck, Sheridan served during the "Siege" of Corinth (April 29–May 30, 1862) after Halleck, having effectively relieved Brigadier

General U. S. Grant, took personal command of Grant's troops and moved with such dilatory deliberation as to allow P. G. T. Beauregard to slip out of Corinth with his army intact.

Thus Sheridan experienced firsthand the corruption and incompetence that pervaded much of the Union army, reaching to the highest levels of command. Although he found some satisfaction as an assistant to the Department of the Missouri's topographical engineer, he longed to get into meaningful combat. Fortunately for him, while serving on Halleck's staff, he met Brigadier General William T. Sherman, who tried to obtain for him a colonelcy of an Ohio infantry regiment. As it turned out, Sherman could not deliver on this, but the momentum of his attempt led to other influential individuals petitioning Governor Austin Blair of Michigan to appoint Sheridan colonel of the 2nd Michigan Cavalry on May 27, 1862.

BATTLE OF BOONEVILLE, JULY 1, 1862

That Sheridan was not trained as a cavalryman did not discourage him from jumping at the appointment. On June 11, the commander of the brigade of which the 2nd Michigan Cavalry was a part received a promotion, catapulting Sheridan into command of the entire brigade. He moved immediately to create a leadership bond with his men. As a former quartermaster, he knew how to get the best available food and clothing for his troops. He did so now. He also closely supervised the layout of encampments to ensure proper sanitation. He avoided assigning busy-work details to his command—"needless sacrifices and unnecessary toil"—so that "when hard or daring work was to be done, I expected the heartiest response and always got it."

On July 1, at the Battle of Booneville, Mississippi, Sheridan led his brigade against a number of regiments of Confederate cavalry under Brigadier General James R. Chalmers. Acting to protect the main force, he blunted Chalmers's attempt at a flanking attack with a diversionary maneuver, hitting the enemy's rear, then dashing off and following up with a quick and daring frontal attack. Stunned, Chalmers's men broke and ran. As for Sheridan, he returned to division with detailed reconnaissance of the Confederate positions.

Coming, it seemed, out of nowhere, Sheridan created a sensation among the Union division commanders, including Brigadier General William S. Rosecrans, who would soon relieve Don Carlos Buell to become commander of a force designated as the Army of the Cumberland. In a virtually unprecedented action, the division commanders wrote an appeal to Halleck, "respectfully" begging him to "obtain the promotion of Sheridan. He is worth his weight in gold." Halleck not only obliged them, but he saw to it that the promotion, approved in September, was made retroactive to July 1 specifically in recognition of Sheridan's achievement at Booneville.

BATTLE OF PERRYVILLE, OCTOBER 8, 1862

Now a brigadier general, Sheridan was given command of the Eleventh Division, III Corps, in what was at the time Major General Don Carlos Buell's Army of the Ohio, and, on October 8, led the division in the Battle of Perryville.

Ordered by III Corps commander Major General Charles Gilbert to transport much-needed water from nearby Doctor's Creek, Sheridan dispatched a brigade under Colonel Daniel McCook to do the job. After McCook skirmished with Confederates and secured the water, Gilbert ordered McCook to hold his position while his cavalry attacked. Hearing the fire of battle, Sheridan rode to the sound of the guns with another brigade. The cavalry Gilbert had sent failed to secure the heights in front of McCook, but the brigade Sheridan led drove the Confederates from the field, discouraging Major General Leonidas Polk, the Confederate commander, from mounting an offensive.

Despite Sheridan's demonstrated willingness to seize and hold the initiative, General Buell did not commit his division to the main fighting at Perryville. A frustrated Sheridan later wrote that time and energy had been wasted in unnecessary maneuvering instead of directed toward a "skillful and energetic advance" that could have "destroyed the enemy before he quit the state." President Lincoln seems to have agreed, since he ordered the relief of Buell by Rosecrans, who became commander of the Department of the Cumberland and its field force, now designated as the Army of the Cumberland.

BATTLE OF STONES RIVER, DECEMBER 31, 1862–JANUARY 2, 1863

Now serving under Rosecrans, one of the generals who had petitioned for his promotion, Sheridan fully revealed his intuitive grasp of a given tactical situation and his equally instinctive impulse to act with proactive aggression. At Stones River, near Murfreesboro, Tennessee, he accurately anticipated a Confederate attack and, on December 31, deployed his division to prepare for it. He was thus able to delay the enemy's advance all along his front until dwindling ammunition forced him to withdraw. Despite having to pull back, Sheridan had bought Rosecrans the time he needed to re-form at a stronger defensive position. Because he knew where to be and when, and because he was willing to hold a position against a superior enemy force, Sheridan was promoted to major general on April 10, 1863, retroactive to the day of the battle, December 31, 1862.

BATTLE OF CHICKAMAUGA, SEPTEMBER 19–20, 1863

Sheridan's rise had been meteoric—first from poor immigrant's son to West Point graduate, and then, in the space of half a year, from captain to major general. Now he found himself thrust into a critical role in the Battle of Chickamauga. Operating in supremely difficult terrain, which caused great operational confusion, Rosecrans, erroneously believing that there was a gap in his line, moved to plug it. In so doing, however, he created the very gap he had sought to close up. Perceiving this, Confederate commander Braxton Bragg launched an attack at the weak point on September 20, 1863. It so happened that, as part of Rosecrans's misguided maneuvering, Sheridan's division was positioned behind the Union battle line precisely where Bragg was concentrating his attack. Sheridan immediately took up a position on Lytle Hill and made a stand against an entire Confederate corps led by Lieutenant General James Longstreet.

As it turned out, Sheridan's most immediate problem was not the vastly superior numbers of the enemy, but the onrushing tide of panic-stricken Union soldiers in retreat. As those troops smashed into his, the confusion exceeded even Sheridan's ability to restore order, and Longstreet drove his division from the field.

Unwilling to join Rosecrans and other principal commanders in headlong retreat, Sheridan fell back toward Chattanooga in good order, gathering up as many men as he could along the way and doing his best to inspirit and inspire them. Before he had gone very far, word reached him that Major General George H. Thomas had not joined the rout, but, on the contrary, was leading his XIV Corps in the stand on Snodgrass Hill that would, by battle's end, earn him the title of the "Rock of Chickamauga." Sheridan decided right then and there to cast his lot with Thomas, and he ordered his division back to the fighting. Although they did not arrive in time to participate in Thomas's counterattack, the fact that he had rallied his troops and was returning them to the field was sufficient to ensure that he was not, like Rosecrans, tainted and relieved of command.

MISSIONARY RIDGE, BATTLE OF CHATTANOOGA, NOVEMBER 25, 1863

The Army of the Cumberland withdrew to Chattanooga and fell under siege by Bragg. At this time, Rosecrans was relieved and replaced by George Thomas, and as Grant closed in on Bragg's besieging army from the outside, Sheridan's division was part of an Army of the Cumberland force detailed to attack it from the inside, its assigned mission to capture Confederate rifle pits on Missionary Ridge.

Preparing to launch the charge on November 25, Sheridan called out to his men: "Remember Chickamauga!" In return, they shouted his name as they began their assault. It was a dangerous uphill climb, with the enemy, well dug in, firing from above. Sheridan was heard to exclaim "Here's at you!" when he saw a clutch of Confederates silhouetted against the crest of the ridge. As if in response, a shell burst nearby, showering him with clods of earth. "That's damn ungenerous!" the gallant commander retorted. "I shall take those guns for that!"

Sheridan's men broke through the Confederate lines, and captured the rifle pits as they had been assigned to do. But spurred on by the momentum of vengeance for Chickamauga, they refused to stop until they had driven Bragg's entire army off Missionary Ridge.

"To Sheridan's prompt movement," Grant wrote in his official report of the engagement, "the Army of the Cumberland and the nation are indebted for the bulk of the capture of prisoners, artillery, and small arms that day. Except for his prompt pursuit, so much in this way would not have been accomplished."

BATTLE OF YELLOW TAVERN, MAY 11, 1864, AND AFTER

Shortly after he was elevated to general-in-chief of all the Union armies on March 12, 1864, Ulysses S. Grant summoned Sheridan to

Sheridan and his generals, 1864. Left to right: Wesley Merritt, David McMurtrie Gregg, Sheridan, Henry E. Davies (standing), James H. Wilson, and Alfred Torbert. NATIONAL ARCHIVES AND RECORDS ADMINISTRATION

Washington to tell him that he was now chief of cavalry and was in command of a separate "Cavalry Corps" of the Army of the Potomac. (Although Grant, in his *Personal Memoirs* of 1885, wrote that Sheridan was the very man he wanted, he had actually first chosen Major General William B. Franklin, but allowed Chief of Staff Henry W. Halleck to persuade him to give the job to Sheridan instead.)

Until this point in the war, the Union army had made less use and far less *effective* use of cavalry than the Confederate army did. Grant wanted to change that, and Sheridan was ready to do so, but while Grant was general-in-chief and traveled *with* the Army of the Potomac, that

army's designated commander was George Gordon Meade. A conventional officer, Meade was not interested in expanding the role of cavalry beyond its traditional functions of screening, providing reconnaissance, and guarding trains and rear areas—the types of missions cavalrymen had been performing so far in the Union army. Understandably, Sheridan chafed under Meade's command.

In the Battle of the Wilderness (May 5–7, 1864), it was not Meade but the densely forested terrain that precluded a significant role for cavalry, and what assignments Sheridan's troopers did have, they discharged poorly. Tasked with clearing the road from the Wilderness toward

Spotsylvania Court House, they failed, which meant that the Confederates came to control the important crossroads at Todd's Tavern.

Justifiably angered, Meade summoned Sheridan to a tongue lashing, accusing him of neglecting his assigned duties of screening and reconnaissance. Sheridan responded as no junior should ever respond to a senior: "I could whip Jeb Stuart if you would only let me. But since you insist on giving cavalry directions without even consulting or notifying me, you can command the cavalry corps yourself. I will not give another order." Muttering something about resigning, he turned his back on Meade and stormed out of his command post.

Meade went to Grant, looking to him for support in bringing charges of insubordination. When Grant asked Meade to repeat what Sheridan had said—"I could whip Jeb Stuart if you would only let me"—he questioned him: "Did he really say that?" Receiving a response in the affirmative, Grant calmly observed, "Well he usually knows what he's talking about. Let him go ahead and do it."

At Grant's request, Meade sent Sheridan and his cavalry on a raid toward Richmond from May 9 to 24, 1864. Grant put him in the position of directly challenging the Confederate cavalry, and although the raid, as a whole, was much less productive than had been hoped for, the Union cavalry more than held its own against the storied Confederate horsemen. Most important, at the Battle of Yellow Tavern on May 11, six miles north of Richmond, Sheridan not only defeated Jeb Stuart, but a dismounted Michigan cavalry trooper managed to shoot and kill him.

The death of Stuart was a tremendous blow to Robert E. Lee, yet the strategic wisdom of Sheridan's raid remains highly doubtful. Because Sheridan neglected the traditional cavalry role of reconnaissance, Grant and Meade were left without critical intelligence for the Battle of Spotsylvania Court House, which put the Army of the Potomac at a severe disadvantage. Sheridan

had proved his point about the fighting capacity of the Union cavalry, but, inadvertently, he had also bolstered Meade's traditional approach to the use of cavalry. Indeed, while Sheridan loudly trumpeted the performance of his Cavalry Corps during the Overland Campaign in his official reports, putting the heaviest emphasis on Yellow Tavern and the death of Stuart, the strategic value he claimed was slight. He came out ahead at the Battle of Haw's Shop (May 28) but suffered heavy casualties while also exposing Union troop dispositions to Confederate cavalry reconnaissance. Although the Cavalry Corps did seize a critical crossroads at the start of the Battle of Cold Harbor (May 31–June 12) and held its own against repeated assaults there, this action had no influence on the costly outcome of the battle. And in action against the Virginia Central Railroad, Sheridan was intercepted and defeated at the Battle of Trevilian Station (June 11–12, 1864), his raid coming to naught.

THE SHENANDOAH VALLEY CAMPAIGN

Certainly, Sheridan's performance in the Overland Campaign did not change Meade's opinion of the proper role of cavalry, and as Grant settled in for what would be the long siege of Petersburg in the summer of 1864, he looked for a new mission to hand Sheridan. It had to be something that would both vindicate Sheridan's concept of the strategic cavalry raid *and* separate Sheridan from Meade's interference.

Since the early days of the war, Confederate armies had been using the Shenandoah Valley as a backyard entrance into Maryland and Pennsylvania and, most of all, as a means of threatening Washington, D.C. So far, Union commanders had been unable to disrupt this pattern, and now, Lieutenant General Jubal A. Early, looking to draw off pressure from Lee at Petersburg, was using the Valley to attack frighteningly close to Washington and to raid towns in Pennsylvania. Pressured by Lincoln and others to protect the capital, Grant grudgingly created the Middle Military Division, which was given control of a field force dubbed the Army of the Shenandoah. Over objections from Secretary of War Edwin M. Stanton, Grant assigned command of both the Middle Military Division and its army to Sheridan.

Thus Grant had liberated Sheridan wholly from Meade and had given the thirty-three-year-old general command of both a department and an army. Taking charge of his new force at Harpers Ferry on August 7, 1864, Sheridan was tasked with three objectives: defeating Early once and for all, permanently closing off the Shenandoah as an invasion route, and executing upon the lush Shenandoah Valley, celebrated as the "breadbasket of the Confederacy," a scorched-earth policy intended to bring the South to the brink of starvation. "Give the enemy no rest," Grant instructed Sheridan. "Do all the damage to railroads and crops you can.... If the war is to last another year, we want the Shenandoah Valley to remain a barren waste."

Despite the ruthless tone of his orders to Sheridan, Grant advised proceeding with caution, warning him to avoid launching an offensive "with the advantage against you," yet complaining when Sheridan failed to move quickly and aggressively. At last, with Lincoln's reelection quite possibly hanging in the balance, Grant conferred with Sheridan on September 16 at Charles Town, and the two agreed that he would launch his major attacks within four days.

Sheridan met and defeated Early in the Third Battle of Winchester (Virginia) on September 19. He kept the pressure on, exploiting this victory on September 22 at the Battle of Fisher's Hill, which Sheridan also won. As the battered Early attempted to regroup his forces, Sheridan turned away from him to begin raking the Shenandoah Valley countryside, appropriating or killing livestock, commandeering whatever provisions the Army of the Shenandoah needed for itself and destroying the rest.

Factories, mills, farms, and railroads—all were ruined in a total-war campaign waged as relentlessly as anything Sherman would do to Georgia in his more infamous March to the Sea. Those who lived in the Valley dubbed Sheridan's operations simply and terribly "The Burning."

To Sheridan's stunned surprise, the badly battered Jubal Early did not regard himself as beaten. After receiving reinforcements, he attacked Sheridan's army on October 19 at Cedar Creek, Virginia, while Sheridan, suspecting nothing, was en route to Washington, D.C., to meet with high command. At Winchester, where he had spent the night on the way to the capital, an aide informed Sheridan of the distant thunder of artillery, and the general immediately rode to the sound of the guns. When he encountered panic-stricken troops and their officers in retreat toward Winchester, he spurred his horse to a gallop and reached the Cedar Creek battlefield by 10:30 a.m.

Instantly, he set about rallying his troops, riding up and down the line, exhorting and inspiring his men. Early's army was, in fact, suffering from acute hunger and exhaustion. His soldiers were less interested in scoring a glorious victory than in pillaging abandoned Union encampments. The Confederates were disorganized, having become more of a mob than an army. Sheridan, through the force of his powerful command presence and with the aid of Major General Horatio G. Wright commanding VI Corps, succeeded in reminding his men that they were an army. Once he had restored discipline and esprit, the tide at Cedar Creek quickly turned. By about four that afternoon, Early was whipped, his army neutralized as an offensive force for the rest of the war.

ENDGAME, MARCH 2–APRIL 9, 1865

The Shenandoah Campaign earned Sheridan the personal thanks of Abraham Lincoln and a promotion to major general in the regular army,

BATTLE OF CEDAR CREEK - OCTOBER 19, 1864

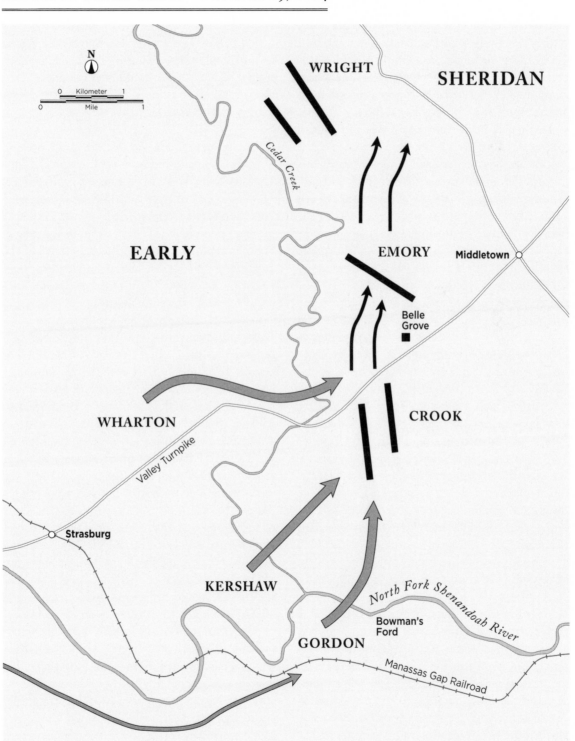

N

Kilometer

Mile

WRIGHT

SHERIDAN

Cedar Creek

EARLY

EMORY

Middletown

Belle
Grove

WHARTON

CROOK

Valley Turnpike

Strasburg

KERSHAW

North Fork Shenandoah River

GORDON

Bowman's
Ford

Manassas Gap Railroad

elevating him to a position behind only Grant, Sherman, and Meade. "Sheridan's ride," which turned the tide at Cedar Creek, inspired a poem of that title by Thomas Buchanan Read, and that martial lyric did much to stimulate Republican turnout in the November general election, which comfortably propelled Lincoln to a second term and ensured that the president's policy of total victory would be pursued. The Confederacy had lost its last hope for a negotiated peace.

After the Shenandoah Campaign, Sheridan fought more or less desultory skirmishes. Grant gave him a loose set of directions, which included choosing either to link up with William T. Sherman in North Carolina or to return to Winchester. Winchester was in Virginia, and, for Sheridan, this was enough of an excuse to turn away from North Carolina and instead join the Army of the Potomac at Petersburg. In his memoirs, he frankly conceded his motive for the move, which was by no means contemplated in Grant's orders: "Feeling that the war was nearing its end, I desired my cavalry to be in at the death."

What had been desultory skirmishing now became intense campaigning. En route to Petersburg, he fought the Battle of Waynesboro (March 2, 1865), enveloping and destroying what little remained of Jubal Early's army. On April 1, he definitively severed Lee's line of supply and communications at the Battle of Five Forks, giving him no alternative but to evacuate Petersburg.

On April 6, at the Battle of Sayler's Creek, he scored a victory against Lee's limping Army of Northern Virginia that resulted in the surrender of nearly a quarter of the men remaining in that force. After the battle, he sent Lincoln a telegram, which the president quoted in one he sent to Grant on April 7: "Gen. Sheridan says 'If the thing is pressed I think that Lee will surrender.' Let the thing be pressed." At the Battle of Appomattox Court House (April 9), Sheridan blocked the only remaining route through which Lee could escape, and, that afternoon, the Confederate commander surrendered the shell that was the Army of Northern Virginia.

"I believe General Sheridan has no superior as a general, either living or dead, and perhaps not an equal," Grant would later remark.

CODA AND RECONSTRUCTION

The surrender of Lee and the Army of Northern Virginia was followed by that of Joseph E. Johnston and the Army of Tennessee on April 26, 1865. The end of the Civil War was a foregone conclusion, but Edmund Kirby Smith still led a Confederate army in Texas. Appointing Sheridan commander of the Military District of the Southwest on May 17, 1865, Grant ordered him to engage and defeat Smith so as to restore Texas and Louisiana to Union control.

By the time Sheridan had gotten as far as New Orleans, word came that Smith had surrendered. Grant then directed Sheridan to occupy Texas with a large force so as to discourage a possible exploitive incursion by some of the forty-thousand French troops stationed in Mexico to prop up the government of Austrian Archduke Maximilian, a puppet of France's Napoleon III. Sheridan quickly mustered fifty-thousand men and sent them to occupy key Texas cities and to patrol the Mexican border. Thanks to Sheridan's quick action in this show of force, coupled with U.S. diplomatic pressure and an increasingly successful Mexican independence movement led by Benito Juárez, Napoleon III withdrew his troops in 1866, and fears that the French would collaborate with Confederate diehards to seize Texas came to an abrupt end.

In March 1867, Sheridan was appointed military governor of the Fifth Military District, which encompassed Texas and Louisiana. He introduced a harsh Radical Republican Reconstruction regime, essentially assuming dictatorial authority and disqualifying former Confederates from voting or serving in most government offices. Although he had not entered the war as an abolitionist or a Radical Republican, his experience had hardened him against the Confederate movement, and he soon fell to disputing with President Andrew Johnson over many aspects of the Military Reconstruction Acts. Johnson removed Sheridan in August 1867, ordering him to change places with Winfield Scott Hancock, Hancock to become the new military governor of the Fifth Military District and Sheridan to take over as commander of the Department of the Missouri headquartered at Fort Leavenworth, Kansas.

INDIAN WARS

Sheridan's new command put him front and center in the Indian Wars. His assignment was to "pacify" the Plains, which essentially meant herding recalcitrant Indians into reservations. Those who refused to live where they were assigned were to be regarded as hostile. Sheridan faced two major problems in his new assignment. The first were uncertain, changeable, and contradictory federal policies with regard to the Indians, with control of Indian affairs continually seesawing between the U.S. Army and the Department of the Interior. The second problem was the diminutive size of the army after it had been demobilized following the Civil War. The troops broadcast throughout far-flung Western outposts were less an army than a small police force.

Lacking the manpower to fight Indian warriors whenever and wherever they showed themselves, Sheridan planned a campaign that drew on his Civil War experience in the Shenandoah Valley. He decided to attack during the winter, the season that was hardest on the Indians and one in which they generally preferred to avoid fighting. His principal targets in 1868 and 1869 were the Cheyenne, Kiowa, and Comanche tribes, and his objective was to destroy their stored crops, their food reserves, and their livestock. Sheridan also promoted civilian hunting of bison herds on the Great Plains, even to extinction. The absence of this staple animal, he reasoned, would leave the starving Indians no choice but to accept a government-subsidized existence on reservations.

Besides the Winter Campaign of 1868–1869, Sheridan planned and ordered the Red River War (1874) and the Great Sioux War of 1876–1877 as well as other campaigns. By the 1880s, the Indian Wars were largely a matter of history. Sheridan's uncompromising "total war" approach in these conflicts led to semi-justified accusations of a policy of genocide, and Sheridan would be stigmatized in popular culture as the man who blithely declared, "The only good Indian is a dead Indian." The origin of this phrase was a reported remark by Chief Tosawi (Silver Knife) of the Comanche who was said to have introduced himself to Sheridan in 1869 by saying, "Me Tosawi. Me good Indian." Sheridan supposedly shot back: "The only good Indians I ever saw were dead." Sheridan repeatedly denied having uttered anything of the kind, and it is most likely that a remark made earlier in 1869 by U.S. Representative James M. Cavanaugh, "I have never seen in my life a good Indian . . . except when I have seen a dead Indian," was misattributed to Sheridan. Given the general's unrelenting total war policy, however, the persistent error is understandable.

OTHER POSTWAR ASSIGNMENTS

Promoted to lieutenant general on March 4, 1869, Sheridan was sent by President Ulysses Grant to observe the Franco-Prussian War of the following year. His official report was terse. To be sure, he wrote, the Prussians were "very good brave fellows [but] there is nothing to be learned here professionally."

As commanding general of the army west of the Mississippi, Sheridan's headquarters were in Chicago. He was living in the city when the

In the years following the Civil War, after he was comfortably established in his Chicago headquarters, Sheridan grew stout, gouty, and took eagerly to all the trappings of high command. FROM PERSONAL MEMOIRS OF P. H. SHERIDAN (1888)

great fire of 1871 broke out on October 7. At the mayor's request, the devastated city was put under martial law, with Sheridan in command. Although he received high praise from the mayor and the city's citizens, especially for the humanitarian relief work his troops carried out, he clashed with the governor, who believed that the federal intervention was an unconstitutional usurpation of the state's authority.

Sheridan succeeded William T. Sherman as Commanding General, U.S. Army on November 1, 1883, but it was not until June 1, 1888, that he was promoted to general in the regular army. The promotion was in large part motivated by the news that Sheridan had suffered a serious heart attack. Members of Congress were eager to honor him and to ensure that his widow—should he succumb—would be amply provided for. A second heart attack, on August 5, 1888, proved fatal. He was only fifty-seven, but when his wife, thirty-three-year-old Irene Rucker Sheridan, was asked whether she planned to remarry, she replied, "I would rather be the widow of Phil Sheridan than the wife of any man living."

BIBLIOGRAPHY

GENERAL WORKS

Allardice, Bruce S. *More Generals in Gray: A Companion Volume to Generals in Gray*. Baton Rouge: Louisiana State University Press, 1995.

Anders, Curt. *Fighting Confederates*. New York: Dorset Press, 1968.

Boritt, Gabor S. *Jefferson Davis's Generals*. New York: Oxford University Press, 1999.

Boritt, Gabor S. *Lincoln's Generals*. New York: Oxford University Press, 1994.

Davis, William C. *Lincoln's Men*. New York: Touchstone, 1999.

Freeman, Douglas Southall. *Lee's Lieutenants*. 3 vols. New York: Charles Scribner's Sons, 1942–1944.

Jones, Wilmer L. *Generals in Blue and Gray: Davis's Generals*. Mechanicsburg, Pa.: Stackpole, 2004.

Jones, Wilmer L. *Generals in Blue and Gray: Lincoln's Generals*. Mechanicsburg, Pa.: Stackpole, 2004.

Warner, Ezra J. *Generals in Blue: Lives of the Union Commanders*. Baton Rouge: Louisiana State University Press, 1964.

Warner, Ezra J. *Generals in Gray: Lives of the Confederate Commanders*. Baton Rouge: Louisiana State University Press, 1959.

Waugh, John C. *The Class of 1846*. New York: Warner Books, 1994.

Williams, T. Harry. *Lincoln and His Generals*. New York: Alfred Knopf, 1952.

BY SUBJECT

P. G. T. BEAUREGARD

Basso, Hamilton. *Beauregard: The Great Creole*. New York: Charles Scribner's Sons, 1933.

Roman, Alfred. *The Military Operations of General Beauregard in the War between the States, 1861 to 1865: Including a Brief Personal Sketch and a Narrative of His Services in the War with Mexico, 1846–8*. New York: Harper & Brothers, 1883.

Williams, T. Harry. *P. G. T. Beauregard: Napoleon in Gray*. Baton Rouge: Louisiana State University Press, 1954.

BRAXTON BRAGG

Hallock, Judith Lee. *Braxton Bragg and Confederate Defeat: Volume II*. Tuscaloosa: University of Alabama Press, 1991.

McWhiney, Grady. *Braxton Bragg and Confederate Defeat: Field Command*. New York: Columbia University Press, 1969.

Seitz, Don Carlos. *Braxton Bragg: General of the Confederacy*. Columbia, S.C.: The State Company, 1924.

AMBROSE E. BURNSIDE

Marvel, William. *Burnside*. Chapel Hill: University of North Carolina Press, 1991.

Poore, Ben Perley. *Life and Public Services of Ambrose E. Burnside*. Providence, R.I.: J. A. & R. A. Reid, 1882.

JUBAL EARLY

Early, Jubal A. *Memoirs*. Baltimore: The Nautical & Aviation Publishing Company of America, 1989.

Osborne, Charles C. *Jubal: The Life and Times of General Jubal A. Early, CSA.* Chapel Hill, N.C.: Algonquin Books of Chapel Hill, 1992.

NATHAN BEDFORD FORREST

Hurst, Jack. *Nathan Bedford Forrest.* New York: Knopf, 1993.

Wills, Brian S. *A Battle from the Start: The Life of Nathan Bedford Forrest.* New York: Harper-Collins, 1992.

Wyeth, John A. *That Devil Forrest.* Baton Rouge: Louisiana State University Press, 1989.

ULYSSES S. GRANT

Grant, Ulysses S. *Personal Memoirs.* New York: Da Capo Press, 1982.

McFeely, William S. *Grant.* New York: W. W. Norton, 1981.

Perret, Geoffrey. *Ulysses S. Grant: Soldier and President.* New York: Random House, 1997.

Simpson, Brooks D. *Ulysses S. Grant: Triumph over Adversities, 1862–1865.* Boston: Houghton Mifflin, 2000.

HENRY WAGER HALLECK

Ambrose, Stephen E. *Halleck: Lincoln's Chief-of-Staff.* Baton Rouge: Louisiana State University Press, 1962.

Anders, Curt. *Henry Halleck's War: A Fresh Look at Lincoln's Controversial General-in-Chief.* Cincinnati: Emmis Books, 2002.

Marszalek, John F. *Commander of All Lincoln's Armies: A Life of General Henry W. Halleck.* Cambridge, Mass.: Belknap Press, 2004.

WINFIELD SCOTT HANCOCK

Jamieson, Perry D. *Winfield Scott Hancock: Gettysburg Hero.* Abilene, Texas: McWhiney Foundation Press, 2003.

Jordan, David M. *Winfield Scott Hancock: A Soldier's Life.* Bloomington: Indiana University Press, 1996.

Tucker, Glenn. *Hancock the Superb.* Indianapolis: Bobbs-Merrill, 1960.

JOHN BELL HOOD

Dyer, John P. *The Gallant Hood.* New York: Smithmark, 1995.

Hood, John Bell. *Advance and Retreat: Personal Experiences in the United States and Confederate States Armies.* Lincoln: University of Nebraska Press, 1996.

McMurry, Richard. *John Bell Hood and the War for Southern Independence.* Lincoln: University of Nebraska Press, 1982.

JOSEPH HOOKER

Hebert, Walter H. *Fighting Joe Hooker.* Lincoln: University of Nebraska Press, 1999.

THOMAS J. "STONEWALL" JACKSON

Alexander, Bevis. *Lost Victories: The Military Genius of Stonewall Jackson.* New York: Henry Holt, 1992.

Bowers, John. *Stonewall Jackson: Portrait of a Soldier.* New York: William Morrow, 1989.

Davis, Burke. *They Called Him Stonewall.* New York: Holt, Rinehart and Winston, 1954.

Douglas, Henry Kyd. *I Rode with Stonewall.* Greenwich, Ct.: Fawcett, 1965.

Farwell, Byron. *Stonewall: A Biography of General Thomas J. Jackson.* New York: Norton, 1992.

Robertson, James I. *Stonewall Jackson: The Man, the Soldier, the Legend.* New York: Macmillan, 1997.

ALBERT SIDNEY JOHNSTON

Johnston, William Preston. *The Life of Gen. Albert Sidney Johnston, Embracing His Services in the Armies of the United States, the Republic of Texas, and the Confederate States.* New York: D. Appleton, 1878.

Moore, Avery C. *Destiny's Soldier: General Albert Sidney Johnston.* San Francisco: Fearon, 1958.

Roland, Charles P. *Albert Sidney Johnston: Soldier of Three Republics.* Austin: University of Texas Press, 1987.

JOSEPH E. JOHNSTON

Longacre, Edward G. *Worthy Opponents: William T. Sherman & Joseph E. Johnston: Antagonists in War, Friends in Peace.* Nashville, Tenn.: Thomas Nelson, 2006.

Symonds, Craig L. *Joseph Johnston: A Civil War Biography.* New York: Norton, 1992.

ROBERT E. LEE

Commager, Harry S., et al. *America's Robert E. Lee.* Boston: Houghton Mifflin, 1951.

Dowdey, Clifford. *Lee.* New York: Bonanza Books, 1965.

Eicher, David J. *Robert E. Lee: A Life Portrait.* Dallas: Taylor, 1997.

Freeman, Douglas Southall. *Lee of Virginia.* New York: Charles Scribner's Sons, 1958.

Horn, Stanley F. *The Robert E. Lee Reader.* New York: Bobbs-Merrill, 1949.

JAMES LONGSTREET

Eckenrode, H. J., and Bryan Conrad. *James Longstreet: Lee's War Horse.* Chapel Hill: University of North Carolina Press, 1986.

Longstreet, James. *From Manassas to Appomattox: Memoirs of the Civil War.* Philadelphia: J. B. Lippincott Co., 1896.

Piston, William Garrett. *Lee's Tarnished Lieutenant: James Longstreet and His Place in Southern History.* Athens: University of Georgia Press, 1987.

Sanger, Donald B., and Thomas Robson Hay. *James Longstreet.* Baton Rouge: Louisiana State University Press, 1952.

Tucker, Glenn. *Lee and Longstreet at Gettysburg.* Indianapolis: Bobbs-Merrill Company, 1968.

Wert, Jeffrey D. *General James Longstreet: The Confederacy's Most Controversial Soldier.* New York: Simon & Schuster, 1993.

GEORGE B. MCCLELLAN

Rowland, Thomas J. *George B. McClellan and Civil War History.* Kent, Ohio: Kent State University Press, 1998.

Sears, Stephen W. *George B. McClellan, the Young Napoleon.* New York: Ticknor & Fields, 1992.

Waugh, John C. *Lincoln and McClellan: The Troubled Partnership between a President and His General.* New York: Palgrave Macmillan, 2010.

GEORGE GORDON MEADE

Bache, Richard Meade. *Life of General George Gordon Meade: Commander of the Army of the Potomac.* Philadelphia: H. T. Coates & Co., 1897.

Cleaves, Freeman. *Meade of Gettysburg.* Norman: University of Oklahoma Press, 1960.

Pennypacker, Isaac R. *General Meade.* New York: D. Appleton and Company, 1901.

Rafuse, Ethan S. *George Gordon Meade and the War in the East.* Abilene, Texas: McWhiney Foundation Press, 2003.

JOHN HUNT MORGAN

Ramage, James. *Rebel Raider: The Life of John Hunt Morgan.* Lexington: University Press of Kentucky, 1986.

Thomas, Edison. *John Hunt Morgan and His Raiders.* Lexington: University Press of Kentucky, 1975.

JOHN POPE

Cozzens, Peter. *General John Pope: A Life for the Nation.* Urbana: University of Illinois Press, 2000.

Cozzens, Peter, ed. *The Military Memoirs of General John Pope.* Chapel Hill: University of North Carolina Press, 2009.

WINFIELD SCOTT

Eisenhower, John S. D. *Agent of Destiny: The Life and Times of General Winfield Scott.* Norman: University of Oklahoma Press, 1999.

Johnson, Timothy D. *Winfield Scott: The Quest for Military Glory.* Lawrence: University Press of Kansas, 1998.

Peskin, Allan. *Winfield Scott and the Profession of Arms.* Kent, Ohio: Kent State University Press, 2003.

PHILIP H. SHERIDAN

Morris, Roy Jr. *Sheridan: The Life and Wars of General Phil Sheridan.* New York: Vintage, 1992.

O'Connor, Richard. *Sheridan: The Inevitable.* Indianapolis: Bobbs-Merrill, 1953.

Sheridan, Philip H. *Personal Memoirs.* New York: Da Capo Press, 1992.

WILLIAM TECUMSEH SHERMAN

Fellman, Michael. *Citizen Sherman.* New York: Random House, 1995.

Lewis, Lloyd. *Sherman: Fighting Prophet.* New York: Harcourt, Brace & World, 1958.

Marszalek, John F. *Sherman: A Soldier's Passion for Order.* New York: Vintage, 1993.

J. E. B. STUART

Davis, Burke. *Jeb Stuart: The Last Cavalier.* New York: Holt, Rinehart and Winston, 1957.

De Grummond, Lena, and Lynn De Grummond. *Jeb Stuart.* Philadelphia: J. B. Lippincott, 1962.

Thomas, Emory M. *Bold Dragoon: The Life of J. E. B. Stuart.* New York: Harper & Row, 1986.

GEORGE H. THOMAS

Cleaves, Freeman. *Rock of Chickamauga.* Norman: University of Oklahoma Press, 1948.

Einolf, Christopher J.. *George Thomas: Virginian for the Union.* Norman: University of Oklahoma Press, 2007.

McKinney, Francis F. *Education in Violence: The Life of George H. Thomas and the History of the Army of the Cumberland.* Detroit: Wayne State University Press, 1961.

Index

A

Advance and Retreat (Hood), 124
Anderson, Robert, 4, 7, 8, 216, 244
Antietam. *See* Battle of Antietam
Appomattox Campaign, 28, 197
    Lee's surrender, 39–40, 208–9, 279
    Longstreet in, 104, 113
Armistead, Lewis A., 254, 255–56, 261
Army of Mississippi, 59
Army of Northern Virginia. *See also* Lee,
    Robert E., 21, 96
    surrender of, 39
Army of Tennessee, 25, 69
    surrender of, 26
Army of Virginia, 166
Aroostook War, 142, 143
asymmetric warfare, 73, 82
Atkinson, Henry, 55
Atlanta Campaign, 15, 211–12, 219–23
    Battle of Kennesaw Mountain, 220–21
    Hood in, 115, 221, 223, 250
    Hooker in, 227, 238
    map, 222
    Thomas in, 241, 249–50
Atzerodt, George, 263
Averett, Thomas Hamlet, 94

B

Baker, Edward Dickinson, 154
Banks, Nathaniel, 47, 49, 166, 203
Barlow, Francis, 131
Barron, James, 140
Barton, H. S., 186
Battle of Antietam, 28, 34–35, 51, 68, 93,
    159, 171, 191–92
    Burnside in, 173, 176–77
    casualties in, 35
    Early in, 126, 129
    Hancock in, 253, 257
    Hood in, 115, 119
    Hooker in, 227, 232

    Jackson in, 42
    Longstreet in, 104, 109
    McClellan in, 148
    Meade in, 267, 270
    photograph of, 160
    Stuart in, 97–98
Battle of Bentonville, 25, 72
    Bragg in, 64
Battle of Brice's Crossroads, 89, 90
Battle of Buena Vista (U.S.-Mexican War),
    57, 65
    Morgan in, 73, 74
    Pope in, 161
    Thomas in, 240, 242
Battle of Cedar Creek, 288, 289
Battle of Cerro Gordo (U.S.-Mexican War),
    30, 138
Battle of Chancellorsville, 28, 35–37, 51,
    111, 234–37
    Early in, 126, 130
    Hancock in, 253, 258
    Hooker in, 227, 258
    Jackson in, 42
    map, 235
    Meade in, 267, 271
    Stuart in, 93, 98–99
Battle of Chapultepec (U.S.-Mexican War)
    Beauregard in, 2, 5
    Grant in, 196, 199
    Hooker in, 226–27, 229, 230
    Jackson in, 41, 44
    Lee in, 30
    Longstreet in, 103, 105–6
    McClellan in, 147, 150
    Scott in, 138, 143
Battle of Cheat Mountain, 28, 33
Battle of Chickamauga, 69–70, 246–49
    Bragg in, 112, 113, 285
    Forrest in, 82–83, 87
    Hood in, 115, 120
    illustration of, 88

Longstreet in, 104, 112–13
map, 247
Sheridan in, 279, 284–85
Thomas in, 241
Battle of Chippawa (War of 1812), 141–42
Battle of Churubusco (U.S.-Mexican War)
    Beauregard in, 2, 5
    Hancock in, 252, 254–55
    Jackson in, 44
    Lee in, 30
    Longstreet in, 105
    McClellan in, 147
    Scott in, 138
Battle of Contreras (U.S.-Mexican War)
    Beauregard in, 2, 5
    Jackson in, 44
    Longstreet in, 103, 105
    McClellan in, 147, 150
    Scott in, 138
Battle of Fort Brown, 65
Battle of Fort Donelson, 85–86
Battle of Fort Sumter, 2, 6–8
Battle of Fredericksburg, 28, 51, 193
    Burnside in, 173–74, 177–78, 180
    casualties in, vi
    Early in, 126, 129–30
    Hancock in, 253, 257–58
    Hood in, 115
    Hooker in, 227, 233
    Jackson in, 42
    Longstreet in, 104, 110
    map, 179
    Meade in, 267, 270–71
    Stuart in, 93, 98
Battle of Gettysburg, 28, 37–38, 258–61, 271–74
    Early in, 126, 130–31
    Hancock in, 253, 258–61
    Hood in, 115, 120
    Lee in, 27, 42
    Longstreet in, 104, 111–12
    map, 275
    Meade in, 267
    Pickett's Charge, 259, 260

    Stuart in, 92, 93, 99–101
Battle of Hartsville, 77
Battle of Kennesaw Mountain, 24, 220
Battle of Kernstown. *See* Valley Campaign
Battle of Monterrey (U.S.-Mexican War), 56–57, 65
    Grant in, 196, 199
    Hooker in, 226–27, 229
    Longstreet in, 103
    Meade in, 266, 268–69
    Pope in, 161, 163
    Thomas in, 240, 242
Battle of Nashville, 122
Battle of Seven Pines. *See also* Peninsula Campaign, 21, 107, 231
    Longstreet in, 104
Battle of Shiloh, 3, 10–11, 53, 155, 189, 190, 202
    A. S. Johnston in, 59–62
    Bragg in, 63, 66–67
    Forrest in, 82, 86
    Grant in, 197
    map, 61
    Morgan in, 73, 75
    Sherman in, 211, 218
Battle of South Mountain, 28, 109, 232
    Meade in, 267, 270
Battle of Stones River, 68–69, 77, 246
    Sheridan in, 279, 284
Battle of the Crater. *See also* Overland Campaign, 173, 174, 267, 277
Battle of the Wilderness. *See also* Overland Campaign, 107, 286–87
Battle of Tupelo, 90
Battle of Veracruz (U.S.-Mexican War), 138
Battle of Waynesboro, 134
Battle of Yellow Tavern, 93, 102, 286, 287
Battle of Yorktown. *See also* Peninsula Campaign, 22
Beauregard, P. G. T., 2–13, 25
    background of, 3–4
    Battle of Fort Sumter, 6–8
    Battle of Shiloh, 10–11, 59, 60, 62, 66, 67, 189, 202

care for Hood's children, 124
early assignments, 4–5
First Battle of Bull Run, 8–10, 19, 20, 46, 106
Mississippi Island No. 10, 165
opinion of Early, 128
principal battles, 2–3
relationship with Sherman, 214
replaced by Bragg, 67
U.S.-Mexican War, 5
withdrawal from Corinth, 189, 190
Bee, Barnard Elliott, Jr., 46, 47
Benedict, George, 261
Bentonville. See Battle of Bentonville
Bermuda Hundred Campaign, 3, 12
Bingham, Henry H., 261
Black Hawk War, 14, 16, 142
Johnston in, 53, 55
Blair, Austin, 283
Blair, Montgomery, 232
Booth, John Wilkes, 182, 263
Bragg, Braxton, 4, 6, 11, 24, 63–72, 77
advisor to Davis, 72
aiding A. S. Johnston, 59
assigned to Florida and coastal defenses, 66
background of, 64–65
Battle of Bentonville, 72
Battle of Chickamauga, 69–70, 112, 113, 246, 247, 248–49, 285
Battle of Shiloh, 60, 66–67
Battle of Stones River, 68–69, 246
Battles of Lookout Mountain and Missionary Ridge, 70–72
Chattanooga Campaign, 67–68, 77, 238, 249
Forrest under, 87
opinion of Thomas, 242, 243
relationship with Morgan, 77–78, 80–81
relationship with Sherman, 214
replaces Beauregard, 67
retreat into Georgia, 23
Second Battle of Fort Fisher, 72
U.S.-Mexican War, 65

Brannan, John, 246, 248
Breckinridge, John C., 12, 60
Brewer, Charles, 102
Brooks, Eliza, 65
Brown, John. See also Harpers Ferry, 28, 32, 95
Bruce, Rebecca Grantz, 74, 75
Buchanan, James, 58, 229
Buchanan, Robert C., 199
Buckingham, Catharinus Putnam, 232, 233
Buell, Don Carlos, 10, 11, 201, 202
Battle of Perryville, 284
Battle of Shiloh, 59, 63, 66, 67
command of Western Department, 187, 189
First Kentucky Raid, 77
pursuit of Bragg, 67–68
relationship with Sherman, 214, 217
relieved of command, 192
in Western Theater, 245
Buford, John, 97, 272
Bull Run. See First Battle of Bull Run; Second Battle of Bull Run
Burnside, Ambrose, 35, 51, 173–82
Battle of Antietam, 176–77
Battle of Fredericksburg, 98, 104, 110, 177–80, 193, 233, 257–58, 270–71
Burnside Expedition, 175–76
First Battle of Bull Run, 175
invention of carbine rifle, 174–75
Morgan's Raid, 78–79
Overland Campaign and Battle of the Crater, 181–82
relieved of command, 180
reorganizes Army of the Potomac, 233
replaces McClellan, 232–33
Second Battle of Bull Run, 176
Burnside, Edghill, 174
Burr, Aaron, 140
Butler, Benjamin, 12, 229

C
Caldwell, John C., 259
Cameron, Simon, 217, 269
Catlett's Station Raid, 92–93, 97

Catton, Bruce, 229
Cavanaugh, James M., 291
Cedar Creek. *See* Battle of Cedar Creek
Chalmers, James R., 87, 283–84
Chamberlain, Joshua, 120, 273
Chancellorsville. *See* Battle of Chancellorsville
Chapman, Reuben, 105
Chase, Salmon P., 148
Chattanooga Campaign, 104, 113, 197, 219
　　Hooker in, 238
　　Sheridan in, 279, 285
　　Sherman in, 211
　　Thomas in, 241, 249
Cheat Mountain. *See* Battle of Cheat Mountain
Chestnut, James, 7, 8
Chickamauga. *See* Battle of Chickamauga
Civil War. *See also* specific battles; generals;
　　maps
　　casualties in, vi
　　cavalry in, 93
　　"political" generals in, vii
　　population of Confederate states, vi
　　population of Northern states, vi
　　romantic view of, 83, 135
　　Scott's Anaconda Plan for, 145–46
　　voluntary enlistees in, vii
Cooke, Flora, 94
Cooke, Philip St. George, 95, 97
Cooper, Samuel, 15, 21
Corinth, "siege" of, 3, 11, 183, 189–90
　　Sheridan in, 279
Crittenden, George B., 244
Crittenden, Thomas Leonidas, 248
Crouch, Darius, 258
Curtin, Andrew G., 269
Curtis, Samuel, 283
Custer, George Armstrong, 101, 134
Custis, George Washington Parke, 32
Custis, Mary Anna Randolph, 29

D
Davis, Jefferson
　　after Lee's surrender, 25
　　assigning A. S. Johnston, 58, 59
　　assigns McClellan to Crimea, 150–51
　　commissioning Longstreet, 106
　　defense of Atlanta, 24
　　early assignments for Lee, 31
　　forms 2nd U.S. Cavalry, 116–17, 243
　　on Jackson's death, 52
　　names Lee general-in-chief, 38
　　opinion of A. S. Johnston, 53, 57, 62
　　opinion of Hood, 118–19, 120, 121
　　relationship with Beauregard, 4, 6, 8,
　　　　10, 11, 12
　　relationship with Bragg, 63, 65, 68, 69,
　　　　72, 113
　　relationship with Johnston, 14, 15, 19,
　　　　20, 21, 23
　　relieves Johnston, 221
　　replaces Johnston with Lee, 33–34
Deal, John, 118
Dearborn, Henry, 141
Delafield, Richard, 150, 151
Dent, Julia Boggs, 105, 198, 199
Dent, Mary Ann, 104
Deslonde, Caroline, 5
Devens, Charles, 154
Dortch, Helen, 114
Downey, John, 58
Duke, Basil W., 79

E
Early, Joab, 126–27
Early, Jubal, 4, 125–35, 280, 287, 288
　　background of, 126–27
　　Battle of Antietam, 129
　　Battle of Gettysburg, 130–31
　　Battle of Williamsburg, 128–29
　　Battles of Fredericksburg and
　　　　Chancellorsville, 35, 37, 129–30
　　Blackburn's Ford and First Battle
　　　　of Bull Run, 128
　　Cedar Mountain and Second Battle
　　　　of Bull Run, 129
　　military governor of Monterrey, 127
　　myth of "Lost Cause," 135
　　opinion of Longstreet, 135

opinion on secession, 128
Overland Campaign, 131
principal battles, 125–26
Second Seminole War and U.S.-Mexican
     War, 127–28
Seven Days Battles, 129
Shenandoah Valley Operations, 131–34
Siege of Petersburg, 38
Edwards, Ninian Wirt, 162
Eggleston, Joseph, 15
Elements of Military Art and Science
     (Halleck), 184, 185
Elzey, Arnold, 129
Emancipation Proclamation, 159
Emory, William, 280
Evans, Nathan George, 119
Ewell, Richard S., 4, 37, 38, 99, 111
     Battle of Gettysburg, 130, 131
     under Jackson, 49
Ewing, Ellen, 214
Ewing, Maria, 213
Ewing, Thomas, 213, 214
Ewing, Thomas, Jr., 214

F
Farley, Henry, 8
First Battle of Bull Run, 2, 4, 8–10, 41,
     46–47, 148–49
     Burnside in, 173, 175
     Early in, 125, 128
     Johnston in, 14, 19–21
     Longstreet in, 103, 106–7
     map, 9
     Sherman in, 211, 216
     Stuart in, 92, 95–96
Flexner, James Thomas, 42
Floyd, John, 85, 86, 201, 229
Foote, Andrew H., 165, 166, 201
Fornance, Joseph, 254
Forrest, Jonathan, 83
Forrest, Nathan Bedford, 70, 82–91, 116,
     203, 221, 223
     background of, 83–84
     battalion and regiment of, 84–85

Battle of Brice's Crossroads, 89, 90
Battle of Chickamauga, 246
Battle of Fort Donelson, 85–86
Battle of Nashville, 250
Battle of Shiloh, 86
Battles of Cedar Bluff, Chickamauga,
     Okolona, 87
closing battles, 90
farewell address to troops, 91
First Battle of Murfreesboro, 86
Fort Pillow Massacre, 87–88
involvement in KKK, 91
skirmish at Sacramento, Kentucky, 85
Fort Donelson. *See* Battle of Fort Donelson
Fort Pillow Massacre, 83, 87–88
Fort Sumter. *See* Battle of Fort Sumter
Fort Wagner, Battles of, 3
Franklin, William, 176, 177, 286
     Battle of Fredericksburg, 178
Fredericksburg. *See* Battle of Fredericksburg
Fremantle, James A. L., 65
Frémont, John C., 49, 164, 166
     assigns Grant, 200
     relieved of Western command, 187
French, Richard, 116
French, William H., 45
From Manassas to Appomattox
     (Longstreet), 114

G
Gardner, William, 149
Garfield, James A., 265
Garland, John, 163
Garland, Maria Louisa, 105, 114
Gates, William, 65
Generals in Blue: Lives of the Union Commanders
     (Warner), 174
Gettysburg. *See* Battle of Gettysburg
Gilbert, Charles, 284
Granger, Gordon, 248, 249
Grant, Jesse Root, 197
Grant, Ulysses S., 196–210
     appointed brigadier general, 200
     Appomattox Campaign, 208–9

attack on Jackson and Vicksburg, 23
Battle of Shiloh, 10, 11, 59–60, 66, 67,
    155, 189, 202
Battles of Lookout Mountain and
    Missionary Ridge, 70
on Bragg, 64
and Buell, 201–2
on Burnside, 173
captures Forts Henry and Donelson,
    189, 201
Chattanooga Campaign, 249
general-in-chief, 194–95, 204, 276
opinion of A. S. Johnston, 53, 54
opinion of Forrest, 82, 87
opinion of Hancock, 252
opinion of Hooker, 226
opinion of Meade, 267, 276, 277
opinion of Scott, 143
opinion of Thomas, 250–51
Overland Campaign, 12, 101, 131, 204–7
Overland Campaign and Siege of
    Petersburg, 38
as president, 209
principal battles, 196–97
promotion of Sheridan, 285–86, 288
relationship with Halleck, 183–84
relationship with Longstreet, 105, 113, 114
siege of Petersburg, 132
siege of Vicksburg, 86
support for Sheridan, 101
taking Fort Henry, 85
U.S.-Mexican War, 31, 198–99
Vicksburg Campaign, 203–4
at West Point, 197–98
Greeley, Horace, 148
Griffin, Eliza, 56
Groesbeck, Olivia Augusta, 239

H
H. L. Hunley, 11
Halleck, Henry Wager, vii, 3, 11, 159–60,
    165, 166, 183–95
    assigning Sheridan, 282–83, 284
    background of, 184–85

Battle of Antietam, 191–92
Battle of Shiloh, 189, 190
on Burnside, 174
career from 1846-1860, 185–86
chief of staff, 194–95, 204
command of Western Department,
    187, 189
general-in-chief, 190–91, 192–94
importance of Vicksburg Campaign, 203
Meade's request to resign, 274, 276
Pope and McClellan's conflict, 168
promotes Thomas, 244–45
relationship with Grant, 183–84, 201–2
relationship with Hooker, 193, 194, 229
relationship with Sherman, 217, 218
replaces Buell, 192
replaces Frémont, 164
"siege" of Corinth, 183, 189–90
Hamer, Thomas L., 197
Hamilton, Elizabeth, 186
Hancock, Benjamin, 253, 254
Hancock, Winfield Scott, 252–65
    assignments after Civil War, 263–65
    assignments before Civil War, 255–56
    Battle of Antietam, 257
    Battle of Gettysburg, 258–61, 273
    Battle of Williamsburg, 256
    Battles of Fredericksburg and
        Chancellorsville, 257–58
    early life and West Point, 254
    principal battles, 252–53
    Siege of Petersburg, 261–63
    U.S.-Mexican War, 254–55
Hanson, Alexander Contee, 29
Hardee, William J., 25, 69
Harpers Ferry, 28, 32–33
    Johnston at, 19, 46
    Stuart at, 92, 95
Harris, Abigail, 54
Harris, Isham G., 60, 84
Hayes, Rutherford B., 114
Hennen, Anna Marie, 124
Henshaw, John, 4–5
Herold, David, 263

Hill, A. P., 98, 99, 111, 129, 131, 263
    Battle of Antietam, 177
    Battle of Gettysburg, 259
    and Ellen Marcy, 150, 151
Hill, D. H., 105, 121, 129, 159, 232
    Battle of Fredericksburg, 271
    Battle of South Mountain, 270
Hines, Thomas, 78, 80
Holmes, Oliver Wendell, Jr., 132
Hood, John Bell, 12, 15, 105, 111, 112,
    115–24, 206, 207
    after the war, 124
    Atlanta Campaign, 121
    background of, 116
    Battle of Antietam, 119
    Battle of Chickamauga, 120
    Battle of Gettysburg, 120
    Battle of Kennesaw Mountain, 220
    Battles of Nashville and Franklin, 83,
        90, 121–24, 250
    command of corps, 121
    defense of Atlanta, 221, 223, 250
    Hood's Texas Brigade, 117–18
    in 2nd Cavalry, 116–17
    principal battles, 115–16
    relationship with Lee, 119, 120
    replaces Johnston, 24–25
    Second Battle of Bull Run, 119
Hooker, Joseph, 4, 51, 99, 177, 226–39
    on A. S. Johnston, 57
    Battle of Antietam, 176, 177, 232, 270
    Battle of Chancellorsville, 35–37, 93, 130,
        234–37, 258, 271
    Battle of Fredericksburg, 233
    Battle of Kennesaw Mountain, 220
    Chattanooga and Atlanta Campaigns,
        238, 249
    command of Army of the Potomac,
        233–34
    early life and West Point, 227–28
    notorious habits of, 229
    Peninsula Campaign, 227
    principal battles, 226–27
    reinstatement in Army, 230–31

    relationship with Halleck, 193–94
    relationship with Pillow, 229
    relieved of command, 237–38
    replaced by Meade, 272
    replaces Burnside, 180
    resigns Army of the Cumberland, 238–39
    Second Battle of Bull Run, 232
    Second Seminole War and U.S.-Mexican
        War, 228–29
    Yorktown siege and Battle of Seven
        Pines, 231
Horton, Clara, 163
Houston, Sam, 56
Howard, O. O., 221, 238
    at Gettysburg, 259, 260
Huff, John A., 102
Huger, Benjamin, 107
Hunt, Henrietta, 74
Hunt, John Wesley, 74
Hunter, David, 126, 187
    Battle of Lynchburg, 131
Huston, Felix, 56

I
Indian Wars. *See also* Seminole Wars,
    161–62, 225
    Black Hawk War, 14, 16, 53, 55, 142
    Plains Indian War, 212
    Sheridan in, 280, 281–82, 291

J
Jackson, Andrew, 142
Jackson, Cummins, 43
Jackson, Thomas J. "Stonewall," 19, 30,
    41–52, 53, 54
    assignment to Harpers Ferry, 45–46
    attacks on Pope, 168, 170
    Battle of Antietam, 51, 97–98, 119
    Battle of Chancellorsville, 37, 51, 98,
        236, 237, 271
    Battle of Fredericksburg, 51, 98
    at Cedar Mountain, 168
    early life and West Point, 42–43
    First Battle of Bull Run, 46–47

on Hood's brigade, 118
Lee's invasion plans, 159
opinion of Early, 129
opinion of Pope, 167
Second Battle of Bull Run, 34, 50, 109
Seven Days Battles, 50
Stuart under, 95
U. S.- Mexican War, 43–44
Valley Campaign, 47–50
wounds of, 51–52
James, George S., 8
Jefferson, Thomas, 140
Johnson, Andrew, 251
    approach to Reconstruction, 280, 291
    Longstreet's pardon, 114
    pardon of Confederate generals, 135
    recalls Hancock, 264
    Sherman's treaty, 225
Johnson, Edward, 49
Johnston, Albert Sidney, 3, 10, 15, 21, 53–62
    attitude toward secession, 58
    background of, 54–55
    Battle of Shiloh, 59–62, 66, 189, 202
    Black Hawk War, 55
    at cavalry post, 31
    heads Army of Mississippi, 59
    2nd U. S. Cavalry, 117, 243
    orders to Morgan, 75
    Texas Republic, 55–56
    U.S.-Mexican War, 56–57
    Utah (Mormon) War, 57–58
Johnston, John, 54
Johnston, Joseph E., 2, 3, 8, 12, 14–26
    armistice with Sherman, 26, 224–25
    Atlanta Campaign, 115
    background of, 15
    Battle of Kennesaw Mountain, 220–21
    Battle of Seven Pines, 107
    First Battle of Bull Run, 8, 10, 19–21, 106
    at Harpers Ferry, 19, 46
    heading Army of Tennessee and Atlanta
        Campaign, 23–25
    Lee replacing, 33–34
    luring McClellan, 155, 157

on Morgan's success, 77
opinion of Hood, 118, 119
opposition to secession, 18
Peninsula Campaign, 21, 22
principal battles, 14–15
reinstatement of, 26
relationship with Davis, 21, 23
replaced by Hood, 121
replacing Bragg, 69, 72
at Sherman's funeral, 26
Vicksburg Campaign, 23
Johnston, Mary Valentine Wood, 15
Johnston, Peter, 15
Johnston, William Preston, 55
Jomini, Antoine-Henri, 185
Junkin, Elinor, 45

K
Kearney, James, 269
Kellogg, Frances Lucretia, 243
Kent, James, 213
Kimball, Nathan, 49
King, Rufus, 170
Knoxville Campaign, 113
Ku Klux Klan (KKK), 91

L
Lamar, Mirabeau B., 56
Law, Evander M., 120
Lawton, Alexander, 129
Ledlie, James H., 182
Lee, George Washington Custis, 31
Lee, Harry, 15
Lee, Henry, 28–29
Lee, Robert E., 27–40
    Appomattox Campaign and surrender, 25,
        38–40, 208–9
    background of, 28–29
    Battle of Antietam, 34–35, 68, 109,
        171, 176
    Battle of Chancellorsville, 35–37, 111,
        130, 234, 235–37
    Battle of Cheat Mountain, 33
    Battle of Fredericksburg, 35, 51, 98

Battle of Gettysburg, 37–38, 42, 99, 101, 111–12, 258, 259, 260, 273, 274
command of 2nd Cavalry, 117
defense of Richmond, 12
evaluation of, 27–28
father of, 15
Harpers Ferry, 32–33, 95
invasion of Maryland and Battle of Antietam, 97, 157, 159
on Jackson's death, 52, 54
Northern Virginia Campaign, 168, 169
opinion of Early, 125, 126, 129, 130, 131, 135
opinion of Meade, 267
opinion of Pope, 167
Overland Campaign, 38, 204, 206
post-war meeting with Meade, 277
principal battles of, 28
rank of pre-Civil War, 15
relationship with Davis, 21
relationship with Hood, 119, 120, 121
relationship with Johnston, 15, 16, 18, 25
relationship with Scott, 144
relationship with Thomas, 243
replacing Johnston, 21, 33–34
Second Battle of Bull Run, 34, 109
Seven Days Battles, 33–34, 129
Siege of Petersburg, 38, 262
as strategist, 59–60
on Stuart's death, 102
U.S.-Mexican War, 5, 30–31
on war, vi
at West Point and early assignments, 29–30
Letcher, John, 18, 45
Lexington Rifles. *See* Morgan, John Hunt
Lincoln, Abraham
description of Sheridan, 280
Emancipation Proclamation, 159
at Fort Stevens, 132
and Frémont, 164
frustration with McClellan, 35, 157, 176, 190, 192, 232, 270
frustration with Meade, 274, 276

Lee's colonelcy, 33
relationship with Grant, 202–3
relationship with Halleck, 184, 192–93
relationship with Hooker, 194, 230, 232, 233–34, 237–38, 271–72
relationship with Pope, 163–64, 166–67
Longstreet, Augustus Baldwin, 105
Longstreet, James, 34, 50, 103–14
after the war, 114
background of, 104–5
Battle of Chickamauga, 112–13, 120, 247, 248, 285
Battle of Chickamauga Creek, 69, 70
Battle of Fredericksburg, 93, 98, 110, 178
Battle of Gettysburg, 37, 38, 111–12, 259
Battle of the Wilderness, 113
Battles of South Mountain and Antietam, 109
Chattanooga and Knoxville Campaigns, 104, 113
First Battle of Bull Run, 106–7
named brigadier general, 106
opinion of Pope, 162
Peninsula Campaign, 107
policy of "tactical defense," 103
principal battles of, 103–4
Second Battle of Bull Run, 50, 97, 108–9, 170
Siege of Petersburg and Appomattox Campaign, 113
U.S.-Mexican War, 105–6

M
Mackall, William Whann, 25
Madison, James, 141
Magruder, John, 117, 157
Mahan, Dennis Hart, 43, 185
Mansfield, Joseph, 163
maps
Atlanta Campaign, 222
Battle of Brice's Crossroads, 89
Battle of Cedar Creek, 289
Battle of Chancellorsville, 36, 235
Battle of Chickamauga, 247

Battle of Fredericksburg, 179
Battle of Gettysburg, 275
Battle of Kernstown - Valley
  Campaign, 48
Battle of Nashville, 122
Battle of Shiloh, 61
Battle of Yorktown, 22
Battles of Lookout Mountain and
  Missionary Ridge, 72
Early's Shenandoah Valley Campaign, 133
First Battle of Bull Run, 9
Morgan's Raid, 76
Northern Virginia Campaign, 169
Overland Campaign, 205
Peninsula Campaign, 22, 158
Pickett's Charge at Gettysburg, 260
Second Battle of Bull Run, 108
Stuart's ride at Gettysburg, 100
Western Theater, 188
Marcy, Ellen Mary, 150, 151
Marcy, Randolph, 150
Mason, Charles, 29
Mason, John Y., 242
McArthur, Pope, 16
McClellan, George B., 147–60, 166
  Battle of Antietam, 34–35, 97–98, 159,
    171, 176–77, 191–92
  on Burnside, 174
  command of U.S. Army, 153–54, 232
  early Civil War skirmishes, 149
  early military assignments, 149–51
  General War Order No. 1, 155–56
  orders from Halleck, 191
  Peninsula Campaign, 21, 47, 103, 107,
    156–59
  and Pope, 168
  principal battles, 147–48
  relationship with Hancock, 256
  relationship with Hooker, 230, 231
  replaced by Burnside, 160, 176
  replaces Scott, 139, 146
  Seven Days Battles, 34
  Stuart's reconnaissance of, 92, 96–97
  in U.S.-Mexican War, 5

McClernand, John, 245
McCook, Alexander McDowell, 248
McCook, Daniel, 284
McDowell, Irvin, 4, 47, 49, 148, 166, 230
  First Battle of Bull Run, 8, 10, 19, 20,
    148–49, 175
McGuire, Hunter, 52
McKinley, William, 114
McLane, Lydia, 17
McLaws, Lafayette, 111
McLean, Wilmer, 208
McNealey, Julia, 128
McPherson, James, 116, 203, 219, 221, 238
Meade, George Gordon, 37, 38, 233,
  266–77
  Battle of Chancellorsville, 271
  Battle of Fredericksburg, 129, 270–71
  Battle of Gettysburg, 258, 259, 260, 261,
    272–74, 275
  Battles of Cold Harbor and the Crater,
    182, 277
  Battles of South Mountain and
    Antietam, 270
  early life and West Point, 267–68
  offers to resign, 276
  opinion of cavalry and Sheridan, 101,
    286–87
  post-war meeting with Lee, 277
  principal battles, 266–67
  replaces Hooker, 194, 237–38, 271–72
  report on Great Lakes, 269
  Second Battle of Bull Run, 270
  Second Seminole War and U.S.-Mexican
    War, 268–69
  Seven Days Battles, 269–70
Meade, Richard Worsam, 267, 268
Memoir of the Last Year of the War for
  Independence in the Confederate States of
  America (Early), 135
Memoirs (Sherman), 213, 225
Milroy, Robert H., 49
Mitchell, W. B., 159, 192
Moore, Andrew, 106
Mordecai, Alfred, 150, 151

Morgan, Calvin, 74
Morgan, John Hunt, 73–81
    background of, 74
    Battle of Hartsville, 77
    Battle of Shiloh, 75
    death of, 81
    First Kentucky Raid, 75, 77
    Morgan's Raid, 77–80
    raises Lexington Rifles, 75
    U.S.-Mexican War, 73, 74
Morgan, Richard, 79
Morgan, Tom, 75, 78
Morrison, Mary Anna, 45
Morton, Oliver P., 78
Murfreesboro, battles in, 82, 83, 86, 90

N
Narrative of Military Operations
    (Johnston), 26
Nat Turner's Rebellion, 14, 16, 241
Nesmith, James, 231
Newton, John, 118

O
Overland Campaign, 28, 38, 204–7
    Battle at Cold Harbor, 206
    Battle of Spotslyvania Court House, 204,
        205, 279
    Battle of the Crater, 181–82
    Battle of the Wilderness, 101, 279
    Burnside in, 173
    Early in, 126, 131
    Grant in, 197
    Hancock in, 253
    map, 205
    Meade in, 267, 276–77
    Sheridan in, 286–87
    siege of Petersburg, 206
    Stuart in, 93

P
Patterson, Robert, 244, 268
Patton, George S., Jr., vi, 197, 198
Pemberton, John C., 15, 23, 218

Peninsula Campaign, 21, 47, 147–48, 156–59
    Battle of Williamsburg, 128–29, 256
    Hancock in, 252–53
    Hooker in, 227
    Longstreet in, 103, 107
    maps, 22, 158
    Seven Days Battles, 157, 269–70
Personal Memoirs of U. S. Grant (Grant), 54,
    198, 199, 210
    account of Lee's surrender, 208
Petersburg Campaign
    Second Battle of, 3, 12
    Siege of Petersburg, 28, 38, 104, 197, 206,
        253, 261–63, 267
Philbrick, Chase, 154
Pickens, Francis Wilkinson, 7
Pickett, George, 105, 106, 111, 112
Pickett's Charge, 259, 260, 273
Pierce, Franklin, 5, 143, 144
Pillow, Gideon J., 201, 228–29
    and Scott, 229
Pinkerton, Allan J., 151, 156
Plains Indian Wars, 212
Pleasants, Henry, 181
Pleasonton, Alfred, 99
Plummer, Joseph B, 165
Political and Military Life of Napoleon
    (Jomini), 186
Polk, James, 143, 229
Polk, Leonidas, 67, 69, 112, 113, 284
Pope, John, 105, 161–72, 245
    Army of the Mississippi and Island No. 10,
        164–66, 189
    Army of Virginia command, 166–68
    background and early assignments of,
        162–63
    Catlett's Station Raid, 97
    at Cedar Mountain, 168
    Jackson's attacks on, 169, 170
    McClellan under, 157
    principal battles, 161–62
    raid on Stuart and Catlett's Station,
        168, 170
    relationship with Halleck, 191

relationship with Lincoln, 163–64
relieved of command, 171–72
Second Battle of Bull Run, 34, 50, 97, 104,
     109, 170–71, 176, 191
U.S.-Mexican War, 163
Pope, Nathaniel, 162
Porter, David, 203
Powell, Lewis, 263
Preston, Henrietta, 55
Price, Sterling, 68
Provisional Army of the Confederate
     States, 33

R

Read, Thomas Buchanan, 290
Report on the Means of National Defence
     (Halleck), 184, 185
Reynolds, John, 259, 271
     Battle of Gettysburg, 272
Riley, Bennet, 186
Ritchey, Thomas, 281
Robinson, David, 140
Rochelle, James, 241
Rodes, Robert E., 98
Rogue River War, 278, 282
Roosevelt, Theodore, 114
Rosecrans, William S., 69, 77, 105, 203
     Battle at Stones River, 279
     Battle of Chickamauga, 112, 246, 247,
          248, 249, 285
     Battle of Stones River, 246, 284
     opinion of Sherman, 213
     replaces Buell, 192
     and Thomas, 245–46
Russell, Almira, 255–56

S

Schenck, Robert C., 49
Schofield, John, 83, 90, 116, 219, 221, 251
     Franklin-Nashville Campaign, 123, 250
Scott, Winfield, 5, 6, 16, 138–46, 148, 198
     arrest of Pillow, 229
     assigning A. S. Johnston, 58
     assigning Halleck, 184

assignments under Jackson, 142
background and early career of, 139–41
on Beauregard, 5
Bragg's criticism of, 65
creating professional army, 142
on Hooker at Chapultepec, 229
Jackson under in Mexico, 44
Lee's colonelcy, 33
Longstreet under, 105
loses 1852 election, 143–44
opinion of Lee, 31
principal battles, 138–39
relationship with Johnston, 18
replaced by McClellan, 153
strategy for Civil War (Anaconda Plan),
     139, 145–46
U.S.-Mexican War, 17, 143
War of 1812, 141–42
Second Battle of Bull Run, 28, 42,
     170–71, 191
     Burnside in, 173, 176
     Early in, 126, 129
     Hood in, 115, 119
     Hooker in, 232
     Longstreet in, 104, 108–9
     Meade in, 267, 270
     Pope in, 34, 50, 161
     Stuart in, 93, 97
Sedgwick, John, 35, 130
Seminole Wars, 63
     Early in, 125, 127
     Johnston in, 14, 16–17
     Meade in, 269
     Scott in, 142
     Thomas in, 240, 242
Sergeant, Margaretta, 268
Seven Days Battles. *See also* Peninsula
     Campaign, 28, 33–34, 157
     Battle of Gaines Mill, 118
     Early in, 126, 129
     Jackson in, 42, 50
     Longstreet in, 104, 107
     McClellan in, 148
     Meade in, 267, 269–70

Shackelford, James M., 80
Shenandoah Valley Campaign, 93, 131–34,
    207, 279, 287–88
    Battle of Cedar Creek, 288, 289, 290
    Early in, 125, 126
Sheridan, Irene Rucker, 292
Sheridan, John, 280–81
Sheridan, Philip H., 38, 126, 264, 278–92
    attitude towards Reconstruction, 290–91
    Battle of Bonneville, 283–84
    Battle of Chickamauga, 284–85
    Battle of Perryville, 284
    Battle of Stones River, 284
    Battle of the Wilderness, 286–87
    Battle of Yellow Tavern, 102, 286, 287
    conflict with Meade, 101
    early life and West Point, 280–81
    final assignments, 291–92
    final Civil War battles, 290
    Indian Wars, 291
    Missionary Ridge, Battle of
        Chattanooga, 285
    Overland Campaign, 287
    principal battles, 278–80
    pursuit of Early, 280
    Shenandoah Valley Campaign, 93, 132,
        134, 207, 287–88, 289
    "siege" of Corinth, 283
Sherman, Charles R., 212–13
Sherman, John, 215
Sherman, William Tecumseh, 4, 211–25
    armistice with Johnston, 224–25
    assigned to Grant, 204, 217–18
    Atlanta Campaign, 15, 23, 24, 25, 121,
        219–23, 249–50
    Battle of Bentonville, 25
    Battle of Shiloh, 11, 202, 218
    breakdown of, 187, 217
    Chattanooga Campaign and Meridian
        Expedition, 219, 249
    early life and West Point, 212–14
    First Battle of Bull Run, 216
    first meeting Lincoln, 215–16
    Indian Wars, 225, 263

    March to the Sea, 206–7, 212, 223
    opinion of Forrest, 82, 83
    principal battles, 211–12
    relationship with Hooker, 229, 238
    Second Seminole War and U.S.-Mexican
        War, 214
    superintendent of Louisiana State
        Seminary, 214–15
    surrender of Johnston, 26
    "total war" concept, 212
    Vicksburg Campaign, 203, 218–19
Shiloh. See Battle of Shiloh
Shubrick, William, 186
Sickles, Daniel, 259, 273
Siegel, Franz, 166
Siege of Petersburg. See Petersburg Campaign
Slidell, John, 5, 6
Slocum Henry, 281
Smith, Andrew J., 90
Smith, Edmund Kirby, 67, 68, 124, 135, 290
Smith, Persifer F., 150, 228
Smith, William F., 12, 174, 256
    Siege of Petersburg, 261
Smith, William Farrar, 206
Smith, William Sooy, 87
Sorrel, Moxley, 106
South Mountain. See Battle of South
    Mountain
Stanton, Edwin, 157, 166
    Burnside's resignation, 182
    Halleck's request to, 189
    opinion of Thomas, 249
    on Sherman's armistice, 225
Stone, Charles, 153, 154
Stoneman, George, 35, 234, 237
Stones River. See Battle of Stones River
Streight, Abel, 87
Stuart, Alexander, 93
Stuart, J. E. B., 31, 92–102
    background of, 93–94
    Battle of Brandy Station, 99
    Battle of Chancellorsville, 35, 98–99
    Battle of Fredericksburg, 98
    Battle of Gettysburg, 37, 38, 99–100

Battle of Yellow Tavern, 102, 287
Catlett's Station Raid, 97, 168, 170
Chambersburg Raid, 98
early assignments, 94
First Battle of Bull Run, 95–96
Harpers Ferry, 32, 95
invasion of Maryland and Battle of
    Antietam, 97–98
opinion of Thomas, 244
Overland Campaign, 101
principal battles of, 92–93
promotion to colonel, 95
reconnaissance of McClellan, 96–97
Second Battle of Bull Run, 97
Sturgis, Samuel D., 90
Sumner, Edwin, 58, 94, 178
Surratt, Mary, 263

T
Taliaferro, N. M., 127
Taylor, Richard, 90
Taylor, Zachary, 143, 268
    and A. S. Johnston, 56, 57
    Bragg under, 65
    Longstreet under, 105
    Thomas under, 242
Tennessee Campaign, 173, 180
Terrill, William R., 281
Texas Revolution, 53, 55
Thomas, George H., 16, 105, 221, 223,
    238, 240–51
    Atlanta Campaign, 221, 249–50
    Battle of Chickamauga, 112–13,
        246–49, 285
    Battle of Stones River, 69, 246
    Chattanooga Campaign, 219, 249
    early life and West Point, 241–42
    Franklin-Nashville Campaign, 90, 116,
        121, 123, 250
    under Halleck and Buell, 245
    loyalty to Union, 244
    in 2nd U.S. Cavalry, 243
    postwar career, 251
    principal battles, 240–41

Second Seminole War and U.S.-Mexican
    War, 242
Thomas, John, 241
Tilden, Samuel J., 265
Toutant-Beauregard, Jacques, 3, 4
Travis, Joseph, 16, 241
Trist, Nicholas, 143
Turner, Nat. *See* Nat Turner's Rebellion
Twain, Mark, 210
Twiggs, David E., 33, 244
Tyler, Erastus B., 49

U
United States. *See also* Civil War; U.S.-Mexican
    War
    army in 1861, vi–vii
    cost of Civil War, vi
    War of 1812, 138, 141–42
U.S.-Mexican War
    Albert Johnston in, 53, 56–57
    Beauregard in, 2, 5
    Bragg in, 63, 65
    Grant in, 196, 198–99
    Halleck in, 183
    Hancock in, 252, 254–55
    Hooker in, 226–27, 229–30
    Jackson in, 43–44
    Jackson's battles in, 41
    Johnston in, 14, 17
    Lee in, 30–31
    Lee's battles in, 28
    Longstreet in, 103, 105–6
    McClellan in, 147, 150
    Meade in, 266, 268–69
    Morgan in, 73, 74
    Pope in, 161, 163
    Scott in, 138–39, 143
    Thomas in, 240, 242
Utah (Mormon) War (Rebellion), 53,
    57–58, 255

V
Vallandigham, Clement L., 180
Valley Campaign, 47–50

Jackson in, 42
Vanderbilt, William H., 209
Van Dorn, Earl, 68, 203
Van Rensselaer, Stephen, 141
Vicksburg Campaign, 15, 23, 197, 203–4
    Grant's siege of, 86
    Sherman in, 211, 218–19
von Clausewitz, Carl, 211, 212, 213

W
Wager, David, 185
Walker, William, 5–6
Wallace, Lew, 126, 132
Warner, Ezra J., 174, 240
War of 1812, 138, 141–42

Warren, Gouverneur K., 273
Welles, Gideon, 195, 249
Wigfall, Louis T., 21, 23, 124
Wilcox, Cadmus, 42
Wilkinson, James, 140
Wilmot, David, 269
Wilson, James H., 83, 90
Wood, John, 248
Wool, John E., 242
Worth, William J., 268

Y
Yakima War, 278–79, 282
Yates, Richard, 164, 200

ABOUT THE AUTHOR

Alan Axelrod is the author of numerous popular titles focusing on military history, general history, and American history. After receiving his PhD in English (specializing in early American literature and culture) from the University of Iowa in 1979, Axelrod taught early American literature and culture at Lake Forest College (Lake Forest, Illinois) and at Furman University (Greenville, South Carolina). He then entered scholarly publishing in 1982 as associate editor and scholar with the Henry Francis du Pont Winterthur Museum (Winterthur, Delaware), an institution specializing in the history and material culture of America prior to 1832. Axelrod is former senior editor of Abbeville Press and vice president of Zenda Inc., a consulting firm to museums and cultural institutions. In 1994 he became director of development for Turner Publishing Inc. (Atlanta), a subsidiary of Turner Broadcasting System Inc., and in 1997, he founded The Ian Samuel Group Inc., a creative services and book-packaging firm.

Axelrod was a featured speaker at the 2004 Conference on Excellence in Government (Washington, D.C.), at the Leadership Institute of Columbia College (Columbia, South Carolina), and at the 2005 Annual Conference of the Goizueta School of Business, Emory University (Atlanta). He has been a creative consultant (and on-camera personality) for *The Wild West* television documentary series (Warner Bros., 1993), *Civil War Journal* (A&E Network, 1994), and The Discovery Channel, and he has appeared on MSNBC, CNN, CNNfn, CNBC, Fox Network affiliates in Philadelphia and Atlanta, and numerous radio news and talk programs, including National Public Radio. He and his work have been featured in *BusinessWeek*, *Fortune*, *Men's Health*, *Cosmopolitan*, *Inc.*, *Atlanta Business Chronicle*, and many newspapers, including the *Atlanta Journal-Constitution* and *USA Today*. Axelrod has served as consultant for the Margaret Woodbury Strong Museum (Rochester, New York), the Airmen Memorial Museum (Suitland, Maryland), and the Henry Francis du Pont Winterthur Museum (Winterthur, Delaware).